Liberalization and Redemocratization in Latin America

Liberalization and Redemocratization in Latin America

EDITED BY
GEORGE A. LOPEZ
AND
MICHAEL STOHL

CONTRIBUTIONS IN POLITICAL SCIENCE, NUMBER 178

GREENWOOD PRESS
NEW YORK
WESTPORT, CONNECTICUT
LONDON

In memory of
Jose Luiz Melo
scholar and friend;
and to the memories of
Rosemary T. Lopez
and
Thomas M. Lopez

Library of Congress Cataloging-in-Publication Data

Liberalization and redemocratization in Latin America.

(Contributions in political science, ISSN 0147-1066 ;
no. 178)
  Bibliography: p.
  Includes index.
  1. Latin America—Politics and government—1980-
2. Representative government and representation—Latin
America. 3. Democracy. I. Lopez, George A. II. Stohl,
Michael, 1947–   . III. Series.
JL976.L53   1987   320.98   87-272
ISBN 0-313-25299-8 (lib. bdg. : alk. paper)

British Library Cataloguing in Publication Data is available.

Library of Congress Catalog Card Number: 87-272
ISBN: 0-313-25299-8
ISSN: 0147-1066

First published in 1987

Greenwood Press, Inc.
88 Post Road West, Westport, Connecticut 06881

Printed in the United States of America

The paper used in this book complies with the
Permanent Paper Standard issued by the National
Information Standards Organization (Z39.48-1984).

10 9 8 7 6 5 4 3 2 1

Contents

Tables

Abbreviations and Acronyms

AMNLAE	Nicaraguan Women's Association
AP	Accion Popular (Peru)
APRA	American Popular Revolutionary Alliance (Peru)
ARENA	National Renovating Alliance (Brazil)
ATC	Association of Rural Workers
B-A	bureaucratic-authoritarian
BANAMERICA	Banco de América
BANIC	Banco Nicaragüense
BIR	Banco Intercambio Regional
CACM	Central American Common Market
CCP	Confederacion Campesinos del Peru
CD	Christian Democrats
CDN	Nicaraguan Democratic Coordinate
CDS	Sandinista Defense Committees
CEA	Consejo Empresario Argentino
CGTP	Confederacion General de Trabajadores del Peru

CIDH	Interamerican Commission on Human Rights (Comisión Interamericana de Derechos Humanos)
CODE	Convergencia Democratica
CODI-DOI	Center of Operations of Internal Defense (Brazil)
COMPASPO	Armed Forces Commission on Political Matters
CONDECA	Central American Defense Council
COR	Revolutionary Labor Confederation
COSENA	National Security Council
COSEP	Superior Council on Private Enterprise
CP	Communist Party
CROC	Revolutionary Confederation of Workers and Peasants
CTM	Mexican Workers Confederation
DCG	Christian Democrat Party
DIT	Division Investigaciones Technicas (Guatemala)
DNC	Joint National Directorate
DPM	Democratic Popular Movement
EAP	economically active population
EEBI	School of Basic Infantry Training
EGP	Guerrilla Army of the Poor
EPS	Sandinista People's Army
ESG	Escola Superior de Guerra
FAO	Broad Opposition Front
FAR	Rebel Armed Forces
FDN	Nicaraguan Democratic Force
FPN	National Patriotic Front
FPR	Patriotic Front of the Revolution
FRS	Sandino Revolutionary Front
FSLN	Sandinista National Liberation Front
GAM	Mutual Support Group
GPP	Prolonged Popular War
GRN	Government of National Reconstruction
IAN	Instituto Agrario de Nicaragua
IDB	International Development Bank

IMF	International Monetary Fund
ISI	import-substitution industrialization
IU	Izquierda Unida
JGRN	Junta of the Government of National Reconstruction
LOPPE	Law of Political Organizations and Electoral Procedures
MAP-ML	Popular Action Movement/Marxist-Leninist
MAUS	Movement Toward Unified Socialism
MDB	Brazilian Democratic Movement
MIR	Leftist Revolutionary Movement (Chile)
MLN	National Liberation Movement
MOBRAL	Mobilization for Brazilian Literacy
MPU	United People's Movement
OAS	Organization of American States
OBAN	Operation Bandeirantes
OPEC	Oil Producing and Exporting Countries
OPRA	Revolutionary Organization of the People
PAC	Civil Self-Defense Patrols
PAN	National Action Party
PARM	Authentic Party of the Mexican Revolution
PCB	Communist Party of Brazil
PCD	Conservative Democratic Party
PCM	Mexican Communist Party
PCP	Partido Comunista Peruano
PDCN	Democratic Party of National Conciliation
PDM	Mexican Democratic Party
PDS	Democratic Socialist Party
PGT	Guatemalan Workers' Party
PLC	Liberal Constitutionalist Party
PLF	Liberal Front Party
PLI	Independent Liberal Party
PMDB	Democratic Movement of Brazil Party
PMT	Mexican Workers Party
PNM	Mexican National Party
PNR	National Renewal Party; National Revolutionary Party

PP	People's Party
PPC	Partido Popular Cristiano
PPS	Popular Socialist Party
PPSC	Popular Social Christian Party
PRI	Institutional Revolutionary Party
PSC	Social Christian Party
PSD	Social Democratic Party; Democratic Socialist Party
PSR	Revolutionary Socialist Party (Peru)
PST	Socialist Workers Party
PSUM	Unified Mexican Socialist Party
PTB	Brazilian Labor Party
RUOG	United Representation of the Guatemalan Opposition
SNI	National Intelligence Service
UCN	Union of the National Center
UDEL	Democratic Union of Liberation
UNESCO	United Nations Educational, Social, and Cultural Organization
UNSCH	Universidad Nacional San Cristobal de Huamanga
URNG	Guatemalan National Revolutionary Unity
USAID	United States Agency for International Development

Introduction

George A. Lopez and Michael Stohl

This volume has had three distinct points of origin. The first emerged in 1983–84 among a number of the contributors who were, like the co-editors, involved in researching the changing character of gross violations of human rights, repression, and state terror in various nations. As we began to assess the demise of some aspects of harsh authoritarian rule in Latin America, we became convinced that a study of how repressive governments "decompose" or "carry within them the seeds of reform" constituted an important query. This quickly led us to communicate with Latin Americanists studying the redemocratization question. That encounter generated a set of panels at the 1983 meetings of the International Studies Association in Mexico City, where first drafts of three of the chapters contained here were presented. The third impetus for this volume came from country experts in the comparative analysis of Latin politics who believed that a multi-nation compilation on this question would complement the important theoretical work on liberalization and redemocratization being conducted under the sponsorship of organizations like the Woodrow Wilson Center. Prominent among these enthusiasts was Stephen M. Gorman, professor at North Texas State University, whose untimely death in 1984 made this collection, and the field of Latin American politics generally, less than what it might be.

This volume, then, is the product of three coalitions of research interests assembled on the basis of the common ground of an important topic of inquiry:

processes of liberalization and redemocratization within authoritarian regimes in Latin America. Except for contributors of the first and last chapters, each author has focused on both a process and a country in a manner that reflects the concerns of those interested in all three of the overlapping interests that spawned this compilation. With apologies for lost patience to those authors who wanted "just a few more weeks to see how events would continue to unfold" and in gratitude to the other contributors who had patience with the editors, we hope that the volume will prove helpful to the study of this critical development.

1

Liberalization and Redemocratization in Latin America: The Search for Models and Meanings

George A. Lopez and Michael Stohl

In the more than two decades that followed Fidel Castro's assumption of power in 1959, a wave of authoritarian regimes has swept Latin America. Although interdiction by military men in the governance of the state had been a recurrent phenomenon in Latin America, some particular features of the political and economic interests that supported this new wave of coercive centralization and the particular structures employed to govern the state distinguished this trend from the ruling style of prior eras. Described by Guillermo O'Donnell and others as the bureaucratic-authoritarian (B-A) regime, pervasive military-civilian technocracies forcibly replaced predominantly civilian (and often democratically elected) national governments in Brazil (1964), Peru (1968), Uruguay (1973), Chile (1973), and Argentina (1966, 1976). The new ruling alliance was spawned in the growth-oriented sixties by economic industrialization policies pursued (or desired) by modernizing elites who now appeared willing to form new management coalitions to control both the national economic future and the expanding political demands emerging from a variety of sectors affected by industrial success or failure.[1]

According to a number of analysts of this process, as well as documented events within the nations themselves, these B-A regimes were inherently corporatist and repressive.[2] Compared to earlier, more personalized dictatorships, B-A regimes were characterized by the rule of the military as an institution. In addition, the civilian B-A supporters were individuals heavily involved in the internationalized (externally dependent) sectors of the economy. These actors envisioned a more staunchly capitalist and more thoroughly integrated agricultural-industrial development model than earlier elites had advocated.[3] Either as a conscious policy taken to actualize these designs or as a response to control the political opposition that certain of the economic policies incurred, B-A regimes resorted to unprecedented levels of coercion. Although the levels of state violence against citizen opponents, both real and perceived, varied from the milder regimes of Peru to the brutality of a regime where thousands disappeared and were murdered in Argentina, the harsh reality of B-A rule could not be denied.[4]

When a number of observers were willing to admit that governing styles in the region were unlikely to change, a period of political thaw and intense discussions about its nature developed in a number of Latin American states. This rapidly led to the military backing out of control in Ecuador in 1979. Peru followed in 1980, with subsequent military dismounts in Bolivia (1982), Argentina (1983), Uruguay (1984), and Brazil and Guatemala (1985). Discussions of the likelihood of similar processes continued to penetrate the politics of Agusto Pinochet's Chile and even of Alfredo Stroessner's Paraguay. Intense debate raged in the hemisphere regarding the nature of the transition of the post-Somoza Nicaraguan regime and the democratic character of the embattled government of El Salvador.

Why this dramatic shift in ruling styles would occur within a relatively short time and follow so dramatically the development of such seemingly powerful regimes presented a major intellectual challenge to students of comparative politics in general and of Latin America in particular. With each new political opening, amidst each dialogue between regimes and opposition groups, or with each pledge to transfer authority back to civilians came new insights as to how and why such developments were occurring. The plethora of literature of the past few years indicates that the scholarly community has responded vigorously to this trend. Investigations both of individual transitions from authoritarian ruling structures and comparative assessments of these transition processes have appeared.[5] Since the literature itself is still developing and because the governments that it examines continue to be fragile and evolving post-authoritarian systems, accurate generalizations about such transitions are relatively few and still tentative. Despite similarities surrounding the decline in B-A regimes that we may be able to uncover, the dynamics of the transition process itself and its outcome appear to vary greatly from country to country. While acknowledging this issue, and thus assembling the chapters in this volume, it is also clear that the literature in this area has provided us with clear definitions and has isolated a number of critical factors affecting the transition process. We focus on these factors in this introduction in order to place the chapters that comprise the volume in their broadest context.

TYPES OF TRANSITION AND THEIR MEANING

The demise and replacement of authoritarian rule may result from the violent overthrow of a government by opposition forces (Castro versus Batista, the Sandinistas versus Somoza), the abdication of rule under pressure (Peron in Argentina, Duvalier in Haiti), or the planned and managed transition to a new system. As this latter form of governance has become more prevalent in Latin America, discussions of what kinds of ruling modes replace existing authoritarian coalitions have focused on three related forms: the liberalizing regime, the democratizing regime, and the redemocratizing regime. Compared to revolutionary and withdrawal types of transitions, these three alternatives represent governmental change with the participation and consent of the elites of the ruling authoritarian regime.[6] Since the evidence indicates that these technocratic elites acquired and retained power through no small amount of energy and societal upheaval, their subsequent participation in transitions to less than authoritarian rule begs some clarification of these options and the question of why they would help architect their own demise.

Our particular focus in this volume is on the liberalization and redemocratization options of post-authoritarian transition. By *liberalization* we mean the curtailment of violent and harsh government practices that threaten citizens who engage in real or perceived dissent and the reinstating of minimal civil and political rights to individuals and groups. Although this process includes a number of discrete dimensions, the recent work of Douglas Chalmers and Craig Robinson specifies four critical decisional arenas involved in the liberalization of the political straightjacket of authoritarian control that distinguish this political phenomenon. They include an assessment of the location of responsibility for authoritative decisions, the basis for the control of dissent, the degree of pluralism that will be permitted, and the openness of the information flows within the society. In the "creation of new political space" that develops as regime elites and others discuss the unfolding of these issues, liberalization builds its own constituency and may provide a fragile, but definitive, phase in the development of regimes of yet a lesser authoritarian mode.[7]

By *redemocratization* we mean the restoration of democratic government as traditionally defined in both its structural and procedural form. As regards the *structural dimensions*, a redemocratized government provides an arena of open, competitive political relationships as part of the institutional character of government. This institutionalization develops both in the factions, be they political parties or collective actors such as unions, that contend for official government positions of authority and in the ongoing character of the ruling bodies themselves. These include the tensions within multi-house legislative bodies or between the legislative and executive branches. For the *procedural dimensions* we mean the (often constitutionally) guaranteed participation of citizens in the competitive modes as structured, as they so choose, without fear of recrimination.[8]

Clearly, the processes of liberalization and redemocratization are intertwined, and from a scholarly perspective they appear to be logically ordered. But in the managed reallocation of political control that has occurred in the political reality of contemporary Latin America, we know in an uncertain way that the appearance of the first phase does not directly predict the development of the second. In fact, liberalization and redemocratization stand as somewhat discrete transition processes. It is also obvious that the term *redemocratization* applies to those situations in which democracy again becomes the preferred governance mode. This applies to the case with Southern Cone countries and Peru. *Democratization*, however, serves as the more accurate depiction of governments, as in the case of a Nicaragua, Haiti, or Bolivia, which moved to this scheme for the first time in their recent political history.

In discussing how these patterns of events and alternative processes have surprised some scholars now attempting to come to grips with them, Juan Linz has noted that social science may have been hampered in our assessment of liberalization modes by our lack of full attention to how B-A regimes actually functioned. Linz maintained that analysts were caught between somewhat contradictory, but equally misleading, perceptions of such governments. These perceptions involved "the expectation of their failure based on their illegitimacy and the assumption of a total lack of support in the society, as well as the opposite based on an overestimation of their repressive capacity and the cohesion of the coalition of social forces supporting them."[9] Although Linz may be correct, students of such transitions have attempted to recover and in so doing have provided a number of alternative explanations of why authoritarian regimes have decomposed. They range from broad theories of the erosion of coercive control to detailed propositions about the structure of choices envisioned by elites as they continue to rule.

One of the more general theories of transition emerges from the work of Veliz on the cycles of the centrist tradition in Latin America. Reflecting on the rise of the authoritarian regimes of the seventies, Veliz noted that although the leaders have resorted to a somewhat unusual level of violence against opposition groups, and they do represent a more direct role of the military in all institutions of governance and society, processes of authoritarian rule have historically fluctuated in Latin America. If contemporary governments are able to achieve a pattern of economic modernization suited to Latin needs and experience, they will, Veliz argued, like the processes associated with their despotic predecessors, soon loosen their rule in favor of more popular government forms.[10] The conclusion to be drawn from Veliz is that prospects for liberalization of authoritarian rule are generally mid-range over time and particularly high during periods of economic success.

A somewhat less ecological explanation for the demise of authoritarian control comes from the generalizations of Juan Linz. This scholar of democratic breakdown and resurgence noted that authoritarian regimes elect different and changing strategies of social control of their population during their reign. These strategies are often based on the number, character, and level of challenge presented by opposition groups. In what appears to be a relatively rational decision rule, the authoritarian regime may devise a modicum of liberalization in the structure or style of rule as the best available means for reducing the power of the opposition or even as a way of co-opting it. Although the regime may clearly control this liberalization, this limited thaw may actually lead to new testing of the scope of regime domination by various political opponents and actors in the system. This intensifies pressure for greater liberalization and raises the temptation of renewed regime repression to limit such trends. To resort to the former obviously increases the pace of reform. To elect the latter is to return to an authoritarian style but this time devoid of the legitimacy level and support of the particular political groups it has just enjoyed. Thus coercive control becomes more cumbersome over time.[11]

Guillermo O'Donnell pushed even further in his explanation of why transitions from authoritarian rule develop. O'Donnell contended that the movement toward greater liberalization, if not some levels of democratization, of the B-A regime becomes pronounced because such alterations in rule alleviate some particular substantive and process shortcomings posed by strict and continued elite domination. As regards the substance of the corporatist policies that the elite have adopted, increased democratization:

(1) satisfies the need of people for participation and a feeling of the character of "citizenship" (even in the face of the domination of the state); (2) if tied to elections, it satisfies the problem of presidential succession, so elusive but necessary for stability and predictability of political and economic policies; and, (3) over the long term, it obscures the harsher aspects of the state coercion necessary to maintain economic domination of the state.[12]

Beyond this, O'Donnell claimed that democratization as a process becomes a *modus vivendi* of sorts for B-A regimes because it speaks to their concern for establishing a society in which large numbers of the populace find themselves in accord with the same values. Plebiscites, elections, and other demonstrations of the *pueblo* are necessary, then, not only to affirm the direction of policy but also to verify the attainment of the new political and social identity that the regime pledged to call forth from the nation.[13] Thus we might posit that B-A systems carry some of the seeds of their own reform, however unanticipated liberalization or redemocratization by the elites may be.

As we come to learn more about the dynamics of and rationale for each transition, we are also able inductively to posit why authoritarian elites elect to loosen stringent reigns of control and often opt for some level of democratization. For example, in their recent studies comparing these processes in Argentina and Brazil, Scott Mainwaring and Eduardo Viola have noted that such transitions usually occur after some kind of regime rupture and involve a combination of controlled transition from above and initiatives from below. Those initiatives from within the society take various forms, not the least of which are social movements that owe their development, in part, to the character of the authoritarian rule itself.[14] Whether they be church, lawyer, or women's groups, these associations widen the political agenda and may become new groups with which the regime must cope. They may even fill the mid-ground of the political space open between the regime and the opposition such that a loosening of the system is dependent on their future participation.

In examining the processes by which elites resort to harsh and violent actions against their own citizens, our own research has uncovered various aspects of the decisional norms and conditions associated with B-A regimes that also have bearing on post-authoritarian transitions. Since we know that regimes employing repression and state terror do so based on an assessment of low opportunity costs and high rewards in resorting to stringent measures, we can posit that political transitions represent a recognition by the ruling elite of a changed calculus of maintaining government by force. This may result from the declining support of local economic elites who do not sense an economic miracle forthcoming and of a general population that will no longer be cowed into submission or from external pressure from allies, as in the case of human rights policies. The leaders of the B-A coalition clearly sense that the costs of preserving their rule have become prohibitive in light of their view of the state or of their concern about their own future in the society.[15] Under these conditions, as implied by the work of Douglas Chalmers and Craig Robinson, the difficult problem then becomes the management of public policies as the disenchanted B-A regime withdraws. Here the major issue will be the extent to which another coalition, acceptable to the outgoing elites, can emerge to rule the state via a different equation of costs and benefits.[16]

Although these theoretical approaches may be somewhat contentious and overlapping explanations of the decline in authoritarian rule, it is clear that a mixture of larger political trends beyond the direct control of the B-A regime and distinctive aspects of the structure of the regime itself provide impetus to and combine with particular choices made by regime members to yield a transition. In fact, if a generalization can be credibly made about post-authoritarian transitions, it may be that they are a function (a) of broad pressures external to the government, (b) of the reform-oriented internal dynamics within the regime, and (c) of the manner in which regime leaders elect to stifle or further the liberalizing or democratizing tendencies that have developed. If another can be posited, it would be that a diverse array of factors influence the transition phase from the post-authoritarian order to the newly liberalized, democratized or redemocratized system.

FACTORS THAT INFLUENCE TRANSITIONS

Although a full discussion of all ingredients that must develop to yield a full and successful replacement of authoritarian rule are beyond the scope of this chapter, we can detail those factors most critical to the transition and the consolidation phases of this process. Four considerations appear most influential as regimes begin to reform or rupture. They include the constellation of and internal cohesion within those political actors with a vested interest in changing the existing B-A rule, the conditions envisioned by the military for its place in a transition, the character of the political-economic environment in which the state operates, and the success of particular processes or "moments" of power reallocation. Although we briefly discuss each factor as distinct and somewhat mutually exclusive dimensions, one of the most intriguing research aspects of these political alterations is their dynamic inter-relationship and self-reinforcing nature. Thus despite the analytical categorization in what follows, the reality of the phenomenon is much less neat and certainly not static.

Probably the most complex influence on the transition from authoritarian rule to some other undetermined governmental form emerges from the constellation of and cohesion within those political groups that envision a more liberalized system of governance. Even within regimes that consciously engineer their own transitions, the formation of clear and reasonably viable coalitions among "new" political elites is a delicate but important step. On its first level, such a coalition-building process may initially unfold within the existing B-A system between hard-line and soft-line factions, with each seeking wider support from the extended political and economic elite of the nation. To the extent to which some clear victory for one over the other can be established and the willing support of the moderate opposition can be secured, an elite leadership base for governmental changes has been forged.[17]

On a second level, the initiation of such transition from within affects both the number of competing replacement elites and the cohesion of groups that support them. As Donald Share has recently sketched, varying degrees of consensus regarding transitions are possible across authoritarian regimes. The goal would appear to be in a position to build a more liberal and/or democratic order "*upon*, not at the expense, of authoritarianism."[18] To encounter resistance among large segments of the authoritarian order may (based on other factors) retard the transition, but such stonewalling will also prove costly to the former ruling elite who will be thoroughly delegitimated after the transition. Thus, simply for utilitarian reasons, various members of the authoritarian coalition may move steadily along with the transition, even if this contradicts their past behavior and ideological disposition.[19]

Finally, as the recent research of Karen Remmer indicates, the development of viable replacement groups that contend for support from both the entrenched elite and the disenfranchised may depend on the character and duration of authoritarian rule in the nation. The longer the B-A regime has held power and the greater its repression, the more likely the political change within the society. Remmer discovered such change indicated by shifts in the strength of major political parties, in electoral realignments, and in the rise of new partisan groups.

Thus the task of transition, even within redemocratizing regimes, is further complicated by bringing into focus a new political spectrum.[20]

Insuring a motivation for and process of extrication from power for the military is a particularly sensitive problem in transition systems. This is true even if the military faction of the authoritarian regime is sponsoring the liberalization and when it has ruled in collusion with civilian technocrats. As a number of analysts have noted, the ease of military dismount may have little to do with either goodwill or political partisanship. It may be more related to such factors as inter-service rivalry, the degree of military staffing of key positions in the social and economic spheres, the solidity of leadership at top echelons, and the particular sense of mission the military has held for itself in the past and will hold for itself in the future political order.[21] The degree of military involvement in repression as regards future prosecution for Nuremberg-like crimes, although a consideration we believe critical in the consolidation phase, has an impact here as well, especially after the conviction of Argentine generals in this area.[22]

A third general factor influencing the pace and character of transition is the broader political-economic environment of the time. This has internal as well as external dimensions of substantial proportion. Internally, the most conspicuous proposition would seem to be that the greater the economic failure of the B-A regime policies, the more likely the onset of transition. Although this is apparent in the Argentine case in 1983, other factors (as David Pion-Berlin discusses in chapter 9) were also at work. Inversely, despite continual economic dislocation at various times in the seventies, Brazil's transition process continued as planned during the earlier "miracle" period. Chile, however terrible the economic indicators or bold the protestors of recent times may be, still gives little indication of imminent transition. Despite intuitive propositions to the contrary, then, this situation has led most analysts to conclude that varying ideas about and support for particular policies, rather than the actual impact of the economic policies themselves, affect the transition process. These ideas and supports do so indirectly, through the formation of new coalitions of political actors as noted above.[23]

An influential part of the larger economic and political environment that breeds smooth transitions from authoritarian rule emerges external to the regime. One obvious source of support or pressure will be key aid providers and political legitimators. Thus human rights policies, foreign aid conditionality, loan reviews by international organizations, and social responsibility concerns of transnational corporations all interact with internal incentives or retardants of reform. Precisely how such external actions impact transitions or sustain reform once established varies widely from state to state. But in recent (as well as future) years, no greater external support structure may exist than the willingness by national and transnational economic actors to deal with the Latin American debt crisis.[24]

Another important impetus for transition is the larger climate for authoritarianism in the hemisphere. It is no coincidence that those Latin states most influenced by Iberian and Mediterranean nations and thus turned to neo-facist regimes from the thirties to the fifties would also reference off the democratization trends within these European states in recent years. Furthermore, the pressure for other states in the region to shun authoritarianism increases as more Latin American states pursue such transitions. Such political momentum toward liberalized and more democratic regimes may clearly be a function of several other variables and policies. But its snowball effect cannot be underestimated.

A final factor influencing the transition phase is how the regime and its coalition of transition supporters architect particular processes that effectively transfer power and portend a changed character of political life. As noted earlier in this chapter, in commenting on the work of theorists of B-A regimes, real pressures do exist both within and external to regimes to hold plebescites and elections in some form. If the regime, as in the case of Brazil and Chile, has appealed successfully to the populace for some legitimation of its authoritarian control, the prospect for some popular voice and process to assist in the transition may be likely. As the case of the Uruguayan citizen rejection of the regime in a national plebescite in 1981 illustrates, it also is possible for an incumbent elite to have its route to a transition sparked by a loss at the ballot box.

In the political engineering that transitions entail, constructing the right moment may not be a conscious process. The entire transition scheme may be opened as an issue because of a leadership or succession crisis, as was the case in Franco's Spain and to a lesser extent in Argentina. Or as in the case of Peru and Brazil, the stage may have been set for a very long period by lower level electoral processes and constitutional guarantees.[25] Whatever the style or vehicle, each of the cases of transition in this volume, and in Latin America generally, can point to a particular time and set of circumstances when the moment of transfer was unquestionable.[26]

THE CHAPTERS IN THIS VOLUME

With these conceptual parameters in mind, the contributors to this volume have undertaken a considerable task. Each examines the contours of the challenge to democratize and to liberalize practices in a single Latin nation. For some states, particularly the Southern Cone countries, this entails some discussion of the character of the authoritarian structure that preceded the transition period. For other states, such as Mexico and Nicaragua, it involves a historical perspective on those forces that have shaped the possibility for democratic institutions to emerge and to be sustained over time. But in each instance, the authors assess the meaning of liberalization and redemocratization in the nation and the factors that inhibit or enhance it.

In the first case study, Laura Nuzzi O'Shaughnessy discusses the prospects for redemocratization in Mexico against the background of that nation's authoritarian one-party political system. O'Shaughnessy's focus on whether electoral reform can be used to increase both the political participation of citizens and viable political parties while also extending power sharing in government poses an important query relevant to the Mexican case and beyond. Gordon Bowen and Richard Stahler-Sholk provide detailed analyses of Guatemala and Nicaragua, respectively. Bowen's chapter constitutes a curious case of whether the democratization of a national political life that has been distinguished by harsh military rule can bring liberalization, enlightened social consent, and a curtailment of factional violence. His identification of the central role of financial conditions and key external actors, such as the United States, in bringing these processes to complete fruition is echoed in the Stahler-Sholk study of Nicaragua. The latter devotes some particular energy to examining the coalition that replaced Somoza and the factors that influenced the Sandinista choices and behavior in the first five years after the revolution.

In the work of Sandra Woy-Hazelton and William Hazelton about Peru, we are presented with the dilemma of the general goodwill of the military to maintain post-transition democratic rule while it is being challenged to guarantee national security against a growing terrorist-guerilla war movement. With his study of the *abertura* in Brazil, Wilfred Bacchus analyzes the case of the most prolonged transition to civilian rule in the region. His study illustrates both the detailed maneuvering that typifies transition processes and the unique issue of the ''critical moment'' of election, crisis, and survival in a redemocratization. For the case of Uruguay, Ronald H. McDonald discusses the number of countervailing forces that ultimately influence the recasting of a new Uruguayan democracy by the mid-eighties.

Chilean social scientist Manuel Antonio Garreton provides both a theoretical discussion and a case study in his chapter on Chile. First, he sketches the dilemmas involved in transitions in Southern Cone countries. Then, he details how in the case of Chile, the future of redemocratization will be a function of the resolution of differences among fragmented political forces, the cohesiveness of the armed forces, and the power of Pinochet's personality. In his discussion of what may be the most celebrated of transitions, that of Argentina returning to civilian democratic rule in 1983, David Pion-Berlin cites the deterioration of military control of particular economic sectors as a major factor in the demise of military control in that state. This both sets the stage for a new democracy and also predicts to the areas of greatest concern of that new government.

In the final chapter, David Carleton and Michael Stohl examine a much discussed force in assessing the prospects for liberalization and redemocratization in the Americas: the role of the United States. The authors demonstrate that, by considering the specific leverage point of foreign assistance, the position of a state in its liberalization or redemocratization phase predicts to relatively little change in foreign aid allocations that have occurred during the past decade. This appears to hold true under both the perceived pro-human-rights Carter administration and the perceived hostile-to-human-rights Reagan administration.

On balance, we believe these chapters make a contribution to our general understanding of the delicacy and complexity of transitions from authoritarian rule to more humane and predictable forms of governance. Viewed as a unit, these chapters also document the challenge to social science to construct accurate generalizations about such fragile processes. To continue to monitor and to assess those factors that enhance or inhibit these processes may constitute a research agenda of large measure.[27]

NOTES

1. The classic analysis of this alliance formation is Guillermo O'Donnell, *Modernization and Bureaucratic-Authoritarianism* (Berkeley: University of California Press, 1973).

2. For these analyses, see the literature on corporatism and B-A regimes, especially O'Donnell, *Modernization and Bureaucratic-Authoritarianism*; James M. Malloy, ed., *Authoritarianism and Corporatism in Latin America* (Pittsburgh: University of Pittsburgh Press, 1977); David Collier, ed., *The New Authoritarianism in Latin America* (Princeton, N.J.: Princeton University Press, 1979), as the best general and theoretical sources distinguishing this trend. In addition to developing the concept of the B-A regime, O'Donnell was the first to point out the "conspicuous capacity for coercion" of these regimes. See Guillermo O'Donnell, "Tensions in the Bureaucratic State and the Question of Democracy," in David Collier, ed., *The New Authoritarianism in Latin America*, (Princeton, N.J.: Princeton University Press, 1979), p. 296.

3. For this formulation, see Collier, *The New Authoritarianism*, p. 368.

4. The policy and scholarly communities were made aware of the extent of the violations by the workings of international monitoring groups, such as Amnesty International and Americas Watch, and by local groups such as the Vicaria de la Solidaridad of the Chilean Catholic Church. For various discussions on the impetus to terror as predicted by the ideological stance of the regime or as a form of dealing with challengers, see David Pion-Berlin, *Ideas as Predictors: A Comparative Study of Coercion in Peru and Argentina* (Ph.D. thesis, University of Denver, 1984); George A. Lopez, "National Security Ideology as an Impetus to State Terror," pp. 73–96, and Ted Robert Gurr, "The Political Origins of State Terror: A Theoretical Analysis," pp. 45–72, in Michael Stohl and George A. Lopez, eds., *Government Violence and Repression: An Agenda for Research* (Westport, Conn.: Greenwood Press, 1986).

5. For individual country studies, see Constantine C. Menges, *Spain: The Struggle for Democracy Today* (Beverly Hills, Calif.: Sage Publications, 1980); Jorge Braga de Macedo and Simon Sarfaty, eds., *Portugal Since the Revolution* (Boulder, Colo.: Westview Press, 1981); Jose Maravall, *The Transition to Democracy in Spain* (New York: St. Martin's Press, 1982); Wayne A. Selcher, ed., *Political Liberalization in Brazil* (Boulder, Colo.: Westview Press, 1985). Comparative analyses include Howard J. Wiarda, ed., *The Continuing Struggle for Democracy in Latin America* (Boulder, Colo.: Westview Press, 1980); Howard Handleman and Thomas J. Sanders, eds., *Military Government and Movement toward Democracy in Latin America* (Bloomington: Indiana University Press, 1981); John Herz, ed., *From Dictatorship to Democracy* (Westport, Conn.: Greenwood Press, 1982); Julian Santamaria, *Transitions to Democracy in Southern Europe and in Latin America* (forthcoming); Guillermo O'Donnell and Philippe Schmitter, eds., *Transitions from Authoritarian Rule: Tentative Conclusions About Uncertain Democracies* (Baltimore: Johns Hopkins, 1986).

6. For a discussion of this issue, see Donald Share, "Transitions to Democracy and

Transition through Transaction'' (Paper delivered at the 1985 Annual Meeting of the American Political Science Association, New Orleans, August 29-September 1, 1985).

7. Douglas A. Chalmers and Craig H. Robinson, ''Why Power Contenders Choose Liberalization: Perspectives from South America,'' *International Studies Quarterly* 26, no. 1 (March 1982): 3–36.

8. Definitional sources for democracy and democratization abound, but most analysts insist on resorting to Robert Dahl, *Polyarchy* (New Haven: Yale University Press, 1971), pp. 6–9.

9. Juan Linz, ''The Transition from Authoritarian Regimes to Democratic Political Systems and the Problems of Consolidation of Political Democracy'' (Paper presented at the Annual Meeting of the International Political Science Association, Tokyo, Japan, March 29–April 1, 1982), p. 13.

10. Claudio Veliz, *The Centrist Tradition in Latin America* (Princeton, N.J.: Princeton University Press, 1980).

11. Linz, ''The Transition from Authoritarian Regimes,'' pp. 10–33.

12. O'Donnell, ''Tensions in the Bureaucratic State,'' p. 313.

13. Ibid., pp. 316–317.

14. Eduardo Viola and Scott Mainwaring, ''Transitions to Democracy: Brazil and Argentina in the 1980s,'' Working Paper #21 (Notre Dame, Ind.: The Kellogg Institute for International Studies, The University of Notre Dame, July 1984).

15. For a full development of the opportunity cost approach, see Raymond D. Duvall and Michael Stohl, ''Governance by Terror,'' in Michael Stohl, ed., *The Politics of Terrorism*, rev. 2d ed. (New York: Marcel Dekker, 1983), pp. 179–220. For an assessment of the norms and conditions associated with the rise of authoritarian terror regimes, see George A. Lopez and Michael Stohl, ''State Terrorism: From Robespierre to Nineteen Eighty-Four,'' *Chitty's Law Journal* (forthcoming); Lopez, ''National Security Ideology as an Impetus to State Terror.''

16. Chalmers and Robinson, ''Why Power Contenders Choose Liberalization,'' pp. 33–34.

17. Richard Sholk, ''Comparative Aspects of the Transition from Authoritarian Rule,'' A Rapporteur's Report. The Working Papers of the Latin American Program of The Wilson Center, Washington, D.C., 1982, pp. 18–20.

18. Share, ''Transitions to Democracy,'' p. 5.

19. Ibid., pp. 3–6.

20. Karen L. Remmer, ''Redemocratization and the Impact of Authoritarian Rule in Latin America,'' *Comparative Politics* 17, no. 3 (April 1985): 253–275. Note especially the generalizations offered on pp. 264–274.

21. Sholk, ''Comparative Aspects of the Transition,'' pp. 20–24.

22. The degree of that impact, however, may very well be dependent on the number of those former military officers who are to be tried and convicted, as the Alfonsin and popular debate of Argentina highlights. For each society, popular response to how elites resolve the tension between structuring guarantees for the full ''dismounting of the military'' and prosecuting human rights violators in the military as part of the restoration of the rule of law will always be a factor necessitating close monitoring.

23. See Sholk, ''Comparative Aspects of the Transitions,'' pp. 12–16, for a useful discussion of this issue.

24. The perspectives on the relationship between debt and democracy are many and shift rapidly with changes in governments and interest rates. Useful recent examples

include Riordan Roett, "Support Brazil's Democracy," *New York Times*, January 22, 1985; Nicholas D. Kristof, "Debt Crisis Called All but Over," *New York Times*, February 4, 1986; George Shultz, "Beyond the Debt Problem: The Path to Prosperity in Latin America," United States Department of State, Bureau of Public Affairs, Current Policy no. 768, December 1985; Alejandro Foxley, "The External Debt Problem from a Latin American Viewpoint," Working Paper #72 (Notre Dame, Ind.: The Kellogg Institute for International Studies, the University of Notre Dame, July 1986).

25. See Linz, "The Transition from Authoritarian Regimes," pp. 32–45, for a fuller discussion of these options.

26. To move to such an analysis is what scholars of redemocratization and liberalization have long hoped. See especially ibid., pp. 11–14, and Sholk, "Comparative Aspects of the Transition from Authoritarian Rule," pp. 18–20.

27. This caution emerges from the best traditions of the study of political change in comparative politics in the form of Samuel P. Huntington, *Political Order in Changing Societies* (New Haven: Yale University Press, 1968), and has been expressed with respect to backsliding" on redemocratization in Sholk, "Comparative Aspects of the Transition from Authoritarian Rule," pp. 32–40.

2

Redemocratization in Mexico: The Unique Challenge

Laura Nuzzi O'Shaughnessy

Legitimacy must result from a transformation of the authoritarian nature of the system. This reform could imply casting aside the limitations to our pluralism, heeding in practice the principles contained in our formal constitutional structures, and pushing the so-called "political reform" to its final consequences. Until now, this reform has implied only allowing opposition party entry into the lower house of Congress and into some local governments. In a true reform, the various social interests would be allowed to organize politically and independently until both populism and authoritarianism disappear. The new legitimacy would not be based on public sector subsidies, especially to the organized lower and middle classes, but on a real interaction of social forces through a true party system. The strength lost in the paternalistic relationship between the state and popular groups would be transferred to a civil society.[1]

The purpose of this chapter is to examine Mexico's past and present attempts at redemocratization within the context of the realities of Mexican politics and within the barriers to reform in a nation that fears its past in its visions of a changing future.

It is clear that any form of political opening must be examined within the context of Mexico's revolutionary past and the authoritarian structure of government that has prevailed since the successful institutionalization of the Institutionalized Revolutionary Party (PRI) in 1938. Also, redemocratization is greatly influenced by the profound economic crises and resultant austerity measures that have placed severe burdens on Mexico's lower and middle classes. Finally, Mexico's role as an "elder statesman" and mediator in revolutionary conflicts in Central America must have influence on domestic politics. Under two administrations, José López Portillo (1976–1982) and Miguel de la Madrid (1982–), Mexico has offered its own revolutionary process as an example of a successful transition to a democratic and stable regime.

Will the economic crises determine the continuation of Mexico's authoritarian regime? Or will economic hardships open up the possibility of changes in state-subject or (state-citizen) relations? Will changes in state-citizen relations be perceived by Mexico's political elite as a threat that may jeopardize the degree of "liberalization" that Mexicans enjoy? Will Mexico's role in Central America lead to an *apertura* in the Mexican system?

Within the context of conflicting national and international pressures we will examine these questions by looking at one important manifestation of Mexico's commitment to redemocratization: the electoral reforms of 1963 and 1979. The first reform, called the Law of Party Deputies, introduced a measure of proportional representation in the lower house of the Mexican Congress, the Chamber of Deputies. The 1979 reform, the Law of Political Organizations and Electoral Procedures (LOPPE), was an expansion of the 1963 reform.

The Mexican political system is undoubtedly one of the most stable in Latin America. After a violent and prolonged revolution, which began in 1910, power changed hands peacefully in the 1934 presidential elections. During the revolutionary conflict several of Mexico's revolutionary leaders organized a constituent assembly to determine the foundations for a new political order. Although some of the members of the assembly were interested in legitimating their political positions, the Mexican Constitution of 1917, which they produced, was an exhaustive document that was both socially innovative and democratically pluralistic in its orientations. Many of the social provisions concerning workers rights, maternal protections, and state ownership of subsoil resources were truly revolutionary for the early twentieth century. At the same time, under the influence of North American democracy, the Mexican Constitution was liberal democratic in its structuring of the Mexican political system. Federalism, the separation of powers, a bicameral legislature (Senate and Chamber of Deputies), and elections by majority vote were established.

The normative and legal precepts of 1917 notwithstanding, the actual evolution of Mexico's political system witnessed the development of a dominant party that the 1917 Constitution did not envision. Yet to understand democracy in Mexico the dual contexts of the constitutional framework and the political structure, of which the party system is an important component, must be interrelated.

Since its creation in 1929 as the National Revolutionary Party, the PNR has remained electorally invincible. Originally an organization of military political leaders, under the unquestioned leadership of General Plutarco Calles, the dominant party evolved in the 1930s from a regionally based coalition of military leaders into a functionally based party under the leadership of President Lazaro Cardenas. The ruling party, which later became known as the Institutional Party of the Revolution (PRI), has won virtually every major electoral competition— for the presidency, the governorships, and both houses of Congress—until 1964 when the Law of Party Deputies was introduced. Before the elections of 1964, the oldest and most viable opposition party, the National Actional Party, had won less than ten seats in the Chamber of Deputies in almost twenty-five years of electoral competition.

THEORETICAL FRAMEWORK

The Mexican regime has been called "authoritarian" following the path-breaking work of Juan Linz. Originally writing in 1964 and 1973, Linz was searching for a way to describe the Spanish regime of Francisco Franco.[2] He rejected the polarized "either-or" classification of totalitarian or democratic systems and argued that another type of regime existed between these two polar extremes, a variant that possessed characteristics of both totalitarian and democratic regimes. He argued that an authoritarian regime is most essentially characterized by limited political pluralism and low subject mobilization of the population. In authoritarian regimes, political parties and interest groups could organize as they could in a democracy, although their pluralism was limited, not autonomous. Citizens may be mobilized temporarily, as they are in totalitarian societies, to show their support for the regime's elite by means of elections or mass demonstrations, but in general, independent political participation is not rewarded.

These formulations have also been used by many to describe Mexico.[3] Indeed, the characterization of Mexico as an authoritarian regime remained essentially unchallenged or unrefined until recently. It is not that contemporary scholars dispute the nature of limited pluralism as a defining characteristic of Mexican politics. It is a case of scholars viewing Mexican democracy from perspectives that include pluralism as one of several important variables. In so doing the notion of low subject mobilization has been reexamined. Daniel Levy and Gabriel Szekely, for example, distinguished between collective rights to organize and individual rights. They maintained that Mexicans as individuals enjoy a large degree of personal political freedom, although the Mexican regime does not allow strong independent organizations to challenge the basic development model.[4]

If mobilization is to be viewed exclusively in terms of organized participation in politics, the original conceptualizations of low subject mobilization will still prevail in Mexico. However, John Booth and Mitchell Seligson found that a

largely democratic political culture exists in Mexico. In their survey of middle-
and working-class Mexicans a strong tolerance for civil liberties was apparent.[5]
Although this contradiction between a politically tolerant civic culture and the
maintenance of an authoritarian Mexican regime are currently difficult to explain
satisfactorily, it is with this context that we must discuss the Mexican political
system. The authoritarian regime is still an accurate portrayal of Mexican politics,
but to use the terms of this book, a high degree of liberalization and the possibility
of redemocratization also describe Mexico.

THE POLITICAL REFORMS OF 1963

Even though the PRI had not lost an election for president, governor, or
senator since 1940, unmistakable signs of systemic strain and loss of regime
support appeared before the passage of both the 1963 and 1979 laws. In introducing these reform measures, the regime demonstrated its flexibility in expanding the rules of the game in a way that did not seriously challenge the
boundaries of the political system. The 1963 reform was designed in part to
defuse the political dissent that occurred after the repression of the teachers and
railroad workers' strikes in 1958 and 1959. In part they were also intended to
strengthen the oldest loyal opposition party in Mexico, the National Action Party
(PAN), which was experiencing severe internal crises during this period. Although it can be argued that the 1963 reforms also benefited the two other
opposition parties, the Popular Socialist Party (PPS) and the Authentic Party of
the Mexican Revolution (PARM), these two parties were already weak and seen
as appendages (*paleros*) of the PRI. In retrospect, they did not revitalize themselves in the manner of the PAN even after the passage of the Law of Party
Deputies.

The 1963 law was to be a combination of election by majority vote in the
Senate, thus preserving the equality of the Mexican state and both proportional
representation and election by majority vote in the Chamber of Deputies. Thus
the Chamber would elect a combination of majority deputies (*diputados de
mayoría*) and party deputies (*diputados de partido*). Specifically, the law intended
to avoid the proliferation of small parties by requiring that a minority party must
gain 2.5 percent of the total vote to be eligible to elect a maximum of twenty
party deputies. If a party won 2.5 percent of the total vote it would receive five
seats in the Chamber of Deputies and one additional seat for each 0.5 percent
above 2.5 percent until a total of twenty seats was reached. Those candidates
who did not win by majority, but who polled the most votes relative to the other
candidates in their party, would become party deputies. Under the 1963 law the
number of deputies could not rise above twenty. One key provision of this law
was revised in 1973 to expand minority representation further. Since 1973 the
percentage of votes needed to become eligible for the system of party deputies
was reduced from 2.5 to 1.5 percent, and the maximum number of seats increased
from twenty to twenty-five.

The history of the 1963 Law of Party Deputies was intertwined with the history of the PAN, the strongest opposition party in Mexico. In the early 1960s the PAN experienced a profound internal crisis concerning its role in Mexican politics. In part, the impetus for the introduction of the 1963 law came from Adolfo Christlieb Ibarrola, president of the PAN from 1962 to 1968. Christlieb worked arduously both to unify and politically modernize the PAN and to make the role of strengthened opposition party acceptable to the rank and file membership. During the 1960s the PAN, which has always been the party of Mexican Catholics, was divided between its more traditional Catholic supporters and those who wanted the PAN to become a Mexican Christian Democratic party. In an effort to unify and politically modernize the PAN, Christlieb reaffirmed Acción Nacional as a Mexican party grounded in Mexico's historical reality. Specifically, the PAN definitively rejected any transformation into a political party of a religious or confessional nature that would invoke constitutional sanctions against the existence of a religiously based party. At the same time the PAN formally rejected any legal association with Latin American Christian Democratic parties.

The political modernization of the PAN under Christlieb's leadership was not so much a radical change in party doctrine or statutes as a change in political orientation. As a reflection of the ambiguity of its political goals, the PAN always avoided being implicated in the Mexican political system. Somehow Acción Nacional in its self-image was above politics; it was not responsible for political corruption and the lack of democracy in Mexico.

Christlieb altered the negative image of the PAN by formulating a positive role for political opposition in Mexico, one that could make a constructive contribution to the operation of the regime. The PAN, as a political opposition, was not to remain above politics, but rather, the party and the government should recognize the need for mutual, revitalized cooperation. To Christlieb, opposition and dialogue were integral parts of a democratic system.[6]

With the 1963 introduction of the law that established party deputies, the influence of the PAN increased greatly. First, the PAN consistently won a majority of party deputies in every congressional election from 1964 to 1976. Second, PAN prestige reached its peak in the Chamber of Deputies during the 1964–67 electoral term. In an unprecedented move, PAN deputy Abel Vicencio Tovar became second vice-president of the Chamber of Deputies, and PAN deputies were included in the membership of the majority of congressional commissions. Finally, Adolfo Christlieb, who was elected as a party deputy for the 1964–67 term, accompanied President López Mateos and PRI leader Alfonso Martínez Domínguez to the opening session of the Chamber of Deputies. Thus by 1967 the PAN seemed to have solved its internal problems and accepted and benefited from the political reform law.[7]

The PAN leadership and the majority of PAN's membership endorsed the system of proportional representation. The statement of Efraín González Mórfin, PAN presidential candidate in 1970, exemplified the prevailing attitude of the party:

In 1963, the PAN deputation supported the system of proportional representation as one way to open Congress to reform. Proportional representation was seen as a transitory reform which was a logical move for this point in time. Christlieb maintained full lucidity about the significance of the risks the party was taking . . . The PAN believed the initiative would open new roads to government and return hope to the party.[8]

Increased PAN prestige and improved PAN/political elite relations also encouraged additional PAN victories not only in the Congress but at the local and state levels. The PAN won municipal elections in Garza García, Nuevo Leon (1965), and in Hermosillo, Sonora, and Mérida, Yucatan (1967), both important state capitals, in addition to thirteen other mayoralities. The following year (1968) the PAN won the mayoralities and gained control of the city councils in Tijuana and Mexicali, Baja California, although the PRI-controlled state legislatures refused to confirm the electoral results.[9]

In retrospect, the nullification of the PAN 1968 municipal victories in Baja California was a preview of worsening relations between the PAN and the political elite. The following year (1969), the PAN candidate Manuel Correa Racho lost the gubernational elections in Yucatan. By all accounts of the foreign and domestic press, Correa Racho was victorious; however, after the vote count, the PRI candidate was declared the winner.[10]

The elite response to the PAN municipal victories and (alleged) state victory in Yucatan quickly negated the attempt to consider the introduction of proportional representation as the full maturation of democracy. PAN electoral victories in an arena of Mexican politics such as the state or local levels, which the political elite could not monitor as effectively, weakened the viability of a responsible role for the opposition. Ironically, the 1963 reforms were not pursued to their fullest implications because they were a success. The PAN was winning more than congressional elections.

PAN's electoral victories jeopardized PAN/political elite relations and ultimately led to an abrupt termination of the policy of dialogue. Beginning in 1967 the political elite attempted to influence Christlieb to insure that the PAN did not continue winning.[11] Throughout 1968 both President Diaz Ordaz and Interior Minister Luís Echeverría, who was responsible for state electoral procedures, tried to negotiate an electoral position with Christlieb to prevent any further embarrassing electoral conflicts or PAN victories. Throughout 1968, as the Echeverria/Christlieb negotiation continued, it became apparent that what the political elite did not want was "a repeat in Chihuahua (in forthcoming municipal elections) of what happened in Baja California."[12] As we have seen the PAN won two important municipal victories in Baja California, which were not confirmed by the PRI-controlled state legislature.

In the last meetings between Christlieb and Luis Echeverria, Christlieb adamantly refused to negotiate electoral positions, believing that victory must be decided by the vote, and in no way would he influence the PAN to invalidate electoral results in Chuhuahua or in upcoming gubernational elections in Yucatan. The policy of dialogue ended in the months before the 1969 elections.

In September 1968 Christlieb resigned from the presidency of the PAN for reasons of health. In his letter of resignation he spoke of the policy of dialogue as a hopeful beginning that was never achieved. In the following excerpt from his resignation speech Christlieb left no doubt about the cause of the termination of the policy of dialogue. He stated:

During my presidency I tried to guide the PAN into political conduct which supposed a minimum of good faith on the part of the group in power, in order to develop independent opposition. I cannot separate the political and personal debilitation that I feel; the over-whelming multiplication of frequently sterile efforts which compelled the incomprehensible political closing (of access to) public power and the attitude of many citizens who from a position of inertia, reduce their political participation to an indictment of everyone and everything. . . . I must acknowledge and give thanks for the understanding and support for this "line" of conduct within the Party, in spite of the official policy of doors closed to opposition, of pressures, disreputable actions, threats and even prosecutions against our dedicated members, who nevertheless, still believe that this line of conduct we have followed, is not only possible, but constructive, in order to achieve greater harmony among all Mexicans.[13]

With Christlieb's refusal to negotiate, the spector of the PAN/PRI conflict in Yucatan was evident to all, especially Christlieb, who was gravely ill. Fifteen days before the gubernational elections in Yucatan, on December 6, 1969, Christlieb died of cancer. In a very controversial election, the PAN candidate Manuel Correa Racho lost the gubernational elections.

POLITICAL REFORMS OF 1979

Against the preceding background we must discuss the 1979 electoral reform and its causes and consequences. During the late 1960s the Mexican regime was threatened with another crisis of legitimacy of great intensity. The government's ruthless response to student protests in 1968, during which police killed many students, provoked a widespread negative public response. The poor quality of many PRI nominees for important national offices had become a source of embarrassment for the regime. Given the control of the electoral machinery, the location of voting booths, voter registration lists, registration of political parties by the Federal Electoral Commission, PRI nomination is tantamount to election, no matter how qualified the candidate. Voter turnout declined dramatically during the years from 1967 to 1979 and to the embarrassment of the regime, López Portillo ran unopposed for the presidency in 1976. The PAN, which usually offered the PRI an opposition presidential candidate, was in the midst of a profound internal debate following its disillusionment with the system of party deputies.

Finally, both legal and illegal opposition to the regime was becoming increasingly visible in the early 1970s. In poorer rural areas, such as Guerrero, guerrilla movements were active. More ''respectable'' yet unsanctioned opposition groups with a long history of subrosa political activity reemerged once again. On the right of the political spectrum the successor to the Sinarquista party of the 1940s (Popular Force) and the Mexican National Party (PNM) of the 1960s was the Mexican Democratic Party (PDM). On the left many parties, such as the Mexican Communist Party, the Revolutionary Workers Party, and the Movement Toward Unified Socialism (MAUS), all claiming to represent the working classes, had formed.

By the middle 1970s it was impossible to maintain the status quo in Mexican politics. The level of individual and collective mobilization was indeed high, yet unchanneled. As in 1963 the means by which to organize this spirited opposition was to expand the range of legal political participation. The 1977 electoral reforms were designed to raise the level of debate within Mexican politics in a manner that did not threaten the ongoing functioning of the regime. But this time, in recognition of the magnitude of opposition, the provisions of the 1977 reform were more generous than those of the 1963 law.

In examining the provisions of the LOPPE, what is most evident are the philosophical and procedural similarities of this law with that of its predecessor, the 1963 Law of Party Deputies. Both laws expressed a need for greater democracy in Mexico; both acknowledged the legitimacy of minority representation to be insured through the introduction of proportional representation in the lower house of Congress. Both laws spoke against the tyranny of minorities and made it clear that the will of the majority must prevail.[14]

To insure that the opposition parties continued to participate in the electoral process the LOPPE also contained a provision that all political parties must participate in elections or risk cancellation of their permanent registration. In other words, the example set in 1976, when López Portillo ran unchallenged, should not be repeated.

However, the law did introduce potentially important changes. The total membership of the Chamber of Deputies was expanded from 235 to 400 deputies: 300 would be elected as majority deputies by simple majority vote from uninomial districts. The remaining 100 deputies were to be elected under the system of proportional representation from plurinomial districts. Minority parties must present lists of candidates; each party will be assigned from its lists a number of deputies in accordance with the percentage of the votes it has received in that district. In practice the system of proportional representation applies only to the minority opposition parties, because those parties that have elected more than 60 majority deputies, such as the PRI, are not eligible to elect party deputies.

An important measure of flexibility associated with the LOPPE was the expansion of political participation to parties on both the left and the right of the political spectrum. In the 1963 period, the passage of the Law of Party Deputies was accompanied by the arbitrary cancellation of the registration of political parties on both the right and left.[15] In contrast, to encourage more political parties to apply for registration, the LOPPE required that a nascent party obtain 2,000 members in at least two-thirds of the states of Mexico (originally 3,000 affiliates were needed). By 1979 when the first elections under the LOPPE were to take place, three new parties had received their legal permission to participate. Two of these parties, the Mexican Communist Party (PCM) and the PDM, were specifically denied participation a decade earlier. The third new party, the Socialist Workers Party (PST) joined the ranks of the PAN, PPS, and PARM as competitors.

Finally, the LOPPE made some attempt to open up the means of communication to the opposition parties. Before 1977 the opposition parties had access only to radio and television time during election periods. Under the LOPPE, opposition parties had free regular access to the communications media every month to publicize their programs and positions.

POLITICAL PARTICIPATION IN THE 1979 AND THE 1982 ELECTIONS

Did Mexico institute the beginnings of a pluralist party system as a result of the LOPPE, or is the LOPPE another extension of an authoritarian regime? Undoubtedly, the electoral results of 1979 and 1982 witnessed the eventual demise of two of Mexico's oldest opposition parties: the PARM and the PPS. The PARM received 2.1 percent of the total vote in 1979 (and twelve party deputies), but by 1982 the party polled slightly less than the 1.5 percent needed to maintain its legal position. Thus its political registration was cancelled. One indication of change might be that in the 1964, 1967, and 1973 elections the PARM received less than 1.5 percent of the vote but was rescued by the political elite and awarded seats in the Chamber. In 1979 the PPS received 2.8 percent of the total vote (and ten party deputies), but by 1982 it had received only 2.2 percent of the total vote and may well be following the destiny of the PARM. Thus, with the exception of the PAN, the older opposition parties have made way for the new.

The PAN reaffirmed its role as the most viable opposition party by winning 11.5 percent of the total vote and elected four majority deputies and thirty-nine party deputies to the Chamber of Deputies in the 1979 elections. The PCM polled 5.1 percent of the vote and elected eighteen party deputies. The other newly registered parties, the PST and the PDM, each elected ten party deputies.

In the 1982 elections the PAN increased its share of the total votes cast in the Chamber of Deputies races to 17.5 percent and elected fifty party deputies. In the presidential elections, PAN candidate Pablo Emilio Madero received 16.4 percent of the vote, a far distant second to PRI candidate Miguel de la Madrid. Arnaldo Martínez Verdugo of the Unified Mexican Socialist Party (PSUM), which in 1981 succeeded the PCM, received only 3.65 percent of the vote. In a slight decline from the electoral success of 1979 the PSUM elected sixteen party deputies in the 1982 Chamber of Deputies. Voter abstention remained high during the 1979 elections when more than 50 percent of those eligible to vote did not do so. However, in the 1982 elections voter abstention declined to 30 percent.[16]

In the 1979–82 session of the Mexican Congress the Chamber of Deputies became an arena for political debate, with the PAN and the PCM dominating congressional discussions.[17] In fact, the PCM appeared to be the most energetic and vocal of the newly registered opposition parties. Mexico's moderate Communists wanted to turn the usually passive Chamber into a European parliament and to call cabinet ministers to testify and account for their policies. The PCM wanted Congress to define the petroleum policy of the nation. Yet at the same time the PCM was enmeshed in the dilemma of being an opposition party in an authoritarian regime. If it does succeed in revitalizing the Mexican Congress its very success will strengthen Congress' role and legitimate the existing regime. Martínez Verdugo, secretary-general of the PCM and 1982 presidential nominee of the PSUM, was aware of this difficulty when he argued that the Communist Party would not "submit itself to the rules of the game . . . and was prepared to return to illegality if necessary."[18] Martínez also predicted the "great alliance of the Mexican left"* would show that participation in the Chamber of Deputies can be done for revolutionary goals.

Yet how far can the opposition go in its attempt to broaden its bases of support? In ideological terms the "conservative" PAN and the "progressive" PCM are far apart; yet one wonders if what happened to the PAN in 1968 as a result of its electoral success beyond the Congress lies in the future of the left? Electoral participation and electoral victory are essential to the life of an opposition party if it is to continue to be a political party and recruit new members. At present, the prevailing view within the left is that it can do more legally than it was able to do illegally, although a notable exception to this view can be found in the Mexican Workers party (PMT). This minority party, founded by Herberto Castillo, did not participate in the elections of 1979 or 1982 and would not officially join the PSUM. It opposed the LOPPE and the government's control of the Federal Electoral Commission.[19]

The creation of a vibrant, broadly based opposition will be a most difficult task. First, opposition parties must participate in the elections to maintain their permanent registration. Second, many parties believe they must nominate as many congressional candidates and alternates as possible, a potential maximum of 800 nominees. Jesus Reyes Heroles, a principal author of the LOPPE, former director of PEMEX, and former president of the PRI, admitted that if the elections were completely honest there would have to be representatives of the opposition parties at all 43,000 voting stations (*casillas*) in the nation. Most importantly, "For power to be transferred to the opposition they would need the infrastructure and power to exercise control over the state—this was far in the future. The

*The PSUM was formed in November 1981.

reform was intended to be gradual, cautious and moderate. No party has the infrastructure and power to control the state at this point in time."[20]

THE ROLE OF THE OPPOSITION, 1983

The PAN has been the most visible beneficiary of Mexico's electoral reforms. In the municipal elections of July 3, 1983, the PAN won the mayoralities of a number of major cities including Ciudad Juárez, Baja California, and Ciudad Comargo, Chihuahua, as well as five other municipalities. Uncharacteristically, the PRI candidates conceded defeat in these elections.[21]

The PAN seemed to have resolved the internal crises over Christian democracy, which deeply divided the party during the 1960s. It also resolved its debate over the merits of electoral participation, which resulted in its non-participation in the 1976 presidential elections. The party has returned to its traditional bases of support among the urban middle classes and the petty bourgeoisie. It is also possible that it has gained some support from the demise of the PARM and from those who are dissatisfied with the economic measures of the de la Madrid administration.

During the summer of 1983 there was an air of expectancy surrounding the PAN. Following its municipal victories in Baja California and Chihuahua the PAN was working for its gubernational candidate in the upcoming September elections in Baja California. Many PAN members conceded that to win a governorship they would have to win by a four to one margin to prevent the all-too-frequent occurrence of electoral fraud. When the ballots were counted the PRI nominee, a candidate chosen by the Mexican Workers Confederation (CTM), won the governorship of Baja California.[22]

If the PAN has found its niche in Mexican politics the PSUM has yet to discover its place. Logic would have suggested that the PSUM would do well in the congressional elections of 1982 and the municipal elections of 1983. This line of reasoning argued that given the degree of economic crisis in Mexico, which reduced the purchasing power of many lower and lower middle-class Mexicans, the PSUM and not the PAN should have received a large protest vote. Yet there are several reasons why this did not occur. First, the PSUM is a new actor on the Mexican scene and was not as well known as the PAN. National Action, since its formation in 1939, has had much higher visibility and has been the party urban Mexicans vote for (if they vote) when they want to cast a protest vote against the PRI.

Second, because many of its ideological statements were similar to those of the PRI, the PSUM was not considered to be that different from the PRI. The PSUM members would argue that they did not win because the PRI cannot allow victories to the left of the spectrum, only to the right.[23] In support of this we must mention the municipal elections in Juchitán, Oaxaca, in which COCEI, a regional movement of marginalized peasants, workers, and students, was involved. COCEI split from the PRI and supported the PSUM in the municipal elections in July 1983. The PSUM won the Juchitán, municipal elections which were then invalidated by the PRI-controlled state legislature.[24]

However accurate these reasons may be, we must add another reason for the PSUM's lack of success. Because it is a coalition party of four organizations of the left—PCM, PPM, MAUS and PST—the PSUM must formulate a coherent ideology to present to the public. This will require much accommodation and seemed to be in process in 1983–84. Despite the notion of many Mexicans that the PSUM was an imitation of the PRI, it must be said that important differences existed between the two parties. The Socialists rejected the capitalist thrust of Mexican development, Mexico's subordination to transnational capital, and the acceptance of IMF regulations. They feared the aggravation of social divisions in Mexico—what has been called the "argentinization" of Mexican politics. Instead they wanted to see a consolidation of a popular movement based in the working classes, the peasantry, and the universities.[25]

To build this popular movement the PSUM must extend its base beyond university circles and rely on those members of its leadership who can increase the party's support within the labor movement. Despite some contentious exchanges between CTM leader Fidel Velasquez and President de la Madrid, most CTM unions seemed set in their patterns of government acquiescence.[26] In fact, the LOPPE was perceived as threatening to the CTM. It reasoned that if the number of party deputy seats was to increase in the Chamber of Deputies there would be fewer seats for labor and consequently less patronage opportunities.[27]

Looking beyond the CTM, what is the possibility for other PSUM-labor alliances with the Revolutionary Labor Confederation (COR) or the Revolutionary Confederation of Workers and Peasants (CROC) or with independent unions that were invited to join the umbrella group, the Labor Congress, in January 1983? Thus far, the severity of the economic crisis, the sharp decline in real wages, and the hardships imposed by economic stabilization measures have not resulted in a commensurate response from the labor unions. Yet the potential for changes in state-labor relations is clearly present, especially when the CTM must deal with the problem of the succession to eighty-four-year-old Fidel Velasquez. The PSUM is a party whose potential has yet to be realized.

CONCLUSION: THE ROLE OF THE ELITE

During the first two years of his administration, de la Madrid has enacted a series of unpopular austerity measures; yet the strongly predicted social unrest has not erupted. De la Madrid has managed thus far to convince many constituencies that the government has done what was necessary to resolve the problems of massive foreign debt, a decline in oil prices, and currency devaluations. In part the campaign of moral renovation, announced in his inaugural address of December 1982, was intended to show the Mexican people that the government also had a commitment to fiscal responsibility and belt tightening. The renovation was intended to fight corruption at the highest levels of the government, to hold officials accountable for past misuse of Mexico's scarce resources, and to bolster the legitimacy of the Mexican regime.[29]

Also, Mexico's insistence on a negotiated settlement of the conflicts in Central America may compel Mexico to further redemocratization. The argument herein is that setting one's own house in order might set an example for the nations of Central America. Although not intending to minimize this possibility, Mexico's role in Central America has had an additional consequence that ironically has worked against further redemocratization. To the extent that de la Madrid can maintain foreign policy independence from North American positions and thus reaffirm Mexican nationalism, he has succeeded in creating more "political space" at home. Thus his administration can continue unpopular domestic economic policies and postpone further efforts at redemocratization.

The focus of this chapter has been on Mexico's electoral reforms from the perspective of the opposition parties. To be sure, within an authoritarian regime there are some actions that the parties themselves can take. They must formulate a coherent ideology, participate in the electoral process, and attract new members. Yet the political elite itself must act boldly as well as symbolically in future years if full redemocratization is to take hold in Mexico. Recent survey data, which attested to the existence of a democratic political culture, would suggest that the citizenry is ready.

The most dramatic move that Mexico's political elite could make to further redemocratization would be to grant the opposition its victories when they occur, at whatever level. The PRI would continue to win the vast majority of elections, but the opposition would elect majority deputies, senators, and governors. The PAN might win the governorships of Yucatan, Baja California, and Nuevo León. A gradual opening of the political system would involve substantial risks for the political elite and would entail new precedents. The patronage functions and candidate selection procedures of the PRI would have to change. Governorships cannot be guaranteed positions for ex-cabinet ministers, ex-senators, and *ex-tapados*. In effect, the task of internal democratization, which the PRI has been reluctant to try, would be stimulated from without—by opposition victories. Moreover, fiscal relations between the federal government and the states would be modified. The political bargaining between members of the elite, which occurs now in private, would become more public if the opposition had a stake in the bargaining process.

By 1984 one could sense a tension within the Mexican elite and within the PRI—a tension between those who want to maintain the status quo, the patronage nominations of the past, and those who are willing to explore other possibilities. Mexicans themselves make a distinction between the technocrats (*técnicos*) and the politicians (*politicos*) and admit that more of the former are to be found in the de la Madrid administration than in previous administrations. One wonders what changes the infusion of technocrats into the Mexican political system will have, especially if the present economic crisis can be surmounted.

A modest restructuring of the political system is possible if the efficiency-oriented, pragmatic values of technocracy can be made to prevail over the old-line coalition-building politics for which the PRI is legendary. In a curious twist of fate the PRI must do what the Democratic Party must do in the aftermath of the 1984 elections: reassess its bases of support, initiate internal reform, and reassess its selection of candidates and its procedures for selection. The patronage functions of the PRI will not disappear overnight, but if the technocrats can set the policy agenda for the PRI, it is possible that the party's slate of nominees for major offices will be more professional in orientation. It is unlikely that some form of primary system would formalize a competition for nominations within the ruling party; yet even a majority of *técnico* candidates would signal an important, informal change, which could have far-reaching implications. Potential PRI candidates would know they would be judged more on the basis of competency, and opposition parties might perceive a greater incentive to participate. Increased competition would also strengthen the democratic system established by the Mexican Constitution more than sixty years ago. For this to happen the economic crisis must be overcome, and the older generation of leaders who have guided the dominant sectors of the PRI and built their personal careers on their patronage power must retire.

Yet many Mexicans, across many walks of life and within the political elite, are afraid of change and the potential violence that could be unleashed.[30] In 1979 Reyes Heroles admitted that there was discussion within the political elite about opposition victories. In a speech he delivered in Spain at the second Meeting of Hispanic Social Scientists Reyes Heroles stated: "With reference to the transfer of a state government when it is won by the opposition, it was very difficult because this transference or its mere possibility provoked prolonged discussion and strong divisions inside the nucleus in power. In the power nucleus there were groups disposed to handling the state government to the opposition if they won, but there were others that were solidly opposed."[30]

In an interesting commentary on the rules of the game in Mexico, *Proceso* reporter Francisco Jose Paoli, who covered the Meeting of Hispanic Social Scientists, was publicly informed by the President of the PRI, Gustavo Carvajal, speaking on behalf of Reyes Heroles, that Paoli did not report his comments with accuracy. In a subsequent issue of *Proceso* Paoli did not retract his coverage but instead amplified it.

We began this chapter by speaking of Spanish authoritarianism as a framework for Mexican politics. We return once again to a comparison of Spain and Mexico. Spanish authoritarianism, institutionalized by forty years duration, collapsed quickly when General Franco died. On balance, even in the midst of economic austerity, attempted military coups, and regional conflicts, a functioning parliamentary democracy has replaced Franco's system. Yet for many in Mexico, Spain's experience does not seem to be in Mexico's future because Mexico is a captive of its past. Mexico never had a strong tradition of liberal democracy in the nineteenth century, and one out of fifteen Mexicans died in a bitter revolution that raged from 1910 to 1934. Mexicans look to the repression of

Chile as a more likely possibility for what type of changes would occur if the Mexican system were to depart from its limited pluralism. At present the path of least resistance is to maintain the political status quo. Yet the burden placed upon legal opposition groups is enormous, and the rewards are meager. At the same time it is difficult to sanction illegal and violent opposition. Mexico's political leaders surely must remember that the Porfirian system, because it closed all routes to genuine power sharing, collapsed of its own weight.

NOTES

1. Lorenzo Meyer, "Mexico: "The Political Problems of Economic Stabilization," in Donald L. Wyman, ed., *Mexico's Economic Crisis: Challenges and Opportunities,* Monograph Series, no. 12 (La Jolla, Calif.: Center for U.S.-Mexican Studies, 1983), p. 122.

2. Juan Linz, "An Authoritarian Regime: Spain," in Erik Allardt and Yrto Littunen, eds., *Clearages, Ideologies, and Party Systems* (Helsinki: Academic Bookstore, 1964), pp. 291–341; idem, "Opposition to and under an Authoritarian Regime: The Case of Spain," in Robert Dahl, ed., *Regimes and Oppositions* (New Haven: Yale University Press, 1973).

3. Most recently, see Kenneth Coleman and Charles Davis, "Preemptive Reform and the Mexican Working Class, *Latin American Research Review* 28, no. 1 (1983): 3–31; José Luís Reyna, and Richard Weinert, *Authoritarianism in Mexico* (Philadelphia: Institute for the Study of Human Issues, 1977); Susan Kaufman Purcell, *The Mexican Profit-Sharing Decision: Politics in an Authoritarian Regime* (Berkeley: University of California Press, 1975).

4. See, for example, the discussion in chapters 3 and 4 of Daniel Levy, and Gabriel Szekely, *Mexico: Paradoxes of Stability and Change* (Boulder, Colo.: Westview Press, 1983).

5. John A. Booth, and Mitchell A. Seligson, "The Political Culture of Authoritarianism in Mexico: A Reexamination," *Latin American Research Review* 19, no. 1 (1984): 106–125.

6. See, for example, "La Oposicíon Democrática," in Adolfo Christlieb, *Solidaridad y Participacíon* (Mexico: Accíon Nacional, 1969); *La Nacíon,* April 1, 1968, pp. 3–4.

7. *La Nacíon,* September 4, 1964, pp. 2–3.

8. Interview with Efrain Gonzalez Morfin, June 20, 1975.

9. In fact, in June 1969 the state assumed control of the municipal police, thus beginning a decline in the quality of Merida's social services. For full coverage, see *Excelsior,* June 13, 1969; *La Nacíon,* June 1969.

10. See the coverage in *Excelsior,* September and October 1969.

11. This section relies on interviews with Sra. Hilda Morales de Christlieb, Adolfo Christlieb Morales, and Javier Christlieb, July and August 1975, Mexico City.

12. Interview with Adolfo Christlieb Morales, son of PAN president Adolfo Christlieb, July 23, 1976.

13. *La Nacíon,* September 16, 1968.

14. For example, the 1963 law recognized "the urgency of giving a legitimate outlet to the expression of minority political parties but it was also necessary to conserve the

former Mexican tradition of electoral majorities.'' Diaz Ordaz, Iniciativa de Ley, *Diario de los Debates*, Mexico City, 1962.

15. For an extended discussion of the exclusion of parties from the 1963 elections, see chapter 4 of Laura N. O'Shaughnessy, "Opposition in an Authoritarian Regime: The Incorporation and Institutionalization of the Mexican National Action Party (PAN)," (Ph.D. diss., Indiana University, 1977).

16. Levy and Szekely, *Mexico: Paradoxes of Stability and Change*, p. 77. See also *La Nacíon*, July 28, 1982, pp. 16–18, for complete voting statistics.

17. See, for example, *Regional Reports: Mexico and Central America, RM79–01*, p. 16 (November 16, 1979).

18. Elias Chavez, "Interview with Arnaldo Martinez Verdugo," *Proceso*, July 9, 1979, pp. 6–9.

19. The views of the PMT are similar to those expressed by many Mexican intellectuals who wanted to see a more inclusive political reform as distinct from an electoral reform. These ideas are presented in Octavio Rodriquez Araujo, *La Reforma Politica y Los Partidos en Mexico* (Mexico City: Siglo XXI, 1979).

20. *Proceso*, October 8, 1979, p. 5.

21. *La Nacion*, July 16, 1983; *Latin American Regional Report: Mexico and Central America*, July 15, 1983.

22. Interviews in Mexico City with PAN deputy Marco Antonio Fragoso, August 15, 1983, and with Lic. Gonzalo Altamirano, press spokesman for the PAN, August 17, 1983.

23. Interview in Mexico City with Miguel Angel Guzman, director of publications for the PSUM, August 11, 1983.

24. See coverage in *Uno Mas Uno*, September 29, 1983, p. 3; and October 1, 1983, p. 5.

25. The support of the PSUM in Mexican intellectual circles can be seen in the preference for a working-class solution to Mexico's problems as expressed in Pablo Gonzalez Casanova, and Enrique Florescano, eds., *Mexico, Hoy* (Mexico City: Siglo XXI, 1979).

26. Miguel de la Madrid was not labor's choice to succeed López Portillo. Velasquez publicly threatened massive strikes if the government took the unions for granted, and the president said publicly that the CTM unions could be expendable and he was not in favor of "irresponsible populism," a reference to the package of social benefits the CTM workers receive.

27. Labor's role in the making of the LOPPE is discussed in Kevin J. Middlebrook, Susan Kaufman Purcell, ed., "Political Change in Mexico," in *Mexico-United States Relations* (New York: Proceedings of the Academy of Political Science, 1981), pp. 55–67.

28. Barry Carr, "The Mexican Economic Debacle and the Labor Movement: A New Era or More of the Same?" in Donald L. Wyman, ed., *Mexico's Economic Crisis: Challenges and Opportunities*, Monograph Series, no. 12 (La Jolla, Calif.: Center for U.S.-Mexican Studies, 1983), p. 20.

29. To date, the indictment of Diaz Serrano, former director of PEMEX, on charges of mismanagement of $34 million has been the most publicized case of "moral renovation." See *New York Times*, August 27, 1983, p. 2.

30. In many conversations with market women, taxi drivers, and newspaper vendors, the possibility of thorough changes in "el sistema" were not taken seriously. The PAN

could never win, according to one woman, because ''the PRI is a monster in the service of the government and it will devour any serious opposition.'' Others told stories about the revolution and how it must never occur again. Given the relative youth of the Mexican population, statements such as the preceding are a strong testimony to the dominant interpretation of the Revolution in Mexican culture.

    31. *Proceso*, October 8, 1979, p. 7.

3

Prospects for Liberalization by Way of Democratization in Guatemala

Gordon L. Bowen

The pageant of Central Americans voting new leaders into office has formed a dramatic accompaniment to contemporary U.S.-sponsored anti-Communist crusades in the region. Can ballot boxes erected in the 1980s prove pivotal in the establishment of liberal regimes if social consensus remains absent? If ballotings can help to nudge violent political systems toward becoming more liberal societies, what additional steps should follow elections?

The object of this chapter is to view these issues more clearly. To do so, we must consider local traditions as well as abstract requisites of tolerant, procedural ways of holding leaders accountable to their subjects. Even in the Western European experience, the fit of economic modernization and the evolution of democratic institutions has been imperfect (e.g., Germany's zigzag course). Western democracy has been most successfully achieved when elite consensus on procedural norms has preceded the extension of voting rights to the masses. In the absence of this, when mass demands for participation (and for distribution of benefits) have occurred simultaneously with the extension of political rights, political decay often has followed.[1]

In this chapter these relationships are explored in regard to one of Latin America's most illiberal societies, Guatemala. Having had authentic, elected governments for only a ten-year span (1944–54) in its 150-year independent history, traditions that form barriers to democracy are many.

THE MAIN POLITICAL ACTORS

For the past thirty-two years, liberal social norms and tolerant popular governments have eluded the Guatemalan people. Civilian leaders have been overshadowed by military rule, both direct and indirect. Since the 1960s, guerrilla insurgents, the official Armed Forces, and their paramilitary allies have created widespread political violence. Most acutely felt since 1978, this climate of violence has made it more difficult to forge consensus on peaceful norms of political competition and basic public policies.

Yet the thirst for change is widespread: nearly three-fourths of the potential adult electorate voted in the fall 1985 presidential and legislative elections. A clear mandate for change was given to the winning Democracia Cristiana Guatemalteca, or Christian Democrats (DCG). DCG party leader Marco Vinicio Cerezo Arevalo was inaugurated as president on January 14, 1986. He took office after having won 68 percent of the presidential vote. Additionally, his party controlled a narrow (but clear) majority of 51 of 100 seats in the unicameral National Congress.

Holding office, however, is not the same as holding power. Major Guatemalan political forces long have opposed open electoral routes to power. In the past, the use of political violence has formed a profound barrier to the creation of a more liberal society and politics. Notably, military regimes consistently have excluded leftists and Communists (Guatemalan Workers' Party [PGT]) from legitimate forums. Political violence also has been the primary mode of interest articulation used by the Guatemalan National Revolutionary Unity (URNG), the organizational rubric for the nation's four underground, leftist guerrilla armies. Spokesman for its political front, the RUOG (United Representation of the Guatemalan Opposition), Raul Molina Mejia expressed this intransigence toward peaceful change clearly when, in 1984, he said that ''the electoral process does not mean anything within a situation of internal armed conflict.''[2] Major elements within both the leftist guerrilla movement and the Armed Forces have continued to oppose reforms under democratically elected leaders' guidance as the route to national conciliation.

Beyond the men and women with guns, the buds of a liberalized leadership still may exist. Some Guatemalans consistently have opted for ballots over bullets. But pervasive violence often has been focused on these above-ground reform movements: assassinations and forcible disappearance of civilian potential leaders in recent decades has stilled many civic-minded voices. Thirty-five thousand (or more) Guatemalans remain missing after abduction. Thousands more have fled this ''dirty war'' into foreign exile. In the middle 1980s, it would appear that civic confidence can be renewed fully only by policies that bring about a complete end to flagrant violence against those peaceably involved in public life.

For a civilian administration to reverse the anti-democratic traditions, it must secure the power to create the rule of law. It must erase the public expectation of rule by gunmen in the night. Extra-legal violence must come to be perceived as having too high a personal price for those used to practicing it. Only from such seeds can a new degree of trust develop among officials, their opposition, and the public. The previously dominant army and the guerrillas must be convinced by the deeds of law-abiding authorities that it is a personal and group necessity to move beyond violent combat both against each other and against those believed to be the civilian supporters of their adversary.

In the best of circumstances, this would be no mean feat. Yet the very process of democratization in some ways may have soured relations between civilian politicians and those who hold the preponderance of lethal power, the Guatemalan military. DCG spokesmen, for example, repeatedly have characterized the situation as one in which "the citizens have suffered at the hands of the authorities." According to Amnesty International, the Organization of American States' (OAS's) Interamerican Commission on Human Rights (CIDH), and numerous other reputable investigators, officially planned assassinations, disappearances, and massacres of civilians were, in fact, the hallmark of the military governments of the 1970s and 1980s.[3] The chastized Armed Forces can find little solace in the election of Cerezo. Within his first month in office, police (though not army) personnel were detained for some of these criminal activities.[4] Military relations with the DCG never have been good: DCG candidates were barred from the 1966 election and had the 1974 victory of a candidate they backed stolen from them by fraudulent vote tallies.

The civilian opposition to the DCG stands to its right but also is hardly pro-military in its public presentations. The leader of the Union del Centro Nacional, or Union of the National Center (UCN), Jorge Carpio Nicole, has been a critical journalist and newspaper publisher (*El Grafico*) for years. As a candidate and politician winning 22 to 32 percent support, 1984–86, he steadily has accused the army of condoning electoral fraud in the past, of ruling by corruption, and of violence so grave as to have created "a moral, economic and social calamity."[5] Understatement is not a well-developed art in Guatemala. Even the stridently right-wing Movimiento de Liberación Nacionál, or National Liberation Movement (MLN), during the election campaigns charged the police and past military governments with complicity in a vast pattern of violent crimes.[6] Short of disbanding Central America's most efficient anti-Communist army, can such widespread distrust be reconciled with policies that sustain progress toward a reformed political process and a liberalized society? This remains the dilemma for civilian government in Guatemala.

THE STAKES INVOLVED

Advocates of liberal societies and elected governments must wrestle with the fit between their values and the protection of U.S. national interests. Although less visible in North America than neighboring El Salvador (which borders Guatemala) and Nicaragua (which does not), the ultimate resolution of the violence in Guatemala may prove to be of more profound significance to U.S. national security. Like the activity in El Salvador, since the late 1970s, large-scale military conflict between guerrilla forces and the official state army has raged. Conservative estimates of non-combatant deaths in each nation note killings in excess of 35,000. But we should not be swayed by superficial similarities.

Little of strategic value to the United States can be lost in El Salvador that has not already been lost due to the 1979 Nicaraguan Revolution and Sandinista consolidation there (e.g., an unfriendly Pacific port and potential Soviet air bases). Guatemala continues to have strategic significance even if Sandinista rule in Nicaragua remains true to its anti-U.S. course. Guatemala not only has a Pacific port, it has ports on both the Caribbean and the Pacific linked by railroads and multiple highways (as Nicaragua does not). Although tiny El Salvador has received nearly $1 billion in U.S. military aid since 1980—and Guatemala has received almost none—among the Central American nations, only Guatemala possesses valuable minerals, oil, and nickel. Five times larger in land area than El Salvador, Guatemala has both the largest economy and the largest population on the isthmus. Of additional interest to Americans is the fact that nearly 200 U.S. corporations conduct production or sales operations in the nation.

Truly vital U.S. regional interests, however, rest further north in oil-rich, debt-laden Mexico. The only hispanic Central American nation to border Mexico is Guatemala. Thus conditions on the southern side of the porous 575-mile border between Guatemala and Mexico are of some indirect but permanent concern to the United States. These border regions long have been the very poorest parts of both nations, a situation that has been of little practical importance to the leaders of each nation in the past. In recent years, however, growing political violence among Guatemalans has been most intense in the very areas that most closely resemble the states of southern Mexico.

Important ethnic similarities also make Guatemala more analogous to southern Mexico than to El Salvador. Poorly assimilated indigenous groups (*indigenas*, or Indians) predominate in the dirt-poor border regions of the state of Chiapas (Mexico) and in restless rural Oaxaca (Mexico).[7] The same is true in the border departments (provinces) of San Marcos, Huehuetenango, and El Quiché (Guatemala). The political fates of these regions are further mingled by recent human migrations. By the middle 1980s, as many as 125,000 Guatemalan refugees, mostly *indigenas*, had fled into Mexico, straining already inadequate social services and forcing a touch of realism onto the Mexican government's usually bellicosely anti-U.S. foreign policy in the region. Accused of collaborating with leftist guerrillas by the Guatemalan military, refugee encampments in Chiapas were repeatedly assaulted by Guatemalan Army troops as many as twenty times in 1982–83; other incursions continued into 1984. This sharply strained the already low level of intercourse between the two nations.[8] Mexican authorities mitigated the problem by relocating some (but not all) of the refugees to Campeche (i.e., well away from the border). U.S. strategists, however, must weigh the more intractable effect that a long inter-ethnic war in Guatemala might have on the stability of multi-ethnic Mexico in the long run.

The preferred vocabulary of the Reagan years cast Third World civil wars (like Guatemala's) into East-West, Communist-Free World terms. To promote democracy, a new quiet diplomacy was said to be unfolding in the background, away from the public embrace given to moderate authoritarian dictators like Guatemala's ruling generals (Romeo Lucas García, 1978–82; Efrain Rios Montt, 1982–83; Oscar Humberto Mejia Victores, 1983–January 1986).[9] Coupled with a "Reagan Doctrine" of aiding anti-Communist freedom fighters, the strategy implied an ideological litmus test of U.S. interests. Worldwide, by 1986 the strategy's results were vaporous: South Africa teetered toward mass revolution; Haiti's "Baby Doc" Duvalier and the Philippines' Ferdinand Marcos were routed by unexpected, popular revolutions.

In the Central American region, the "Reagan Doctrine" placed peripheral interests (e.g., Nicaragua) at center stage, downplaying the important connection of Mexico to U.S. national security. But in 1986 oil prices slid steeply lower, threatening the financial foundations of Mexican popular government. Despite a tremendous 1985 earthquake, inexplicably, only minor increases were proposed in U.S. foreign aid to Mexico or to the fledgling Guatemalan democracy (to $85 million) on its border. Ideology appears to have required that underwriting democracy be defined in the region principally in terms of mobilizing a U.S.-backed army, "the contras." At least $100 million publicly was sought for these adversaries of the Sandinista government in Nicaragua. In fact, much more was raised and spent.

There are sound strategic and (pro-democratic) ideological reasons to question these priorities. Guatemalan democratization is important: failure to stabilize the situation may contribute to the further destabilization of Mexico at the worst possible time. Developments to the south rarely have affected Mexico, but they now do. In the 1950s, during Guatemala's last democratic experiment, President Jacobo Arbenz (1951–54) pursued a non-aligned foreign policy and purchased arms from Czechoslovakia, but this had no real impact on Mexico's internal security. As recently as the early 1970s, the conventional wisdom in Guatemala was that the Indian half of the 8 million total national population constituted a buffer, as resistant to radicals' appeals as to government development plans. Studies confirmed that in terms of national politics, the Indians were politically quiescent and that the Indian locales were the least likely to have experienced political violence.[10] This changed.

By 1983 nearly 29 percent of the 11,500 victims of extra-judicial executions and unsolved abductions (i.e., disappearances) were in the border departments named earlier.[11] Radical movements among Mexican Indians in Chiapas and Oaxaca also surfaced. Thus violence against Indians in the Guatemala highlands and against Indian refugees in southern Mexico presented a difficult internal and foreign policy challenge to the perpetually ruling Mexican PRI party (Institutional

Revolutionary Party). This challenge may be expected to continue to fester, for even as the PRI lionizes itself as historic champion of the indigenous Mesoamericans, rhetorical posturing uneasily marries with the unfulfilled aspirations of Mexico's own southern Indians.

It is in the interest of both the United States and Mexico to limit the "demonstration effect" of Guatemalan violence by encouraging changes in Guatemala that will stem the migration of refugees to Mexico and encourage those already there to return to Guatemala. According to many reputable international human rights organizations, the hallmark of Guatemalan Army policy during 1981–84 was the grisly massacre of Indians (men, women, and children), concurrent with the plague of disappearances among both mixed-ethnic ladino and indigenous groups.[12] In some measure these state actions have reflected the long-gestating crises among ladino elites regarding how to respond to Indian masses who have begun to demand public policies to meet their basic needs.

Guatemala has entered an era of crisis over societal authority. The Roman Catholic Church no longer stands together with the army as a pillar of the status quo, rationalizing and enforcing existing societal priorities (respectively).[13] Since the 1960s, much of the energy of many Guatemalan church people was placed firmly behind the cause of changing existing economic priorities. After the elevation of Prospero Penados del Barrio to archbishop of Guatemala in 1984, the authority of top church officials also was committed to reversing the cold facts that nearly half of all Guatemalans are illiterate and that eight in ten children are malnourished.[14] Again, these issues are relevant to Mexican and U.S. national interests, for similarly intractable social problems exist (to a lesser degree) north of the Guatemalan-Mexican border.

Visiting Guatemala in March 1983, Pope John Paul II joined in Penados' (and other bishops') criticisms of the social priorities of the Guatemalan state as obstacles to needed change. But he went further, declaring that "God will punish those who harm the Indians." In response, the long-resident Guatemalan ambassador to the Vatican, Luis Valladeres Aycinela, was recalled from Rome.[15]

In Guatemala, the primary beneficiaries of these authoritative criticisms were the Catholic activists, ladino and Indian, of the DCG. In December 1984 a second sharp papal criticism, this time of General Mejia's ruling group, further undermined claims by conservative Catholics (especially in the MLN party) to the effect that the DCG and the activist Archbishop Penados were exceeding appropriate guidelines on church activism. Penados and the other bishops issued a series of more than fifteen pastoral letters and public denunciations, 1983–86, all calling for respect of human rights and social, economic, and land reform. Typical of these messages was that found in one issued on February 14, 1986, which denounced the "unjust and unequal distribution of goods" in Guatemala and which stated that "it is necessary that the sectors with the greater part of the material goods take into account the suffering and desperation of those who have little or nothing." Thus the mobilization of organized religion on behalf of a reform agenda represented a dramatic shift from the unequivocal support the church gave to the army during the overthrow of Arbenz by the CIA and the army in 1954. This legitimization of a reform agenda by the Catholic church plays differently in Mexico, however: the ruling PRI and the church long have been antagonists, making the growing regionwide campaign for social justice less easily converted into broadened support for current rulers and the democratic system. The 1986 embrace of revolution by the Catholic hierarchy in the Philippines should foreshadow to all the potential inherent in the situation should Cerezo's efforts to reform Guatemala by stymied. As Cerezo himself told U.S. reporters in 1986, ''This is Guatemala's last chance to avert civil war.''[16]

THE POLITICAL TRADITIONS

With but one brief interlude (1966–70), Guatemalan military rulers have been at the helm of the ship of state from 1954 to January 1986. They became Central America's largest and most effective military force. Buttressed by substantial U.S. military aid from 1954 to 1977, these rulers repeatedly ignored international critics and silenced local ones. For a tolerant political system to evolve in the later 1980s, the major challenge will be to devise a set of incentives to spur the military into a pattern of behavior consistent with international standards of human rights. Unless broad support for authentic democratization can be created within the military, the electoral mandate held by Cerezo and the DCG may prove hollow.

The absence of the effective rule of law under the military regime also inhibited the development of social attitudes and behavior conducive to democracy. A new (1985) Constitution now extends a laudable range of rights to citizens, but so did the inoperative 1965 Constitution that was technically in effect from 1966 to 1982. As the past president of the CIDH told the U.S. Congress about that 1965 basic law:

The Constitution of Guatemala guarantees the full panoply of human rights. Persons opposed to perpetual government by the Armed Forces who attempt to exercise these rights are murdered by the security forces or paramilitary auxiliaries. Hence, opponents of the government have, in effect, no rights. More than any other country, we [CIDH] concluded, murder was the principal instrument for maintaining the existing allocation of societal power.[17]

Today's Guatemalan political organizations have been shaped by this hard reality. Ironically, it is the leadership of anti-electoral, clandestine Communist and other guerrilla forces that have remained most intact, while above-ground opposition parties have been more systematically decimated. The U.S. interest in stable, non-Communist government bordering Mexico requires that advocates of democracy for Guatemala clearly perceive these limitations and act in ways to strengthen pro-democratic, non-military forces and the rule of law. Thus far the Reagan administration has shown little sensitivity to these facts or to the enormity of the task at hand. As early as May 1984 President Reagan stated blandly that "in Guatemala, political parties and trade unions are functioning," even as dozens of political activists (and unionists) were then being killed. This plague continued well into 1986, but aside from one April 29, 1985, denunciation of killings of Grupo de Apoyo Mutuo, or Mutual Support Group (GAM), human rights workers (published in the daily *Prensa Libre*), the U.S. administration failed to criticize publicly the anti-democratic violence in Guatemala.[18] No U.S. official attributed responsibility to the Mejía government even in the cases of the dead GAM martyrs Rosario Godoy de Cuevas (April 4, 1985) and Héctor Orlando Gómez (March 31, 1985), whom witnesses saw abducted by security officials.

Meaningful democratization will require that civic faith be nurtured so that the legitimacy of government by elected rulers can withstand episodic setbacks (e.g., hard economic choices or dramatic assassinations). These conditions now are absent in Guatemala: the last government to propose needed tax reforms— Ríos Montt's—was overthrown by a coup d'etat within a month. Why the system has been unable to respond to challenging problems can be traced to its etiology, which unfolded in a four-step process: a revolutionary period, 1944–54; a purgative anti-Communist transitional era, 1954–66; a constitutional era, 1966–82, which relied on institutionalized state terrorism; and an even more brutal era of direct extra-constitutional military rule, March 1982–January 1986.[19] At each critical crossroads, state violence rather than conciliation and reform determined outcomes.

Throughout most of the first three periods, Guatemala's banana- and coffee-exporting economy grew and diversified, but this growth did not reduce the highly polarized distribution of resources among social classes and ethnic groups. Guatemala developed Central America's largest industrial economic sector, but the work force remained largely agricultural. Access to the rich land always has been a vital fact of life. Guatemala has the greatest inequality (as measured by the GINI index of inequality) in all Latin America. While 2.6 percent of farm families controlled 66.0 percent of the arable land in 1970, a 1983 USAID study found that fewer still—1 percent—actually controlled more than 78 percent of the land.[20]

Technical legal rights to form unions and farming cooperatives, to strike, and to undertake other collective non-violent actions were not meaningful tools in the context of state terrorism. This was also true of the modern economic sector: Donald Schulz has shown that real wages of wage-earning workers actually fell in these same recent eras.[21] In the mid–1970s, and again in 1983–85, rapid inflation compounded the difficulties of the masses. Poorer sectors developed habits of political action divorced from the electoral process. Protest movements in 1960, 1962, 1976–78, and September 1985 were direct challenges, "politics of the streets," not fronts for political parties.

Legal political parties by and large were unable to incorporate the masses' grievances into institutionalized forms (i.e., elections, party programs, and public policies) due to the state tradition of responding with lethal violence. George

Lopez has suggested the relevant general theory of state violence of this kind.[22]
In terms of responses to political opposition by state organs of repression, a state
may (1) pass discriminatory legislation; it may more threateningly (2) do nothing
to protect opponents from the crimes of other civilians; or it may (3) arbitrarily
detain and abuse the opponents. Each type of response involves life-threatening
tactics of social control and rule. These theoretical concepts can be usefully employed to understand state violence in Guatemala, as long as they are seen as dynamic choices within a waxing and waning cycle of state violence, rather than as
irrevocable, one-way signposts in the totalitarianization of the state.

Thus the isolated, occasional assassination of the revolutionary era (1944–54)
gave way to recurring bursts of state violence. Significant roundups of "enemies"
occurred in 1954–55 and again in 1970–71. Hundreds, then thousands, were
violently made to disappear. Between these orgies of officially targeted intimidation, vigilante organizations in support of state repression became refined. By
the mid–1960s paramilitary allies of the army, associated with the MLN party,
terrorized the rural ladino peasantry first in the eastern departments of Izabal
and Zacapa, where leftist guerrillas had been attempting to develop a base of
operations. Later, these organizations menaced opponents of the regime nationwide, earning the grim nickname "death squads."

By late 1971 these manifestations of official violence and official indifference
to vigilante violence were well understood by the public. Anomic protests, short-
lived marches, and other spontaneous, anonymous actions were the only rational
outlets in such an environment. Association with opposition activity had already
been demonstrated to involve clear hazards, since organized protests ipso facto
must have leaders, meetings, membership lists, and other dimensions that could
make the protests more easily targeted for violence. Yet social learning is never
perfect, and during a period of slackening official violence in the middle 1970s,
a new generation of opposition again became visible. Unable to resolve the issues
that cooperatives, rural trade unions, and urban workers raised, a more active
cycle of state violence resumed.

From 1978 to early 1986 labor leaders, Roman Catholic priests and seminarians, schoolteachers and university personnel, medical professionals, and others
working directly to improve the lot of the poor were systematically killed or
disappeared. After nearly a decade of burgeoning self-help projects, by 1981
nearly half of all rural-development projects run by private organizations were
forced to close. In these seven most violent years in Guatemalan history, dozens
in each of these professions were exterminated by either army and National
Police units or by their death-squad allies.

To try to chart this violence precisely is simply to come to know its vast scale.
Americas Watch, in April 1983, stated that "at least 12,000 civilian non-com-
batants have been killed by Guatemalan Armed Forces since 1978." The bishops
of the Guatemalan Roman Catholic Church, in September 1984, put the figure
at 100,000 political murders since 1954. The president of the Guatemalan judiciary during the Mejía military government lent credibility to these shocking

sums when he declared that 24,000 orphans from the violence were to be found in just one department, El Quiché. By late 1985 another well-informed human rights team used censuses of orphans and other figures to peg the overall body count at between 50,000 and 75,000 since 1978.[23]

By any measure, the cycle of violent disappearances and massacres since 1978 was substantially more comprehensive than in any earlier repression. Although massacres of Spanish-speaking ladinos were frequent in Eastern Guatemala in 1966–69, in each year from 1981 to 1983 more were massacred than in that entire first counterinsurgency war. Recent tabulations of documented cases of unresolved extra-judicial mass executions indicate between 178 and more than 300 incidents of mass murder in the 1978–85 period.[24] At least 2,000 perished in each of 1984 and 1985. The CIDH found 80 new cases of 'disappearances' per month in 1983–84, a rate that fell to only 40 to 50 per month by early 1986.[25]

The 1985 election campaign proceeded under this cloud. It is small wonder that party leaders tended to present non-threatening, innocuous formal programs at election time. Indeed, it was a minor miracle that any sharp criticisms at all were aired during the fall 1985 campaign. Overall, the event was sharply different from all elections under the 1965 Constitution in which, except for 1966, all winners were army officers. These military leaders were chosen to head civilian political parties under somewhat less than free conditions. In 1985 civilians represented themselves. In the past, sitting governments always "certified" their choice as the winner of the actual voting; in 1985 all parties accepted the accuracy of Cerezo's mandate (although MLN leaders claimed that the voter registration rolls had been fattened). In 1974 and 1982 "certified" winners General Kjell Laugerud and General Anibal Guervara were widely believed to have "won" after having finished second (or even third) in the real voting.[26] This perception was so widespread that when junior officers blocked General Guevera's 1982 "election" by the military coup of that year (ultimately leading to the Ríos Montt "presidency"), they legitimized their usurpation, saying that "the Guatemalan people have been the victims of repeated electoral frauds which have caused them to lose faith in democratic institutions."[27]

In regard to policy, even the last civilian before Cerezo to hold the presidential office, Julio Méndez Montenegro (1966–70), was, in the words of one (Mejía era) Guatemalan diplomat, "given the oath of office with his hands tied behind his back" by the army.[28] Cerezo, too, must operate under the constraint their gaze imposes on his discretion. Although the 1985 Guatemalan Constitution bars any but military courts from trying military defendants, the precedent of transcending such limitations on war-crimes trials was established in Argentina by the Alfonsín government's December 1985 murder convictions of former presidents based on civilian appeals courts' review of reluctant military courts there. Can the seed of Guatemalan democracy flower without rooting it in a similar soil of justice? How else can the alienated be reassured that the era of massacres and hushed-toned rumors is over?

Elections under the 1965 Constitution failed to appeal to the broad popular classes, and turnout was low. Leaders who tried to appeal to these groups simply were killed. The small affiliate to the Socialist International, for example, the Partido Social Democrático, or Democratic Socialist Party (PSD), and its leader Alberto Fuentes Mohr (finance minister under Méndez) stood with Ríos Montt for the vice-presidency in 1974. Fuentes Mohr was assassinated in broad daylight as he drove past an army base in the capital in January 1979; an eyewitness was killed the next day.[29] Within weeks the leading popular figure likely to have led the pro-lower-class opposition in the wake of Fuentes Mohr's killing, former Guatemala City Mayor Manuel Colom Argueta, was murdered by twenty gunmen while an official helicopter hovered overhead.[30] In light of the several hundred DCG workers killed between 1981 and 1984, it is noteworthy that only a few died during the 1985 campaign. No murders of leading figures in any party occurred during the 1985 campaign. However, at least 30 lower-level UCN and DCG party workers were killed, among them Abelino Godinez Garcia (November 12, 1985) and a rural vice-mayor and his wife in San Marcos (October 29, 1985).[31] By indicting more than 100 National Police of the Division Investigaciones Technicas (DIT) squad, Cerezo conveyed to all that a day of reckoning may await gunmen who would shoot down democracy. But if top officials and the army were involved in the great preponderance of past violence, the public may retain a rational civic hesitancy.

It is revealing that the old system always was merciful toward some. During the period of pseudo-democracy under the 1965 Constitution, no such lethal stakes surrounded the generals who at election time headed the political parties' tickets. The DCG's 1974 standardbearer, General Ríos Montt, moved off to a paid exile as Guatemala's military attaché to Spain; General Anibal Guevara simply was retired from active duty after the 1982 fraud was voided by military coup. When a relatively clean balloting for the Constituent Assembly that drafted the 1985 Constitution was held, Guevara polled less than 5 percent of the ballots.[32]

It was apparent, therefore, that two separate political processes were at work under the 1965 Constitution, both of which laid a weak foundation for democratic politics. High stakes surrounded civilian opposition behavior but not that of military figures. The illiberal essence of this two-tier political process became most visible during the seventeen-month rule of General Ríos Montt (March 1982-August 1983), ostensibly an opposition-linked figure. Although he had been the 1974 DCG presidential candidate, Ríos ruled much as had all of the elected military presidents once a coup brought him the presidency. Tellingly, his actions against the positions and interests of his former DCG allies were frequent, numerous, and of both a de jure and a practical kind. Voting rights as well as the right to form political parties formerly were guaranteed under Articles 14 and 27 of the 1965 Constitution. By decree, Ríos ended them on April 26, 1982, enunciating a "Fundamental Statute of Government" (Decree law 24–82) instead. This extra-constitutional act, at Article 112, declared all existing political parties suspended.[33] Technically put into hibernation, the dangerous times for DCG officials and their families continued at the practical level. DCG leaders were assassinated in Huehuetenango and El Quiché; five others disappeared in the weeks following Christmas 1982. Later, all were found dead. Party headquarters were bombed and forced to close. Cerezo only narrowly escaped several grenade and machinegun attacks at his home and office. His response was to send his family into exile in the United States and to begin living at no fixed address. By mid-summer 1983 the DCG had prepared formal written denunciations, released after General Mejía's August 1983 coup, which faulted their former "ally's" brand of tyranny.[34]

From this example it is clear that parties and military factions did not develop meaningful ties under the 1966–82 rules of the political game. Moreover, it shows that the Cerezo administration cannot rely solely on military factions as automatic allies (even though Cerezo personally has stated that "if I didn't have friends in the military, I'd be dead").[35]

The moral force behind the DCG and many of its supporters long has been the Guatemalan Roman Catholic Church, to which more than 80 percent of all Guatemalans at least nominally belong. Catholic religious leaders also have lacked steady allies in the military. Under General Lucas (1978–82), times were worst for the church, but anti-clerical state violence continued under Generals Ríos Montt and Mejía as well. Hundreds of catechists and members of Catholic Action in Indian (and other) areas were executed by army troops, often after only specious evidence of involvement in the cause of social justice was found (e.g., graduation certificates from church-sponsored courses; membership in a Catholic cooperative). In some areas, discovery of the Bible by soldiers as they ransacked peasant homes proved to be sufficient cause for execution of whole families, or so many Indian families came to believe.[36] It was also true that the officer corps was highly divided on the use of such tactics in the service of anti-communism. Indeed, pointed criticisms of Ríos' anti-Catholicism aired by General José Echeverría Vielman helped to stimulate the August 1983 ouster of the eccentric evangelical Protestant dictator. However, under the (professedly) very Catholic General Mejía, new dozens of catechists, a priest, a Catholic missionary, and several seminarians were killed under suspicious circumstances. These problems have remained ongoing: during the final days before the first balloting for president in 1985, catechist Luis Ché was murdered after abduction by army troops in El Estor, Izabal. Even on the eve of Cerezo's victory, social worker, Catholic, and former seminarian Rafael Yos Muxtay violently disappeared.[37]

WELLSPRINGS OF CHANGE

The two-tier political process of the earlier constitutional era (1966–82) did not produce solid linkages between candidates, parties, social bases, and public policies, but the system itself was not entirely flimsy. No plots against its presidents succeeded for a remarkably long sixteen years. The regular, if fraudulent, ballotings enhanced the stature of the regime internationally and were valuable in helping to secure U.S. foreign assistance from 1966 to 1977. Yet when the system collapsed, a more candid form of military government (1982–86) also failed; why?

Three factors appear significant. First, by the early 1980s, pseudo-democratic practices no longer effectively absorbed the energies and aspirations of an ever-more-divided Armed Forces. (These issues were amply developed earlier.) Second, the state terrorism they practiced created a crisis in Guatemala's international relations. When the methods of counterinsurgency war in the early 1980s became visible, Guatemala's international isolation became nearly complete. Third, heavy international borrowing and the effects of the worldwide economic recession after 1981 made the inaccessible international relief ever more important; without it, the economy took the steepest nosedive in Guatemala's history. This combination of unpropitious developments convinced General Mejía, many other officers, and most Guatemalans that national development under military auspices was an inept failure. Let us examine this interplay between a "successful" counterinsurgency war and the international isolation that contributed to it becoming a Pyrrhic victory.

Counterinsurgency war began as a small part of the Guatemalan Armed Forces' mission but grew to become their raison d'être. Initially, the guerrilla movement began in the wake of a November 13, 1960, young officers' coup that had failed. Taking to the hills of eastern Guatemala, and joined within a year by leftists of the *Fuerzas Armadas Rebeldes*, or Rebel Armed Forces (FAR), these guerrillas proved to be more of an annoyance than a significant military threat. The army's mission, under the dictator Colonel Enrique Peralta Azurdia (1963–66) and under President Méndez (1966–70), gradually expanded to one not merely of eradicating the guerrillas and their suspected supporters, although this they fiercely accomplished (aided by death-squad vigilantes); guided by a perverse conception of national security that viewed all domestic critics as carriers of infectious ideas, a comprehensive repressive apparatus capable of ferreting out and purging all subversive influences was refined. This state of terrorism would continue unperturbed by any notion of due process of law, human rights, or other restraints; this was the price exacted from those who would play at politics under the 1965 Constitution.

Given virtually no other outlet for political expression, a much more significant guerrilla challenge developed in the late 1970s. The two new major guerrilla forces (Guerrilla Army of the Poor [EGP] and Revolutionary Organization of the People in Arms [ORPA]) were strongest in the mountainous western highlands, among the twenty-two Guatemalan Indian minorities. By 1980 virtually the entire Indian population in many locales tacitly, and in some areas actively, supported the guerrilla fighters. For the Guatemalan military, this mobilization presented problems, because U.S. police aid and U.S. military aid had been terminated (in 1975 and 1977, respectively), owing to the abysmal human rights record of the regime.

Basking in anti-U.S. nationalism, the Guatemalan rulers (especially General Lucas) unleashed a wave of disappearances and group executions during the

Carter administration that did little to address the basis of the insurgents' appeal. Violating the sanctity of a foreign embassy (that of Spain, January 31, 1980) in order to murder "subversives" en masse further reduced the international standing of the regime.[38] Yet the guerrilla movement continued to spread in 1980 and 1981, bringing ever higher army casualties with which the top commanders eventually had to reckon. Betting on a promised resumption in U.S. military aid (which failed to materialize) to turn the tide, by mid–1982 General Ríos had concluded that only much more comprehensive repression would break the by-then-united URNG guerrilla movement. Thus the massacres of Indians, which had begun in May 1978, reached alarming levels in 1982–83. Despite steady efforts by the Reagan administration to assist Ríos and Mejía in the operation, congressional assertiveness, and the inept 1983 Guatemalan Army murders of several USAID contract workers forced the Reagan team to maintain only low levels of aid.[39]

Guerrillas, in theory, are as fish in the (peasant) waters. The Guatemalan Army strategy appears to have sought to dry up the water to kill all of the fish. Under Ríos and Mejía, firm control over the entire rural Indian population was established. First, suspected guerrilla-collaborating villages were massacred. In villages whose loyalty was in doubt, food supplies (both planted and stored) were confiscated or burned, the villages razed, and the population forced into protected villages, a modern version of the strategic hamlets of the 1960s in Southeast Asian wars. Government food distributions enticed others to relocate away from the zone of greatest guerrilla strength. All of these migrations were joyless affairs, since it was broadly recognized that the supplies were, by and large, the fruit of seizures from other Indians. (U.S. food assistance also played a supporting role). These model villages formed the hub of development poles; residents then were organized into mandatory Patrullas de Autodefensa Civil, or Civil Self-defense Patrols (PACS). By late 1985, 900,000 were members of these groups, obliging most Indian families to do without their male PAC "patrolmen" for several days a month (and more in some cases). Although the rate of massacres slowed by late 1984, sporadic rural violence continued throughout 1985, especially in Chimaltenango.

ECONOMIC COLLAPSE

Had material prosperity been able to have been gleaned from this Dante-esque landscape, the generals might still rule. But coincident with the expensive counterinsurgency war, the economy took a nosedive unmatched in modern times. National income slumped for reasons not unrelated: a wandering and dislocated rural labor force, coupled with guerrillas' sabotage in the countryside, and steep declines in export harvests occurred in the early 1980s. Prices for coffee and other exports remained low throughout the 1985 season, further depressing a GDP that already had fallen 2.7 percent in 1983, remained flat in 1984, and dipped a further 1.6 percent in 1985. By 1984 all segments of the Guatemalan economy were contracting, except textiles production. Although a coffee price boom was experienced by American consumers in 1986 (owing to a Brazilian frost), much of the potential profit from Guatemalan beans was lost to the national treasury. General Mejía's team sold one-third or more of the unharvested 1986 crop to middlemen in the fall of 1985. These advance sales of the 1986 harvest were made at low, pre-inflation prices.[40]

Aggressive public-sector borrowing in the early 1980s also saddled the government with double-digit interest and rapid repayments, draining dollar reserves entirely by the time Cerezo took office. The interest due ($710 million) to service the 1986 Guatemalan debt (about $3 billion) was nearly as great as the entire debt principal had been only seven years earlier ($759 million, 1979). Although only 2 percent (1979) to 6 percent (1982) of the value of Guatemala's exports previously were required to service the debt, in 1986 more than half of the export earnings were needed to repay foreign lenders (private and institutional). The generals burned most bridges to a quick change of direction by civilians: an emergency 1983 International Monetary Fund (IMF) austerity package (raise taxes, cut spending) remained unimplemented by Mejía, so the funds (half of $121 million) were frozen by the IMF in 1984. With no bank window of last resort available, multi-lateral lenders (Interamerican Development Bank and the World Bank) stopped new loans. Private finance sources became more expensive or dried up entirely. Even regional governments closed their borders to imports from Guatemala due to disputes over outstanding accounts (Costa Rica) and disadvantageous trade balances (El Salvador).[41]

In the wake of a "successful" counterinsurgency war several of the Guatemalan classes also had begun to speak with their feet, further exacerbating economic activity. Refugee Indians slipped into Mexico by the thousands; upper-class Guatemalans walked onto jets and flew their cash to Miami. In the charnel house that Guatemala had become, few riches were to be made. By late 1984 unemployment soared to more than 44 percent of the work force (up from 40 percent in 1983; including those underemployed). Guatemalans who could do so scurried to convert quetzales to dollars rather than investing them in productive directions: according to official Guatemalan reports, more than $1.16 billion illegally left the country between 1980 and 1985.[42] To attract capital back, in November 1984 the quetzal was allowed to float on a free, parallel-exchange market. Immediately, its value began to fall: from its former parity with the dollar, it bottomed out around twenty-five U.S. cents (August 1985) before stabilizing around thirty-five U.S. cents (spring 1986). In the wake of falling world oil prices, even that moderating external trend contained a touch of bad news: concessionarily inexpensive Mexican and Venezuelan oil shipments on which Guatemala had depended were jeopardized as those nations sought full-price customers. (Guatemala's crude oil is not suitable for domestic use without refining, which is not available locally).

In such a context the options available to the Cerezo administration were narrow, providing few alternatives on which to lay a foundation for popular democracy.

LIBERALIZATION FROM DEMOCRATIZATION?

It is difficult to envisage conditions less conducive to the evolution of a durable liberal society than these. How much can these traditions and problems be overcome by a short run of relatively open party competition? It is undeniable that vigorous campaigns accompanied many parties vying for seats in the 1984 Constituent Assembly and in the 1985 legislative and presidential elections. In them, support for the intransigent right evaporated, as Table 3.1 clearly illustrates. These are buds of improvement; to flower, a more comprehensive liberalization must also take place. Despite Cerezo's massive (68 percent) electoral mandate, no social consensus exists about the allocation of benefits that could be distributed among Guatemalans.

Even the accurately counted balloting in 1985 may mark only minor progress toward stable government, economic prosperity, and protection of human rights if vigorous steps are not taken to assure the people that a thorough change has begun. Underneath a deceptive calm in the Guatemalan highlands are unaddressed economic injustices and ripe, recent traumas that prevent the national community from pulling together. Among the urban ladinos, a renewed campaign of illiberal disappearances, begun shortly after Cerezo's election, threatened to drive the people away from an active democratic life. In the past, officials' violence eroded the legitimacy of state institutions (especially the army and the National Police). By indicting some of the most despicable state terrorists shortly after assuming office, Cerezo attempted to reverse the endemic lack of confidence in the legitimacy of the law that had become second nature to many Guatemalans. To take further steps, Cerezo will need help.

Legal and land reforms can provide the olive branch of conciliation, if Cerezo can come to believe that it is anything other than personal suicide to extend it. With support, the Cerezo government may be able to create a positively received and viable land reform that could address the deeper reasons why the guerrillas were able to establish a base of operations in the first place. In combination with vigorous prosecution of common and political criminals, the basis for peace negotiations announced in August 1987 could be fortified.Even though he foreswore land reform during the campaign, the will to create a changed Guatemala betrays the public persona of Cerezo; discretion on the land issue was required until after he survived the electoral gauntlet.

The Reagan Latin American team often has expressed that it is "ideologically committed to democracy, . . . that there is a clear connection between respect for human rights and a democratic form of government."[43] The problem with relying on U.S. diplomatic pressure alone to midwife this birth in Guatemala lies in getting the administration to see liberalization after the elections as a necessary

Table 3.1

1984–85 Election Results

Party	1984[1] Votes	%	1st ballot Nov. 1985[2] Votes	%	2nd ballot Dec. 1985[3] Votes	%
DCG	318,300	28.8	648,681	42.1	1,133,517	68.37
UCN	269,448	24.4	339,522	22.0	524,306	31.63
MLN	245,514	22.2	210,806	13.7		
PDCN	142,565	12.8	231,397	15.0		
PSD			57,362	3.7		
PNR	129,664	11.7	52,941	3.4		

DCG = Christian Democrat Party

UCN = Union of the National Center

MLN = National Liberation Movement

PDCN = Democratic Party of National Conciliation
(Revolutionary Party in coalition)

PSD = Democratic Socialist Party

PNR = National Renewal Party

Source: [1]Infor Press, *Centroamericana*, #559, July 12, 1984, p. 3; *Enfoprensa*, vol. 2, #28, July 13, 1984, p. 3; *The Washington Post*, July 7, 1984, p. 11.
[2]*Enfoprensa*, vol. 3, #43, November 29, 1985, p. 1.
[3]*Enfoprensa*, vol. 3, #46, December 20, 1985, p. 1.

priority worthy of substantial U.S. support. In February 1984 the Reagan administration seemed to endorse the $8.9 billion in economic and military aid recommended by the (Kissinger) Bipartisan Commission on Central America, a report that called for hundreds of millions for Guatemala, soon. But by 1986 aid to the anti-Nicaragua contra rebels rated higher in actual dollars publicly requested ($100 million) than did aid to Guatemalan democracy ($85 million).[44]

Moreover, it often has appeared that the administration's ardor for genuine popular government is paper thin and for television audiences alone. Only at the insistence of the U.S. Congress was U.S. foreign assistance to Guatemala from 1983 to 1986 conditioned on demonstrated progress toward democracy. Liberalization in the late 1980s most realistically must be pursued by similar conditioning. For the survival of the Cerezo administration and for its ultimate consolidation of true power, vitally needed U.S. and multi-lateral financial aid must be closely monitored by tieing it to further steps toward a real liberalization. It must be made abundantly clear that the certain consequence of another military coup would be termination of all U.S. assistance.

Enough partisanship has surrounded the U.S. policy in Central America in the 1980s. Around the restoration of a civil society and politics in Guatemala consensus should be able to be formed. To achieve U.S. national security objectives in Mexico and the Central American region, as well as to advance the human rights concerns that are the essential distinctive feature of our shared values as a nation, these specific suggestions are offered as a guide to the development of U.S. policy toward redemocratization and liberalization in Guatemala:

- U.S. economic aid alone should be extended to the Cerezo government. Unless a genuine threat from guerrilla forces imminently menaces Guatemalan democracy, no U.S. officials should even allude to the need to grant aid to, or sell weapons to, the Guatemalan Army. Only if the Cerezo government requests military aid in a manner that convincingly persuades the U.S. Congress of the direct relation of such military aid to the progress toward liberalization should military aid be extended.

- U.S. economic aid given to support democratization and liberalization should be conditioned on continuous, good faith efforts toward legal, land, and other (e.g., penal) reforms.

- Efforts to involve the URNG guerrillas in the process of national reconciliation through democratization should be acceleratd. Representatives of the government, the guerrillas, and the Guatemalan Armed Forces should carry forward the spirit of the August 1987 agreement among Central American presidents and begin the dialogue to end this long war. Encouragingly, URNG guerilla leaders now appear willing to negotiate a cease fire agreement. By excluding all foreign military advisors from the region, a formula for peace may be at hand.

- Most fundamentally, the end of the era of rule by violence must be clearly established. Rule under law to which all are equally liable must become the expectation of all. To achieve this, the scope established by Cerezo for prosecution of officials' past crimes (100+ members of the former DIT police) should be expanded. Those responsible for war crimes, especially between 1981 and 1983, must be tried and punished, army and guerrilla alike.

NOTES

1. Samuel P. Huntington, *Political Order in Changing Societies* (New Haven: Yale University Press, 1968); Myron Weiner, "Political Participation: Crisis in the Political Process," in *Crises and Sequences in Political Development*. Studies in Political Development no. 7. (Princeton N.J.: Princeton University Press, 1971), pp. 159–204, esp. 175–177. See also Gabriel Zaid, "Enemy Colleagues: A Reading of the Salvadoran Tragedy, " *Dissent*, Winter 1982, p. 38.

2. *Latin America Regional Report: Mexico/Central America* 84, no. 6 (July 13, 1984): 1.

3. Amnesty International, *Massive Extrajudicial Executions in Rural Areas under the Government of General Efrain Ríos Montt* (London, July 1982); idem, "Guatemala Campaign Circular Number 5: Repression of Politicians in Guatemala," in Amnesty International, *Country Dossiers, 1975–1979* (Zug, Switz.: Interdocumentation, 1981); idem, *Disappearances in Guatemala under the Government of Gen. Oscar Mejía Victores, August 1983–January 1985* (New York, March 1985); idem, *Amnesty International Report, 1985* (London, 1985), pp. 152–156; Organization of American States' Comisión Interamericana de Derechos Humanos (hereafter CIDH), *Informé Anual de la Comisión Interamericana de derechos humanos, 1983–1984* (Washington, D.C.: Organization of American States, October 2, 1984), pp. 101–110; CIDH, "Informe sobre la situación de los derechos humanos en Guatemala" (October 5, 1983); CIDH *Report on the Situation of Human Rights in Guatemala* (Washington, D.C.: Organization of American States, 1981); Comisión de Derechos Humanos de Guatemala, *Addendum to the Report on Human Rights in Guatemala Presented to the United Nations Commission on Human Rights* (Geneva, Switz., February 1986); Comisión de Derechos Humanos—Guatemala/USA, *Preliminary Report Submitted to the United Nations on the Situation of Human Rights and Basic Liberties in Guatemala* (Washington, D.C., October 1983); idem, "Professionals Disappeared in Guatemala Since August 1983" (n.d., circa. March 1984); idem, *Report Submitted to the 40th Session of the United Nations Human Rights Comission [sic] on the Situation of Human Rights and Basic Liberties in Guatemala* (Geneva, Switz., and Washington, D.C., February 1984); idem, *Report to the Subcommission on the Prevention of Discrimination and the Protection of Minorities of the United Nations, on the Human Rights Situation of the Guatemalan Indigenous Population* (Geneva, Switz., August 1984); Comisión de Derechos Humanos—Guatemala/Mexico D.F., *An Armed Conflict, Not of an International Nature, Which Obliges the Contending Parties to Obey the Norms of International Rules of War* (Mexico City: Comisión de Derechos Humanos— Guatemala, 1983); Comisión de Derechos Humanos—Guatemala/USA, *Report for the 39th General Assembly of the United Nations on Human Rights in Guatemala*, (Washington, D.C., and New York, November 1984); Comisión de Derechos Humanos— Guatemala, *Regarding the Status of Human Rights for the Indigenous Population of Guatemala* (Geneva, Switz. August 1985); Comisión de Derechos Humanos—Guatemala/ USA, *Guatemala: Ejecuciones Extrajudiciales Colectivas, enero 1981–julio 1985* (Mexico City: Comisión de Derechos Humanos—Guatemala, September 1985); Chris Krueger and Kjell Enge, *Security and Development Conditions in the Guatemalan Highlands* (Washington, D.C.: Washington Office on Latin America, August 1985).

4. *Enfoprensa* 4, no. 3 (February 14, 1986): 2; *Latin America Regional Reports: Mexico/Central America* 86, no. 2 (February 14, 1986): 1; *Latin America Weekly Report* 86, no. 8 (February 21, 1986): 5; *Washington Post*, February 8, 1986, p. 18.

5. *Enfoprensa* 2, no. 23 (June 8, 1984): 3; 2, no. 26 (June 29, 1984): 2; 2, no. 24 (June 15, 1984): 2.

6. *Enfoprensa* 2, no. 25 (June 22, 1984): 7. This truly was a case of the kettle calling the pot black. Frequently, in the past, the MLN officials bragged about their role in the liquidation of subversives. See Amnesty International, *Guatemala* (London and New York, 1976), pp. 3–4.

7. Wayne Cornelius, "Politics in Mexico," in Gabriel Almond and G. Bingham Powell, eds., *Comparative Politics Today*, 3d ed. (Boston: Little, Brown, 1984), p. 456; Alan Riding, *Distant Neighbors* (New York: Knopf, 1985), pp. 222–228.

8. Americas Watch, *Creating a Desolation and Calling It Peace* (New York, 1983),

p. 7; Alan Riding, *Distant Neighbors* (New York: Knopf, 1985), pp. 211–212, 292–294, 357–363; *Washington Post*, July 23, 1984, p. 14; *Latin America Regional Reports: Mexico/Central America* 84, no. 2 (February 17, 1984): 5; *Excelsior* (Mexico City) March 22, 1983, p. 1; CIDH, *Informe Anual de la Comisión Interamericana de derechos humanos, 1983–1984*, p. 104; Victor Perera, "A Political Dilemma for Mexico," *Nation*, September 8, 1984, pp. 176–177; Olivia L. Carrescia and Robert Dinardo, "The Yaxan Story," *Commonweal* 110, no. 14 (August 12, 1983): 429–431.

9. See Gordon L. Bowen, "U.S. Policy toward Guatemalan State Terrorism, 1977–1985," in Michael Stohl and George Lopez, eds., *Terrible Beyond Endurance? Foreign Policy and State Terror* (Westport, Conn.: Greenwood Press, 1986).

10. John A. Booth, "A Guatemalan Nightmare: Levels of Political Violence, 1966–1972," *Journal of Interamerican Studies and World Affairs* 22, no. 2 (May 1980): 201, 210. Booth's study is not entirely comparable on this point since he groups San Marcos with the South Coast departments, not with the Indian highlands as I have done here.

11. Comisión de Derechos Humanos de Guatemala, *Boletín Internacionál* 6, no. 3 (Mexico City: March 1984), p. 8.

12. See *Latin America Regional Reports: Mexico/Central America* 84, no. 6 (July 13, 1984): 1. See also Sheldon Davis and Julie Hodson, *Witnesses to Political Violence in Guatemala* (Boston: Oxfam America, 1982).

13. Gordon L. Bowen, "No Roadblocks to Death: Guatemala's War on the Church," *Commonweal* 111, no. 12 (June 15, 1984): 361–364; Penny Lernoux, "Revolution and Counterrevolution in the Central American Church," in Donald Schulz and Douglas Graham, eds., *Revolution and Counterrevolution in Central America and the Caribbean* (Boulder, Colo.: Westview Press, 1984), pp. 141–152; and "A Priest among the People: An Interview with Father Celso," in Jonathan Fried et al., eds., *Guatemala in Rebellion: Unfinished History* (New York, Grove Press, 1983), pp. 223–228.

14. World Bank, *World Development Report, 1980* (Washington, D.C., 1980), p. 110; World Bank, *Guatemala: Social and Economic Position and Prospects* (Washington, D.C., 1978), p. 20; Donald Fox, *Human Rights in Guatemala* (New York: International Commission of Jurists, 1979), p. 6.

15. Linda Drucker, "A Talk with Guatemala's Vinicio Cerezo Arevalo," *New Leader* 66 (March 21, 1983): 5; Comisión de Derechos Humanos—Guatemala/USA, *Information Bulletin* 2, no. 8 (June 1984): 1–4; *Current History* 82, no. 484 (May 1983): 236; Americas Watch, *Creating a Desolation and Calling it Peace* (New York, May 1983), pp. 12–33.

16. CBS News, "60 Minutes: Caught in the Middle" (New York: CBS television program, February 2, 1986); *Enfoprensa* 4, no. 4 (February 21, 1986): 2; Most instructively, see Guatemalan Episcopal Conference (on the present political movement), "To Build Peace: A Collective Pastoral Letter," letter with fifteen signators (Guatemala City, June 10, 1984), 16 pp. For general coverage of the 1954 events, see Stephen Schlesinger and Stephen Kinzer, *Bitter Fruit* (Garden City, New York: Doubleday, 1982); Richard Immerman, *The CIA in Guatemala* (Austin: University of Texas Press, 1982); Jose Aybar de Soto, *Dependency and Intervention* (Boulder, Colo.: Westview Press, 1978); Gordon L. Bowen, "U.S. Foreign Policy toward Radical Change: Covert Operations in Guatemala, 1950–1954," *Latin American Perspectives* 10, no. 1 (Winter 1983): 88–102.

17. Tom J. Farer, "Testimony before the Subcommittee on Human Rights and International Affairs," U.S. House of Representatives' Committee on Foreign Affairs (Memorandum copy, November 17, 1983), pp. 11–12.

18. *New York Times*, May 10, 1984; Comisión de Derechos Humanos—Guatemala/ USA, *Information Bulletin* 3, no. 7 (July 1985): 4.

19. Gordon L. Bowen, "Guatemala: The Origins and Development of State Terrorism," in Donald Schulz and Douglas Graham, eds., *Revolution and Counterrevolution in Central America and the Caribbean* (Boulder, Colo.: Westview Press, 1984), pp. 269–300. See also George Black, *Garrison Guatemala* (New York: Monthly Review Press, 1984); Marlene Dixon and Susanne Jonas, eds., *Revolution and Intervention in Central America* (San Francisco: Synthesis Publishers 1983), pp. 281–331; Susanne Jonas et al., eds., *Guatemala: Tyranny on Trial* (San Francisco: Synthesis Publishers 1984); Gabriel Aguilera Peralta, "The Militarization of the Guatemalan State," in Jonathan L. Fried et al., eds., *Guatemala in Rebellion: Unfinished History* (New York: Grove Press, 1983), pp. 114–121.

20. World Bank, *Guatemala: Social and Economic Position and Prospects*, p. 73; *Latin America Weekly Report* 83, no. 9 (March 4, 1983): 5. For further elaboration, see Gordon L. Bowen, "The Political Economy of State Terrorism: Barrier to Human Rights in Guatemala," in George Sheperd and Ved Nanda, eds., *Human Rights and Third World Development* (Westport, Conn.: Greenwood Press, 1985), pp. 83–124.

21. Donald Schulz, "Ten Theories in Search of Central American Reality," in Donald Schulz and Douglas Graham, eds., *Revolution and Counterrevolution in Central America and the Caribbean* (Boulder, Colo.: Westview Press, 1984), pp. 12–20.

22. George A. Lopez, "A Scheme for the Analysis of Government as Terrorist," in Michael Stohl and George A. Lopez, eds., *The State as Terrorist* (Westport, Conn.: Greenwood Press, 1983).

23. Comisión de Derechos Humanos Guatemala/USA, *Report Submitted to the 40th Session of the United Nations*, p. 32; Americas Watch, *Human Rights in Central America* (New York, April 27, 1983), p. 11; *Enfoprensa* 2, nos. 36/37 (September 14, 1984): 10; 2, no. 38 (September 21, 1984): 6; Chris Krueger and Kjell Enge, *Security and Development Conditions in the Guatemalan Highlands* (Washington, D.C.: Washington Office on Latin America, August 1985), p. v.

24. Comisión de Derechos Humanos—Guatemala/USA, *Guatemala: Ejecuciones Extrajudiciales Colectivas, enero 1981–julio 1985*, 25 pp.; Gordon L. Bowen, "Appendix: Extrajudicial Mass Executions and Unresolved Mass Abductions in Guatemala, 1978–1984," in George Sheperd and Ved Nanda, eds., *Human Rights and Third World Development* (Westport, Conn.: Greenwood Press, 1985), pp. 118–124.

25. Comisión de Derechos Humanos—Guatemala/USA, *Information Bulletin* 3, no. 2 (February 1985): 5; CIDH, *Informe Anual*, p. 102; *Enfoprensa* 3, no. 45 (December 13, 1985): 4. The U.S.Department of State, however, admitted "only" 950 victims of political violence in 1984: *New York Times*, March 2, 1985.

26. Among the Guatemalans who publicly would state that fraudulent voting riddled the 1966–82 system, see the statement to that effect by the Roman Catholic bishops: Guatemalan Episcopal Conference (on the present political movement), "To Build Peace: A Collective Pastoral Letter," pp. 4, 15.

27. Quoted in Comisión de Derechos Humanos—Guatemala/USA, *Report Submitted to the 40th Session of the United Nations*, p. 37. See also Donald Fox, *Human Rights in Guatemala* (New York: International Commission of Jurists, 1979), p. 35; Thomas and Margarita Bradford Melville, "Oppression by any other Name," in June Nash, Juan Corradi, and Hobart Spaulding, eds., *Ideology and Social Change in Latin America* (New York: Gordon and Breach, 1977), p. 276.

28. Carlos Urrutia-Aparicio, "When Democracy Returns to Guatemala," *Washington Post* May 9, 1985, p. 18.

29. Amnesty International, "Guatemala Campaign Circular Number 5: Repression of Politicians in Guatemala" in Amnesty International, *Country Dossiers, 1975–1979* (Zug, Switz.: Interdocumentation, 1981) p. 5; Amnesty International, "Memorandum to the Guatemala Government Concerning Human Rights," in U.S. House of Representatives, Committee on Foreign Affairs, Subcommittee on International Organizations, *Hearings: Human Rights and the Phenomena of "Disappearances," September 20, 1979* (Washington, D.C.: U.S. Government Printing Office, 1980), p. 607; Washington Office on Latin America, *Guatemala: The Roots of Revolution* (Washington, D.C., 1983), p. 13.

30. Amnesty International, "Guatemala: Leading Politicians Murdered," *Amnesty International Newsletter* 9, no. 5 (May 1979): 1; J. Michael Luhan, "The Next El Salvador," *The New Republic*, April 11, 1981, p. 24.

31. Linda Drucker, "A Talk with Guatemala's Vinicio Cerezo," *New Leader* 66 (March 21, 1983): 5; Comisión de Derechos Humanos—Guatemala/USA, *Information Bulletin* 3, no. 10 (November/December 1985): 3; *Enfoprensa* 3, no. 42 (November 22, 1985): 3.

32. *Latin America Regional Reports: Mexico/Central America* 84, no. 5 (June 8, 1984): 6. For a critique of the weaknesses in the 1984 election, see Gordon L. Bowen, "No Gain in Guatemala," *The New Republic* 191, no. 16 (October 15, 1984): 4.

33. Americas Watch, *Human Rights in Guatemala: No Neutrals Allowed* (New York, 1982), pp. 70–75.

34. Washington Office on Latin America, *Update* 8, no. 1 (January/February 1983): 4; Americas Watch, *Creating a Desolation*, p. 35; *Washington Post*, August 10, 1983, p. 1.

35. CBS News, "60 Minutes: Caught in the Middle" (New York: CBS television program, February 2, 1986).

36. Davis and Hodson, *Witnesses*, pp. 7–9, 24–26.

37. Regarding Yos, see Clara Nuñez Pérez, *Testimonio . . . en relación a la desaparicion de mi esposo Rafael Yos Muxtay* (Mexico City: Comisión de Derechos Humanos de Guatemala, January 10, 1986), 11 pp.; Amnesty International, 337/85: "Fear of Extrajudicial Execution: Rafael Yos Muxtay, Aged 27, Social Worker," *Urgent Action* December 5, 1985, p. 1; *Enfoprensa* 3, no. 45 (December 13, 1985): 1; Comisión de Derechos Humanos—Guatemala/USA, "Disappearances in Guatemala," December 4, 1985, p. 1. Regarding Che, see Amnesty International, "Urgent Action 307/85: Disappearance: Guatemala: Luis Che, Catechist from El Estor, Department of Izabal," October 31, 1985, p. 1. More generally, see Bowen, "No Roadblocks"; Lernoux, "Revolution and Counterrevolution"; idem, "A Priest among the People."

38. Pedro Burgos, "Analisis juridico de los sucesos ocurridos en la embajada de España en Guatemala," *Revista de Estudios Internacionales* 1, no. 1 (January/March 1980): 107–127.

39. See Bowen, "U.S. Policy." On the USAID cases in 1983, see *Current History* 82, no. 484 (May 1983): 236; Amnesty International, *Guatemala: Update* (New York, December 1983), p. 14; Comisión de Derechos Humanos—Guatemala/USA, *Report Submitted to the 40th Session of the United Nations*, pp. 72–73; CIDH, *Report on the Situation of Human Rights in Guatemala*, p. 16; Americas Watch, *Guatemala: A Nation of Prisoners* (New York, January 1984), pp. 21, 184.

40. *Latin America Weekly Report* 86, no. 9 (February 28, 1986): 9; *Washington Post*, March 12, 1986, p. 30.

41. *Latin America Regional Reports Mexico/Central America* 83, no. 9 (October 28, 1983): 1; 83, no. 10 (December 2, 1983): 1; *Enfoprensa* 22, no. 30 (July 27, 1984): 3; 2, no. 31 (August 3, 1984): 3; 2, no. 42 (October 19, 1984): 3; World Bank, *World Development Report* (Washington, D.C., 1981), p. 158; idem, *World Development Report* (Washington, D.C., 1984), p. 248; *Washington Post*, December 26, 1984, p. 31.

42. *Enfoprensa* 2, no. 47 (November 23, 1984): 4; 3, no. 14 (April 19, 1985): 6.

43. Elliott Abrams, "Letters," *Foreign Policy* 53 (Winter 1984): 174.

44. *Report of the National Bipartisan Commission on Central America* (Washington, D.C.: U.S. Government Printing Office, 1984).

4

Building Democracy in Nicaragua

Richard Stahler-Sholk

I. THE NICARAGUAN REVOLUTION IN COMPARATIVE PERSPECTIVE

While South American authoritarian regimes faced mounting pressure in the late 1970s and 1980s to liberalize and to transfer power to democratic governments (in Argentina, Brazil, Chile, Peru, and Uruguay), authoritarian regimes in Central America were increasingly challenged by revolutionary movements. These parallel trends, although different in many respects, together held out the prospect of a region-wide turn away from authoritarian rule. Juxtaposing the two trends may stimulate general propositions about the processes of liberalization and redemocratization.

The most decisive transition from authoritarianism in Central America occurred in Nicaragua, where the Sandinista National Liberation Front (FSLN) overthrew the 43-year-old Somoza family dictatorship on July 19, 1979. To examine the Nicaraguan revolution within the conceptual framework of "redemocratization," which has been constructed principally from South American experience, it is

The author is grateful to Laura J. Enriquez for many helpful suggestions; all errors are my own. This chapter is dedicated to the memory of Benjamin Ernest Linder, age 27, killed on 28 April 1987 by U.S.-backed contras while working to bring electricity and drinking water to rural Nicaraguan communities.

important to first put the Nicaraguan case into historical context. A careful analysis of the Nicaraguan revolutionary transition will reveal an accumulation of contradictions at the *political* level, which highlighted the underlying tensions of the Central American economic model.

The wave of South American military coups in the late 1960s and 1970s, in some of the countries with the longest democratic traditions and most well-developed political institutions in the region, confounded the expectations of Modernization theorists. Economic development and industrialization had not produced stable, democratic polities. Social scientists sought to explain the authoritarian phenomenon in terms of a syndrome of overlapping economic crisis and political polarization.[1] Components of the syndrome included (1) bottlenecks associated with a particular phase of dependent industrialization; (2) the rapid mobilization of the popular sectors and collapse of the populist coalitions which had been characteristic of the "easy phase" of import-substituting industrialization; and (3) the growing autonomy of a state bureaucracy composed of middle-class technocrats and a newly professionalized military. The resulting "bureaucratic-authoritarian" regimes relied on coercion to repress wage demands and promoted capital accumulation by an alliance composed of foreign interests, an internationalized fraction of the domestic bourgeoisie, and state managers.[2]

In Central America, as in South America, "modernity" proved to be too undifferentiated a concept to explain regime change. Central America's authoritarian regimes have rather different histories, generally dating back to the "Depression dictators" of the 1930s. The militaries were initially called in to protect the interests of the coffee-exporting oligarchies against the threat of peasant uprisings in the wake of the Depression.[3] These military regimes were supported by the U.S. government, which in the early twentieth century sought to solidify its emerging economic and military predominance in Central America. The case of Nicaragua's Somoza was typical; in Roosevelt's words, "he may be an S.O.B., but he's *our* S.O.B." Before World War II, agroexport elites were firmly entrenched in power in Central America, middle classes were virtually nonexistent, and industrialization was actually restricted by law.

Dramatic changes in Central American societies between the end of World War II and the 1970s brought a cycle of repression and polarization which led the region's authoritarian regimes to a point of rupture. The dramatic expansion of cotton, cattle, and sugar cultivation in the 1950s and 1960s brought an export-led boom with highly concentrated distributive impact. A "modernizing" bourgeoisie used its control of agricultural credits and state resources (including coercion) to squeeze peasants off land that had previously been devoted to food crops and to convert that land to more capital-intensive production of cash crops. This shift converted the peasantry into landless and landpoor, seasonal wage laborers and brought increasing concentration of income and decreased production of basic foodstuffs. It also stimulated massive migration to the cities, causing dramatic acceleration of both urbanization and unemployment. Consequently, demand for government services increased sharply while cyclical downturns in export earnings cut into government revenues. The ranks of the middle class and the urban marginals swelled.

The 1960s saw some industrialization, fostered by the Central American Common Market (CACM); but economic growth and urbanization were not matched by industrial job-creation. The CACM stimulated a burst of capital accumulation by a dynamic fraction of the national bourgeoisies, and also provided attractive incentives for foreign investors to produce in Central America for the artificially expanded regional market. However, the CACM was not accompanied by any redistributive structural reforms to broaden the internal markets within each member country. By the 1970s, this model of regional import substitution was already reaching its limits.[4] Problems of maldistribution and balance of payments crisis loomed. The unraveling of the CACM coincided with a period of accentuated fluctuation in the world prices of Central America's exports in the 1970s.

The region's export-led economic growth spurt of the 1960s, which had masked some of the implications of the profound socioeconomic changes of the post-World War II period, was faltering by the 1970s. The sharp increase in petroleum import bills was momentarily offset by foreign loans and good prices for Central American exports from 1971 to 1977; but capital markets subsequently became restrictive and export prices collapsed, plunging the region into economic crisis.

The consequences of these social and economic changes of the postwar period, followed by economic crisis in the late 1970s and 1980s in Central America, bear some resemblance to the processes of transition from authoritarian rule in the South American cases, which have been examined in detail elsewhere.[5] Among the similar patterns: (1) The authoritarian regimes were eroded by the fracturing of the bourgeoisie, with divisions particularly aggravated by conflict between nationalist and foreign-aligned capital.[6] (2) A major impetus for liberalization came from the mobilization of the popular classes through the vehicles of the previously organized workers' movements in South America and the newly-organized "mass organizations" in Central America.[7] (3) The militaries began to develop their own institutional and economic interests, distinct from the interests of their initial oligarchic sponsors. Lines of fissure emerged between the economic elites and the armed forces, as well as within the armed forces themselves, thus weakening the internal cohesion of the authoritarian regimes. In Central America, the proliferation of private military and paramilitary forces obstructed efforts by the elites to reconstitute a stable power bloc. (4) Adverse economic circumstances contributed at key moments to delegitimizing authoritarian rule. In the Nicaraguan case, the 1972 earthquake that leveled the capital city, and the sharp drop in economic activity in the 1977–79 insurrectionary period, are important examples. (5) At an ideological level, the Catholic Church's renewed focus on social justice and human rights, expressed in the Latin American Bishops' Conferences in Medellín (1968) and Puebla (1979), awakened grassroots religious movements in both Central and South America that pressed for social change.

Despite the broad similarities in these two processes of transition from authoritarian rule, there are several distinguishing features of the Central American transitions in general and the Nicaraguan case in particular. These differences have left a distinctive imprint on the processes of liberalization and redemocratization. First, Central America (with the exception of Costa Rica) lacks a tradition of democratic political institutions. In Nicaragua, for example, political competition was restricted to squabbling between the nineteenth-century Liberal and Conservative parties representing different factions of the landowning elite, followed by U.S. military occupation in the early twentieth-century and then the 43-year Somoza family dynasty. Consequently, "liberalization" in the Nicaraguan context cannot be defined in terms of the *status quo ante*. Rather, liberalization has to be conceived in terms of the aspirations of the majority of participants in the overthrow of the authoritarian regime—or conversely, the process of correcting those conditions that most motivated the aggrieved population to act. Liberalization required the construction of an entirely new order. Since pre-revolutionary political institutions were thoroughly discredited, the transition from authoritarianism in Nicaragua was an open-ended process.

A second feature which obviously distinguishes the Central American transitions is the fact that they have taken the form of mass-based, armed revolutionary movements. The strength of the oligarchic hard-liners in Central America is such that attempts by the bourgeois "moderate opposition" forces to encourage compromise—e.g. the October 1979 junta in El Salvador, or the Broad Opposition Front (FAO) in the 1970s in Nicaragua—are violently resisted by the right.[8] Non-revolutionary liberalization paths have been blocked by the spiral of hard-line repression on the one hand and radicalized opposition on the other. The revolutionary path has important implications for liberalization and redemocratization options. Mass-based armed revolution suggests that the post-authoritarian regime will face a higher level of popular expectations, as well as a less propitious climate for political pacts and compromises. This form of transition also creates an extended period of emergency and instability, which translates into a set of tasks that lend themselves to greater centralization of governmental authority.

Third, transitions from authoritarianism in Central America are distinguished by their special geopolitical context.[9] U.S. interests and influence have historically had a more decisive impact on politics in Central America than in South America. Nicaragua in particular has been considered strategically important, dating back to the nineteenth-century U.S. interest in monopolizing trans-isthmian canal privileges. In the name of democracy, the United States practiced decidedly undemocratic policies in Nicaragua, invading some fourteen times, maintaining the country under military occupation, and installing favored governments. For Nicaragua, therefore, "redemocratization" came to be associated with the reassertion of national sovereignty.

In the 1970s and 1980s, the development of Central American revolutionary movements coincided with a period of palpable decline in U.S. hegemony and a new "rollback" ideology reminiscent of the Cold War,[10] a combination which produced an intense new wave of U.S. involvement in Central American politics. All this suggests that revolutionary movements seeking to dislodge authoritarian regimes in Central America will tend to regard the United States more as an adversary than as a model; and that the geopolitical context will significantly affect the processes of liberalization and redemocratization.

The following section will examine the Nicaraguan authoritarian period in an effort to explain the circumstances that produced the crisis of the *somocista* state. A close look at the Nicaraguan case shows that Kissinger Commission-type prescriptions for bringing democracy to Central America—more export promotion, a stronger private sector, and a modest injection of foreign capital— cannot solve the underlying structural problem, which is a marginalizing and exclusionary economic and political model.[11] Section Three will analyze the development of the revolutionary coalition. The Nicaraguan case shows how the reformist option in Central America was completely blocked by the mid–1970s, in large part because U.S. policy itself repeatedly favored undemocratic forces rather than permit fundamental social change. Finally, Section Four assesses the redemocratization process in the 1979–87 period, in which the Sandinistas have sought to establish a new model of participatory democracy in the midst of persistent U.S. efforts to overthrow the revolutionary government.

II. SOMOCISMO: NICARAGUA UNDER AUTHORITARIAN RULE

The Nicaraguan revolution was more than just a rebellion against an abusive autocrat. Rather, it was a reaction against an exploitative socioeconomic system, sustained by an undemocratic political order and a powerful repressive apparatus which were reinforced by U.S. backing. From 1936 to 1979, the Somoza dynasty ran what was almost a caricature of a U.S. client state. The National Guard of Nicaragua, which functioned as the personal army of the Somozas, attracted worldwide notoriety in the 1970s for its repression of real and imagined dissent.[12]

Formal institutions of democracy lost their substantive meaning under the Somoza regime, as constitutions were rewritten and elections manipulated to legitimize the dictatorship. During its tenure, the Somoza family amassed an enormous economic empire, establishing alliances and dividing the spoils with the other powerful economic groupings in the nation. These four characteristics of *somocismo*—the special relationship with the United States, the repressive practices of the National Guard and its total fealty to Somoza which delegitimized it as a "national" institution, the manipulation of democratic symbols to create the illusion of legitimacy, and the Somozas' use of state power to promote personal accumulation of capital in alliance with major groupings of the national bourgeoisie—defined the direction of the opposition movement which would eventually topple the regime.

U.S. intervention in Nicaragua dated back to the mid-nineteenth century, when the United States sought to displace British hegemony and monopolize trans-isthmian transit rights.[13] U.S. military force was employed to impose "stability" on post-independence Nicaragua politics, which were marked by frequent civil warfare between the Conservatives, representing traditional aristocratic large landowners and ranchers, and the Liberals, representing coffee-growing interests favoring free trade. U.S. Marines were landed in 1909 to remove the Liberal José Santos Zelaya, whose nationalism ran afoul of the Monroe Doctrine, and install the Conservative Adolfo Díaz. A Liberal revolt in 1912 brought a new U.S. invasion, followed by fraudulent "elections" to ratify the Díaz regime. After a period of continued civil strife, the U.S. Marines imposed a 1927 pact installing a non-nationalist faction of the Liberals under Juan Bautista Sacasa, and requiring all arms to be surrendered to the Marines, who would train a Nicaraguan National Guard.

One general from the Liberal army, Augusto César Sandino, opposed the pact and organized an army in the northern mountains to wage guerrilla warfare against the occupying U.S. Marines.[14] Sandino recruited his opposition forces from the nationalist elements of the Liberal bourgeoisie, as well as from the peasantry and the small working class clustered around the foreign mining and lumber enclaves. The United States trained the National Guard of Nicaragua, headed by Anastasio "Tacho" Somoza García, to replace the U.S. Marines, who were withdrawn in 1933. In 1934, Sandino was assassinated by the National Guard, apparently with the complicity of the U.S. ambassador,[15] when he came to Managua for negotiations with the Sacasa government. By that time, effective power was in the hands of Anastasio Somoza García and his National Guard. In 1936, Somoza García seized the presidency, inaugurating the 43-year family dictatorship.

Nature of the Pre-Revolutionary State

The Somoza dictatorship proved to be remarkably long-lasting. Upon taking power in 1936, Somoza García moved quickly to co-opt the Conservatives, signing pacts to guarantee them a degree of representation in Congress as well as economic space. Elections were held, but they were routinely fraudulent: The Somozas often created their own opposition, "mosquito" (zancudo) parties; and special identification cards were given to Somoza voters to help them get jobs and avoid harassment.[16]

The dictatorship assiduously cultivated U.S. backing, and also carefully preserved the trappings of constitutionality. Whenever constitutional obstacles prohibited the "reelection" of a Somoza, either the constitution was changed or an interim puppet president was installed. Five such caretaker presidents punctuated the 43-year Somoza reign, nominally holding office for a total of three and a half years.[17] When Anastasio Somoza García was assassinated in 1956, his older son, Luís Somoza Debayle, became president, while his younger son, Anastasio

"Tachito" Somoza Debayle, became head of the National Guard. When Luís died in 1967, "Tachito" assumed the Presidency.

Aside from the dissident Conservatives, the political opposition to Somoza family rule included two smaller parties: the Independent Liberal Party (PLI), which split with Somoza's Nationalist Liberal Party in 1947, and the Social Christian Party (PSC), a Christian Democratic party formed in 1957. Sporadic plots by these bourgeois and middle-class fractions were brutally repressed by the National Guard in the 1940s and 1950s. The Moscow-oriented Nicaraguan Socialist Party (PSN), founded in 1944, followed the accommodationist line typical of Latin American communist parties in the postwar period, but it was nevertheless severely repressed from 1947 onward. The Sandinista National Liberation Front (FSLN), founded in 1961, carried out a series of guerrilla actions in the 1960s, but the National Guard had inflicted heavy casualties on the guerrilla columns by 1970. In moving against each of its domestic opponents, the dictatorship was careful to invoke U.S. assistance and indeed to exaggerate for domestic consumption the actual degree of U.S. support for the regime:

In dealing with resistance, Somoza adroitly identified his opposition with the current enemy of the United States. After his flirtation with Fascism in the 1930s, he declared war on the Axis powers in December 1941, allowing the USA to install naval and airforce bases inside Nicaragua, and receiving in return large amounts of military equipment which would never be used against an external enemy. The War was used as an excuse to declare a state of siege and suspend constitutional guarantees. After 1945, he abruptly labelled all opposition as 'agents of international Communism' and continued to count on American support in his moves to eradicate it.[18]

In short, while the official opposition performed largely symbolic functions, real opposition was quickly and forcefully repressed.

The repressive agency with sustained the dictatorship was the National Guard of Nicaragua, a combined army and police force whose principal loyalty was to the Somoza family.[19] The Somozas used control over personnel policy, promotions, kick-backs, spies, etc. to insure this loyalty. Officers lived in luxury. Salaries for enlisted men were kept deliberately low, but troops were free to collect bribes and protection money and other "fringe benefits." (Interestingly, when the FSLN pulled off a dramatic commando raid in 1974 and held a houseful of *somocista* notables hostage, one of their demands was for a wage increase for enlisted men.)[20] The Guard routinely engaged in arbitrary killing and torture, especially in periods of active opposition activity.[21] FSLN guerrilla actions in the late 1960s and from 1974 to 1979 triggered the most intense waves of indiscriminate violence, particularly directed against the peasantry in the northern mountains.

The National Guard of Nicaragua received extensive U.S. military aid and training. From 1946 to 1975 Nicaragua received $23.6 million in U.S. military aid. Both military and economic aid escalated sharply in the 1960s as the United

States expanded its counterinsurgency programs in the wake of the Cuban revolution. Nearly 5,000 National Guardsmen received U.S. military training between 1950 and 1975; more troops were trained in Nicaragua than in any other Latin American country.[22] In return, the Somoza dictatorship offered to send troops during the Korean and Vietnam wars, and allowed Nicaraguan territory to be used for the CIA's overthrow of Guatemalan President Jacobo Arbenz in 1954 and for the launching of the Bay of Pigs invasion in 1961. Nicaraguan National Guardsmen were sent to participate in the occupation of the Dominican Republic in 1965 and to help put down a reformist coup in El Salvador in 1972. Nicaragua also joined the Central American Defense Council (CONDECA), participating in joint counterinsurgency operations in the 1960s and 1970s with the other Central American military regimes and the U.S. Southern Command. Not surprisingly, the hated Guard was associated very closely with the United States in the minds of most Nicaraguans.

Personal corruption was another hallmark of the dictatorship. Anastasio Somoza García, founder of the dynasty, starting with virtually nothing when he became head of the National Guard in 1933, quickly amassed a fortune. Some $400,000 in annual bribes were exacted from U.S. companies for mining and lumbering concessions and tax exemptions.[23] During World War II, German-owned property was confiscated and sold to Somoza family members for a fraction of its value. Land sales and loans were rigged for personal gain. By 1944, Somoza was the largest coffee producer in Nicaragua. In the 1950s and 1960s, the Somozas moved into the transportation industry (including the national airlines and merchant marine company), the nation's only milk pasteurizing plant, textiles, cement, and other light industries stimulated by the Central American Common Market. After the 1972 earthquake in Managua, the family economic empire expanded into real estate speculation, construction, insurance and finance. By 1979, the Somoza fortune was estimated at nearly a billion dollars, and included over 20 percent of all arable land in the country.[24]

The Somoza economic empire coexisted with the two other major groupings of the bourgeoisie which emerged with the cotton boom of the 1950s.[25] The Banco Nicaragüense (BANIC) group was formed by Liberal landowners who moved into the dynamic cotton-export sector and then invested their profits in regional integration industries. The Banco de América (BANAMER) group was controlled by Conservative families, with initial investments in cattle and sugar. All three groups profited from the industrial boom stimulated by the CACM in the 1960s, a period when the economic alliances and joint ventures formed among these groups (plus growing U.S. investments) served to mitigate real intra-bourgeois divisions. These divisions would re-emerge in the 1970s, ultimately creating the conditions in which a mass-based opposition movement could successfully challenge the dictatorship.

Two factors served to aggravate the divisions between elite factions: First, the 1960s export-led boom was replaced by fluctuating terms of trade and slowed growth in the 1970s. Second, and more important, "Tachito" Somoza alienated the other fractions of the bourgeoisie after the 1972 Managua earthquake, not only by his blatent theft of international relief funds, but also by monopolizing opportunities for post-earthquake profiteering in construction, real estate, and finance.

From its inception, the Somoza regime was characterized by corruption, un-democratic political institutions, repression, and the subordination of national interests to U.S. priorities. This characterization, however, does not by itself explain how and why the transition from authoritarian rule occurred. To discover the catalysts, it is necessary to examine the socioeconomic impact of *somocismo*. In particular, the 1950s and 1960s saw dramatic changes in Nicaragua's social structure. These changes, which formed part of a general Central American pattern, marked the consolidation of an agroexport model characterized by highly unequal income distribution and rigid political structures.

Somocismo: **The Political-Economic Model**

Coffee cultivation had tied the Nicaraguan economy to the world economy since the late nineteenth century, and also provided the source of capital accu-mulation for the modernizing agrarian bourgeoisie, whose political influence grew at the expense of the traditional *latifundistas*. Agricultural production for domestic consumption (maize, rice, beans, sorghum) still accounted for the bulk of the labor force and land utilization between 1935 and 1948[26] but the attraction of cash crops had led to a steady expansion of coffee cultivation and displacement of small subsistence farmers. This trend was accelerated by world market con-ditions in the 1950s: Coffee prices, which averaged 6–8 cents per pound between 1930 and 1946 in the wake of the Depression, shot up over 50 cents per pound in the early 1950s. The Somoza dictatorship used its control of the state apparatus to rig sales of national lands in the northern hills of Matagalpa and cash in on the coffee boom.[27]

The 1950s and 1960s saw a major agroexport boom which laid the basis for the *somocista* economic/political model. While the model has been extensively examined by others,[28] it is important to review its implications for income distribution and the workforce in order to understand the revolutionary transition.

The coffee boom of the early 1950s financed investments in cotton in a period when cotton prices were soaring, boosted by the Korean War. In 1950, coffee accounted for 50 percent of Nicaragua's total exports, while cotton was only 5 percent; by 1955, coffee had fallen to 35 percent of total exports, and cotton had become the principal Nicaraguan export. Cotton production grew at a rate of 33 percent per year in the early 1960s, and by 1966, Nicaragua was the tenth largest cotton producer in the world.[29]

The cotton boom of the 1950s brought dynamic expansion of the Nicaraguan economy, marked by sharply increased dependence on exports. Between 1950 and 1964, GDP growth averaged an impressive 5.9 percent per year. However, this growth was accompanied by severe oscillations in the economy. For example, from 1950–53, exports rose 58 percent, and the GDP grew 27.9 percent; but in 1955–56, exports fell 19 percent, and the Nicaraguan economy stagnated.[30]

Benefits from the cotton boom were highly concentrated: by 1977, 6 percent of cotton growers controlled 52 percent of cultivated land.[31] The expansion of cotton cultivation also brought a dramatic expulsion of small maize growers from the fertile lowlands of León and Chinandega. Once the "granary of Central America," three-fifths of cropland in those two departments was taken over by cotton growers by 1963.[32]

After 1965, cotton prices on the world market fell. The resulting decline in cotton production provoked an even greater displacement of rural workers to urban areas in search of employment in the industrial and service sectors. This displacement was accelerated by the expansion of land-intensive cattle ranching, responding in part to the growing demand for cheap beef for the U.S. fast-food industry. The amount of land dedicated to pasture doubled between 1960 and 1975. Needless to say, ownership was highly concentrated in the cattle industry: In 1971, 2 percent of the ranchers owned 27 percent of all cattle and over half of all pasture land in Nicaragua. The Somoza family controlled most of the slaughterhouses, giving them greatest control over the profits. Despite a quad-rupling of beef exports in the second half of the 1960s, per capita protein consumption *within* Nicaragua actually declined.[33]

Besides beef, export diversification in the 1960s included sugar cane produc-tion, stimulated by U.S. reapportionment of the Cuban sugar quota to Central America after the Cuban revolution. Four of the country's five sugar mills in the 1970s were owned by the Somoza family. Some diversification into tobacco and shrimp and lobster also occurred. By the 1970s, the four main agricultural exports—coffee, cotton, sugar, and beef—accounted for 60 to 70 percent of total exports; agricultural and agroindustrial products represented 80 percent of foreign exchange earnings; and foreign trade accounted for one-third of the country's economic production.

As the economy became increasingly vulnerable to world price swings, small farmers were much less able to cope with fluctuating earnings than large farmers, particularly since the country's financial/credit institutions were tightly controlled by the Somozas and the other two clusters of the agroexport bourgeoisie (BANIC and BANAMER). A 1966 study by the United Nations Economic Commission for Latin America showed that small farmers received only 5 percent of all agricultural and ranching credits in Nicaragua.[34] Small and medium producers were generally excluded from the cotton boom by limited access to capital and technology. This political/economic structure meant that the benefits of the agroexport boom were distributed in a highly inequitable fashion.[35]

Another consequence of the reorientation of the economy toward cotton and other cash crops was the stagnation of food crop production. The total land area under cultivation in Nicaragua grew 62 percent between 1950 and 1962, but domestic consumption crops fell from 60 percent to 43 percent of agricultural production in this period.[36] The differential profit rate between export crops and domestic consumption crops meant that the best lands went to export crop cultivation. Whereas in 1945 the majority of the agricultural labor force was devoted to production of domestic consumption crops, by 1962, 62.5 percent of all those employed in agriculture were engaged in the production of export crops and another 16.5 percent were employed in the growing cattle industry.[37]

Accompanying the shift in crop production was a reorganization of land ownership. In a predominantly agricultural country, the distribution of land is importantly linked to the distribution of wealth. By 1963, half the land under cultivation was controlled by 2 percent of landowners, while 50 percent of the country's landholdings were crowded onto 3.5 percent of arable land.[38] Export crops were predominantly grown by large landowners, whereas *campesinos* predominated in food crop production. Average yearly income of a large landowner in the mid–1960s exceeded US$ 18,000 as opposed to approximately $380 for a small *campesino*, $370 for a landless agricultural worker, and a national average of $900.[39]

These figures suggest the negative distributive implications of the shift toward export crop production in Nicaragua in the 1950s and 1960s. Furthermore, the stagnating production of food crops was accompanied by very rapid rates of total population growth and urbanization (hence increasing demand for food crops). The urban sector in Nicaragua grew from 19 percent of the total population in 1950 to 42 percent in 1980, the most dramatic shift in Central America. Meanwhile, agricultural unemployment rose steadily after 1965, hitting 16 percent in 1977 and 32 percent in 1979.[40]

Cotton cultivation tended to consolidate capitalist relations of production in agriculture, first introduced with coffee production for export. By the mid-1950s, cotton production in Nicaragua was highly capital-intensive and technology-intensive. Fertilizers, insecticides, and tractors dramatically increased yields. The total number of tractors in Nicaragua jumped from less than 500 in 1950 to over 2,500 by 1955, and cotton productivity rose 180 percent from 1951 to 1963.[41] Rapid mechanization also contributed to growing rural underemployment and migration to the cities. A large seasonal workforce was required only for the cotton harvest period (three or four months per year). Those who had been left landless or squeezed onto sub-subsistence sized plots of land became available for wage labor in the harvest season. This availability was further assured by Somoza government policies which kept food prices low, in effect forcing food crop producers to supplement incomes by selling their labor at least part of the year.[42]

By the 1970s, the seasonal workforce in cotton alone averaged around 150,000–200,000, or half the economically active population (EAP) in agriculture. By 1978, 90 percent of the agricultural EAP lacked year-round employment.[43] As cotton and cattle production for export expanded, the process of concentration and subdivision of land accelerated.

The 1950s and 1960s also marked the beginnings of significant industrialization in Nicaragua, as well as the rapid growth of the commercial and service sectors of

the economy. Under Somoza family rule, the state invested in infrastructural projects designed to increase the profitability of the family investments in export agriculture and agroindustry. The network of roads expanded from 1,880 km. in
1950 to 6,165 km. in 1960 and 12,000 km. by 1971; electrical generating capacity
grew 16.5 percent annually from 1960 to 1964. Accordingly, export agricultural
production grew 19.5 percent per year from 1960 to 1965, compared to only 4.4
percent per year for crops consumed domestically. The rate of investment in this
period grew 17 percent per year.[44] This high rate of domestic accumulation was
supplemented by growing foreign investment after the formation of the Central
American Common Market (CACM) in 1960, which encouraged the expansion
of light industry for export within the Central American region.

The CACM model promoted a type of industrialization that was highly import-
intensive, uncompetitive outside the protected regional market, and based mainly
on consumer goods for the urban middle class and elites.[45] Manufacturing for
export outside the region tended to be of the "final assembly" type, taking
advantage of cheap local labor while generating few domestic economic linkages.

Although industrial production in Nicaragua grew by 10.8 percent annually
in the 1960s, employment did not grow correspondingly: industry accounted for
11.7 percent of the economically active population in 1963, and only 12.3 percent
by 1971. In the same period, agriculture's share of the EAP fell from 59.7
percent to 47 percent, which actually represented a loss of jobs in absolute
terms.[46] Both the agroexport and industrial components of the prevailing economic model depended on the availability of a large marginalized, "informal"
sector of the workforce.[47]

The agroexport and CACM-industrial booms of the 1950s and 1960s left a
distinct imprint on Nicaragua. The growth of industry, commerce, and government meant greater social differentiation, as the middle class and the urban
proletariat expanded. For the poor, however, the boom period brought mostly
frustration. While expectations rose, income distribution was, if anything, worsened; by the 1970s the poorest 50 percent of the Nicaraguan population received
15 percent of the national income, while the richest 5 percent received 30 percent
of income.[48] Over half the population remained illiterate (75 percent in rural
areas), and the life expectancy in Nicaragua (53–55 years) was the lowest in
Central America. Over 80 percent of the rural population lacked access to health
services, and only 2 percent of all children who enrolled in the first grade
completed the sixth grade.[49]

The trends described above for the 1950s and 1960s in Nicaragua had a
tremendous impact on the social structure of the country. Wealth became concentrated in the hands of the Somoza family and a small agroexport bourgeoisie.
As export crop production and cattle grazing encroached on subsistence agriculture, the numbers of landless peasants grew, as did the ranks of the semi-
proletarianized *campesinos* who were forced to earn part of their livelihood via
seasonal wage labor on the cotton, coffee, and sugar plantations. Food production
stagnated. The urban areas swelled with the expansion of the marginalized pro-

letariat and commercial petty bourgeoisie. And the rapid economic growth of the 1950s and 1960s, however unequally distributed its payoffs, was decelerating by the 1970s.

III. THE OVERTHROW OF THE SOMOZA REGIME

If objective conditions in the 1950s and 1960s contributed to mobilizing new groups of disaffected Nicaraguans, it was conscious actions and conjunctural circumstances in the 1970s that determined the specific political shape of opposition to the dictatorship. Through painful political learning, the FSLN transformed itself from a tiny Cuban-style guerrilla band in the northern mountains into the spearhead of an effective mass movement. The 1972 earthquake dramatically exposed the full measure of Somoza's greed, rousing the bourgeoisie to cautious opposition. The United States and the Nicaraguan bourgeoisie maneuvered to preserve selected elements of *somocismo* while pondering ways to eject the dictator himself. Finally, the FSLN seized the moment and led the final offensive that brought down the Somoza dynasty.

Social Base of the Opposition

Like its namesake, the Sandinista National Liberation Front (FSLN) focused its early organizing efforts on the rural northern region. Rural workers, suffering from the boom-and-bust cycles of cotton and coffee prices, had begun to organize strikes and land takeovers to protest brutal working conditions in the late 1950s. The Somoza regime responded violently, using the National Guard to repress peasant movements. Land invasions accelerated in the 1960s. It was in this climate that the FSLN was created in 1961.

Founded by former university students, the FSLN slowly built up peasant support for guerrilla operations against the National Guard in the 1960s. Influenced by the Cuban example, the Sandinistas sought to establish guerrilla *focos*, or focal points from which to launch armed attacks against the regime.[50] But a series of military defeats, culminating in the National Guard's destruction of the major Sandinista guerrilla columns at Pancasán in 1967 (the same year Che Guevara was killed in Bolivia), forced the FSLN to reconsider its strategy. Departing from the *foquista* approach, the FSLN began to concentrate on building mass support and establishing links between urban and rural organizing. This subjective factor—political learning by the FSLN—left an imprint on the revolutionary process which would overthrow the Somoza regime.

The FSLN's shift from *foquismo* to mass organizing was facilitated by the mobilization of new mass constituencies. The socioeconomic changes of the 1950s and 1960s had brought major dislocations in both the rural and urban sectors. By the 1970s, opposition to the dictatorship was broadening. The development of a capital-intensive, export-oriented agricultural sector created a concentration of wealth, but it also meant that some 15,000 jobs were lost in

Table 4.1
Rural Class Structure in Nicaragua, Late 1970s

Fraction	Economically Active Population (EAP)	
	Percentage	Thousands
Proletariat	29.3	125.0
Semiproletariat (poor peasants)	38.4	164.5
Middle peasants	22.3	95.5
Wealthy peasants	8.0	34.5
Bourgeoisie	2.0	9.0
TOTAL	100.0	485.5

Source: Carlos M. Vilas, *The Sandinista Revolution: National Liberation and Social Transformation in Central America* (New York: Monthly Review, 1986), p. 66.

the agricultural sector between 1963 and 1973, and industrialization failed to create an equivalent number of new jobs. Efforts at unionization were repressed. The large urban middle stratum, which by 1963 comprised nearly one-fifth of the EAP in Nicaragua, suffered from arbitrary harassment by Somoza's National Guard.[51] Following the earthquake in Managua in 1972, living standards fell sharply for the urban poor.

By the late 1970s, the overwhelming majority of the rural population in Nicaragua was composed of landless agricultural workers and seasonal wage laborers on large plantations who did not own enough land to provide for their own subsistence (i.e., the semiproletariat), as illustrated in Table 1.

The *campesino* population displaced by the agroexport boom from the 1950s onward formed an important part of the constituency of the revolutionary movement of the 1970s. It is no accident that in the fertile lowlands of León and Chinandega, where peasant production of corn was dramatically displaced by cotton-growers, some 240 land invasions were recorded between 1964 and 1973.[52] Similarly, the eastern part of Matagalpa, which in the 1950s produced more corn and beans than the rest of the country, saw a drastic displacement of *campesinos* in favor of cattle production for export. This was accompanied by USAID-sponsored counterinsurgency aimed at undermining the FSLN stronghold in the area.[53]

The Nicaraguan "agrarian reform" of the 1960s, administered by the Instituto Agrario de Nicaragua (IAN), was typical of counterinsurgency programs promoted by the United States in Latin America, generally in the aftermath of the Cuban revolution:

Since land redistribution in the Pacific coastal region (and even in the more attractive parts of the Central region) was unthinkable in the Nicaraguan political context, agrarian reform essentially meant the resettlement of dispossessed small producers in a few colonization projects and the provision of land titles in these and other remote areas to which they migrated. Thus, IAN 'mediated' landlord-tenant conflicts by offering some land in Nicaragua's large agricultural frontier region and through its titling program, it legitimized some of the spontaneous migrants to this region who had established themselves on public or unclaimed land.[54]

Far from addressing the socioeconomic injustice which lay at the root of rural unrest, the "agrarian reform" was aimed at removing peasants from areas of FSLN activity to distant forest regions.[55]

Another important part of the revolutionary constituency came from the urban informal sector, which had expanded steadily since the 1950s as a product of the economic model, which tended to expel labor from rural areas but failed to provide a compensatory expansion of salaried urban employment.[56] Empirical evidence of the class composition of the insurrectionary movement of the 1970s reveals that students and artisan/tradespeople (mostly from the "informal sector") accounted for the majority of participants.[57]

Popular Organization Against the Dictatorship

Throughout the 1970s, the Sandinistas organized Revolutionary Workers Committees in factories and Civil Defense Committees in the poor urban *barrios*. At the same time, both rural and urban organizing efforts were stimulated by an important ideological element represented by the growing progressive movement within the Latin American Catholic Church.[58] In the mid–1970s, the FSLN began organizing Committees of Rural Workers in collaboration with religious workers inspired by Liberation Theology. The demands of the rural workers were initially centered around working conditions, but they quickly became more political after the National Guard was called in to repress the Committees. These urban and rural committees were the prototypes of the "mass organizations" which would form the FSLN's political base (discussed in section IV below).

The constellation of opposition forces changed shape in the course of the 1970s. In the mid–1970s the FSLN split into three factions or "tendencies," divided in their analysis of the Nicaraguan situation and of the appropriate strategy of opposition to the dictatorship. The Proletarian Tendency (TP), perhaps most influenced by orthodox Marxist analysis, felt that opposition organizing should capitalize on the growing proletarianization (both urban and rural) which characterized the Nicaraguan social formation since the 1950s. The Prolonged Popular War (GPP) tendency, influenced by Maoist thought, focused on creating bases for rural guerrilla struggle. A third, perhaps more ideologically eclectic option was represented by the Insurrectional Tendency (TI), also known as the *Terceristas*.[59]

The *Terceristas*, rejecting the notion of the "passive accumulation of forces" which underlay the calculations of both the TP and the GPP, believed in striking while the dictatorship was weak, without waiting for "objective conditions" to catch up. Also, in contrast to the TP and GPP, the *Terceristas* favored a strategy of alliances with the anti-Somoza bourgeoisie. The force of events tended to vindicate the *Terceristas* on both counts, so that by the time the three tendencies reunified in early 1979, the insurrectional strategy prevailed.

Events of the 1970s shifted the position of the bourgeoisie from grumbling cooperation with the Somoza regime to widespread opposition. General economic downturn, combined with Somoza's greed following the 1972 earthquake, revived intra-bourgeois divisions. While the expansion of the Somoza economic empire into new tertiary-sector activities directly infringed on capital accumulation by the non-Somoza bourgeoisie, the widening ripples of opposition and repression threatened to destabilize the capitalist system as a whole in Nicaragua. In 1974, the growing elements of the reformist bourgeoisie and middle classes which saw little alternative to Somoza's ouster, joined to form the opposition Democratic Union of Liberation (UDEL). In October 1977, the opposition newspaper *La Prensa* published a statement by twelve prominent Nicaraguan businesspeople and professionals—"Los Doce"—praising the participation of the FSLN in the struggle against the dictatorship.

In January 1978, the UDEL Chairman, Pedro Joaquin Chamorro, editor of *La Prensa* and outspoken critic of the dictatorship, was assassinated. The association had the effect of galvanizing and unifying the opposition movement. The bourgeois and middle class elements of the opposition moved closer to the militant position staked out by the FSLN, which drew its strength from the popular sectors.[60] In May 1978 the Broad Opposition Front (FAO) was formed, linking the old UDEL to the pro-FSLN Los Doce as well as a variety of other reformist opposition groups. While UDEL and FAO mobilized Church and foreign opposition to the dictatorship and organized several general strikes, by early 1979 the momentum had clearly passed to the FSLN.

Shifting Correlation of Forces

When the Somoza regime finally crumbled in July 1979, it was the FSLN that came to power. Several factors explain how the FSLN assumed leadership of the revolutionary class alliance that overthrew the dictatorship. In an abstract sense, the FSLN functioned as a vanguard force because the Sandinistas most effectively expressed the interests of the exploited masses. More concretely, the Sandinistas were propelled to the forefront by a combination of factors which included decisive military actions by the *Terceristas*, wavering on the part of the fragmented bourgeoisie, and ill-timed U.S. attempts to influence the course of events.

A close scrutiny of the transition process is required to understand how it led to the polarization that culminated in the revolutionary victory of the FSLN. A major turning point in the opposition movement occurred in 1974, when a group of Sandinista guerrillas invaded a Christmas party of Managua's elite. In exchange for release of the hostages, the FSLN successfully demanded a $2 million ransom, publication of several communiqués, and release of a number of imprisoned Sandinista leaders. The daring raid gave the FSLN instant international visibility and shattered the myth that the dictatorship was invulnerable. Also, the role of Archbishop Miguel Obando y Bravo in these and subsequent negotiations helped solidify the identification of the Catholic Church with the opposition, even though the archbishop and Church hierarchy remained committed to a negotiated settlement that would head off a Sandinista victory.[61]

Somoza overreacted to the 1974 raid, declaring a state of siege that lasted three years. Under cover of martial law, the National Guard launched a massive campaign of indiscriminate repression, directed particularly against the northern region where FSLN strongholds were located. While the FSLN probably had fewer than 150 armed and trained guerrilla fighters in 1974, some 3,000 people were killed by the National Guard during the state of siege.[62] The massacres had a major effect in intensifying domestic and international opposition to the dictatorship.

In September 1977, Somoza lifted the state of siege, and the country erupted in expressions of pent-up protest. The dictator himself had suffered a serious heart attack in July and had been flown to the U.S. for treatment. International pressures contributed to the decision to end martial law. In April 1977 the newly-inaugurated Carter administration, embarrassed by the National Guard's massacres and seeking to define a new human rights policy, had attempted to send Somoza a message by restricting military and economic aid to Nicaragua; in September, the aid restrictions were lifted. The *Terceristas* stepped up military operations in October, and Los Doce issued their endorsement of the FSLN. The endorsement threw the bourgeois-dominated UDEL into disarray,[63] and once again the Sandinistas had seized the initiative.

The assassination of UDEL leader and *La Prensa* editor Pedro Joaquín Chamorro in January 1978 was a watershed event that outraged the opposition bourgeoisie and the public. In protest, UDEL called a general strike that was 80 percent effective. But as the FSLN and Los Doce encouraged more active popular resistance,the strike committee, under pressure from the U.S. embassy, called for an end to the strike.[64] As UDEL wavered, the bourgeoisie lost control of the action. Los Doce returned from exile in July and joined FAO, the reorganized opposition grouping that for the first time formally linked middle class and bourgeois opposition groups to pro-FSLN groups. FAO and leftover elements of UDEL called another one-day strike in July 1978 to protest the Guard's killing of three students; the strike was 70 percent effective. FAO by this time had eclipsed UDEL.

On 22 August 1978, the FSLN once again moved decisively to capture opposition initiative. A *Tercerista* unit led by Edén Pastora seized the National Palace while Congress was in session and held over 2,000 hostages. The daring action won popular admiration as well as concessions similar to those obtained in the December 1974 raid. Equally significant for the eventual course of redemocratization, the raid also apparently forestalled a palace coup intended to install a compromise government which would have excluded the FSLN.[65]

In the days following the August 1978 National Palace takeover, FAO called another general strike, coordinated with FSLN armed operations. The strike quickly boiled over into open insurrection in a number of cities, beginning in the northern city of Matagalpa. The insurrections were spontaneous, but the FSLN quickly threw its units into combat and, on 9 September, endorsed a general insurrection. Somoza responded by once again declaring a state of siege, ordering artillery and aerial strafing and bombing of cities (including incendiary bombs) to crush the insurrections. The bombardment was followed by brutal National Guard mop-up operations in October, setting off a new wave of international condemnation of the regime.

The September 1978 general insurrection solidified the identification of the FSLN with the mass opposition movement. The Sandinistas had set up their own radio station, organized combat training sessions in poor neighborhoods, and expanded the ranks of FSLN troops from between 500 and 1,000 in early 1978 to about 3,000 in late 1978 and 5,000 by July 1979.[66] Also, the three "tendencies" of the FSLN were by this time coordinating their armed actions and had begun talks that would lead to their reunification in early 1979. To broaden its political base the FSLN joined with a number of unions and political organizations to form the United People's Movement (MPU).

While the FSLN was pulling together the bourgeoisie was dividing over the content of opposition demands. Ironically, U.S. policy contributed to the revolutionary denouement—not by "abandoning" Somoza, as unsophisticated critics often claim,[67] but rather by reinforcing regime intractability and undermining the credibility of the non-revolutionary opposition.

U.S. Efforts to Alter the Opposition Coalition

In February 1978, the U.S. embassy had prevailed on the opposition to end its general strike, promising to back reforms in the regime and to cut off U.S. military aid to Somoza for the rest of the year. The bourgeois-dominated National Strike Committee called off the strike, but the popular sectors under the FSLN continued. On 16 February 1978, Carter announced that the United States would not cut off military aid for 1978 after all. In May 1978, Nicaragua was given $12 million in new U.S. credits. In July, Carter wrote a letter to Somoza congratulating him on his improved human rights record. U.S. waffling undermined the position of the reformist elements within the Nicaraguan opposition movement.

While the National Guard bombed Nicaraguan cities to quell the September 1978 insurrection, the United States was encouraging "dialogue" between Somoza and the opposition. FAO and the FSLN had agreed in early October 1978 that both groups would hold out for Somoza's resignation and exile, and that they would not accept direct negotiations with the dictator.[68] Throughout the Fall of 1978, however, the United States continued to back a mediation effort which proposed that power be turned over to an interim government composed of FAO and Somoza's Liberal Party, with the FSLN excluded and the National Guard remaining intact. Even the bourgeois elements within FAO were embarrassed by the unrealism of the proposal:

By pressuring the FAO to abandon its call for Somoza's immediate resignation and negotiate with the regime, the United States destroyed the moderates' unity and their credibility. When the mediation began, the FAO included 16 opposition groups; by the end, fewer than ten remained. As it became increasingly isolated, the FAO could only have recovered if Washington had made up its mind to force Somoza out of office. This it was not willing to do.[69]

U.S. intransigence prompted Los Doce and other groups to quit FAO in late October. The United States apparently hoped at this point that Somoza would resign, and that the successor government would incorporate Somoza's Liberal Party and National Guard (but not the FSLN). Somoza still refused to resign, and a smaller FAO broke off negotiations on 21 November 1978. Under U.S. pressure, FAO agreed on 10 December to violate its compact with the FSLN by beginning direct talks with Somoza, provoking more defections from FAO. A number of the disaffected parties and groups which left FAO were recruited to join with the MPU in a National Patriotic Front (FPN), organized by the FSLN in February 1979. By this point, the lines of polarization were drawn: The FSLN was at the head of a broad-based revolutionary alliance seeking to overthrow the dictatorship.

International alignments became more polarized as well. Somoza terminated negotiations in January 1979, gambling that the United States would prefer to support him rather than risk an FSLN victory. Sure enough, the United States backed a $40 million IMF loan to the Somoza regime in April 1979, and another $25 million loan in May. Besides symbolizing U.S. unwillingness to let Somoza fall, the IMF loans also brought with them an economic austerity program and devaluation whose impact fell disproportionately on the poor.[70] After the IMF loans, Mexico cut off diplomatic relations with the Somoza regime and Venezuela led a group of Andean countries in transferring recognition to the provisional revolutionary Junta, which was announced in Costa Rica. Brazil broke diplomatic relations on 26 June, and FAO endorsed the revolutionary Junta on 27 June.

The U.S. had made a last-ditch proposal for an OAS "peace-keeping force" to install an interim government of U.S. liking, but the OAS overcame U.S. pressure and voted it down on 22 June. As late as July 1979, the United States was still bargaining for the addition of two more "moderates" to the five-person Junta of the new Government of National Reconstruction, plus a guarantee that the National Guard and Liberal Party would remain. On 6 July, Somoza indicated his willingness to resign, but the U.S. Air Force reportedly continued to supply the National Guard.[71]

Both Somoza and the U.S. lacked the necessary leverage at this point to influence the composition of the new government. On 17 July, Somoza resigned and flew to Miami. In a bizarre finale, the interim president, Francisco Urcuyo, who was supposed to turn over power to the new government, announced his intention to remain in power. But the government quickly collapsed, Urcuyo fled to Guatemala, and the remnants of the National Guard surrendered to the FSLN on 19 July 1979.

Although the struggle was long, the final collapse of the Somoza regime came more suddenly than anyone expected. The FSLN itself had not been prepared for the intensity of the September 1978 insurrections. Both Somoza and the United States were apparently counting on a managed transition to an acceptable non-FSLN government as late as June 1979. The Soviet Union—which had long supported the Nicaraguan Socialist Party (PSN) and opposed guerrilla "adventurism"—was caught largely by surprise and opted to reserve judgment on the revolution.[72] Cuba, which in defiance of the Soviets had provided support and encouragement to the Sandinistas, urged moderation on the new government. Cuban President Fidel Castro advised the Sandinistas to maintain a mixed economy and diversified international relations rather than repeat the costly Cuban experience.[73]

Having completed the overthrow of the authoritarian regime, the Sandinistas still faced the enormous task of creating a framework for open and democratic politics. The nature of the Nicaraguan transition process complicated this task. In contrast to the South American model of transition from authoritarian rule, the opposition had not wooed supporters of the regime with promises of self-restraint. In the Nicaraguan case, the composition of the liberalizing coalition was in a state of flux on the eve of the dictator's overthrow. Nicaragua lacked either legitimate political institutions, as in the South American cases, or the equivalent of the king in post-Franco Spain, whose national credibility could replace the mutual trust necessary for establishing new rules of political competition. Political pacts, and indeed electoral politics, had a rather unsavory history in Nicaragua. And once the Sandinistas were in power, the loyalty of the "moderate opposition" was immediately suspect due to its links with the United States and the ancien regime.

IV. A NEW KIND OF DEMOCRACY

The ouster of Somoza inaugurated a process of democratization in Nicaragua. The nature of that process during the period considered here (1979–87) was shaped by the inherited social formation and political tradition, the revolutionary experience itself, and the international context in which the new government was inserted.

The type of democracy conceived by the Sandinistas was not limited to formal democracy in its representative variant, but also encompassed the notion of *participatory* democracy with a substantive commitment to the interests of the poor majority. The Sandinista revolution was not just a political revolution; it was also a social revolution drawing not only on the Lockean vision of tacit consent under the social contract but also on the egalitarian/participatory tradition of Rousseau and the French Revolution.[74] As expressed in 1980 by a member of the FSLN National Directorate,

For the Sandinista Front, democracy is not defined in purely political terms, and is not reducible to popular participation in elections. It is something more, much more.... Democracy first appears in the economic order, when social inequalities begin to diminish, and when the workers and peasants improve their conditions of life.... Once these goals are attained, democracy immediately spreads to other areas: the field of government is broadened; the people exerts influence over its government, determines its government, whether that is agreeable or not. At a more advanced state, democracy means workers' participation in the management of factories, cooperatives, cultural centers, and so on. In short, democracy is mass intervention in every aspect of social life.[75]

The construction of democracy in revolutionary Nicaragua generated tensions between the propertied classes, whose conception of democracy emphasized the rule of law, and the popular classes, who prioritized the substantive content of the revolutionary project. In liberal capitalist democracies, bourgeois rule requires some form of ''mystification,'' some claim that government institutions guarantee class neutrality and a degree of social control over private accumulation of capital.[76] In Nicaragua, the myth was swept away by the process of *concientización*—the development of political consciousness that accompanied mass participation in the struggle against Somoza.

The concept of popular hegemony is central to the Sandinista project. The government rules explicitly in the interests of the poor—who constitute the majority of the population, as well as the majority of those who participated in the insurrectionary movement—and therefore has less need to artificially create a belief in the neutrality of its institutions. At the same time, the Sandinistas recognized from the beginning the diverse composition of the revolutionary alliance; as well as the incomplete crystallization of a new political subject—*el pueblo*—capable of consolidating hegemony in the post-revolutionary society.[77]

The resulting Sandinista model of transition is one that is unique to the Nicaraguan experience. As conceived by its protagonists, the model's central principles are: (1) political pluralism, (2) a mixed economy, and (3) international non-alignment; all within the framework of a participatory democracy which insures that priorities are determined according to a new ''logic of the majorities.''[78]

At a minimum, liberalization in Nicaragua called for ending the generalized repression that the population had suffered at the hands of Somoza's National Guard. This involved more than just a restitution of the pre-war or pre-Somoza situation. Rather, popular expectations, mindful of the gross distributive inequities and corruption which had siphoned off resources under *somocismo*, called for actual improvements in the quality of life.

Democratization, similarly, was no simple matter of reviving old institutions. The old structures did not protect political and civil rights, precisely because the *somocista* state was not conceived and structured toward that end. Besides creating new institutions for the competition of political programs, the Sandinistas were obliged by the revolutionary social contract to radically democratize access to channels of political expression. Nicaragua in 1979 lacked the level of organization of civil society or the tradition of democratic political institutions that had existed in pre-military Argentina, Brazil, Uruguay, or Chile. Yet in contrast to post-Duvalier Haiti, the insurrectionary process itself in Nicaragua had given rise to the new phenomenon of "mass organizations" and conferred enough legitimacy upon the FSLN to lay the foundations for creation of a new democratic political order.

The international context imposed additional complications on the Nicaraguan revolution. The overthrow of Somoza was a war of national liberation against a U.S. client, in a period of growing right-wing backlash within the United States against declining U.S. hegemony (punctuated by the defeat in Vietnam and the 1979 Iran hostage crisis).[79] Nicaragua represented a fundamental challenge to the twenty-year-old U.S. formula of reform plus counterinsurgency to forestall social revolution in Latin America. The result was the initiation of an unrelenting U.S. campaign of "low-intensity warfare,"[80] aimed at destabilizing the Sandinista government through a combination of military hostilities, economic pressures, and diplomatic isolation. The external threats became inextricably intertwined with domestic politics, blurring the distinction between the "loyal opposition," willing to operate within consensually defined rules, and the seditious "disloyal opposition." The redemocratization process therefore has to be evaluated in the context of protracted wartime emergency and economic siege conditions.

Formal Institutions of Government

The first step toward liberalization in Nicaragua was to bring an end to the terror that had marked the dictatorship. In contrast to most revolutionary precedents, no wave of recriminations followed the FSLN victory. Amnesty International reports approximately 100 vengeance killings of *somocistas* "captured by residents in provincial Nicaraguan towns" in 1979, a phenomenon that was soon stopped when the FSLN established discipline over its irregular forces and began collecting the arms that had circulated freely during the insurrection.[81]

Captured National Guardsmen suspected of having committed atrocities were brought before Special Tribunals, open to the press and to international observers. The new government abolished the death penalty and set the maximum allowable sentence at thirty years' imprisonment. While the proceedings of the Special Tribunals were somewhat irregular by the standards of U.S. jurisprudence, the revolution generally lived up to its promise of generosity in victory. Of 7,000 close collaborators of the dictatorship (*somocistas*) initially detained, charges were brought against some 6,000; 4,331 were convicted, and 38 percent of those received sentences of five years or less.[82]

A transitional Government of National Reconstruction (GRN) replaced the old structures of government during the period from 1979 to 1984. The Constitution left from the Somoza regime was nullified and replaced by the Fundamental Statute of the Republic (20 July 1979), which established the structure of the transitional government, and by the Statute on the Rights and Guarantees of Nicaraguans (21 August 1979), the functional equivalent of the U.S. Bill of Rights. The *judiciary* was overhauled, and corrupt judges from the Somoza regime were replaced by "new justices and judges, chosen for expected competence and honesty and not necessarily associated with the FSLN."[83] Formal executive powers passed to the Junta of the Government of National Reconstruction (JGRN), which had been formed in exile in Costa Rica before the fall of the dictatorship. Legislative powers were shared between the Junta and the Council of State, a 51-member representative assembly inaugurated in May 1980.

The composition of the first Junta reflected a balance between the forces that had allied to overthrow Somoza: Daniel Ortega, a Tercerista and member of the FSLN's National Directorate; Moises Hassan, from the MPU; Sergio Ramírez, writer and intellectual and member of Los Doce; Violeta Barrios de Chamorro, widow of *La Prensa* editor Pedro Joaquin Chamorro; and Alfonso Robelo, wealth industrialist of the BANAMER group and private-sector leader. When the latter two, representing the non-Somoza bourgeoisie, resigned in April 1980, they were replaced by Rafael Córdova Rivas, a cattle rancher and leader of the Conservative Democratic Party (PCD); and Arturo Cruz, international banker and member of Los Doce. The Junta was again reorganized and reduced to three members in 1981, when Arturo Cruz was appointed ambassador to the United States and Moises Hassan was shifted to a cabinet post. Each of these reorganizations of the junta preserved the symbolic balance between the different elements of the revolutionary coalition.[84]

While formal executive powers rested in the junta from 1979 to 1984, general lines of policy were formulated by the nine-member Joint National Directorate (DNC) of the FSLN. The DNC, composed of three representatives of each of the three old "tendencies," functioned as the collective leadership of the FSLN. The National Directorate consulted on major policy issues with an 81-member Sandinista Assembly of party leaders. Within the first year of the revolutionary government, a number of conservative Ministers were replaced by Sandinistas— including the key Ministries of Defense, Agriculture, and Planning.[85] The new Sandinista People's Army (EPS) and police forces were put under the authority of the FSLN's National Directorate rather than the junta. The Nicaraguan re-volutionaries were taking no chances of a Chile-style military coup, which would probably receive support from the United States and elements of the Nicaraguan right. Sandinista control of the reorganized armed forces, a legacy of the rev-olutionary struggle, was a source of constant objection by the bourgeois oppo-sition.

During the five-year period of transitional government, the Sandinistas moved to consolidate their power within the GRN and to direct the process of social and economic transformation. In the process, they tended to disconfirm predic-tions by critics on the left who saw the revolution as degenerating into a petty bourgeois, reformist government, while also belying the predictions of critics on the right who foresaw a takeover by dogmatic Marxists.[86] Four Catholic priests and various non-Sandinistas continued to serve at the Cabinet level, and the Sandinistas themselves proved to be ideologically diverse and flexible in their policy outlooks.[87]

In the initial period following the revolutionary victory, most legislative ini-tiatives originated in the Junta, subject to review and recommended changes (but not veto power) by the Council of State. Major decrees in the first year focused on the confiscation of *somocista* properties and nationalization of the mines, both of which passed to the state-owned Area of People's Property (APP), nationalization of foreign trade and the banking system, and extensive admin-istrative reorganization aimed at improving efficiency and honesty in government. By the 1981–82 legislative session, the Council of State was introducing as many laws as the junta, and by 1982–83 was doubling the Junta's legislative initia-tives.[88] Increasingly, the Council of State took responsibility for debating and legislating on the thornier political issues, moving beyond simple administrative reform.

The main substantive political contest in Nicaragua after 1979 was between the Sandinista project of fundamental transformation and the much more re-stricted project of the non-Somoza bourgeoisie.[89] Part of this contest took the form of procedural conflict over the form of the transitional government. The Council of State was originally planned to have 33 members, with functional representation apportioned among the various political parties and interest as-sociations, according to a formula worked out among the opposition groups in exile. By the time of Somoza's overthrow, however, the formula was already obsolete, as political power had shifted to the popular forces.[90] The Council was therefore expanded to 47 (and later 51) to include representatives of the new groups that had emerged—principally, the Sandinista-mobilized mass organi-zations.

Alfonso Robelo resigned from the Junta in protest, hoping to provoke a boycott of the Council of State by the rest of the opposition. However, the FSLN promptly rebalanced the junta; and the bourgeois opposition, after some wavering, gen-erally decided to continue participating. Robelo subsequently joined the U.S.-backed armed opposition seeking to overthrow the government.

Two coalitions of political parties emerged in the 1981–84 period. The Patriotic Front of the Revolution (FPR) was formed by the FSLN; the Independent Liberal Party (PLI), a 1940s breakaway from Somoza's party with a primarily urban middle class and professional base; the Nicaraguan Socialist Party (PSN), the Moscow-oriented communist party also dating back to the 1940s; and the Popular Social Christian Party (PPSC), a center-left grouping which broke away from the Social Christian Party (PSC) in the 1960s. The opposing coalition on the right was the Nicaraguan Democratic Coordinator (CDN), composed of the PSC; the tiny Constitutionalist Liberal Party (PLC), which had originated from a split with Somoza's party; and the Social Democratic Party (PSD), a right-wing party formed in 1979. Also participating in the CDN were the big-business based Superior Council of Private Enterprise (COSEP) and small two union groupings, the Nicaraguan Workers' Confederation (CTN) and the Confederation of Union Unification (CUS).

Three parties that remained outside these coalitions were the Democratic Conservative Party (PCD), the traditional party of the landed elite with a religious and "law-and-order" appeal; the Communist Party of Nicaragua (PCdeN), a 1967 splinter from the PSN; and the far left Marxist-Leninist Popular Action Movement (MAP-ML), with a small organized base among students and agricultural workers in the sugar cane plantations.

The transitional structure of government was superseded in November 1984, when national elections were held for president and vice president, and for a 96-member National Assembly; replacing the junta and the Council of State. The new National Assembly, in addition to assuming full legislative powers, was also charged with drafting a new Constitution, which was ratified and entered into force in February 1987.

The FSLN had promised general elections by 1985 as part of the revolutionary program drawn up in exile. The timetable was accelerated in response to opposition demands. Preparations began with the Council of State drafting a Law of Political Parties, approved in August 1983. Of the FSLN's original draft legislative proposal, some 30 percent was altered by opposition party initiatives.[91] The Council of State approved an Electoral Law in March 1984 and elections were scheduled for 4 November 1984. The law established the Supreme Electoral Council (CSE), a five-member body composed of representatives of various political parties, as a fourth branch of government to oversee national elections. The law provided for direct elections of the president and vice president and a 96-member National Assembly (90 deputies directly elected by a proportional representation system and another six seats guaranteed to minority parties).

The FPR coalition dissolved as the four member parties decided to run separate candidates in the 1984 elections. The three small right-wing parties in the CDN coalition boycotted, arguing that the government had failed to provide conditions for fair elections. The Reagan administration made similar charges, and opposition parties reported attempts by the U.S. embassy to pressure and bribe them to withdraw from the elections.[92] In the end, a total of seven parties fielded candidates, ranging from the far-left MAP-ML to the right-wing PCD. The U.S.-based Latin American Studies Association, one of dozens of organizations which sent an observer delegation, concluded that the election was fair and that "the only parties that did not appear on the ballot were absent by their own choice, not because of government exclusion."[93]

For most of the voters and many of the parties, it was the first time they had participated in elections.[94] The campaign illustrated the striking programmatic and organizational weakness of the opposition. For the parties of the CDN coalition, an attempt to discredit the process by abstention appeared more attractive than competing.

The FSLN won a solid two-thirds majority of the presidential vote and 61 of 96 Assembly seats (see Table 2) in heavy voter turnout. Voter registration, which was mandatory, had incorporated 93.7 percent of the estimated voting-age population, and voter turnout, which was voluntary, reached 75 percent of registered voters, despite an abstentionist campaign. Invalid (blank or spoiled) ballots amounted to 6.1 percent of votes cast.[95] Even assuming that all the non-voters and all the void ballots represented supporters of the abstentionist coalition, the FSLN still won by a landslide. The newly elected government was inaugurated on 10 January 1985, with former junta coordinator Daniel Ortega assuming the Presidency.

The new National Assembly formed a Constitutional Commission in April 1985 that included representatives of the seven political parties. The Commission spent the next year in national and international consultations, writing a draft of the new Constitution. Comments were specifically invited from each of the political parties and mass organizations. Beginning in May 1986, the draft was submitted for public discussion in a series of open assemblies (*cabildos abiertos*) and then sent back to the Commission for redrafting. An estimated 100,000 people participated in these assemblies, with thousands of comments and suggested revisions registered.[96] The final draft was submitted to the whole National Assembly in early 1987 and was formally ratified in February 1987.

The Mass Organizations

While not part of the formal institutions of government, the *organizaciones de masa* (OM) or "mass organizations" played an important role in the participatory democracy under construction in Nicaragua since 1979. The OM arose primarily from Sandinista-led popular organizing efforts against the Somoza dictatorship in the 1970s. By the mid–1980s they incorporated over half the adult population (at varying levels of involvement) and constituted the FSLN's main organized base of support.[97] Table 3 shows the approximate membership of the principal mass organizations.

One of the first steps toward expanding popular participation was a National Literacy Crusade (CNA), launched in 1980.[98] Through the mobilization of thousands of volunteer teachers in the national campaign, illiteracy was reduced from

Table 4.2
1984 Election Results

Party	(presidential)		(assembly)
	No. of Votes	% of Valid Votes	No. of Seats
FSLN (Sandinista National Liberation Front)	735,967	67.0	61
PCD (Democratic Conservative Party)	154,327	14.0	14
PLI (Independent Liberal Party)	105,560	9.6	9
PPSC (Popular Social Christian Party)	61,199	5.6	6
PCdeN (Communist Party of Nicaragua)	16,034	1.5	2
PSN (Nicaraguan Socialist Party)	14,494	1.3	2
MAP-ML (Popular Action Movement-Marxist Leninist)	11,352	1.0	2
(null)	71,209	--	--
TOTAL	1,170,142	100.0	96

Source: Latin American Studies Association (LASA), *The Electoral Process in Nicaragua: Domestic and International Influences* (Austin, TX: 19 November 1984).

pre-revolutionary levels of over 50 percent (and perhaps 75 percent in rural areas) to around 13 percent. The literacy campaign was seen both as essential for preparing citizens for meaningful democratic participation and as a political/educational experience for the thousands of high-school students and other volunteers sent out to the furthest reaches of the country.

The OM with the largest membership was constituted by the Sandinista Defense Committees (CDS), which originated in the network of Civil Defense Committees organized in the *barrios* during the struggle against Somoza. Since 1979, one of the main activities of these neighborhood committees consisted of organizing local food distribution to help cope with shortages. The CDS also mobilized tens of thousands of volunteers for highly successful popular health campaigns, including vaccinations and mosquito control. The CDS also set up

Table 4.3
Approximate Membership of the Principal Mass Organizations, 1987

CDS	Sandinista Defense Committees	485,000
UNAG	National Union of Farmers and Ranchers	125,000
CST	Sandinista Workers' Central	113,000
AMNLAE	Nicaraguan Women's Association "Luisa Amanda Espinosa"	80,000
ATC	Rural Workers' Association	50,000
JS-19	Sandinista Youth "19th of July"	30,000

Sources: Gary Ruchwarger, *People in Power: Forging a Grassroots Democracy in Nicaragua* (South Hadley, MA: Bergin & Garvey, forthcoming); and *Barricada*, 9 November 1986 and 2 January 1987.

a neighborhood night watch program which by 1984 involved some 250,000 volunteers, in an effort to cut down on crime and dissuade counterrevolutionary sabotage.[99] With varying degrees of success, CDS committees organized neighbors around issues of local concern and pressured government agencies for solutions.

The Sandinista Workers' Central (CST) and the Association of Rural Workers (ATC) had antecedents in pre–1979 organization of urban and rural workers, respectively. Once Somoza-era labor repression was ended, union organizing expanded rapidly, from about 11 percent of the salaried workforce in 1979 to some 56 percent (260,000 organized workers) by 1986.[100] Each of the seven major union confederations was associated with one of the political parties, with the pro-Sandinista confederations (CST and ATC) leading in membership.[101] Other labor groups which tended to support the Sandinista government included the teachers' association ANDEN, with 20,000 members in 1986; the health workers' federation FETSALUD, with 23,000; and the public employees' union UNE, representing 29,000.

The ATC played an active role in the agrarian reform. The CST organized campaigns against decapitalization by factory owners (1980–81) and promoted increased productivity as well as better distribution of basic goods to workers (1984–87). Both organizations faced dilemmas in attempting to defend workers' interests, while at the same time supporting a government which imposed strike bans and austerity measures in the context of economic crisis and an external military threat. At the level of the workplace, some advances were made in worker participation and control (particularly in agricultural enterprises in the state sector), but progress was slowed by the perceived need to prioritize "defense and production."[102]

Small and medium farmers, initially organized together with agricultural laborers in the ATC, broke away in 1981 to form the National Union of Farmers and Ranchers (UNAG). The organization grew in size and prestige after 1984, when UNAG began to take more independent initiative in pressing for land redistribution to individual farmers, and organized its own distribution network of farm supplies to complement the often inefficient state channels.[103] By the mid–1980s, a growing recognition of the importance of small and medium producers—impelled both by pressure from UNAG and by wartime realities— brought about a major shift in the emphasis of the agrarian reform.[104]

AMNLAE, the women's association, had its origins in AMPRO-NAC, which mobilized poor and middle-class women in collective struggle against the dictatorship. Since 1979, AMNLAE pressed successfully for a law against sexist advertising and modifications in the divorce and family support laws. Expansion of child care facilities was slowed in part by wartime financial limitations. The issue of legalizing abortion surfaced in the public debate in 1985–86, but the FSLN appeared unwilling to further complicate relations with the Catholic Church. In general, AMNLAE forced some of the same dilemmas as the workers' organization, i.e., tension between strategic defense of the revolution and more immediate demands of their respective constituencies.[105]

The Sandinista Youth organization (JS–19) mobilized 50,000 young Nicaraguans to participate in the 1980 Literacy Crusade, as well as subsequent adult education and popular health campaigns.[106] The JS–19 also organized Student Production Brigades (BEP) to alleviate labor shortages in the cotton and coffee harvests.

The exact relationship between the mass organizations, the FSLN party, and the State is important to the issue of popular democracy. The FSLN itself was not conceived as a mass party; membership was restricted to about 16,000 in 1984.[107] The OM were allocated 44 percent of seats under the functional representation system in the Council of State,[108] and OM leaders (most of whom were FSLN members) continued to enjoy ample representation in the National Assembly after the 1984 elections. The OM, however, functioned with relative autonomy from both the party and the state, and the FSLN on various occasions warned against the OM being converted into mere transmission belts or cheerleaders.[109]

While the OM generally supported the Sandinista government, on a number of occasions they differed on significant policy issues:

- In early 1980, the ATC organized a march of 30,000 *campesinos* to the Government House in Managua, protesting court rulings returning some "spontaneously confiscated" lands to their owners. The government eventually compromised, ceding the land to the occupiers and paying compensation to owners.[110]

- In 1980–81, CST pressure and factory takeovers induced the government to pass stricter sanctions against decapitalization. Continued confrontation eventually led to the September 1981 "Social and Economic Emergency" laws, forbidding strikes, lockouts, and unauthorized takeovers.[111]
- In 1983, pressure from AMNLAE resulted in modification of the Military Service Law to allow voluntary integration of women. Continued insistence at the second AMNLAE congress in 1986 on the need for attention to women's issues resulted in the formation of a special commission in the Sandinista Assembly, and a 1987 FSLN declaration.
- UNAG pressure in 1983 resulted in a waiver of *campesino* debt arrears. Demonstrations organized in the Masaya region in 1985 led to a review and substantial expansion of the agrarian reform.[112]
- FSLN criticism of the CDS in 1985–86 for bureaucratism and petty abuse of privilege prompted a shakeup and new national CDS elections.[113]

The expansion of popular participation since 1979 tended to consolidate a mobilized base of support for the Sandinistas. This is not unique to revolutionary Nicaragua; the hegemonic forces in any society inevitably define and structure political participation. The bourgeois opposition initially viewed the mass organizations, and particularly the CDS, with considerable trepidation.[114] By the mid-1980s, however, the CDS were suffering flagging participation; while the mass organizations that showed the most autonomy, such as UNAG, tended to gain in influence.

The relative *de*mobilization of the OM in the 1979–81 period in the interests of national unity (for example, via the Social and Economic Emergency laws) tended to convert the state into the "authorizer" of popular demands, particularly economic demands. This had the negative consequence of promoting verticalist and bureaucratic tendencies in the state apparatus, and disillusionment at the base level of the OM. The problem was clearly recognized in 1984–85 when agrarian reform policy was sharply revised in favor of individual land redistribution, after state planners realized that their assumptions did not coincide with *campesino* preferences.[115]

Also in 1984–85, the government undertook a major shift in economic policy. A fragmented state apparatus, attempting to reconcile multiple interests (whose direct manifestation of economic demands was partly suppressed), had led to considerable disorder.[116] The stabilization measures of late 1984/early 1985 were put forth as an explicit rectification of errors, and the measures inaugurated a reopening of national debate on economic policy in which the unions took an active part.[117]

Civil Liberties

Protection of basic civil liberties was formally guaranteed under the transitional government by the Statute of the Rights and Guarantees of Nicaraguans (15

August 1979); and subsequently codified in the new Constitution, ratified in February 1987. However, certain civil rights were periodically suspended under various states of emergency enacted in the 1979–87 period.

From July 1979 to April 1980, a Law of National Emergency (allowed for in the Statute of Rights and Guarantees) suspended some rights of people detained for suspected crimes committed during the Somoza dictatorship. This state of emergency was lifted when the trials ended and the Special Tribunals were dissolved.[118] In addition, a Law of Appeal was enacted which provided for judicial review of administrative errors.

In September 1981 the GRN decreed a State of Social and Economic Emergency, which suspended the application of the Law of Appeal in matters related to the economic emergency. The 1981 decree also banned strikes, lockouts, and land and factory takeovers, as well as publication of "false and destabilizing" economic news. On 15 March 1982, a Law of National Emergency was passed, in accordance with provisions of the Statute of Rights and Guarantees. The 1982 law renewed the strike ban, instituted press censorship, restricted public demonstrations, and suspended *habeas corpus* only in cases affecting national security. The restrictions on assembly and press were relaxed in July 1984 to permit election campaigning, and were partially restored on 15 October 1985.

The emergency decrees of 1981 and 1982 were enacted in response to mounting threats to the stability of the revolutionary government. Among the factors contributing to economic instability were U.S. economic destabilization efforts; attacks by U.S.-backed counterrevolutionaries ("contras"), which by late 1981 were beginning to concentrate on economic targets; speculation and hoarding of goods, and deliberately-sown rumors of impending shortages; and decapitalization by elements of the private sector, often triggering spontaneous takeovers by angry workers (and vice versa). Real per capita income had already been set back to 1962 levels by the war against Somoza. The Social and Economic Emergency measures were aimed at restraining both labor and capital in order to establish stable conditions for economic reactivation.[119] Several Communist Party union leaders were arrested under the emergency measures for illegal strike action, and prominent COSEP figures were also jailed for several months for publishing a statement accusing the Sandinistas of "preparing a new genocide."

The 1982 State of Emergency was decreed the day after CIA-backed commando teams blew up two key bridges in northern Nicaragua. By that time, extensive U.S. involvement in the armed effort to overthrow the Nicaraguan government was an open secret.[120] The war intensified in 1983 as the CIA mined Nicaragua's principal harbors and blew up oil storage and pipeline facilities and the United States cut Nicaragua's sugar export quota. A CIA manual circulated in 1984 called for assassination of Sandinista leaders and urban sabotage. U.S. economic and diplomatic hostilities included blocking Nicaragua's access to multilateral loans, a U.S. trade embargo imposed in May 1985, and pressures on Western Europe and Mexico to isolate Nicaragua.[121] By 1985, when the state of emergency was renewed, the contra war had already caused 25,000 casualties, provoked economic losses equivalent to a full year's production, and was absorbing about half the government budget.[122] By 1987 total casualties reached 40,000.[123]

The boundaries of legitimate political competition in Nicaragua tended to be blurred by U.S. support for both the armed contra forces and the internal bourgeois opposition. The central domestic contest was between the Sandinistas and the bourgeois opposition, over the shape of the revolutionary project. In an initial "war of maneuver," the main weapon of the bourgeoisie was the capital strike, while the main weapon of the Sandinistas was mass mobilization. The battle for hegemony spread quickly to ideological institutions such as the media and the Church, which became highly polarized.[124]

Prominent members of the internal opposition periodically merged with the contra forces, thus reducing political trust. On 9 November 1980, the Sandinistas refused to allow former Junta member Alfonso Robelo and his opposition Nicaraguan Democratic Movement, MDN, to hold a public rally in the town of Nandaime, citing security concerns. Eight days later, Jorge Sálazar, vice president of the big business council COSEP, was killed when he ran a police roadblock in a truck full of arms.[125] Robelo left Nicaragua in 1982 and joined with Edén Pastora in Costa Rica to form an armed alliance, ARDE, aimed at overthrowing the Sandinista government. Banker Arturo Cruz, whose opposition CDN coalition boycotted the 1984 election, subsequently joined the contra leadership.

The issue of press censorship illustrates the more general dilemma of distinguishing between seditious and legitimate opposition in wartime. The GRN closed down the small MAP-ML newspaper *El Pueblo* in January 1980 after the paper called for overthrow of the government and after several leaders of the MAP-ML's labor organization were caught with illegal arms caches.[126]

Censorship subsequently fell primarily on *La Prensa*. What had once been the anti-Somoza newspaper veered sharply rightward in 1980 when the paper's directors fired progressive editor Xavier Chamorro. Most of the staff left to form the pro-FSLN (private) newspaper, *El Nuevo Diario*.[127] Those who remained at *La Prensa* turned it into an organ of the bourgeois opposition, while a third paper, *Barricada*, reflected the official FSLN line. *La Prensa* was periodically suspended for a day or two and, with the 1982 Law of National Emergency, subject to prior censorship, created a curious political dynamic:

. . . *La Prensa's* power was not derived from bringing news and opinion to mass audiences. Rather, its sizable international and domestic reputation was based almost entirely on the fact that it was censored by the government.

Therefore, it was in the best interests of *La Prensa* to provoke continued censorship. Without censorship, it would be judged on its dubious editorial quality by a very limited audience. Consequently, a cat-and-mouse game between *La Prensa* and the government emerged. The editors almost gleefully baited the government in print and, in turn, the censors, made paranoid by wartime pressures and *La Prensa's*, seditious tradition, searched for hidden meanings in every line of copy.[128]

The resulting censorship was erratic. *La Prensa* in any event posted all censored articles on public bulletin boards at its offices and distributed photocopies to foreign embassies and domestic opposition leaders.

In June 1986 *La Prensa* co-director Pedro Joaquin Chamorro, Jr., on a trip to the U.S., lobbied in favor of proposed legislation to provide U.S. $100 million in further aid to the contras. *La Prensa* itself was already receiving $100,000 from the National Endowment for Democracy, a quasi-official U.S. agency. Following publication of a *Washington Post* opinion piece by Chamorro favoring contra aid, the government announced the "indefinite suspension" of *La Prensa*.

Closure of *La Prensa* in mid–1986 was accompanied by expulsion of Bishop Pablo Antonio Vega and Archdiocese spokesperson Fr. Bismarck Carballo. Vega had lobbied for contra aid, while Carballo had violated media laws with publication of an unauthorized newspaper, *Iglesia*, whose first numbers attacked the military draft.[129] These 1986 events marked a new low in relations between the Sandinista government and the conservative hierarchy of the Catholic Church. Earlier in the year, newly promoted Cardinal Miguel Obando y Bravo had stopped in Miami to celebrate a mass with the contra leadership on the way back from his investiture in Rome. Obando's return was followed by an intense itinerary of speaking trips throughout Nicaragua, focusing on criticism of the government and the military draft.[130] Tensions were abated in late 1986/early 1987, when the Vatican's new nuncio, Paolo Giglio, pressed for resumption of Church-State talks.

Despite conflicts with the conservative Church hierarchy, religious activity itself was not restricted by the revolutionary government. The phenomenon of popular religiosity in fact appeared to have grown during the revolutionary period, inspired by the spread of Liberation Theology, which formed an important ideological component of the Sandinista revolution.[131] Freedom of religion was specifically guaranteed in a 1980 FSLN declaration and in the 1987 Constitution.

Human rights organizations found substantial improvement in respect for human rights in Nicaragua since the revolution, but expressed concern over the state of emergency. Particular concern was expressed over detention of suspected contra collaborators—some of whom were also opposition political party and trade union figures—under the emergency laws. Amnesty International identified twelve such questionable arrests in 1986.[132] The general human rights evaluation, however, was favorable:

In Nicaragua there is no systematic practice of forced disappearances, extrajudicial killings or torture—as has been the case with the 'friendly' armed forces of El Salvador. While prior censorship has been imposed by emergency legislation, debate on major social and political questions is robust, outspoken, even often strident.[133]

Ethnic Minorities

The Miskitu Indians of Nicaragua's sparsely populated Atlantic Coast bore a disproportionate burden under the emergency laws, although their situation was exaggerated by regime opponents for propagandistic purposes.[134] Relatively isolated from the struggle against Somoza for reasons of geography, language and history, the Miskitus and other ethnic minorities of the Coast soon found themselves locked into mutual misunderstandings with the Sandinista government.[135] These tensions were exploited by opportunistic Miskitu leaders and by contra forces, who recruited a number of Miskitus into the armed bands that raided Nicaraguan territory from across the Honduran border.

The Sandinista government attempted from the beginning to integrate the peoples of the Atlantic Coast into national political life; but early efforts were often characterized by cultural insensitivity and ignorance. Implementation of the Literacy Crusade on the Coast had to be delayed to allow preparation of instructional materials in indigenous languages and in Creole English. One of the most serious early errors was the appointment of self-proclaimed Miskitu leader Steadman Fagoth to the Council of State. Fagoth turned out to have been a Somoza security agent, and his arrest in February 1981 provoked riots on the Coast.[136] Upon his release one month later, Fagoth fled to Honduras and began organizing Miskitus to fight alongside the contra forces.

As fighting intensified, in February 1982 the government relocated some 8,500 indigenous people from their homes along the Rio Coco, which marks the Honduran border, to resettlement areas farther from the border. U.S. government officials were quick to accuse the Sandinistas of atrocities, but investigations by Americas Watch and other human rights organizations, while critical of the relocation, disconfirmed the U.S. allegations.[137]

Policy toward the Coast began to shift in mid–1983, when Interior Minister Tomás Borge offered a public apology for past errors and announced an amnesty for Miskitus jailed for security-related offenses. The Sandinistas acknowledged that some excesses had occurred in responding to the security threat on the Coast, and the Army launched an investigation of reported abuses, leading to court martial and imprisonment of convicted officers.[138] The government also proceeded to negotiate ceasefire agreements with armed indigenous groups in 1985 and allowed the return to relocated Miskitus to the Rio Coco area. A special Autonomy Commission was also set up to conduct a grassroots consultation among Coastal peoples and draft legislation providing for regional autonomy.[139]

Social and Economic Democracy

The Sandinista vision of redemocratization emphasized economic as well as political participation. The program of government drawn up by the provisional Junta in Costa Rica in June 1979 envisioned a mixed economy, with extensive state powers to appropriate and redistribute surplus. Similarly, the August 1979 Statute on the Rights and Guarantees of Nicaraguans set forth a radical reconceptualization of the notion of ''private property'':

Property, whether individual or collective, fulfills a social function. Therefore it may be subject to restrictions with respect to ownership, benefit, use and disposition, for reasons of security, public interest or utility, social interest, the national economy, national emergency or disaster, or for purposes of agrarian reform.[140]

The economic policies of the Sandinistas often clashed with the views of most of the bourgeoisie, who also spearheaded the domestic political opposition.[141] In the Sandinista democratization project, economic policy was guided by "the logic of the majorities," meaning that the private property rights of a privileged minority would be tempered by the rights of the poor majority to not be marginalized from satisfaction of basic human needs.[142]

Concretely at issue was the "freedom" to make investment and consumption decisions. Nationalization of property was basically limited to *somocista* holdings and the foreign-owned mines; by 1982, some 37 percent of material production was in state hands, while the large private producers controlled 25 percent and small/medium private producers accounted for the remaining 38 percent.[143] Despite private ownership of the majority of production, however, state control of foreign trade and banking were used to mobilize resources for an ambitious public investment program that shifted the "center of accumulation" to the public realm.[144] Foreign exchange controls prioritized imports of productive inputs and basic consumption items, clashing with the foreign-oriented consumer preferences of elites.[145] Allocation of agricultural credit, formerly monopolized by agroexport capitalists, was broadened to include small producers and the state sector.[146]

The result of these economic policies was a mixed economy with considerable tensions. Indicators of the democratizing economic logic included the sharp drop observed in the intensity of labor following the overthrow of the repressive Somoza regime, and the much more favorable indices of basic consumption than non-basic consumption after 1979.[147] Per capita food consumption improved steadily until 1983, but then leveled off as the contra war began to intensify.[148] By the mid–1980s, wartime inflation had sharply reduced real wages,while the agroexporters continued to receive large state subsidies through the "guaranteed price" system; yet the capitalist sector remained generally unresponsive to production incentives, citing a climate of uncertainty and excessive controls.[149]

The attempt to sustain a project of "national unity" was constantly in tension with the redistributive goals of the revolutionary government. An Export Incentives Program favored by capitalist growers in 1982, for example, was ultimately amended to reimpose foreign exchange controls, provoking the resignation of the Central Bank President. A limited program of dollar cash incentives was later established for agroexporters, but was opposed by small farmers organized by UNAG.

Agrarian reform was one of the centerpieces of economic democratization in Nicaragua. Confiscated *somocista* properties, amounting to some 20 percent of arable land, were organized into state enterprises under the Area of People's Property. A comprehensive agrarian reform law of 1981 provided for redistribution of large tracts of land left idle, as well as abandoned properties. In addition, credit and technical services were expanded for small farmers and cooperatives.[150]

Though private farms being actively worked were not subject to confiscation under the 1981 law, regardless of their size, the COSEP-affiliated farmers' and ranchers' associations complained about the climate of "uncertainty." Their concern was heightened by UNAG pressure and land seizures by landless and land-poor *campesinos* in the Masaya region in 1985, which prompted the government to declare a new "agrarian reform zone" and redistribute some properties of COSEP President Enrique Bolaños. A new agrarian reform law of 1986 eliminated the size requirement for idle land subject to confiscation, and also specifically provided for compulsory sale of land to the state for redistribution in special cases of social necessity. Bolaños, in protest against this expansion of the agrarian reform, refused the state's offer of equivalent land elsewhere.

In fact, Bolaños was still the largest landowner in the region after the land redistribution. The action was aimed at providing relief for some 30,000 *campesinos* in a region where population pressure on the land was twelve times the national average.[151] As in other critical cases where "national unity" collided with the interests of the popular sectors, the revolutionary government inclined toward the latter.

By 1986, farms of over 355 hectares had dropped from a pre-revolutionary 36 percent of total cultivated land to 10 percent, and cooperatives accounted for 22 percent of land. Some 100,000 *campesino* families, or about half the rural population, had benefited from the agrarian reform by 1986 by receiving either redistributed land or legal title to the land they worked.[152]

Social policy also reflected the democratizing tendency of the Sandinista revolution. The 1980 Literacy Crusade, for which Nicaragua was awarded a UNESCO prize, was followed by an adult education program that reached 160,000. Illiteracy dropped from over 50 percent to 13 percent. School enrollments doubled between 1978 and 1984, and university fees were reduced to token levels. Social security coverage of various kinds rose from 7.7 percent of the population in 1979 to 50 percent in 1986. The national health system was expanded, with new emphasis on primary health care and rural coverage, resulting in a drop in infant mortality rates from 121 per 1,000 to 76 and special recognition by the World Health Organization.[153] All these improvements in the quality of life for the majority of the population, however, were slowed by the war from 1981 on—both by diversion of scarce resources and by contra attacks directed specifically at health and education workers and social service facilities.[154]

Economic democracy for the Sandinistas also extended to the international plane, where Nicaragua sought a more equitable insertion into the international economy. Investment policy focused on agricultural and agroindustrial projects designed to restore food self-sufficiency, and to increase the industrial value-added of Nicaragua's primary products.[155] Diversification of foreign trade and aid links was also part of a strategy to reduce and balance external dependence.

The U.S. economic destabilization campaign, however, forced a costly acceleration of this diversification.[156] Nicaragua's international terms of trade also fell sharply in the 1980s, further complicating efforts to alter the basis for Nicaragua's insertion into the international economy.

V. OPPORTUNITIES AND OBSTACLES FOR CONTINUED DEMOCRATIZATION

A number of factors influence the prospects for continued democratization in post-Somoza Nicaragua. The major negative factors include the continued operation of a counterrevolutionary "disloyal opposition" based in neighboring countries; serious external economic constraints; and the multifaceted U.S. destabilization campaign. Positive factors include the efforts of the Contadora and Lima Support Groups and other moderating external actors; and the institutionalization of a political structure in which the non-seditious opposition can function. In addition, major shifts in the agrarian reform, economic planning, and policy toward the Atlantic Coast beginning around 1984[157] indicate flexibility and increased space for internal debate within the Sandinista project.

The activities of the U.S.-backed contras hurt the prospects for continued democratization by providing justification for emergency legislation which restricts civil and political rights, and by narrowing the scope for tolerating legitimate opposition. Diversion of some 25 percent of economic production and over 10 percent of the workforce into the defense effort[158] reduces the government's capacity to deliver on its promise of economic and social democratization. The Sandinista military build-up, though privately recognized even by the CIA as a defensive response to the external threat,[159] is nevertheless criticized by both domestic and foreign opponents—reinforcing Sandinista suspicions that the two are in league to overthrow the government. Lest there by any doubt, President Reagan in 1985 expressed his commitment to "remove the present structure" of the Sandinista government by force if necessary.[160]

A variety of external pressures have contributed to worsening economic constraints on the Nicaraguan government, thus restricting the room for political compromise. U.S. economic warfare has included blocking Nicaragua's access to international financial institutions, ending bilateral aid, cutting the quota for Nicaraguan sugar exports to the U.S., mining the country's main harbors, and finally imposing a trade embargo in 1985. Declining terms of trade and a severe foreign exchange shortage have added to the pressure. Government policy responses included such measures as the restrictive Social and Economic Emergency Law, as well as new austerity measures imposed since 1985.[161]

The bourgeois opposition, whose international contacts once gave them some political clout during Nicaragua's debt renegotiations in 1980–81, lost leverage as new aid and loans from Western financial institutions dried up. Financial flows to all of Central America became highly politicized in the 1980s.[162] Since 1984–85, when IMF pressure led Mexico to suspend petroleum credits to Nicaragua, trade credits from socialist countries come to represent Nicaragua's main source of external finance.[163] The Soviet Union, however, indicated unwillingness to write Nicaragua a blank check. Loans and credits from Social Democratic governments of Western Europe and Latin America clearly depended on continued domestic political opening.

The undeclared U.S. war against Nicaragua reinforced the hardliners and undercut the compromisers on all sides. U.S. funding and support for the contras tended to intensify the security fears of the Sandinistas and increase the difficulty of distinguishing between dissent and counterrevolution. U.S. efforts to enlist Honduras and Costa Rica as proxies in the war against Nicaragua, including virtually uninterrupted military "exercises" in Honduras since 1983, undermined democratic processes in those countries and exacerbated regional tensions. The U.S. campaign to foment international hostility against the Sandinistas undercut the potential moderating influence of external actors, and limited the space for pluralism within Nicaragua.

On the positive side, the efforts of the Contadora Group (Colombia, Mexico, Panama, and Venezuela) to promote regional negotiations found international resonance. The initiative of the Contadora countries was joined by the Lima Support Group (Peru, Brazil, Argentina, and Uruguay) in July 1985. The alternative of regional negotiations was bolstered by the June 1986 ruling of the International Court of Justice in The Hague, that the U.S. war was in violation of international law. Nearly universal opposition among U.S. allies[164] probably helped dissuade the United States from invading Nicaragua to "redemocratize," Grenada-style. Increasing discord within Honduran political and military circles, as well as domestic opposition within the United States itself, were other important factors working against an invasion and reversal of the Nicaraguan transition.

Various internal factors point toward continued democratization as well. Following the successful 1984 elections, the parliamentary opposition took an active part in the process of drafting the new Constitution. The Nicaraguan Catholic Church, though divided and politicized, continued to function as a relatively protected dissent channel, and the Vatican since 1986 served as promotor and mediator of dialogue between the Church hierarchy and government. Increasingly autonomous functioning of the mass organizations, particularly UNAG, was a positive sign. Finally, within the FSLN itself, continued respect for the principle of collective leadership, as well as a willingness to admit and correct major policy errors, suggested a tendency toward internal democratization.

The overthrow of Somoza was a tremendous step toward democratization, but it was only the *beginning* of the revolutionary process. The outlook will be significantly affected by the international correlation of forces, particularly U.S. support for the contras. This, in turn, will be influenced by U.S. public opinion and "Contragate"-type contradictions, as well as by the ability of the United States to influence its proxies and allies.

Within Nicaragua, the scope for political compromise will be significantly affected by economic conditions, which will be a function of diverse elements, including U.S. blockade measures, alternative sources of aid and trade, and the government's capacity to adapt economic policies to the exigencies of wartime survival. Continued democratization will also depend on the intangibles that create confidence within governing circles. This self-confidence is essential for opening up internal policy disputes, and for creating mutual trust among the FSLN leadership, trust in the responsibility of the mass organizations, and trust in the intentions of the opposition. The real test is how far the Sandinistas are willing to go in "institutionalizing uncertainty"[165] at each of these levels of political activity.

Creating democracy is a difficult challenge in a country where political institutions were historically never designed to register the popular will. Democratization by revolution endows the new government with a different set of popular expectations regarding economic and social participation, as well as a different set of calculations regarding the possibility of compromise. Building a new democracy in Nicaragua was further complicated by persistent U.S. efforts to abort the revolution. For all these difficulties, however, the 1979–87 period saw lively political discourse among the diverse elements of the revolutionary class alliance. By 1987, the Sandinista revolution was substantially consolidated, and the long process of democratization continued.

NOTES

1. Guillermo O'Donnell, *Modernization and Bureaucratic-Authoritarianism* (Berkeley: University of California Press, 1973); David Collier, *The New Authoritarianism in Latin America* (Princeton: Princeton University Press, 1979); Juan J. Linz and Alfred Stepan, *The Breakdown of Democratic Regimes: Latin America* (Baltimore: Johns Hopkins University Press, 1978).

2. Peter Evans, *Dependent Development: The Alliance of Multinational, State, and Local Capital in Brazil* (Princeton: Princeton University Press, 1979); "Why the Generals Were Necessary," NACLA *Report on the Americas* (Mar.-Apr. 1979).

3. For examples, see: James Dunkerley, *The Long War: Dictatorship and Revolution in El Salvador* (London: Verso Editions, 1983), Chs. 1 and 2; Thomas P. Anderson, *Matanza: El Salvador's Communist Revolt of 1932* (Lincoln: University of Nebraska Press, 1971); Ralph Lee Woodward, Jr., *Central America: A Nation Divided* (New York: Oxford University Press, 1976).

4. John Weeks, *The Economies of Central America* (New York: Holmes & Meier, 1985), pp. 140–51.

5. See forthcoming collection edited by Laurence Whitehead and Guillermo O'Donnell.

6. Benjamin L. Crosby, "Divided We Stand, Divided We Fall: Public-Private Sector Relations in Central America," Florida International University, *Occasional Papers* No. 10 (Miami: April 1985).

7. See Daniel Camacho and Rafael Menjivar, eds., *Movimientos populares en Centroamérica* (San José, Costa Rica: EDUCA, 1985).

8. See Richard R. Fagen and Olga Pellicer, eds., *The Future of Central America: Policy Choices for the U.S. and Mexico* (Stanford: Stanford University Press, 1983).

9. George Irvin and Xabier Gorostiaga, eds., *Towards an Alternative for Central America and the Caribbean* (London: Allen & Unwin, 1985).

10. On the Nicaraguan application of the "Reagan Doctrine," see Kent Norsworthy and William Robinson, *David and Goliath* (New York: Monthly Review, forthcoming).

11. For critiques of the Kissinger Commission position, see: William M. LeoGrande, "Through the Looking Glass: The Kissinger Report on Central America," *World Policy Journal*, Vol. I, No. 2 (Winter 1984); Policy Alternatives for the Caribbean and Central America, *Changing Course: Blueprint for Peace in Central America and the Caribbean* (Washington, D.C.: Institute for Policy Studies, 1984); Richard Feinberg and Bruce M. Bagley, eds., *Development Postponed: The Political Economy of Central America in the 1980s* (Boulder, Colo.: Westview, 1986).

12. See Richard Millett, *Guardians of the Dynasty: A History of the U.S.-Created Guardia Nacional de Nicaragua and the Somoza Family* (Maryknoll, N.Y.: Orbis Books, 1977).

13. Walter LaFeber, *Inevitable Revolutions: The United States in Central America* (New York: W. W. Norton, 1984).

14. See Gregorio Selser, *Sandino* (New York: Monthly Review, 1981); Donald C. Hodges, *Intellectual Foundations of the Nicaraguan Revolution* (Austin: University of Texas Press, 1986).

15. George Black, *Triumph of the People* (London: Zed Press, 1981), p. 15.

16. John A. Booth, *The End and the Beginning: The Nicaraguan Revolution* (Boulder, Colo.: Westview, 1982), p. 90; Henri Weber, *Nicaragua: The Sandinist Revolution* (London: NLB, 1981), p. 30.

17. Weber, *Nicaragua*, p. 18.

18. Black, *Triumph*, p. 31.

19. For detail on the National Guard, see Millett, *Guardians*.

20. Black, *Triumph*, pp. 51–52 and 88.

21. Booth, *The End*, pp. 91–5.

22. Black, *Triumph*, pp. 47–8; Booth, *The End*, pp. 75–7; Weber, *Nicaragua*, pp. 30–1. See also Michael T. Klare and Cynthia Arnson, "Exporting Repression: U.S. Support for Authoritarianism in Latin America," in Richard R. Fagen, ed., *Capitalism and the State in U.S.-Latin American Relations* (Stanford: Stanford University Press, 1979).

23. Black, *Triumph*, pp. 34–36; Booth, *The End*, pp. 67–69; Weber, *Nicaragua*, pp. 15–18.

24. William M. LeoGrande, "The Revolution in Nicaragua: Another Cuba?," *Foreign Affairs*, Vol. 58, No.1 (Fall 1979), p. 29; Joseph R. Thome and David Kaimowitz, "Agrarian Reform," in Thomas W. Walker, ed., *Nicaragua: The First Five Years* (New York: Praeger, 1985).

25. Harry W. Strachan, *Family and Other Business Groups in Economic Development: The Case of Nicaragua* (New York: Praeger, 1976); Jaime Wheelock Román, *Nicaragua: imperialismo y dictadura* (Havana: Editorial de Ciencias Sociales, 1980).

26. CSUCA, *Estructura agraria, dinámica de población y desarrollo capitalista en Centroamérica* (San José, Costa Rica: EDUCA, 1978), p. 207.

27. Wheelock, *Nicaragua*, p. 82.

28. Jaime M. Biderman, "Class Structure, the State and Capitalist Development in Nicaraguan Agriculture," Ph.D. thesis, Dept. of Economics, University of California/ Berkeley (1982); Francisco Mayorga, "The Nicaraguan Economic Experience, 1950–

1984: Development and Exhaustion of an Agroindustrial Model,'' Ph.D. thesis, Yale University (1986); Orlando Nuñez, *El somocismo: desarrollo y contradicciones del modelo capitalista agroexportador en Nicaragua (1950–1975)* (Havana: CEA, 1980).

29. Pedro Belli, ''An Inquiry Concerning the Growth of Cotton Farming in Nicaragua,'' Ph.D. thesis, University of California/Berkeley (1968); and Biderman, ''Class Structure.''

30. CSUCA, *Estructura agraria*, pp. 223–24; and Mayorga, ''The Nicaraguan Economic Experience.''

31. Nuñez, *El somocismo*, p. 19.

32. Robert Williams, *Export Agriculture and the Crisis in Central America* (Chapel Hill: University of North Carolina Press, 1986), pp. 54–60.

33. Biderman, ''Class Structure,'' pp. 118–19.

34. CSUCA, *Estructura agraria*, p. 227.

35. See Weeks, *The Economies*; Williams, *Export Agriculture*.

36. CSUCA, *Estructure agraria*, pp. 226–27; and Jaime Biderman, ''The Development of Capitalism in Nicaragua: A Political Economic History,'' *Latin American Perspectives*, Vol. X, No. 1 (Winter 1983), p. 17.

37. CEPAL/FAO/OIT, *Tenencia de la tierra y desarrollo rural en Centroamérica*, 3rd ed. (San José, Costa Rica: EDUCA, 1980), p. 175; CSUCA, *Estructura agraria*, p. 207. See also Peter Dorner and Rodolfo Quirós, ''Institutional Dualism in Central America's Agricultural Development,'' *Journal of Latin American Studies*, Vol. 5, Part 2 (Nov. 1973); and Anthony Winson, ''Class Structure and Agrarian Transition in Central America,'' *Latin American Perspectives*, Vol. V, No. 4 (Fall 1978).

38. Biderman, ''Class Structure,'' p. 107.

39. CEPAL/FAO/OIT, *Tenencia*, 188.

40. Robert W. Fox and Jerrold W. Huguet, *Population and Urban Trends in Central America and Panama* (Washington, D.C.: Inter-American Development Bank, 1977), p. 27; Booth, *The End*, p. 84.

41. Biderman, ''The Development of Capitalism,'' p. 15.

42. Laura J. Enriquez, ''Social Transformation in Latin America: Tensions between Agro-Export Production and Agrarian Reform in Revolutionary Nicaragua,'' Ph.D. thesis, University of California/Santa Cruz (1985). See also Peter Utting, ''Domestic Supply and Food Shortages,'' in Rose J. Spalding, ed., *The Political Economy of Revolutionary Nicaragua* (Boston: Allen & Unwin, 1987).

43. Biderman, ''Class Structure,'' pp. 137–38.

44. CSUCA, *Estructura agraria*, pp. 236–38.

45. Weeks, *The Economies*, Ch. 6.

46. CSUCA, *Estructura agraria*, pp. 239–40.

47. PREALC, *Cambio y polarización ocupacional en Centro-américa* (San José, Costa Rica: EDUCA, 1986).

48. Booth, *The End*, pp. 77–82, 84–85.

49. Biderman, ''Class Structure,'' pp. 139–40.

50. Black, *Triumph*, Ch. 6. See also Regis Debray, *Revolution in the Revolution?* (New York: Grove Press, 1967).

51. Harald Jung, ''Behind the Nicaraguan Revolution,'' *New Left Review*, No. 117 (Sept.-Oct. 1979), p. 73.

52. Biderman, ''Class Structure,'' p. 140.

53. Williams, *Export Agriculture*, pp. 129–34.

54. Biderman, "The Development of Capitalism," p. 21.

55. Booth, *The End*, p. 84.

56. PREALC, *Cambio y polarización*; and E. V. K. FitzGerald, "Notas sobre la fuerza de trabajo y la estructura de clases en Nicaragua," *Revista Nicaragüense de Ciencias Sociales*, No. 2 (Mar. 1987).

57. Carlos M. Vilas, *The Sandinista Revolution: National Liberation and Social Transformation in Central America* (New York: Monthly Review, 1986, Ch. 3); and Orlando Nuñez, "La tercera fuerza social en los movimientos de liberación nacional," *Estudios Sociales Centroamericanos*, No. 27 (Sept.-Dec. 1980).

58. Michael Dodson and Laura Nuzzi O'Shaughnessy, "Religion and Politics," in Walker, ed., *Nicaragua: The First Five Years*.

59. See Black, *Triumph*, pp. 91–97; David Nolan, *The Ideology of the Sandinistas and the Nicaraguan Revolution* (Coral Gables, Fl.: Institute of Interamerican Studies, University of Miami, 1984).

60. See Black, *Triumph*.

61. Black, *Triumph*, pp. 318–19; Booth, *The End*, p. 137.

62. Black, *Triumph*, p. 89; Booth, *The End*, p. 143.

63. Black, *Triumph*, p. 105.

64. Black, *Triumph*, pp. 110–12.

65. Booth, *The End*, pp. 144–45, 162–63.

66. Booth, *The End*, p. 150.

67. See, e.g., Jeane Kirkpatrick, "Dictatorships and Double Standards," *Commentary*, Vol. 68, No. 5 (Nov. 1979).

68. Booth, *The End*, pp. 165–67.

69. LeoGrande, "The Revolution in Nicaragua," p. 34. See also Richard R. Fagen, "Dateline Nicaragua: The End of the Affair," *Foreign Policy*, No. 36 (Fall 1979).

70. Black, *Triumph*, pp. 148–51.

71. Jung, "Behind," pp. 84–89; LeoGrande, "The Revolution in Nicaragua," pp. 33–36.

72. Cole Blasier, "The Soviet Union," in Morris J. Blachman, William M. LeoGrande, and Kenneth Sharpe, eds., *Confronting Revolution: Security Through Diplomacy in Central America* (New York: Pantheon, 1986). See also: Richard E. Feinberg, "Central America: The View From Moscow," *Washington Quarterly*, Vol. 5, No. 2 (Spring 1982); Jerry F. Hough, "The Evolving Soviet Debate on Latin America," *Latin American Research Review*, Vol. XVI, No. 1 (1981).

73. William M. LeoGrande, "Cuba," in Blachman et al., eds., *Confronting Revolution*.

74. See Michael Dodson, "Democratic Ideals and Contemporary Central American Politics," presented at International Studies Association meeting (Atlanta: 27–31 Mar. 1984); and Ilja A. Luciak, "Popular Democracy in the New Nicaragua: The National Union of Farmers and Ranchers (UNAG)," presented at Western Social Science Association meeting (Reno: 23–26 Apr. 1986).

75. Comandante Humberto Ortega, 23 Aug. 1980 speech at close of the Literacy Campaign; quoted in Weber, *The Sandinista Revolution*, p. 112.

76. Adam Przeworski and Michael Wallerstein, "Democratic Capitalism at the Crossroads," *Democracy*, Vol. 2, No. 3 (July 1982). See also James Petras, "Authoritarianism, Democracy and the Transition to Socialism," *Socialism and Democracy* (Fall 1985).

77. Vilas, *The Sandinista Revolution*, Ch. 3; José Luís Coraggio, *Nicaragua: rev-*

olución y democracia (Mexico: Editorial Linea, 1985), pp. 30–31; Richard R. Fagen, "The Politics of Transition," in Richard R. Fagen, Carmen Diana Deere, and José Luís Coraggio, eds., *Transition and Development: Problems of Third World Socialism* (New York: Monthly Review, 1986).

78. JGRN, *Principles and Policies of the Government of Nicaragua* (Managua: 1982). See also Xabier Gorostiaga, "Los dilemas de la Revolución Popular Sandinista," INIES/CRIES, *Cuadernos de Pensamiento Propio* (Managua: 1982).

79. Roger Burbach, "The Conflict at Home and Abroad," in Richard R. Fagen et al., *Transition and Development.*

80. See Sara Miles, "The Real War: Low-Intensity Conflict in Central America," NACLA *Report on the Americas*, Vol. XX, No. 2 (Apr.-May 1986); and Tom Barry, *Low Intensity Conflict: The New Battlefield in Central America* (Albuquerque: The Resource Center, 1986).

81. Amnesty International, *Nicaragua: The Human Rights Record* (London: March 1986), p. 3.

82. See Amnesty International, *Nicaragua.*

83. Booth, "The National Governmental System," in Walker, ed., *Nicaragua: The First Five Years*, p. 40.

84. See Richard Sholk, "The National Bourgeoisie in Post-Revolutionary Nicaragua," *Comparative Politics*, Vol. 16, No. 3 (Apr. 1984).

85. Stephen M. Gorman, "Power and Consolidation in the Nicaraguan Revolution," *Journal of Latin American Studies*, Vol. 13, Part I (May 1981); and Stephen M. Gorman and Thomas W. Walker, "The Armed Forces," in Walker, ed., *Nicaragua: The First Five Years.*

86. See, e.g.: James Petras, "Whither the Nicaraguan Revolution?," *Monthly Review*, Vol. 31, No. 5 (Oct. 1979); and Constantine Menges, "Central America and Its Enemies," *Commentary*, Vol. 72, No. 2 (Aug. 1981).

87. See Walker, ed., *Nicaragua: The First Five Years.*

88. Booth, "The National Governmental System," in Walker, ed., *Nicaragua: The First Five Years*, pp. 35–39.

89. Dennis Gilbert, "The Bourgeoisie," in Walker, ed., *Nicaragua: The First Five Years.*

90. Black, *Triumph*, pp. 244–49.

91. Booth, "The National Governmental System," in Walker, ed., *Nicaragua: The First Five Years*, p. 39.

92. Latin American Studies Association (LASA), *The Electoral Process in Nicaragua: Domestic and International Influences* (Austin, Tex.: 19 Nov. 1984), pp. 29–32.

93. LASA, *The Electoral Process.*

94. Coraggio, *Revolución y democracia*, pp. 100–104.

95. LASA, *The Electoral Process.* For detailed interpretation of electoral returns, see *Envio*, No. 41 (Nov. 1984) and No. 46 (Apr. 1985).

96. *Envio*, No. 53 (Nov. 1985).

97. Gary Ruchwarger, *People in Power: Forging a Grass-roots Democracy in Nicaragua* (South Hadley, Mass.: Bergin & Garvey, forthcoming); Luís Héctor Serra, "The Grass-Roots Organizations," in Walker, ed., *Nicaragua: The First Five Years*; CIERA, *Participatory Democracy in Nicaragua* (Managua: 1984).

98. Valerie Miller, *Between Struggle and Hope: The Nicaraguan Literary Crusade* (Boulder, Colo.: Westview, 1985); Jan Flora et al., "The Growth of Class Struggle: The

Impact of the Nicaraguan Literacy Crusade on the Political Consciousness of Young Literary Workers," *Latin American Perspectives*, No. 36 (Winter 1983).

99. Serra, "The Grass-Roots Organizations," in Walker, ed., *Nicaragua: The First Five Years*, p. 74.

100. Richard Stahler-Sholk, "Organized Labor in Nicaragua," in Sheldon L. Maram and Gerald Michael Greenfield, eds., *Latin American Labor Organizations* (Westport, Conn.: Greenwood Press, forthcoming).

101. See Weber, *The Sandinista Revolution*, and Black, *Triumph*, for details on early labor conflicts.

102. See: Marvin Ortega, "Workers' Participation in the Management of the Agro-Enterprises of the APP," *Latin American Perspectives*, Vol. 12, No. 2 (Spring 1985); *Envio*, No. 35 (May 1984); debate between union leaders, in *Barricada*, 6–7 July 1986.

103. See Luciak, "Popular Democracy."

104. Carmen Diana Deere et al., "The Peasantry and the Development of Sandinista Agrarian Policy, 1979–1984," *Latin American Research Review*, Vol. XX, No. 3 (1985); Peter Marchetti, "War, Popular Participation, and Transition to Socialism: The Case of Nicaragua," in Fagen et al., eds., *Transition and Development*; Eduardo Baumeister, "Estado-mundo agricola: una relación cambiante," *Pensamiento Propio*, No. 34 (June 1986).

105. Maxine Molyneux, "Mobilization Without Emancipation? Women's Interests, State, and Revolution," in Fagen et al., eds., *Transition and Development*.

106. Serra, "The Grass-Roots Organizations," in Walker, ed., *Nicaragua: The First Five Years*, p. 71.

107. Comandante Bayardo Arce, interviewed in Gabriele Invernizzi et al., *Sandinistas* (Managua: Editorial Vanguardia, 1986), p. 67.

108. Serra, "The Grass-Roots Organizations," in Walker, ed., *Nicaragua: The First Five Years*, p. 76.

109. Gary Ruchwarger, "Las organizaciones de masas sandinistas y el proceso revolucionario," in Richard Harris and Carlos M. Vilas, eds., *La revolución en Nicaragua* (Mexico: Ediciones Era, 1985), pp. 169–70.

110. Joseph Collins, *Nicaragua: What Difference Could a Revolution Make?*, 2nd ed. (San Francisco: Institute for Food and Development Policy, 1985), p. 81.

111. Sholk, "The National Bourgeoisie."

112. *Envio*, No. 51 (Sept. 1985); Baumeister, "Estado-mundo agricola."

113. Ruchwarger, "Las organizaciones de masas." See also speech by National CDS Coordinator Leticia Herrera in *Barricada*, 29 August 1985.

114. Coraggio, *Revolución y democracia*, pp. 49–50.

115. Marchetti, "War, Popular Participation," in Fagen et al., eds., *Transition and Development*, pp. 120–21; and José Luís Coraggio, "Economia y politica en la transición: reflexiones sobre la revolución sandinista," in José Luís Coraggio and Carmen Diana Deere, eds., *La transición dificil: la autodeterminación de los pequeños paises periféricos* (Mexico: Siglo XXI, 1986), p. 274.

116. Coraggio, "Economia y politica," p. 274.

117. Roberto Pizarro, "The New Economic Policy: A Necessary Readjustment," in Spalding, ed., *The Political Economy*.

118. Amnesty International, *Nicaragua*, pp. 4–7.

119. Bill Gibson, "A Structural Overview of the Nicaraguan Economy," and E. V. K.

FitzGerald, "An Evaluation of the Economic Costs to Nicaragua of U.S. Aggression: 1980–1984," in Spalding, ed., *The Political Economy*.

120. "America's Secret War," *Newsweek*, 8 Nov. 1982.

121. FitzGerald, "An Evaluation of the Economic Costs"; Michael Conroy, "Economic Dependence, External Assistance, and Economic Aggression Against Nicaragua," *Latin American Perspectives*, Vol. 12, No. 2 (Spring 1985); Daniel Siegel et al., *Outcast Among Allies: The International Cost of Reagan's War Against Nicaragua* (Washington, D.C.: Institute for Policy Studies, 1985); and a leaked National Security Council directive on the "isolation of Nicaragua" in *The New York Times*, 7 Apr. 1983.

122. Deborah Barry et al., "Nicaragua: pais sitiado," INIES/CRIES *Cuadernos de Pensamiento Propio* (Managua: June 1986).

123. *Barricada*, 28 Apr. 1987.

124. John Spicer Nichols, "The Media," and Michael Dodson and Laura Nuzzi O'Shaughnessy, "Religion and Politics," in Walker, ed., *Nicaragua: The First Five Years*.

125. Gilbert, "The Bourgeoisie," in Walker, ed., *Nicaragua: The First Five Years*.

126. Black, *Triumph*, pp. 335–39.

127. Nichols, "The Media."

128. Nichols, "The Media," in Walker, ed., *Nicaragua: The First Five Years*, p. 188.

129. Margaret E. Crahan, "Nicaragua: Political Legitimacy and Dissent," paper for Conference on "Conflict in Nicaragua: National, Regional and International Dimensions," organized by University of Miami and The Royal Institute of International Affairs (London: 28–30 Apr. 1986).

130. Alfonso Dubois, "El proyecto tras el Cardenal," *Pensamiento Propio*, Vol. IV, No. 31 (Mar. 1986).

131. Hodges, *Intellectual Foundations*, pp. 268–91; and Conor Cruise O'Brien, "God and Man in Nicaragua," *Atlantic Monthly*, Aug. 1986.

132. Amnesty International, *Nicaragua*.

133. Americas Watch, *Human Rights in Nicaragua: Reagan, Rhetoric and Reality* (New York: July 1985), p. 3.

134. Washington Office on Latin America, "Nicaragua: The State Department, the Miskito Indians and Covert Operations," WOLA *Update*, Vol. VII, No. 2 (Mar.-Apr. 1982); Americas Watch, *The Miskitos in Nicaragua, 1981–1984* (New York: November 1984).

135. Philippe Bourgois, "Ethnic Minorities," in Walker, ed., *Nicaragua: The First Five Years*.

136. Bourgois, "Ethnic Minorities."

137. Americas Watch, *The Miskitos*, pp. 15–34.

138. Americas Watch, *Human Rights in Central America: A Report on El Salvador, Guatemala, Honduras and Nicaragua* (New York: June 1984), pp. 23–26.

139. *Envio*, No. 52 (Oct. 1985) and No. 57 (Mar. 1986).

140. Quoted in Black, *Triumph*, pp. 198–99.

141. Gilbert, "The Bourgeoisie," in Walker, ed., *Nicaragua: The First Five Years*; Carlos M. Vilas, "Unidad nacional y contradicciones sociales en una economia mixta: Nicaragua 1979–1984," in Harris & Vilas, eds., *La revolución en Nicaragua*; and CINASE/Fundación Ebert, eds., *La economia mixta en Nicaragua: proyecto o realidad* (Managua: 1986).

142. See: Franz J. Hinkelammert, "Democracia, estructura económico-social y for-

mación de un sentido común legitimador," in Coraggio and Deere, eds., *La transición difícil*.

143. Richard L. Harris, "Transformación económica y desarrollo industrial de Nicaragua," in Harris and Vilas, eds., *La revolución en Nicaragua*, p. 92. The proportions remained basically unchanged in 1984; see David F. Ruccio, "The State and Planning in Nicaragua," in Spalding, ed., *The Political Economy*.

144. George Irvin, "Nicaragua: Establishing the State as the Centre of Accumulation," *Cambridge Journal of Economics*, No. 7 (1983).

145. Sylvia Maxfield and Richard Stahler-Sholk, "The Economy: External Constraints," in Walker, ed., *Nicaragua: The First Five Years*.

146. Laura J. Enriquez and Rose J. Spalding, "Banking Systems and Revolutionary Change: The Politics of Agricultural Credit in Nicaragua," in Spalding, ed., *The Political Economy*.

147. E. V. K. FitzGerald, "Notes on the Analysis of the Small Underdeveloped Economy in Transition," in Fagen et al., eds., *Transition and Development*; and Vilas, "Unidad nacional," in Harris & Vilas, eds., *La revolución en Nicaragua*.

148. Utting, "Domestic Supply," in Spalding, ed., *The Political Economy*.

149. John Weeks, "The Mixed Economy in Nicaragua: The Economic Battlefield," in Spalding, ed., *The Political Economy*; and Collins, *Nicaragua: What Difference*, Ch. 5.

150. Thome and Kaimowitz, "Agrarian Reform," in Walker, ed., *Nicaragua: The First Five Years*; Deere et al., "The Peasantry."

151. *Envio*, No. 51 (Sept. 1985).

152. MIDINRA, *Informaciones Agropecuarias*, No. 20 (Oct. 1986).

153. Serra, "The Grass-Roots Organizations," in Walker, ed., *Nicaragua: The First Five Years*, p. 71; Deborah Barndt, "Popular Education," in Walker, ed., pp. 328–31; Thomas John Bossert, "Health Policy: The Dilemma of Success," in Walker, ed., pp. 350 and 361; Nicaraguan Institute of Social Security and Welfare (INSSBI), *Seis años de revolución en el INSSBI* (Managua: July 1985); *Barricada*, 13 July 1986; and Inter-American Development Bank, *Economic and Social Progress in Latin America, 1985* (Washington, D.C.: 1985).

154. FitzGerald, "An Evaluation of the Economic Costs," in Spalding, ed., *The Political Economy*.

155. Jaime Wheelock Román, *Entre la crisis y la agresión: la reforma agraria sandinista* (Managua: Editorial Nueva Nicaragua, 1985).

156. Michael E. Conroy, "Patterns of Changing External Trade in Revolutionary Nicaragua: Voluntary and Involuntary Trade Diversification," in Spalding, ed., *The Political Economy*.

157. José Luís Coraggio and Rosa María Torres, *Transición y crisis política: la revolución en Nicaragua (1979–1986)* (Managua: CRIES, 1986, pre-edition), pp. 61–71.

158. Carlos M. Vilas, "El impacto de la guerra en la revolución sandinista," *Revista Nicaragüense de Ciencias Sociales*, No. 2 (March 1987), p. 5.

159. Dennis Gilbert, "Nicaragua," in Blachman et al., *Confronting Revolution*; Colin Danby et al., *The Military Balance in Central America: An Analysis and Critical Evaluation of Administration Claims* (Washington, D.C.: Council on Hemispheric Affairs, 5 April 1985).

160. *The New York Times*, 22 Feb. 1985.

161. Pizarro, "The New Economic Policy," in Spalding, ed., *The Political Economy*.

162. Jim Morrell and William Jesse Biddle, "Central America: The Financial War," *International Policy Report* (Washington, D.C.: Center for International Policy, Mar. 1983); and Eugenio Rivera Urrutia et al., *Centroamérica: politica económica y crisis* (San José, Costa Rica: Editorial Dei, 1987), pp. 17–24.

163. Richard Stahler-Sholk, "Foreign Debt and Economic Stabilization Policies in Revolutionary Nicaragua," in Spalding, ed., *The Political Economy*; and Rubén Berríos, "Economic Relations Between Nicaragua and the Socialist Countries," Wilson Center/ Latin American Program, *Working Papers*, No. 166 (Washington, D.C.: 1985).

164. Siegel et al., *Outcast Among Allies*.

165. Adam Przeworski, "Some Problems in the Study of the Transition to Democracy," Wilson Center/Latin American Program, *Working Papers*, No. 61 (Washington, D.C.: 1979).

5

Sustaining Democracy in Peru: Dealing with Parliamentary and Revolutionary Changes

Sandra Woy-Hazelton
and William A. Hazelton

The restoration of democracy in Latin America is usually greeted with a mixture of optimism and pessimism. The optimism stems from the promises of democracy. For both individuals and societies as a whole, democracy fulfills psychological desires for self-control, self-governance, and self-determination through political participation and government accountability in periodic elections. Theoretically, a democratic system should at the very least protect basic individual liberties, political freedoms, and minority rights; provide for popular participation in government; be responsive to the popular will; and honor the rule of law. Yet even these basic requirements have been difficult to attain or maintain, with the result that most governments are not "democratic." Scholars and practitioners alike have sought to identify the prerequisites of democracy, for example, an educated population, economic prosperity, consensus on rules, political parties, and institutional legitimacy. Democracy, however, has proved not to be the inevitable result of particular social, economic, or political developments, nor once established has it proved immune to breakdown. Likewise, once destroyed, democracy has not been forever lost, in that the psychological urge to have a voice in the way we are governed has given democracy a certain resilience, especially among Latin American nations.

The pessimism, which frequently greets the restoration of democracy in Latin America, results from traditional skepticism that new conditions will be any more conducive to sustaining a democratic system than the old ones. Each time the pendulum swings between military and civilian governments, dictatorship and democracy, the same questions arise. Will democratic institutions and procedures take hold, are democratic values shared widely enough to engender strong popular support, are the politicians dedicated to preserving the democratic process and to making the system work? In other words, has the political environment really changed so as to enhance democracy's chances of success?

All of these questions have been raised with regard to the redemocratization of Peru in 1980 when the military handed the reins of government to Fernando Belaunde Terry for the second time. In 1963 he was the left-of-center hope for reform, supported by a progressive military and the United States, a perfect representative for the Alliance for Progress. His initial reforms were thwarted by an entrenched oligarchy, and his government was at the mercy of mercurial coalition partners. In the face of guerrilla threats, economic instability, and business scandals, the military removed him from power in a bloodless coup in October 1968. When he returned to power a dozen years later, the context of Peruvian politics had changed to the point that Belaunde was now the center-right candidate. For Belaunde and his party, Accion Popular (AP), the 1980 elections represented not only a restoration of democracy but also the return to their rightful place of authority. Any illusions of continuity brought about by Belaunde's election, however, ignored the fact that this time Peru's redemocratization involved major political reforms, not the least of which was expanding the electorate to include illiterates.

In part because of these changes, Peru's reconstructed democracy stood a better chance to survive than did its predecessors, as witnessed by the fact that on July 28, 1985, Belaunde actually did turn over power to an elected successor, Alan Garcia, an event that had last occurred in 1914. Yet enthusiasm for direct political participation in a civilian government has been tempered by a prolonged economic crisis, repeated acts of terrorism, and Peru's authoritarian tradition. Indeed, Peruvian anthropologist Rodrigo Montoya has lamented that ''no one has taught democracy in this country. What we are familiar with are examples of authoritarianism and verticalism. . . . Democracy remains to be invented in Peru.''

Sustaining a democracy, as Peru knows only too well, is a far more difficult task than simply reinstating civilian rule through free and fair elections. The greatest challenge for any democratic regime, and especially a newly reconstituted one, is how to deal with significant opposition, both in-system (legal) and out-of-system (illegal), without undermining the principles and procedures upon which the regime is based. The Peruvian experience from 1980 to 1985 illuminates the dilemmas that confront fledgling democracies that are hard pressed by both a significant political opposition and a growing guerrilla threat. In this chapter, the redemocratization of Peru is examined from the perspective of the Belaunde administration's attempts to deal with both of these challenges and how its efforts affected the nature, process, and prospects of Peruvian democracy.

TRANSITION TO DEMOCRACY

There were few illusions that the going would be easy for Peru in the early 1980s. The military's voluntary withdrawal from power was due primarily to its reluctance to continue governing in the face of serious economic difficulties and rising popular discontent. The twelve-year revolutionary military experiment, known as the *docenio*, encountered numerous problems, and in 1975 the initial reforms of General Juan Velasco Alvarado were reversed by an internal coup. Velasco's successor, General Francisco Morales Bermudez, became even more isolated as he lost support among those popular sectors wishing to accelerate the revolutionary process and failed to gain the loyalty of those groups wanting to eradicate the Velasco reforms. By 1977 the armed forces, divided over how the country should be run, had become more concerned about preserving their institutional integrity than continuing with their failing experiment in governing.[2] The military's willingness to extricate itself from governing was made easier by the existence of reformist groups to whom they were willing to hand over power and a process—the holding of a constituent assembly—through which they could exercise control over the gradual transition to civilian rule.

The general consensus of Peruvian analysts is that despite its many problems, the *docenio* brought about some long overdue reforms.[3] Although hesitant steps toward reform had been taken by the first Belaunde administration (1963–68), the military government succeeded in removing the underpinnings of an entrenched, intransigent oligarcy by completely altering the land-tenure system, modernizing parts of the economic system, instituting national planning, expanding state enterprises, and overhauling the educational system.[4] The result was a shift in the distribution of power from conservative autocrats to liberal bourgeois democrats. At the same time that the military's reformist policies benefited the middle class, they also stimulated the political consciousness and non-electoral participation of popular sectors that had never before played a significant role in Peruvian national politics.[5] Thus not only did the military leaders promote different policies and interests than previous civilian and military regimes, but they also expanded the number of political participants, with Peru experiencing the greatest mass mobilization and politicization in its history between 1977 and 1980.

When the armed forces decided to return the responsibility of governing to civilians, they wanted as much control as possible over the transition. Although the military had no intention of presiding over a restoration of the traditional political elites, they also did not want a "people's democracy." Therefore, to smooth the way for the establishment of a liberal democratic system dominated by reformist political elements, the generals convened a constituent assembly to write a new constitution. Such an assembly provided the military with an opportunity to reactivate the political organizations and reinstitute electoral activity without immediately transferring power. Moreover, free and fair elections for the seats in the assembly gave the military an opportunity to assess the distribution of political support among the participating parties.

The 1978 election results for the hundred-member assembly showed a highly politicized and polarized electorate. Twelve parties contested the election, and representation in the assembly broke down ideologically into three relatively equal camps: four night-of-center parties received 28 percent of the vote and twenty-nine seats in the assembly, the centrist party won 35 percent of the vote and thirty-seven seats, and seven leftist parties accounted for 36 percent of the vote and got thirty-four assembly seats.[6]

That the Peruvian Aprista Party (APRA) represented the center and had the support of the military is testimony to the significant political shift that had come about by the end of the *docenio*. For almost fifty years the APRA, under Victor Raul Haya de la Torre, had been the largest mass-based party in Peru. Its doctrine was reformist, innovative, nationalistic, and anti-oligarchic, and because of this the party was periodically banned.[7] In 1931, 1962, and 1969, the APRA's chances of becoming the governing party were blocked by military intervention. Despite repeated setbacks, the party continued to seek incorporation into the political system, and when the opportunity arrived in the form of the 1978 Constituent Assembly elections, APRA leaders were willing to cooperate with their bitter historical rivals, the military. From the military's perspective, at least initially, the APRA was a valuable ally in that it was increasingly moderate, avidly anti-Communist, and popularly based.[8]

The APRA's "understanding" with the military government meant that the assembly was duly constrained in any attempts to act like a legislature, and the final document drafted by the assembly differed little from the 1933 Constitution, providing the framework for a liberal capitalist system that incorporated few of Velasco's reforms. Overall, the Constitutional Assembly fit the military's plans. It even avoided efforts to impose constitutional controls on the military during the transitory period by postponing the date for the Constitution's implementation until the civilian president's inauguration.

Postponement was also necessitated by the fact that the political forces had yet to consolidate in such a way that the military felt confident it could sanction presidential and parliamentary elections. What the armed forces wanted was a popularly based government, with a stable governing party and a president who would respect the military's position within Peruvian society.[9] However, soon after his moment of glory as president of the Constituent Assembly, Haya de la Torre died, and the APRA disintegrated in a bitter struggle over the selection of his successor. As ideological and generational disputes split the party's popular support, the military abandoned the APRA in favor of Belaunde's AP as the party to lead the redemocratization of Peru. Ironically, the AP had not participated in the Constituent Assembly elections, contesting instead their legitimacy. Nevertheless, party leaders began returning from exile as the AP prepared to campaign in the subsequent national elections. With the APRA's fortunes declining, the

AP's chances of becoming the governing party steadily mounted, and it soon became apparent that the military would be handing power back to the very man they had ousted in 1968.

The results of the 1980 national elections reflected a marked change in the three-way ideological split seen in 1978. The left and far right declined in support, with 17.0 percent and 10.0 percent of the vote, respectively, whereas the two center reform parties accounted for 73.0 percent, with the APRA receiving 27.4 percent and the AP winning with 45.4 percent of the vote. Belaunde's convincing victory helped provide the AP with a comfortable majority of ninety-eight to eighty-two in the Chamber of Deputies and, in a coalition with the Partido Popular Cristiano (PPC), control of the Senate by a margin of thirty-two to twenty-eight.[10] In addition, the AP did extremely well in the provincial and municipal council elections. Thus the military turned power over to a fairly stable, popularly elected government with widespread legitimacy.

This legitimacy derived largely from major systemic reforms. One factor contributing to the vulnerability of previous civilian regimes to military intervention had been the very narrow base of political support upon which they rested. But the reconstituted political system, instituted by the military, provided for universal suffrage, organizational freedom, and proportional representation. The electorate was enlarged to include eighteen-year-olds and, more important in terms of numbers, illiterates. No legal restrictions were placed on the formation of parties, and despite some minor harassment of leftist politicians, all groups have been allowed to vie for support at the polls. Diversity of political opinions was enhanced through proportional representation, insuring nearly every ideological tendency a legitimate outlet of expression. Consequently, the 1980 election gave representation to nine political parties and several independent factions distributed across a broad ideological spectrum.

Another important facet of Peruvian redemocratization is the relationship that was instituted between the military and the new civilian government. Military intervention into politics has historically been justified on the grounds of protecting national interests that were either being ignored or subverted by civilian politicians. As guarantors of the nation's security against both external and internal threats, the Peruvian military has occasionally chosen to place this sacred duty above the law. In addition, the armed forces constitute an important interest group that seeks to protect its influence over certain key policy areas.

Nineteen days before Belaunde took office, the military decreed a wide-ranging Mobilization Law that insured their continued involvement in any matter that could be connected to national defense.[11] An important provision of this law permits the mobilization of the armed forces not only in time of war but also during acts of internal subversion and national disasters, which includes arson and sabotage. Under this law, analysts believe, the military can maintain its autonomy and exert considerable influence over government attempts to deal with domestic violence.[12] Thus democracy, as it was restored in Peru, did not place the military entirely under civilian control; to the contrary, the armed forces made sure that the more unstable the new democracy, the greater their potential role would be in governing the country.

Broad-based participation, fair elections, a stable governing party, and a military content to remain in the barracks are not the only requirements for a successful democracy, however. Continued support from the general population, key interest groups, and party leaders is also important, and this depends upon a constant evaluation of how well the system and its institutions are performing. This evaluation is more than simply a cost-benefit analysis of current policies. It includes an assessment of the government's legitimacy, based in part on its respect for civil liberties and political rights, its responsiveness to popular demands, and its commitment to the rule of law, as well as the perceived benefits of working within the framework of a democratic system.

During his term of office, Belaunde and his party faced several serious challenges. The economy declined to its worst point in this century. Growth stopped, and rampant inflation averaged more than 100 percent annually, causing a 30–40 percent drop in real wages since January 1983.[13] The country's prosperity was mortgaged through international loans and a debt burden of $12.4 billion by mid–1984 that virtually shut off what meager public spending the International Monetary Fund (IMF)-imposed austerity plans allowed.[14] Compounding these problems, natural catastrophes in 1983 destroyed 60 percent of the nation's agricultural production, and the government continued to face a bloody anti-systemic challenge from the militant revolutionary group Sendero Luminoso ("Shining Path"). Because of the government's inability to deal with these problems, the AP suffered a stinging defeat in the 1983 municipal elections and was thoroughly routed in the April 1985 national elections. In other words, the post–1980 situation in Peru has been very conducive to social and political unrest, placing the fragile foundations of democracy under considerable strain. Despite serious problems, the Belaunde government managed to survive and transfer power to a popularly elected successor. However, the question remains whether Peru's commitment to democracy is strong enough that popular discontent will be channeled largely through the electoral process, or if it will add fuel to the ongoing guerrilla war and trigger yet another military intervention.

To a substantial degree the answer to this question depends upon the Garcia government's respect for democratic norms, its treatment of the in-system opposition, and its response to revolutionary terrorism. It also depends upon the population's capacity to distinguish between the real and potential merits of a democratic system and the actual performance of a particular regime. If those who are unhappy with the policies of the current administration have some assurance that alternatives are available within the democratic process, their continued support for the institutions of government may still be forthcoming. However, this will be true only if the integrity of those institutions is respected and maintained.

In retrospect, a major challenge for the Belaunde administration was to define the rules of democratic competition so as not to restrict political participation unnecessarily or to undermine basic democratic tenets. Simply stated, Belaunde and his coalition had to avoid a common temptation of regimes under pressure, that is, to subvert democracy under the pretense of saving it. In the next section the Belaunde government's relationship with the legal opposition is examined in three controversial areas: (1) expanding executive authority, (2) the centralization of government, and (3) the expression of political dissent.

THE PARLIAMENTARY OPPOSITION AND RULES OF DEMOCRATIC COMPETITION

In parliament the political opposition to the AP and its coalition partner until March 1984, the PPC, was composed of the following elements: (1) the APRA, or at least its leftist faction; (2) the Marxist coalition Izquierda Unida (IU), whose heterogeneous membership includes two fronts—the Maoist Union Democratica Popular and the pro-Beijing Union de la Izquierda Revolucionaria, and four parties—the pro-Soviet Partido Comunista Peruano (PCP), the Velasquista Partido Socialista Revolucionario, the Partido Comunista Revolucionario, and the Trotskyist Frente Obrero, Campesino, Estudiantil y Popular; and two small regionally based parties, Frente de Trabajadores y Campesinos and the Trotskyist Partido Revolucionario de los Trabajadores.

The overarching goals of the parliamentary opposition were to press for reforms that would provide socioeconomic benefits for the Peruvian masses and to protect the constitutional and legal rights of political dissent. The strength of the government's parliamentary majority meant that the APRA and the IU had virtually no chance of gaining approval for their own legislative initiatives, and consequently, their tactics were largely defensive, that is, seeking to modify or block legislative proposals introduced by the government. Their main objective was simply to be heard. The role of the opposition was by necessity one of protest that it had to play both inside and outside of parliament depending upon which yielded better results. While the AP and the PPC charged that outside protests violated the rules of the game, the APRA and the IU argued that the government's narrow definition of legal political dissent left them with little choice but to air their positions on issues publicly.

Despite persistent government fears to the contrary, an electoral alliance between the APRA and the IU was never likely. The recent histories of the APRA and the IU had witnessed such extensive internal divisiveness that maintaining their own integrity had become a high priority, and each group remained adamant about preserving its ideological independence. However, during the Belaunde years, they often acted in concert as consistent and unrelenting critics of the government's economic policies and its efforts to restructure the political system.

The opposition charged that an accumulation of structural changes, instituted by the government, fundamentally altered the nature of the regime, primarily through the granting of legislative powers to the executive and extending the power of the national government over provincial and municipal authorities. Expanded executive authority, they believed, was directly contrary to a system of representative democracy in which the legislature made laws in response to the popular will. Moreover, the leftist opposition argued that important legislative functions, which had been delegated to the executive, effectively created a "civilian dictatorship."

Belaunde's government did not, however, illegally usurp the role of legislator. Under Article 188 of the 1979 Constitution, congress could delegate to the executive the power to legislate through *decretos legislativos* on specified issues. The AP claimed this provision allowed for "flexibility, collaboration, and interdependence" between the two branches, and parliament passed *Ley* 23230 giving the executive this power. Opponents argued that the Belaunde government abused this provision because the Constitution intended such delegations of power to be granted only in extraordinary circumstances, not as an inherent attribution of the executive.[15]

During its first year in office, the Belaunde government promulgated 212 *decretos legislativos*, whereas fewer than twenty laws were passed by parliament. Not just the quantity but also the substance of the *decretos* alarmed the opposition. Article 194 of the Constitution clearly established that organic laws must emanate from the legislature; yet the executive branch decreed the expansion of presidential and ministerial functions in several areas that had the substantive effect of altering the structures of the state. Especially frustrating to the opposition was the fact that among those functions delegated to the executive were items of major national import that demanded open public debate. They included the law of agrarian promotion and development that sought to alter the entire agrarian reform program of the Velasco government; the return of newspapers, radio, and television stations to their pre–1968 owners; the national regulation of municipalities; tax laws; the centralization of regional planning in the Council of Ministers; and the authority to revise most of the laws decreed during the military *docenio*.[16] Worse yet, half of these *decretos* were promulgated in the seventy-two-hour period before the authorization expired. While supporters applauded the government's actions as a "democratic and constitutional revolution of the whole," the opposition was appalled. Luis Negreiros (APRA) called the rain of laws "impudent and excessive . . . especially when AP controls both houses," and Enrique Bernales (IU) asked, "If the executive legislates, for what is parliament?"[17]

This trend persisted throughout the Belaunde administration. Bernales calculated that by April 1984 the executive branch had initiated 739 laws of which 276 were *decreto legislativos*, whereas parliament had initiated only 211. The IU delegate placed part of the blame on the slow, inefficient, underpaid parliamentary bureaucracy, as well as on obsolete rules of parliamentary procedure, poor attendance by delegates, and the social composition of congress. However, Bernales still maintained that the concentration of legislative powers in the hands of the executive was primarily due to government actions deliberately calculated to achieve this end.[18]

In addition to concentrating power in the hands of the executive, the administration's policy was to centralize government operations at the national level. A good example of this was the Municipalities Law, *Decreto Legislativo* 51, promulgated in March 1981. Here it should be noted that the administration's tactics of instituting major changes without a parliamentary debate or vote was used not only to diminish the impact of leftist opponents but also to bypass recalcitrant members of the AP on particular issues. The Municipalities Law, for example, was bitterly denounced by AP's most prominent mayor, Eduardo Orrego of Lima, and by a faction of the party that opposed Prime Minister Ulloa's vision of a highly centralized state.[19]

Administrative centralization is not new to Peru; in fact, it follows in the Iberian authoritarian tradition of concentrating power at the top and giving little discretionary authority to subordinate entities. But Belaunde was not expected to adopt this course since he had championed greater autonomy for regional governments during his first administration. The process of *dismunicipalizacion*, advocated by his government, meant that city budgets would have to be approved by the central government, transportation controlled by the minister of transport, construction and urban expansion overseen by the minister of housing, water and heat regulated by the minister of health, and so on.[20] Little wonder that Mayor Orrego called the Municipalities Law "lacking in respect for municipal government" and an "attack on democratic life by substantially restraining their functions."[21] One possible explanation of Belaunde's reversal on this issue is that with the wider participation of the popular sectors, local power was now more likely to be in the hands of opposition parties.

Belaunde's effort to decentralize and promote regional autonomy was confined to a reorganization plan under which twenty-eight new districts and sixteen new provinces were created. The plan, however, had virtually no impact on the existing relationship between the national and regional governments. In short, there was to be no devolution of power to local authorities. Meanwhile, critics pointed out that the consequences of splitting scarce resources more ways in the rural provinces would result in a net loss for these jurisdictions and their increased dependence upon the central administration.[22]

The unfortunate result of concentrating power in the hands of the chief executive is that regional governments and municipalities must direct their demands to Lima's presidential palace, a move that has proved detrimental to both governmental efficiency and democratic accountability. Instead of working through parliamentary representatives or relying on their own resources, local governments felt forced to draw presidential attention to their plight. Therefore, whole cities went on strike to command the national government's attention. Puno, for example, threatened a strike of all municipal employees if the government failed to respond to its problems of high malnutrition, mortality, and illiteracy rate.[23]

A year later its representatives went on a hunger strike in parliament to underscore the need for emergency assistance in coping with a severe drought. In 1982 workers in Cuzco struck for a new airport, a paved road to Lima, and better hospital conditions.[24] Two years later, the mayor threatened to "capture an airliner" to force the government to respond to his concern for expanding social welfare programs.[25] In yet another city, fifty persons, including the mayor, kidnapped two health officials and seventeen employees of the Ministry of Health to demand a permanent doctor.[26] Thus instead of being "taught democracy" through effective participation in local institutions, citizen confidence in a democratic system's ability to produce results declined, while traditional patron/client relations were reinforced at the national level.

Not only was the national parliament deprived of some of its legislative powers by the Belaunde government, but within the body, opponents alleged that devices were employed to limit their right to be heard. One method was to flaunt the chamber's rules when the government parties thought it was expedient to do so, such as accepting a simple majority of those present, instead of the required absolute majority of ninety-one members on certain votes.[27] Another was to adopt rules of procedure that, critics contended, were designed merely to enhance the majority's position and showed a total disregard for custom and parliamentary practices. For example, in the interim between the two yearly sessions of parliament when a permanent commission meets, Dr. Trelles (AP), who at the time was president of the Senate, ruled that motions for order would not be allowed in the commission even though they were part of both chambers' normal procedures. These motions, which are pronouncements on policy, homages, demands, and recommendations, had no binding force, but when approved, they did express parliament's intent and could therefore be an important outlet for minority views.[28]

In December 1982 President Belaunde attempted to use the interim period to ride out the transition between the resignation of Ulloa's cabinet and the formation of a new cabinet under Fernando Schwalb. Parliament was not convened until three months after the crisis began and one and a half months after the new cabinet was installed. In view of the fact that the majority determines when and how often the permanent commission meets during the interim, this tactic would have allowed the AP to consolidate its strength before confronting the opposition in parliamentary debate. The tactic ultimately failed, however, in that the public outcry over the country being left essentially in limbo until April 1 was so great that Belaunde was forced to call an extraordinary session of parliament in late January.[29]

In addition, the majority can organize the legislature so as to minimize the impact of the opposition. Initially structured like most Western parliaments, with proportional partisan representation on all legislative committees, Senate president Javier Alva Orlandini (AP), in August 1981, restructured committee representation and work loads, thereby diluting minority representation on key committees. Consequently, the IU, which had been represented on every committee, with even two chairmanships, during the Senate's first session, found itself one year later with no members on some committees and with three of its ten senators on the Sports Committee.[30]

Despite these tactics, the opposition still voiced its views as members introduced motions, made pronouncements, and otherwise participated in legislative debate. In addition, calling ministers before the chamber to explain their actions provided a potential means for subjecting government policies to public scrutiny, especially when debate had been avoided earlier by issuing *decretos legislativos*. This type of accountability was not easily obtained, however, since it takes one-third of the chamber to request a minister's presence, thus requiring the cooperation of the IU and the entire APRA delegation. On some issues they succeeded; for example, Foreign Minister Arias Stella was called to brief the legislature during the border conflict with Ecuador.[31] The danger of failure, however, was always present as in the case of trying to question the Ministry of Industry about the sale of state enterprises when the right-wing faction of the APRA broke and voted with the AP-PPC majority.[32]

It was the successful use of this tactic by the opposition, however, that marked the beginning of the end for Prime Minister Ulloa. In September 1982 the opposition in the Chamber of Deputies coalesced to pass a petition of interpellation (i.e., a formal summons) to the Council of Ministers to explain its policies. The APRA-initiated petition had eight points of inquiry that included the government's inability to control terrorism, the high unemployment rate, refinancing the 1983 budget deficit, and corruption in high government offices. Belaunde initially welcomed the interpellation as "an opportunity for democratic dialogue," where Ulloa could explain the government's positions. After twenty hours of uninterrupted debate, the beleagured prime minister eventually secured a vote of confidence, but the ordeal proved very taxing for the AP. The party was clearly put on the defensive, causing internal dissension within its ranks to spring into public view. Meanwhile, the mere approval of the summons was considered a victory for the opposition parties, greatly enhancing their public image as legitimate spokesmen for policy alternatives.[33]

Another way that opposition delegates had input was in the formation of investigative committees. These committees needed the concurrence of the AP members, however, and thus were formed only on rare occasions when they did not directly relate to the Belaunde government's program. Consequently, only investigations of actions by the previous military government and ex-officials won parliamentary approval. The administration thought that problems should be investigated by the appropriate ministry or executive office, rather than by the legislature. Not surprisingly, repeated attempts by the opposition to create a parliamentary committee to investigate terrorism failed.

Finally, non-traditional methods of drawing attention to its demands were also used by the opposition. The fact that the political socialization of most leftist delegates had occurred in out-of-system, non-electoral activities had a great impact on their notion of political participation. For instance, when the AP-PPC majority impeded discussion of a medical strike, two doctors, Antonio Meza

Cuadra (IU) and Santiago Carranza Vargas (APRA), went on a hunger strike in the chamber.[34] The entire opposition at times walked out of the chambers en masse when votes were taken with which they vehemently disagreed. These non-traditional means of parliamentary protest usually met with strong denunciations from the majority, including calls to limit "congressional immunity" because of the questionable political activities of some opposition leaders.[35] The AP-PPC coalition was especially unsympathetic to parliamentarians working outside of the chambers to influence legislation when those activities involved "illegal" strikes. However, the IU and the APRA claimed that they were prevented from using parliamentary and other "legal" means to influence government policies.

POPULAR OPPOSITION TO THE GOVERNMENT'S ECONOMIC PROGRAM

Belaunde and the AP saw their electoral success as a repudiation of the policies of the military *docenio*. A moderate who believed in gradual reform, Belaunde was committed above all to a program for capitalist economic development that would in turn provide the resources necessary for carrying out major social reforms. To lead the government, Belaunde appointed Manuel Ulloa prime minister and minister of finance. Like many prominent AP members, Ulloa had spent the *docenio* in the United States, in this case, working in international banking. Not surprisingly, given his experience and background, Ulloa's economic program featured the monetarist and stabilization policies of Milton Friedman and was introduced with the blessing of the IMF. These policies, to be continued by Ulloa's successors in the Finance Ministry, had three basic aims: (1) reversing the statist policies of the military government, (2) emphasizing traditional export products and easing import restrictions, and (3) allowing the market to determine the price of domestic necessities in order to stimulate agricultural production and eliminate costly government subsidies for basic goods and services.[36]

The liberalized economy, envisioned by Ulloa and the Finance Ministry, failed to produce the hoped-for economic miracle, in part because of unfavorable worldwide economic conditions beyond the government's control. The domestic political consequences arising from the government's program of stimulating free enterprise and liberalizing foreign trade, however, became the major source of concern. Rising prices, currency devaluations, declining exports, and natural disasters quickly eroded Belaunde's hope for a broad-based coalition of support, and his economic program served instead to unify the political opposition.

Critics of the government's economic program charged that it caused massive suffering and large-scale economic dislocation among the country's poor. Government revenues were increased through regressive taxes, while budget cuts eliminated public subsidies and social programs. Moreover, the benefits of the government's program accrued to the "able" sectors of the economy, with increased tax incentives and government credits for private businesses, more military spending, and an expanding foreign debt to underwrite development projects serving the interests of transnational corporations investing in Peru. The opposition attacked the ''reprivatization'' of the economy, namely, the government's attempt to repeal agrarian reform legislation and sell off state enterprises created under Velasco's military regime for those industries like mining, fishing, sugar, and cotton that used basic resources. Even worse, nationalist opponents charged, was the favoritism shown to foreign businesses by the government in such areas as tax incentives for developing petroleum and mineral deposits and the lifting of protectionist trade barriers.

As prices on essentials rose and salaries eroded with run-away inflation, the number and severity of strikes increased. The opposition claimed that the strikes were economically motivated by intolerable living conditions, but the government persistently denounced the strikes as ''political'' and ''threatening to democracy.''[37]

A labor law passed in September 1981 defined as illegal those strikes that ''interrupt vital public services and paralyze fundamental economic activities, [and] that place in danger the execution of the budget and national defense.'' When the president, with the approval of the Council of Ministers, decides that a conflict involves ''an indispensible service'' or ''gravely threatens a general national interest,'' that conflict must be submitted to binding arbitration.[38] The law defined wage demands, working conditions, and an employer's failure to fulfill legal obligations as legitimate reasons for striking. The law's specific provisions were not so much of a problem as what the opposition feared was its underlying intent and how it might be administered, that is, as means for repressing popular opposition. Such concerns were not totally unwarranted, for Minister Ulloa had warned that ''the government [would] not tolerate politically motivated strikes in essential sectors, and [would] deal drastically with those who try to solve labor problems with violence.''[39]

Economic frustration had led to ten general strikes in Peru from 1977 to mid–1985. Under Belaunde the most important were on March 10, 1983, and March 22 and November 29, 1984, when all four labor confederations—the Communist Confederacion General de Trabajadores del Peru (CGTP), the Christian Democratic Central Nacional de Trabajadores, the Velasquista Central de Trabajadores de la Revolucion Peruana, and the APRA Confederacion de Trabajadores de Peru—joined together in protest. During the first strike, an estimated 30 percent of the work force participated nationwide, and in the second, more than 60 percent, making it the second most successful general strike after the 1977 strike, which precipitated the military's opening to democracy.

In both the 1983 and 1984 protests, the government maintained that the intent was clearly political, not economic, and therefore the strike was illegal. Officials argued that the unions and leftist political parties were ''manipulating the workforce in order to destabilize the democratic regime, subvert the rule of law, . . . [and] push the government into taking repressive measures which would serve the left's purposes of undermining authority.''[40] But the deteriorating economic position of workers obviously could not be ignored. In asking for a 15 percent salary increase in March 1984, protesters argued that their so-called political demands—freezing prices on necessities, protection for regional products, agricultural subsidies, national support for municipal services and so on—were all necessary if the wage increase were to have any real value.[41]

The government's response to these strikes was a mixture of persuasion, concession, and repression. Although the government declared a state of emergency and suspended all constitutional guarantees for a seventy-two-hour period during each strike, it also relied heavily upon inducements and rewards. Appeals were made to "be patriotic, not subversive"; transportation bonuses were offered to workers, along with two hours' tolerance in arriving late to work. Moreover, after the call for a general strike in 1983, Minister of Labor Alfonso Grados agreed to settle an existing miner's strike, raise the minimum wage, and reestablish controls over bread. This significantly eased the general strike's intended impact; ironically, it also demonstrated that the threat to strike could be an effective mechanism for changing government policies.[42]

Despite the concessions and threats, compliance with all three national strikes during Belaunde's administration was high, and violence frequently erupted when police clashed with demonstrators in attempting to disperse the crowds. Four persons were killed in 1983, and scores of strikers were wounded and hundreds detained in each protest.[43] The leftist opposition alleged that labor, neighborhood, and political leaders had been deliberately stopped and physically abused by the military and police. In March 1984 Senator Jorge del Prado (IU), leader of the PCP, was hospitalized after being hit by a tear gas bomb, and several IU mayors around the country were detained.[44] The government's willingness to use force appeared to result from the fear that uncontrolled protests in the cities would only contribute to the guerrilla violence raging in the highlands.

THE REVOLUTIONARY CHALLENGE OF *SENDERO LUMINOSO*

When the fanatics of the Sendero Luminoso stole a ballot box and hung dead dogs from lampposts on election day in 1980, most people thought this was the last gasp of a dissident Marxist group that would soon disappear. Yet five years later, the Belaunde administration found itself fighting a guerrilla war against the *senderistas* in which more than 5,000 persons had died and thirteen provinces were governed by a military-political command under a state of emergency, with 5,000 government forces deployed in anti-guerrilla and security activities.[45]

The Sendero Luminoso had its origins in 1964, with the splintering of the Peruvian Communist Party into pro-Soviet and pro-Chinese factions. Abimael Guzman, the Sendero's founder, abandoned the pro-Chinese PCP-Bandera Roja in 1970, when it adopted a more moderate stance in support of some of General Velasco's reforms. Basically, a small regional group, the strength of Guzman's

PCP-Sendero Luminoso is centered in the campesino areas of the highlands, which because of their remoteness have traditionally been ignored by political organizers. Guzman's immediate goal was to radicalize the agrarian reform movement by organizing peasant unions and land invasions in Ayacucho.[46] Consequently, the Sendero became one of the first parties on the left whose nucleus and general activity was provincially focused but whose objectives and aspirations were clearly national in scope.

The Sendero's philosophy is a mixture of Jose Carlos Mariategui's teachings on Peruvian reality and Mao's model for protracted struggle set in the Quechuan context of the Andean highlands. The *senderistas* argue that nothing has changed in Peru since the 1930s and that democratic civilian government is no different from a military one in that elections merely serve to disguise the "fascist continuum." According to the Sendero's theorists, every Peruvian institution has been "co-opted by fascism," except the university, which must be defended. This view initially led to an isolated, fanatical existence within the confines of a few universities. While Guzman and the majority of his adherents were at the Universidad Nacional San Cristobal de Huamanga (UNSCH) in Ayacucho, the Sendero could also claim followers among academic circles in Lima, Ica, and Huaraz.[47]

Senderistas have separated themselves from the rest of the left in Peru, claiming that the major labor union, the CGTP, and the major peasant union, Confederacion Campesinos del Peru (CCP), were contaminated by "revisionism and reformism." For example, they labeled the national strike of July 19, 1977, "a game of Soviet socialist imperialism." They also parted ways with the rest of the Marxist left by charging that the *electionistas* are not true Marxists because they do not really accept the use of violence. Thus the IU arrangement was ridiculed as a "servant of reactionary opportunism." This deep division dates from 1978 when the leaders of the Sendero decided at their ninth Plenary to reconstitute the party in preparation for an armed struggle. After one and a half years of no communication, the *senderistas* announced in March 1980 that the prerequisites for launching a prolonged popular war had been accomplished and their targets would soon include not only the bourgeoisie but also the parliamentary left.[48]

From its creation in 1970 to its declaration of armed struggle in 1980, the Sendero Luminoso recruited, trained, and organized cadres of followers. Its initial adherents were largely students, teachers, and middle-class professionals, and its organizational efforts were concentrated in the *barriadas* of the highland towns. Estimates of the Sendero's size vary, but in 1981, the Peruvian news magazine *Caretas* estimated that the organization had 400 professors and 6,000 students supporting its activities.[49] Foreign news sources claimed there were fewer than 100 active members.[50] However, by June 1985 official estimates claimed that close to 8,000 *senderistas* had been killed or arrested since 1980.[51]

According to an interview with a *senderista*, members are organized militarily into companies, detachments, squads, militias, and cells, all under a unified command. The militias are formed by people in a community who are not necessarily party members. This tight-knit organization apparently carries over into the civilian sector as well.[52] A journalist from the leftist publication *Equis X*, who had been taken into a zone controlled by the Sendero, reported that they had an infrastructure in Ayacucho that paralleled that of the government and operated twenty-four hours a day. He claimed that support for the Sendero was to be found in most sectors of Peruvian society—from state officials to policemen and members of the civil guard, to clergy, teachers, and students, as well as among the rural and urban poor.[53] It remains difficult to tell, however, how much of this alleged support stemmed from genuine loyalty and shared aspirations and how much rested on intimidation, blackmail, and coercion.

The Sendero's strategy calls for four major stages of struggle. During the first stage, the disciples of Guzman sought to mobilize cadres in the isolated highlands of south central Peru. Then in 1980 the group began its less clandestine phase of creating the social basis for a people's army and capturing weapons and needed supplies, during which time the *senderistas* made their presence known through symbolic attacks on public buildings. In 1982 the so-called third stage marked the initiation of the armed struggle in rural areas and the establishment of support bases in liberated zones. From there the *senderistas* hoped to send detachments throughout the nation to bring about conditions for the fourth stage— a people's war.[54] Chillingly close to its plan, during 1983 and 1984 violent attacks spread from Ayacucho to the central sierra to the coca growing regions in Huanuco to the coast and even to Lima itself.

Yet despite years of government and partisan neglect, the campesinos of the sierra are not necessarily a "sea in which the guerrillas swim like fish," as the Maoists would like to believe. To the contrary, there are many areas in which the campesino's interests have diverged from those of the Sendero Luminoso. Whereas the *senderistas* desire the destruction of the existing regime, most campesinos have concrete aspirations such as title to their land, government assistance in production and marketing, and improved educational and health services.

Moreover, in their struggle the Sendero has used tactics that tend to be counterproductive in winning over tradition-bound and suspicious campesinos. Leaving calling cards of dead dogs, red flags, or a blazing hammer and sickle on hillsides, *senderista* revolutionaries have employed intimidation and fear to produce strikes that paralyze whole towns and death threats to obtain the "collaboration" of businessmen in lowering prices on basic necessities. Given the assassinations of local officials and attacks on symbols of authority, the *senderistas* have created many liberated zones simply by default as government, business, and church officials fled for safety. Although they claim their sabotage activities are intended to draw attention to the extreme poverty and government repression found in the region, the destruction of agrarian research institutes and what little infrastructure that did exist, along with the summary executions of alleged opponents, have served to undermine the legitimacy of the Sendero's cause.[55] Besides their fanaticism, another reason for weak *senderista* support in rural regions has been their decreased ability to protect sympathizers from the government's anti-terrorist measures since the military took control of the area in 1983.[56] The real tragedy has been that the campesinos are the major victims, rather than the beneficiaries, of this guerrilla war, serving as targets for both the *senderista* attacks and the military's reprisals.

THE GOVERNMENT'S RESPONSE

There is little doubt that the Sendero's strategy was to discredit and destabilize Belaunde's administration by provoking repressive military measures against the popular masses and bringing about a direct confrontation between the government and the leaders of the political opposition. With 7.5 billion soles worth of damage from 1,230 terrorist attacks between April 1983 and March 1984 alone, the Belaunde government was under strong pressure to halt the *senderista* threat.[57] But how does a democracy deal with a violent group that rejects the principle of representative democracy? Given the revolutionaries' antipathy for the system, many in the government questioned the necessity of according the *senderistas* any of the civil and political rights guaranteed in the Constitution. The problem was that a democracy always demands some protection for its critics, and the methods employed by the Belaunde government to combat terrorism soon raised questions regarding human rights violations. The dilemma confronting the government was how to be strong and decisive enough to meet the terrorist challenge, without infringing upon constitutional procedures and basic civil liberties.

The consensus in the literature on counterguerrilla tactics is that if a democratic system is to survive, the elected government must be able to undermine the guerrillas' appeal so as to deny them a popular basis of support, and that this requires observing the law while firmly prosecuting those responsible for criminal acts, maintaining tight civilian control over the military, and insuring unified government support behind any extraordinary measures employed.[58] If it was to undermine the appeal of the Sendero, the Belaunde government had to be mindful of the "political" competition, not only with in-system opponents but also with out-of-system dissidents like the *senderistas*. In other words, the government had to accept that certain segments of the population would necessarily associate their future well being with either the government's survival, the election of opposition political parties, or even the victory of a revolutionary terrorist movement. Thus to deprive the *senderistas* of popular support, the government had to address the perceived needs and desires of those Peruvians who were most frequently either alienated from or ignored by the political system.

Initially, the Belaunde government downplayed the ideological appeal of the *senderista* message by labeling it foreign, fanatic, and destructive. They concentrated instead on the most visible elements of the *senderista* strategy—its campaign of terror. More importantly, Belaunde's cabinet, which tended to be transnationally oriented in both its economic strategy and conception of political events, also downplayed the impact that its policies might have in fomenting political unrest. But policies that sought to reverse the agrarian reform and alter the terms of trade for many agricultural products, that looked to large-scale high-tech projects rather than the development of rural infrastructure, and that generally neglected the needs of the poorest regions of the country did little to inspire widespread regime support, especially in the sierra.

If there is any validity to the theory of relative deprivation, the objective conditions for political violence certainly exist throughout much of Peru.[59] As Cynthia McClintock has convincingly documented, the income of peasants in Peru's southern highlands has fallen below subsistence levels, making their lives more miserable and difficult than they had been in the 1950s and 1960s.[60] This in large part was due to intense demographic pressure on very poor land. Ayacucho, for example, has one-fifth of a hectare of arable land per capita. The region has also tended to be a political vacuum. With 80 percent of the population illiterate (three times the national average), there was little incentive to organize or campaign in Ayacucho before the extension of the franchise in 1978.[61] After the somewhat stunted implementation of the military's agrarian reform, the peasants became more politicized. Some leftist parties did attempt to mobilize in the more remote areas of the sierra for the 1978 and 1980 elections, but these groups were really urban in orientation, and their alien concerns, as well as factional in-fighting, cost them support among the rural population. In their wake, the Sendero Luminoso found patches of fertile ground in which to organize. The most susceptible were disaffected educated youth who, because of poor economic conditions in rural as well as urban areas, could not find professional jobs for which they had trained.[62] Yet despite conditions that literally seemed to invite revolutionary violence in the highlands, the government was very slow to respond; in fact, it was not until January 1984 that the political-military commander of the emergency zone, General Huaman, decided to incorporate these socioeconomic problems "as an indispensible part of pacification."[63]

A popular government in a stable democracy can afford to assume that the number of out-of-system dissidents is relatively small in proportion to the target population. But the more fragile the democratic system, the more likely the government is to perceive a revolutionary threat in ever-expanding terms. Although there were many arrests during the Belaunde years, the police and military failed to crack the Sendero's security network, and little still is known about the organization. This lack of accurate information has contributed to the "artifical" growth of terrorist forces in Peru. Part of this artificial growth is a numbers game, which ironically served the interests of both guerrilla and anti-guerrilla forces. On the one hand, the guerrillas were happy to impress the government and their in-system rivals with exaggerated accounts of their strength and range of operations, but on the other hand, government officials were reluctant to discount these reports because they desired additional manpower and supplies to fight the guerrillas.

Another part of this artificial growth is increasing the enemy by definition or, in other words, guilt by alleged association. Frustrated by the lack of success in stopping the *senderistas*, some government politicians sought to place blame on their political opponents. Hard-liners in the AP-PPC coalition, with the assistance of pro-government newspapers, launched a vicious campaign against the parliamentary left. One AP deputy said that "IU leaders must be suspected of having ties with *Sendero Luminoso*."[64] Lima's *Expreso* identified all problems relating to terrorism as "emanating from foreign communist contacts with the leftist members of parliament who are dedicated to the destruction of democratic representation."[65]

The left interpreted these statements as a change in government attitude. Previously, only the recalcitrant right had indiscriminately identified the left with the terrorists.[66] But members of the government soon joined in making the parliamentary opposition a scapegoat. For instance, in April 1982 Minister Ulloa branded the government's leftist opponents "conspirators, irresponsible supporters of extremists promoting a climate of violence."[67] Although he claimed there were individuals in parliament who openly initiated subversion and applauded the Sendero Luminoso, he refused to name anyone when specifically asked to do so.

The IU has consistently denounced the Sendero Luminoso's terrorist activities because they are "contrary to majority feelings, originating in impatient, marginal cliques, [and] not representative of the masses."[68] Fully aware that terrorism provides conservative and military hard-liners with their strongest arguments to limit democratic freedoms, the IU has always maintained that the *senderistas* constitute a serious obstacle to creating a popular Marxist movement in Peru. In defending their legal and political rights, the IU and other leftist deputies attempted to intervene when innocent labor union officials and political leaders were caught in the government's security net, only to be criticized by the AP and PPC for hampering the drive against terrorism.

The government's patience with its in-system opposition was strained not only by its support for political "troublemakers" but also by its continual charges that the Belaunde administration was ultimately to blame for the guerrilla violence. The Marxist left that chose to pursue the non-violent, electoral route to power naturally felt some competition with the *senderistas* for popular support. Thus while the IU quickly and vehemently condemned terrorist attacks on the country's infrastructure, factories, and public buildings, its members argued that terrorism was necessitated by the government's policies and aggravated by its unresponsiveness to popular needs. As IU leader Alfonso Barrantes saw the situation, the guerrilla terrorism was only a response to the "terrorism of prices going up daily."[69] Such comparisons helped spur bitter attacks on groups and organizations that the administration considered far more critical of government actions than of the outrages committed by the *senderista* revolutionaries. Among the government's targets were research organizations in Peru funded by foreign sources, international organizations investigating human rights violations such as Amnesty International, and the international press that Belaunde claimed launched a "campaign to discredit Peru."[70]

Actually, there is little evidence of foreign links to the Sendero. Although an M–19 defector from Colombia said that the *senderistas* were in contact with other guerrilla movements in Latin America, their most important material support probably comes from international drug traffickers who allegedly paid the Sendero not to interrupt their operations in Ayacucho, Peru's third largest center of coca paste production.[71]

With domestic rather than foreign support being a key element, one of the most detrimental ways of adding to the anti-systemic opposition is through a backlash resulting from police and military excesses. As previously stated, the Belaunde regime was aware of this danger, and it consistently maintained that the strikes and terrorism were deliberately perpetrated to provoke such an over-reaction. But how does a democratic government respond effectively and justly when faced with such provocation? It would appear that the closer the association between these acts and generally recognized forms of violent or criminal behavior, the easier it is for the government to respond within the legal system. Conversely, the closer the association is to promoting a political objective or belief, the greater the danger of the government encroaching upon democratic principles. In other words, a democracy must separate beliefs from actions, and laws must respect those beliefs without putting the system at undue risk, all of which creates a very fine line for those who are responsible for formulating and implementing anti-terrorist measures.

The Anti-Terrorist Law, decreed in February 1981, was the work of government hard-liners. It was immediately criticized as draconian by the left, and even some conservative PPC members worried about its vagueness.[72] The law defines *terrorism* as "acts committed to provoke or maintain a state of alarm or terror, creating danger to life, health, or property of persons, destruction of public or private buildings, communication or transportation." Punishment for such acts ranges from ten to twenty years in prison. The most objectionable aspects of the law are those that make the law applicable to groups or organizations of three or more that use or advocate terrorism to achieve their aims. Indeed, being a member or leader of such a group can bring two to six years imprisonment. Using print, television, or radio to incite or commit acts of terrorism is punishable by four to twelve years, and one can receive a sentence of three to five years for publicly apologizing for either a terrorist act or a person accused of such an act. Not only was the opposition greatly concerned about the possibilities for abuse in interpreting and applying these articles, but some members of the governing majority, including former Minister of Interior de la Jara, also thought that enforcement rested too much on subjective judgments of intent, thus threatening individual liberties of free expression and association.[73] More importantly, de la Jara declared that the initial timing of the law was wrong in that the number of terrorist incidents was actually declining in early 1981, and there was still no loss of life directly attributable to the attacks.[74]

The success of such extraordinary legislation depends upon the perceived equity and efficacy of its application. The law's impact, in other words, has as much to do with civic psychology as it does with the government's enhanced capabilities for apprehending terrorists. In rural areas the 1981 Anti-Terrorist Law had little effect because, just as many suspected, it reflected a pronounced urban bias, and that is exactly where it was most often employed. As the Sendero's attacks became more audacious and destructive, the public demanded more protection. But curfews, spot identification checks, mass arrests, and other measures by the government contributed more to a growing atmosphere of suspicion and distrust than they did to the country's internal security.

Labor and neighborhood leaders, schoolteachers, and popular leftist politicians were harassed at demonstrations, strikes, and public gatherings. They and their followers were searched for "subversive" material such as books my Marx, Mariategui, and Lenin. After each of the Sendero's daring attacks in Lima, thousands of persons, including prominent opposition leaders, were detained in mass roundups generally conducted in the poorer areas of the city suspected of harboring guerrilla sympathizers. Most were released eventually since there was no evidence against them to warrant conviction. Nevertheless, hundreds of these individuals spent as many as two years in detention centers awaiting trial. These centers with their confined, monotonous environment have in similar situations around the world served as "staff colleges" for terrorism. In Peru, El Fronton prison was declared the country's "first liberated zone" when the *senderistas* began organizing the inmates.[75]

Given the civilian authorities' lack of success in dealing with the *senderistas*, a political-military command was established under General Noel y Moral in January 1983, creating a military "zone of emergency" in five of the seven provinces of Ayacucho. Calling in the military was seen as an act of last resort. Similar experiences outside of Peru suggested that increased military presence tended to escalate the level of violence and polarize opinion because the military's goal is usually to "identify the enemy and kill," as opposed to the police credo of apprehension and punishment.[76] Although Belaunde's cabinet knew that such a move would play into the hands of revolutionary propagandists as well as elicit parliamentary criticism, they were still not fully prepared for its eventual ramifications. By September 1983 Amnesty International had, for the first time, reported human rights violations in Peru, charging that security forces were involved in the torture, "disappearances," and extrajudicial executions of hundreds of persons in the process of counterinsurgency operations.[77]

The full scope of the tragedy in the Andes was finally brought to bear on the nation when on January 26, 1983, eight journalists were massacred in Uchurracay, Ayacucho. Although hundreds of peasants had already died in the highland turmoil, the deaths of these urban reporters focused national and international attention on the lack of government control in the area.[78] Although the opposition in parliament had been trying in vain for three years to establish a commission on terrorism, Belaunde moved quickly to create a blue-ribbon investigatory committee in the wake of protests over the Uchurracay killings. The committee's report sought to deal with all of the issues involved.[79] But the result was generally viewed as unsatisfactory because few relevant facts of the case were ever examined. It also contained no specific allegations of illegal activity on behalf of the government, nor did it hold anyone directly responsible for the death of the journalists. Instead, the commission said, "the larger historic blame for the bloodstained rocks and clubs in Uchurracay belongs to the great majority of us Peruvians."[80]

If nothing else, the report seemed to indicate that fault rested with the government's failure to maintain order in the highlands. Meanwhile, civil authorities were unable to proceed in the case because of a lack of cooperation from the political-military command in Ayacucho. As many editorials in both pro-government and opposition publications pointed out, the report, along with the military's defiant stance, was evidence that the indiscriminate killing of suspected senderistas was being legitimized in the name of state security.[81] To those concerned by these developments, the fine line between protecting and subverting democracy had now been crossed, and instead of bringing law and order to the region, the intervention of the military into Ayacucho had resulted in tragically confusing friend and foe and in drastically escalating the level of violence.

After the Uchurracay massacre, there was no appreciable decline in terrorist activity, despite government claims of increased numbers of senderistas killed. Although the statistics indicated that the Sendero should have had little support or should soon have been exterminated, many feared that the number of innocent campesinos killed had dramatically risen, but for official reasons the victims were being classified as senderistas. Indeed, the difficulty of determining who is killing whom had been a major problem since the military took control in Ayacucho. The death of the journalists, however, made an important difference in terms of government accountability, with more extensive coverage and monitoring of counterguerrilla operations by the press and independent agencies, both domestic and foreign. Claims that the military was defending democracy and protecting the public order met with charges that the armed forces employed Southern Cone tactics (i.e., kidnapping, torture, illegal detention, and indiscriminate helicopter bombings) to achieve their ends.[82] In addition, there were disclosures that the special counterinsurgency forces, the sinchis, who often dressed like campesinos, were responsible for some deaths attributed to the senderistas. Allegations also surrounded General Noel y Moral, former commander of the emergency zone: that he lied about several important aspects of the Uchurracay massacre and that he deliberately hindered attempts to investigate the incident thoroughly.[83] The general responded to these charges by stating that Ayacucho was in a state of war and that normal legal procedures did not apply.

Many hard-liners were tempted to call the situation in the highlands a "war"

Table 5.1
Estimates of Numbers of Persons Killed in Terrorist Activities (1980–85)

	Prior to Military Zone 1980-Dec. 31 1982[a]	Jan-Feb[b] 1983	1980- Aug 1983[c]	1980- March 1984[d]	1980[e] April 1985
Senderistas	48	243	1,033	1,620	4,700
Civilians/Campesinos	71	56	465	1,660	
Civil Authorities	9		18		
Police	37		59	148	
Military	1	—	3	12	——
Total	166	299	1,578	3,340	
Attacks			2,507		
Detained			2,119	800-1,000	3,000
Missing				1,500	

a) Special Commission Report in U.S. JPRS: 149.
b) Latin American Weekly Report, March 4, 1983: 4.
c) DESCO, Resumen Semanal, August 19-25, 1983: 3.
d) Latin American Weekly Report, July 13, 1984: 8. The
   difficulty with these figures is that they were hinted at in
   January (January 13, 1984: 10). As the results of a National
   Defense Council Report, the figures were repleased in March
   and still being presented as official totals in July 1984;
   however, they should be taken as indicative of trends only.
e) Latin American Weekly Report, June 28, 1985: 4-5. This is two
   times the number previously estimated!

to justify circumventing normal procedures. Former Minister of War Luis Cisneros Vizquerra argued that the Sendero could never be eliminated if every time the military confronts the enemy a lawyer, a journalist, and a photographer are present. His stated position is clear: "In wars there are no human rights . . . first get rid of subversion then worry about rights." General Cisneros even went so far as to suggest publicly that Peru should look to the Argentine military and learn from their "success" in saving the country for democracy.[84] Yet it was precisely the Argentine analogy that haunted the Belaunde administration. The government originally decided not to allow the military to launch an all-out offensive against the guerrillas because they not only feared a military coup but also "were afraid to create another repression like Argentina."[85] These concerns, though seemingly well founded, were apparently lost as the government's deepening paranoia led to counterproductive tactics of fighting terror with terror.

Until mid–1984 Belaunde had insisted that the government was able to control the Sendero without replacing the police with the military and without instituting martial law. However, the capability of the police became increasingly suspect when not only were their successes few but a major second front opened up in the jungle around Tingo Maria. Meanwhile, more than 8 percent of the police force (5,218 men) was being prosecuted on the basis of complaints from the emergency zone that ranged from negligence and inefficiency to extortion, robbery, and murder.[86] Thus in July 1984 a new phase of the counterinsurgency campaign was inaugurated by mobilizing 6,000 soldiers, marines, and airmen; granting the armed forces nationwide control over all anti-subversive activities; and creating a news commission comprised of the military chiefs of staff and representatives of government news bureaus to control counterintelligence information as well as material for the daily press.[87] In addition, rural militias were organized to provide armed, around-the-clock patrols for outlying communities, although critics quickly warned that such a move would only increase the number of civilian casualties.[88]

Despite the hard-liner's view that the regime had no duty to protect the enemy during wartime, government support can easily be eroded when the population perceives that the innocent are more likely to be the government's victims than the terrorists. Self-defined government exigencies were labeled as excesses. Indeed, so many hundreds died or disappeared that the reports out of Lima reached almost numbing proportions. But particular incidents like the massacre in Uchurracay focused enormous public attention on the problem of terrorism. In late August 1984 evidence was disclosed that implicated the police in the death of peasant leader and PSR party member Jesus Oropesa; a journalist, Jamie Ayala, disappeared after last being seen walking into the marine barracks in Huanta; the government publicly acknowledged that six missionaries had been killed by police; and fifty tortured and mutilated bodies were found by the attorney general's staff as they searched for individuals who had "disappeared."[89] These incidents so shocked and repelled Peruvians that the Catholic church and even pro-government newspapers and magazines spoke out against the way in which the counterinsurgency campaign was being conducted.[90] The staunchly pro-government journalist Manuel D'Ornelles, for one, called these actions "a gift to the extreme left," claiming that "nothing justifies the cowardice of nighttime anonymous disappearances."[91]

Government excesses in responding to terrorism and persecuting the guerrilla war drew the attention of international human rights organizations such as Amnesty International, Americas Watch, and the U.N. Commission on Human Rights. In August 1983 Amnesty International wrote to President Belaunde

asking for an investigation into reports of torture, disappearances, and extrajudicial executions by security police. Accompanying the letter was a memorandum
documenting more than 100 cases of alleged abuse. When Belaunde did not
respond, Amnesty International went ahead and published the information, an
action that immediately brought about vigorous denials by the government and
charges that the report was biased.[92] Yet by 1984 Amnesty International had
singled out Peru as the only country in Latin America where such abuses had
actually increased over the previous year.[93] In a concise, well-documented report,
Americas Watch (1984) summarized numerous policies and practices that it
alleged subverted democracy in the name of national security. At the forty-first
session of the U.N. Human Rights Commission in Geneva in February 1985, it
was reported that Peru accounted for the largest number of newly documented
cases of disappearances in 1984.[94] Belaunde thought that such international
criticism was distorted not only in that the government's actions were judged
far more harshly than those of the Sendero but in that it compounded the government's problems by playing directly into the hands of the guerrillas.

Criticism of the administration's policy was also heard from the commander
of the emergency zone, General Adrian Huaman Centeno. Huaman had replaced
the discredited General Noel y Moral in January 1984. A Quechua speaker,
Huaman pressed for significant increases in government social and economic
programs in the remote Andean regions that harbor the *senderista* terrorists. He
also showed a marked willingness to cooperate with civilian investigators regarding human rights violations and was largely responsible for securing the first
indictments against civil guardsmen accused of the massacre at Uchurracay.[95]

Huaman had persistently argued that the solution in Ayacucho was not military,
because if it were, "I could resolve it in minutes," he said.[96] "We are talking
about human beings, of forgotten towns. . . . ignored for 170 years for which we
are now reaping the results." General Huaman asked for more than 70 million
soles in assistance for the region, but by August only 1.5 million had been
received. Ironically, it was Huaman's reiteration of his position that led to his
abrupt dismissal by Belaunde on August 28, 1984. Seeking a scapegoat after
the discovery of the mass graves near Huanta, the government charged that the
general's emphasis on socioeconomic and political problems was "mistaken";
pacification must come first. The primary reason for the general's downfall,
however, was due to the fact that he had become a major political liability for
the government. As the pro-government publication *Caretas* described Huaman's
predicament, he was scorned by the right for his views on increasing government
economic assistance, while the left, in praising him, temporarily overlooked his
previous responsibility for alleged military excesses.[97] Huaman was succeeded
by Colonel Wilfredo Mori.

The continuing problem was the administration's inability to formulate successful policies to erode the *senderista's* base of support and to concentrate
instead on counterinsurgency programs that failed to eliminate the guerrillas
through increased firepower. Stricter laws and executive *decretos* resulted in

bulging prison populations and overcrowded court dockets but had little effect on deterring terrorist attacks. Instead, the government appeared weak and vulnerable as the Sendero repeatedly, and at times spectacularly, disrupted public services, especially electric power and rail transportation between the highlands and the coast. Moreover, the government seemed uncaring in that while willing to suspend constitutional guarantees, it was reluctant to extend economic assistance to the areas under siege.

The combined weight of the country's serious economic problems and a guerrilla war denied the government a broad basis of support for its programs, either in parliament or among the population. The depth of popular dissatisfaction with the government became apparent in the 1983 municipal elections, when the AP suffered a cataclysmic defeat by polling only 15 percent of the vote, one-third of its presidential total. The AP lost in all of the departmental capitals but one, and in Lima only a single district mayor was elected from the AP, down from twenty-three in 1980. The most significant opposition victory was that in Lima of the IU's leader, Dr. Barrantes, who became the first Marxist ever elected mayor of a South American capital.[98]

The election represented a clear rejection of the economic, social, and political policies of the Belaunde regime, and for the first time in Peruvian history, parties representing the masses won significant control at the local level as the APRA polled 34 percent and the IU 30 percent of the vote nationwide. But the election was also a rejection of the Sendero Luminoso, which attempted to have the government cancel the elections by launching a major terrorist offensive in the weeks before the November voting date.[99] Nevertheless, elections were cancelled in only four Ayacuchan provinces, and turnout nationwide was a respectable 70 percent. More importantly, as the election results showed, there were viable political alternatives within the Peruvian democratic system, as the AP's vulnerability was exposed with the 1985 national elections looming on the horizon.

PROSPECTS FOR THE FUTURE

The survival of Peruvian democracy depends upon the country's continued commitment to the democratic process, the willingness of the population to seek alternatives within the system, and the military's acceptance of their constitutional role of remaining on the sidelines despite Peru's serious internal problems. Although struggling against seemingly insurmountable difficulties, there is still reason to believe that Peru's redemocratization of the 1980s has been qualitatively different from previous attempts at reform, thus providing a better chance for democracy's survival.

The first of several positive signs was the 1985 national elections and the resulting transition as the AP peacefully turned power over to its major opponent, the Apristas. Key to this turnover was Belaunde's personal commitment to democratic government and his concern for his legacy to Peru. The fatherly leader was gravely disappointed by his party's crushing defeat in the 1985 elections. His party had underestimated the substantive changes made during the military *docenio* and was consequently out of step with the times and popular demands. The AP's economic policies, which promoted large-scale public works projects and long-term investment, provided few immediate gains for the masses who were experiencing a sharp decline in their standard of living. The government was plagued by charges of corruption regarding construction contracts, government purchasing policies, import-export irregularities, and even drug dealings. Embarrassed by international allegations of government repression and human rights violations, frustrated by the continued guerrilla threat, and plagued by weak internal organization, the AP appeared to have little choice but to accept its defeat. Now that the party is out of power, it is reasonable to expect the AP's fifteen congressmen will work just as diligently as had the APRA and the IU delegates before them to maintain respect for minority rights and representation. The question is what role the party will play in opposition. Assuming the leaders remain dedicated to reviving the AP, their options include aligning with the center-right Convergencia Democratica (CODE) or staking out a position for the AP in the center with a better grassroots organization.

The military's acceptance of the APRA's legitimate claim to govern was yet another milestone in Peruvian political development. Although the military and the APRA made their peace in 1977, the demise of Haya de la Torre and the question of the party's composition and future direction may still be a cause of concern for some members of the armed forces. APRA leaders, however, appear confident that the armed forces have become "more committed to democracy" and are "willing to let APRA have its chance to rule." Indeed, the military seems to have little desire to take on responsibility for governing the crisis-ridden nation. It believes, probably with good reason, that international assistance will be more readily forthcoming to a civilian regime, and perhaps most important, it sees its role as best defined in defeating the guerrilla challenge. The goodwill of the military may have been gained in June 1985, when the AP, with the APRA's active assistance, passed legislation allowing the military and police personnel to be tried in military tribunals when charged with offenses committed in the emergency zone. This gave the military authority it had long sought in its campaign against the *senderista* threat.[101]

The best indicator for the reconstituted system's chances of success is the overwhelming popular support for democratic processes and political competition. In April 1985 the Peruvian people renewed their democratic contract when 92 percent of the eligible voters turned out, a high percentage even in a nation with obligatory voting. In the face of the worst economic situation in the century, they gave a resounding majority to the opposition parties (70 percent). Just as resolutely they denounced the violent path to change as the Sendero's call to boycott the elections went unheeded despite threats, intimidation, and minor disruptions.

Finally, the enthusiasm and optimism generated in mid–1985 by the APRA victory may serve to revitalize sagging national confidence. The youthful, charasmatic president, Alán Garciá, won by such a margin over the second-place candidate, the IU's Alfonso Barrantes, that the latter withdrew from the scheduled run-off election. More importantly, the APRA has a working majority in both houses of congress, enhancing the chances for political stability and a coherent policy orientation.

But treatment of the opposition is still a major question. The Belaunde government's response to in-system political competition, as well as to revolutionary terrorism, was to strengthen its control over the reins of power. This involved attempts to depoliticize certain issues by issuing executive *decretos*, to control regional and municipal politics through state centralization, to reduce public political protests by outlawing strikes, and to eliminate guerrilla violence by counterinsurgency operations. However, none of these maneuvers succeeded in lessening either popular dissent or the terrorist threat. Likewise, the AP's frustration with the leftist opposition in parliament resulted in infringements upon democratic rights, but again these actions did nothing to improve the economic and social conditions that contributed to popular disaffection.

For the AP, the democratic challenge was more potent than the revolutionary one, and it is likely to be the same for the APRA. As a party whose experience has consisted almost entirely of opposition, obstructionist tactics with little practice at negotiating, compromise, or coalition building from a majority position, García and the APRA must cultivate the capacity to guarantee others the rights that the APRA has previously been denied. This challenge will not be easy for a party that has inherited a bankrupt nation wracked by popular unrest and a persistent guerrilla movement. Thus the APRA is confronted by the dual dilemma of how to alleviate a revolutionary threat without violating democratic freedoms and how to respond to opposition challenges without subverting the democratic process.

NOTES

1. *U.S. Joint Publication Research Service*, 84006, pp. 59–60.

2. David Scott Palmer, "Reformist Military Rule in Peru, 1968–80," in Robert Wesson, ed., *New Military Politics in Latin America* (New York: Praeger, 1982), p. 143; Julio Cotler, "Democracy and National Integration in Peru," in Cynthia McClintock and Abraham F. Lowenthal, eds., *The Peruvian Experiment Reconsidered* (Princeton, N.J.: Princeton University Press, 1983), p. 35; Victor Villanueva, "Peru's 'New' Military Professionalism: The Failure of the Technocratic Approach," in Stephen M. Gorman, ed., *Post-Revolutionary Peru: The Politics of Transformation* (Boulder, Colo.: Westview Press, 1982), p. 166.

3. Gorman, *Post-Revolutionary Peru*; Abraham F. Lowenthal, "The Peruvian Experiment Reconsidered," in Cynthia McClintock and Abraham Lowenthal, eds., *The Peruvian Experiment Reconsidered* (Princeton, N.J.: Princeton University Press, 1983), pp. 414–430.

4. Lowenthal, "The Peruvian Experiment Reconsidered," pp. 420–422.

5. Henry Dietz, *Poverty and Problem-Solving under Military Rule: The Urban Poor*

in Lima, Peru (Austin: University of Texas Press, 1980); Evelyne Huber Stephens, *The Politics of Workers' Participation: The Peruvian Approach in Comparative Perspective* (New York: Academic Press, 1980); Cynthia McClintock, *Peasant Cooperation and Political Change in Peru* (Princeton, N.J.: Princeton University Press, 1981).

  6. Sandra L. Woy-Hazleton, "The Return of Partisan Politics in Peru," in Stephen M. Gorman, ed., *Post-Revolutionary Peru: The Politics of Transformation* (Boulder, Colo.: Westview Press, 1982), p. 36.

  7. Robert J. Alexander, ed., *Aprismo: The Ideas and Doctrines of Victor Raul Haya de la Torre* (Kent, Ohio: Kent State University Press, 1973); Grant Hilliker, *The Politics of Reform in Peru: The Aprista and Other Mass Parties of Latin America* (Baltimore: The John Hopkins University Press, 1968); Harry Kantor, *The Ideology and Program of the Peruvian Aprista Movement* (Berkeley: University of California Press, 1953); Peter F. Klaren, *Modernization, Dislocation, and Aprismo: The Origins of the Peruvian Aprista Party* (Austin: University of Texas Press, 1973).

  8. Villanueva, "Peru's 'New' Military Professionalism," p. 167.

  9. Woy-Hazleton, "The Return of Partisan Politics in Peru," pp. 48–49.

  10. Ibid., pp. 54–55.

  11. Villanueva, "Peru's 'New' Military Professionalism," p. 176.

  12. Ibid., p. 178, Palmer, "Reformist Military Rule in Peru, 1968–80," p. 143.

  13. *Latin American Weekly Report*, May 25, 1984, p. 4.

  14. Ibid., July 20, 1984, p. 9.

  15. DESCO, *Resumen Semanal*, June 27-July 3, 1981, p. 3.

  16. Ibid., November 8–14, 1980, pp. 12–14; June 27-July 3, 1981, pp. 10–11.

  17. Ibid., June 13–19, 1981, p. 11.

  18. *Caretas*, October 22, 1984, p. 12.

  19. DESCO, *Resumen Semanal*, March 14–20, 1981, p. 1.

  20. Fernando Tuesta Soldevilla, *Elecciones Municipales: Cifras y Escenario Politico* (Lima: DESCO, 1983), p. 27.

  21. DESCO, *Resumen Semanal*, March 14–20, 1981, p. 1.

  22. Ibid., November 2–8, 1984, p. 3.

  23. Ibid., March 13–19, 1982, p. 1.

  24. Ibid., June 26-July 2, 1982, p. 7.

  25. Ibid., January 20–29, 1984, p. 5.

  26. Ibid., February 3–23, 1984, p. 6.

  27. Ibid., October 10–16, 1981, p. 3.

  28. Ibid., January 17–23, 1981, p. 3.

  29. Ibid., January 15–21, 1983, p. 4.

  30. Ibid., August 6–14, 1981, p. 4.

  31. Ibid., October 17–23, 1981, p. 4.

  32. Ibid., October 10–16, 1981, p. 3.

  33. Ibid., September 4–10, 1982, p. 2: September 18–25, 1982, p. 2.

  34. Ibid., August 16–22, 1981, p. 3.

  35. Ibid., November 28-December 4, 1981, p. 4; December 5–15, 1981, p. 9.

  36. David Werlich, "Peru: The Shadow of the Shining Path," *Current History* 83 (February 1984): 78.

  37. DESCO, *Resumen Semanal*, January 10–16, 1981, p. 1.

  38. Ibid., September 12–18, 1981, p. 1.

  39. *El Comercio*, January 16, 1981, p. 1.

40. DESCO, *Resumen Semanal*, February 25-March 3, 1983, p. 2; March 23–29, 1984, p. 1.

41. Ibid., March 2–8, 1984, p. 1.

42. Ibid., March 4–10, 1983, p. 1; March 11–17, 1983, p. 1; *Latin American Weekly Report*, March 18, 1983, p. 7.

43. DESCO *Resumen Semanal*, March 4–10, 1983, p. 1; March 11–17, 1983, p. 1; *Latin American Weekly Report*, March 18, 1983, p. 7.

44. DESCO, *Resumen Semanal*, March 16–23, 1984, pp. 1–2.

45. *Latin American Weekly Report*, January 13, 1984, p. 10; March 2, 1984, p. 6.

46. *U.S. Joint Publication Research Service*, 82202, p. 58.

47. Cynthia McClintock, *"Sendero Luminoso:* Peru's Marxist Guerrillas," *Problems of Communism* 32 (September-October 1983): 19–34; David Scott Palmer, "From Mao to Mariategui in Rural Peru: The Origins and Evolution of *Sendero Luminoso,* 1963– 1983" (Unpublished paper, New England Council of the Latin American Studies Association, University of New Hampshire, 1983).

48. *Caretas*, December 22, 1981, p. 30; *Latin American Regional Report*, January 23, 1981, p. 2.

49. *Caretas*, November 2, 1981, pp. 49–50.

50. *Latin American Regional Report*, January 23, 1981, p. 2.

51. Ibid., June 28, 1985, pp. 4–5.

52. *U.S. Joint Publication Research Service*, 82202, p. 58.

53. Ibid., 82154, p. 173.

54. Ibid., 82202, p. 58; *Oiga*, November 29, 1982, pp. 20–34.

55. *U.S. Joint Publication Research Service*, 82202, p. 57.

56. Cynthia McClintock, "Government Policy, Rural Poverty, and Peasant Protest in Peru: The Origins of the *Sendero Luminoso* Rebellion" (Unpublished paper, American Political Science Convention, Chicago, 1983), p. 14.

57. DESCO, *Resumen Semanal*, May 11–17, 1984, p. 2.

58. Juliet Lodge, ed., *Terrorism: A Challenge to the State* (Oxford: Martin Robertson, 1981); Nathan Leites and Charles Wolf, Jr., *Rebellion and Authority: An Analytic Essay on Insurgent Conflicts* (Chicago: Markham Publishing Co., 1970); G. Bingham Powell, Jr., *Contemporary Democracies: Participation, Stability, and Violence* (Cambridge: Harvard University Press, 1982); Paul Wilkinson, *Terrorism and the Liberal State* (London: Macmillan, 1977); Grant Wardlow, *Political Terrorism: Theory, Tactics, and Counter-Measures* (Cambridge: Cambridge University Press, 1982).

59. Ted Robert Gurr, *Why Men Rebel* (Princeton, N.J.: Princeton University Press, 1970), pp. 22–56.

60. McClintock, "Government Policy, Rural Poverty, and Peasant Protest in Peru," pp. 8–10.

61. Werlich, "Peru: The Shadow of the Shining Path," p. 80.

62. McClintock, "Government Policy, Rural Poverty, and Peasant Protest in Peru," p. 13.

63. *U.S. Joint Publication Research Service*, 84027, p. 138.

64. DESCO, *Resumen Semanal*, April 17–23, 1982, p. 2.

65. Ibid., February 27-March 5, 1982, p. 2.

66. Ibid., March 20–26, 1982, pp. 2–3; September 4–10, 1982, p. 3.

67. Ibid., April 14–20, 1982, p. 2.

68. Ibid., March 20–26, 1982, pp. 2–3.

69. Ibid., December 30, 1983-January 5, 1984, p. 2.

70. Ibid., August 19–25, 1983, p. 3; *Latin American Weekly Report*, August 26, 1983, p. 2.

71. *U.S. Foreign Broadcast Information Service*, December 13, 1983, p. 1; McClintock, *"Sendero Luminoso,"* p. 23.

72. DESCO, *Resumen Semanal*, March 7–13, 1981, p. 2; February 25-March 3, 1983, p. 2.

73. Ibid., March 7–13, 1981, p. 2.

74. Ibid., February 1–20, 1981, p. 10.

75. *San Francisco Chronicle*, March 20, 1983.

76. Wilkinson, *Terrorism and the Liberal State*, p. 150.

77. Amnesty International, *Peru: Amnesty International Briefing* (London: Amnesty International Publications, 1985), p. 4.

78. DESCO, *Resumen Semanal*, January 29-February 4, 1983, pp. 1–3; July 22-August 4, 1983, p. 5; *Latin American Weekly Report*, June 10, 1983, p. 3; Mario Vargas Llosa, "Inquest in the Andes," *New York Times Magazine*, July 31, 1983, pp. 18–22.

79. *U.S. Joint Publication Research Service*, 83262, pp. 133–157.

80. Ibid., 83262, p. 157.

81. DESCO, *Resumen Semanal*, January 29-February 4, 1983, p. 3.

82. Ibid., June 17–23, 1983, p. 2; *Peru Update*, July 1983, p. 3.

83. DESCO, *Resumen Semanal*, June 1–7, 1983, p. 3.

84. Ibid., September 14–20, 1984, p. 3.

85. *New York Times*, September 2, 1984.

86. *Latin American Weekly Report*, July 29, 1984, p. 9; *New York Times*, September 2, 1984.

87. *Latin American Weekly Report*, August 24, 1984, p. 2; July 27, 1984, p. 9.

88. Ibid., September 21, 1984, p. 8.

89. DESCO, *Resumen Semanal*, August 24–30, 1984, pp. 2–3.

90. Ibid., September 7–13, 1984, p. 3.

91. Ibid., August 24–30, 1984, p. 3.

92. Amnesty International, *Peru*, p. 4.

93. *Latin American Weekly Report*, November 2, 1984, p. 7.

94. *International Herald Tribune*, February 13, 1985, p. 5.

95. *U.S. Joint Publication Research Service*, 84027, p. 137.

96. DESCO, *Resumen Semanal*, August 24–30, 1984, p. 2.

97. Ibid., August 31-September 6, 1984, pp. 1–2.

98. Tuesta Soldevilla, *Elecciones Municipales*, pp. 17–19.

99. *U.S. Joint Publication Research Service*, 84007, pp. 66–68.

100. *Latin American Weekly Report*, June 8, 1984, p. 3.

101. Ibid., June 14, 1985, p. 9.

6

Controlled Political Transition in Brazil: *Abertura* as a Process for a Gradual Sharing of Political Power

Wilfred A. Bacchus

Because of the size and complexity of the Brazilian polity, analysts have resorted to various models as a means to better describe the present military regimes. The choice of fascist examples, however, contributes more confusion than clarity in depicting Brazil's political system. In the sense of closely resembling aspects of the Salazar-Caetano governments of the 1932–74 period, Brazil is not now nor is it approaching a "Portugalized" system.[1] Even less similarity can be found to warrant comparison with the Italian Model of Mussolini.[2] The closest comparison one could make would be to note certain similarities between the five military governments of Brazil since 1964 and Getulio Vargas's *Estado Novo* dictatorship of 1937–45. The two principal aspects of similarity lie in the planned effort to remake the former, allegedly corrupt political systems of the 1930s and 1960s into broader (but hardly democratic) systems and in the ultimate polarization of their fragmented political elites into pro/anti-regime camps.[3] Beyond those points, comparisons become too strained and inaccurate to be useful.

How, then, shall we describe Brazil's military governments? They were never purely military, although civilian politicians, who at times wielded more significant decision powers than military presidents, seemed always to understand clearly that there could be no serious contention on their part for nominal leadership of the government. It was never a personalist dictatorship, although at times in each president's tenure, when faced with challenge from the legislative or judicial branches, the executive authority resorted to use of decree powers to impose his will. Brazil is best judged as belonging to the genre of bureaucratic-authoritarian (B-A) systems of types but with its own, unique Brazilian character.[4]

The B-A typology is appropriate in that the Brazilian regimes have been decidedly bureaucratic in structure, delineation of authority, and behavior and highly authoritarian in that the regimes' linkages to a popular majority have been weak or non-existent. Even following extensive liberalization under the Figuereido government's *abertura* (opening) program, which terminated the long period of military rule, the leadership has not surrendered its most comprehensive, emergency powers under the broad aegis of the Law of National Security.[5] Briefly, that law leaves to military authorities the latitude to define offenses deemed threatening to the national security of the country, the concepts of which are dealt with further in the following section, and to military high courts the right to rule on the constitutional/civil rights interpretations involved.

The idea of the "Brazilian character" presents the greatest difficulty to attempt to define. Various observers have used the term *pragmatism* to explain what it is to be a Brazilian politician (or even a citizen contesting another for a parking space). Combativeness, as an approach, is generally considered much less admirable than gaining the desired end by wits alone. Even in those times of apparent testing of a regime's very survival, as in the 1969–71 period, there was a demonstrated willingness on the part of the powerful to accept compromises for the sake of what were seen as higher, long-range objectives. As Miguel Arraes explained, on many occasions when tensions arose between the central government and various elements of the population, they were resolved by the introduction of small changes.[6] The last phrase, put in the familiar Brazilian expression *fazer um jeito*, really means that when an impasse threatens to halt all parties, you can merely take a little leap over the obstacles, as a hurdler would do. But there is more to the Brazilian character than this pragmatism. There seems to be a natural sense of willingness to accommodate, a bonhommie, that is fundamental to being Brazilian. Thus the uses of police brutality and torture, as a means to extract vital counterguerrilla intelligence in the middle three military regimes (Artur da Costa e Silva, Emilio Medici, and Ernesto Geisel), have seriously offended too many. Their orientation does not incline them toward defense of the heavily security-minded posture taken then in combatting what was not a very large guerrilla threat. Those excesses have been more than adequately chronicled elsewhere in the North American news media and academy but less well investigated—and now no doubt too late to be very effective or fair—by juridical bodies such as the United Nations and Inter-American Human Rights Commissions or by independents such as Amnesty International.[7]

If we are to insist upon allowance for a particularly benevolent cultural trait among Brazilians, one must logically ask how those excesses could take place.

Without entering into an attempted defense of the governments involved, it appears there was inadequate supervision in many if not most cases, in an atmosphere that placed far too much emphasis upon security and, in terms of middle-to-lower rank officers and sergeants, expectation of reward for effectiveness with too little regard for the methods employed.

It would be much too simplistic to imply that the past twenty years' history can be summed up as a bad era, followed by entry of one of authentic goodwill (Figuereido). In fact, the story is complex and convoluted, as I will attempt to explain. By definition, *liberalization* need not necessarily imply immediate or even eventual *democratization*, as that term is understood in the modernized world. Confusion enters, however, in deciding if in each of the past military regimes the leadership fully intended all that the term implies, in promising— as each leader did—to return to democratic political processes during his administration. Since the end result in each of the first four military governments was to leave to the successor a more rigid and authoritarian system than was inherited, we have in store a complicated object for study in Brazil's authoritarian period. Since the object of this particular study is the process and the difficulties encountered in attempting liberalization or redemocratization, we are limited to referring the reader to adequate analyses of Brazil's past authoritarianism. Fortunately, Brazil has been an object of many good studies, of its political system during the past few years.[8]

Growing controversies concerning the increased maldistribution of personal incomes had greatly troubled the administrations of General Ernesto Geisel (1974–79) and continued in the Figuereido government (1979–85). From an already poor income inequality index (GINI) of 0.49 in 1960, past policies of investment had so aggravated the condition that the index reached 0.60 by 1976.[9] It is unclear whether the result was fully anticipated, for it certainly impacted upon the governments' popular support. The supreme objective was to lower inflation from the 100 percent range it had reached briefly in 1964 to a low of 15 percent in 1972, at which point the slight easing of austere wage policies and modest redistribution caused the inflation rate to rise slowly.[10]

The governmental austerity policy necessitated a tightening of authority, beginning with the inauguration of Marshal Artur da Costa e Silva in March 1967, concurrently with the redrafted Constitution. As a result, the government's powers of investigation, decision making, appointment, and enforcement were highly centralized from 1967 until changes were instituted early in the Figuereido administration. In this chapter consideration focuses on the question of whether this centralization of power was a behavioral syndrome typical of many militarized regimes, or if it was, as often claimed, a means toward the regimes' nationalistic aims. As the analysis of steps taken in the liberalization process unfolds, it will be equally important to consider what factors led the Geisel and Figuereido governments voluntarily to surrender some authoritarian controls in proclaimed motives of opening the system.

If overdue, it is nevertheless true that a genuine liberalization has taken place in Brazil in the 1980s. Within his first two years as president, Figuereido emptied the prisons of "political prisoners" (best defined as those whose offenses are based upon the Law of National Security), welcomed back several thousand potential enemies of his regime from exile abroad, and abolished the artificial, unpopular, two-party political system by which Congress had been kept under control. He also did away with the absolute decree powers that previous presidents had wielded under Institutional Act #5, which allowed congress to be dismissed, political and civil rights of individuals to be suspended, and tight controls over public media and speakers to be imposed.

Although *abertura* may have been based on genuinely democratic motivations, its primary intent was to divide and thereby diminish the effectiveness of the government's opposition. In this, it succeeded to the extent that there was immediate fragmentation of the Brazilian Democratic Movement (MDB) Party, but at the same time, the pro-government National Renovating Alliance (ARENA) Party also split. Congress has not been as docile and controllable ever since; the government's ploy has in fact backfired. Yet *abertura* has had beneficial impact by stimulating the nascent, combative spirit of the politicians, rejuvenating the whole political arena in unanticipated ways.[11] Although it did not work perfectly, it proved to be more effective than repression as a means to counter radical opposition, and it earned respect abroad at a point when investor confidence was dwindling. Those were useful gains.

Redemocratization now faces an uncertain future, due to deep economic problems such as prolonged recession, astronomical inflation rates, rising poverty, years of drought in the Northeast region, and the world's highest cumulative external debt burden. The 1980s and probably much of the 1990s will surely entail an uphill struggle for even marginal economic growth and recovery, unless relief from each of these problems is somehow obtained. Just to repay interest on the country's $100 billion indebtedness absorbs almost half of Brazil's external foreign exchange earnings. This issue—whether to declare default or a debt moratorium, to join a suggested "debtor's cartel," or to continue sacrificially paying on that debt—occupies and divides both the administration and opposition political parties.

In addition to mentioning the influence of economic crises upon redemocratization, I earlier identified questions in need of explanation such as the authenticity of prior presidents' declaration of wanting to see liberalization begin and of president Figuereido's motives in relinquishing authoritarian controls. At the outset, I turn to the approach taken toward democratic processes in the first regime.

THE POLITICAL HERITAGE OF THE FIGUEREIDO REGIME (1964–79)

In the first year after 1964, when the military leadership claimed an absolute monopoly of political power, the national Congress represented an ornamental nuisance. True, it had a legitimizing constitutional function, but it was recessed at will in those rare instances when the legislators tried to oppose or even modify executive policy or to use the office to embarrass one of the presidents. The Costa e Silva (1967–69) and Medici (1969–74) administrations were noted for authoritarianism, but Ernesto Geisel also saw fit to dismiss Congress late in his term (1974–79) in order to decree constitutional changes that could insure the election of his chosen successor. There were periods when liberalization seemed imminent, and the leading civilian politicians seemed eager to play the accommodation game, but they faded with the appearance of new pressures or crises. As tabulated actions, taken with such apparent purposes, might suggest (see Appendix), one spate of liberalizations did occur in the first year of the government of General Emilio Garrasazu Medici.

Is it being too cynical if one asserts that liberalizations are routinely proclaimed, in most authoritarian regimes, when they amount only to convenient platitudes aimed at appeasing their critics? Based upon the vast differences between each president's words and his government's deeds, such a judgment has unquestionable merit. If there is any other valid assessment, its explanations will have to come through a review of the record, from a closer examination of the circumstances for policy-making in those days.

The "Liberal" Authoritarianism of Castello Branco

Several actions taken by President Humberto Castello Branco, shortly after his "election" by an obedient Congress (at the direction of the revolutionary high command), seemed highly authoritarian. Using arrogated emergency powers, he purged the legislature, had some members imprisoned or exiled, and thereafter controlled it. He decreed unprecedented investigative powers for many military commissions (IPMs), directed to ferret out subversive Communists in high positions within state, federal, or public corporation posts. Yet those who knew him best regarded Castello Branco as moderate, even liberal, in his sociological ideas, although he was known also as a soldier-scholar, somewhat reclusive and puritanical, and most decidedly anti-Communist. As army chief of staff (yet junior to the war minister and several other generals), he knew his support would be critical to the civil-military movement conspiring to oust President João Goulart. Therefore, he held out and agreed to support a coup only if and when the president committed any of several specified, threatening, unconstitutional acts. He did not seek the office but had the presidency urged upon him by virtue of his qualifications as an apolitical leader who, while subcommandant of Brazil's military "think tank," the Escola Superior de Guerra (National War College), had a central role in formulated national recovery plans. Since the Escola Superior de Guerra (ESG) combined civil-industrial leaders with military students in the nine-month course, his contacts were also useful.[12]

At the end of his second year as president, Castello Branco declared, in his speech inaugurating a new ESG course, "For a society to be democratic, it must have freedom of expressions of disagreement; for it to be viable, it is necessary that the areas of agreement outweigh those of disagreement.[13] The statement of high principle stands on its merits; however, evidence is clear that, for Castello Branco, keeping Brazil's society viable took precedence over democratic freedoms. He seems to have blundered for the sake of democracy (or democratic appearances) in October of the preceding year (1965), thereby encountering strong opposition with the high command, when he not only allowed direct election of state governors but also seemed to welcome this symbolic referendum on his regime's popularity. When the results appeared to be a repudiation instead, by the election of known opponents in several important states, he was able to see their right to take office preserved but only at great personal cost. Not only was his personal position weakened, but he became the reluctant sponsor of some draconian constitutional restrictions, including the abolition of existing political parties, by which the election of Costa e Silva as successor was insured.

Failed "Humanization" under Costa e Silva

Despite the absence of an opposition candidate for the presidency, General (in retirement, Marshal) Costa e Silva vigorously campaigned in all regions of Brazil, pledging to popularize and humanize what he and his military colleagues had named the "Revolution" of 1964. With his installation as second military president in March 1967, high public expectations existed concerning changes from the aloofness, technocratic authoritarianism, and especially unpopular favoritism toward American industrialists. An example of the latter was the approval by the Castello Branco government of the Hanna Mining Company's license application—an American multi-national, unsuccessful under the two previous administrations in gaining entry into competition with Brazil's own Rio Doce (CVRD) steel corporation.[14] For a while, by turning to a new cadre of civil and military technocrats of his own choosing, the Costa e Silva government seemed to have achieved some popularity. Because of the austerity policies decreed by the first military government and a number of reform measures promulgated in the last days of Castello Branco's government, Costa e Silva collected benefits without reaping the anger from those adversely affected by the new orders.

Disappointment over slowness and harder rather than softer socioeconomic policies soon lead to serious problems for the next president. Actually, he had been the target of a failed bomb attack in Recife several months before his inauguration, while he was no longer on active duty, no longer a governmental minister, and in an odd sense "between duties" as he carried his pre-election campaign to the Northeast in the popularization efforts cited above. Then, just before Brazil's independence anniversary day, in September of 1968 a leftist, opposition deputy enjoying legislative immunity brought the full wrath of the president down on the lower house of Congress by making a derogatory speech against the army. Pressed by the executive powers to adopt a special bill that would have lifted Moreira Alves' immunity (after which he would have been punished), enough ARENA legislators joined with the MDB opposition to defeat the measure. Frustrated and infuriated by that defiance, which persisted even after being recalled into special session, Costa e Silva closed Congress (never to be recalled during his term) and issued Institutional Act #5. Following that with purges, not only of Deputy Moreira Alves but of various supporters of his cause, the president did not seem to recognize that winning his battle on a relatively minor point might mean losing the war for higher causes.

Although the economy was improving rapidly, internal turmoil and increasingly brazen guerrilla attacks on banks, trade centers, and television stations raised public consciousness of the regime's naked authoritarianism. Costa e Silva's justice minister and other close advisers began preparing to reopen Congress under a revised Constitution, while also attempting a rapprochement with civil leaders, including for the first time leaders of the MDB opposition. But this confused others, so, responding to the reasonable question as to which political party would be his supporter group, Costa e Silva declared, "My party is the Olive Green [Army]; it is strong, and I can always call upon it when I have need of it."[15] Justice Minister Game e Silva confirmed the belief, shared by the president, that political parties ought to be monoliths, tightly controlled by their chosen leadership, and that Brazil's parties were unforgivably irresponsible in this respect.[16]

We can never know whether Costa e Silva's broken regime had enough vitality to have endured to its expected 1972 termination date, because the president was felled with a serious (ultimately fatal) stroke on August 29, 1969. His three service ministers, rather than see the government powers transferred to civilian Vice President Pedro Aleixo, declared the offices vacant (first, merely in emergency status) and ruled as a governing council for the next two months. Hardly had this unsettling news reached the public when, on September 4, American Ambassador C. Burke Elbrick was kidnapped and held for political ransom by the MR–8 revolutionary guerrilla group. Aside from demanding publication of their charges against the government, they required freedom for fifteen of the most notorious revolutionaries being held prisoner and safe transport for all to Cuba.[17] Perhaps no other governing body in Brazil except the temporary Junta could have allowed freedom for the Cuba-bound group; within a few days, that is what the Junta chose to do, in order to free Ambassador Elbrick unharmed.

Having decided that a new president should be selected, when in the early days of his illness it became clear that Costa e Silva would not soon recover, the problem of choosing a successor became urgent and also complex. During the next month an unusual form of "military democracy" took place, as each of the three military branches canvassed its leadership—in some cases down to the field commanders' level—about whom they preferred to have elected. Although several contenders came under serious consideration, finally it became clear that the choice would be the conservative protégé of Costa e Silva, General Emilio Garrastazu Medici, who then headed Brazil's National Intelligence Service (SNI). Medici was not only already present, familiar with the problems, and well regarded by his senior colleagues, but his SNI position made him the government expert on the growing guerrilla menace.

From Guerrilla Warfare to Great Plans under Medici

In a nationwide speech, before assuming the office, Medici delighted his radio and television audiences by calling for a renewed dialogue between the people and the government. He said, "In the march to development, the people cannot be mere spectators. They must be the principal protagonists. . . . Democracy and development are not resolved by government initiatives; they are the acts of the collective will that it is for the government to coordinate into national objectives."[18] Later, in public speeches in which he seemed to excel, Medici acknowledged that although the nation was prospering economically, the people were not doing so well, and he thought they should be better rewarded through redistributive wages.[19]

Although there continued to be periods of high drama and a few setbacks in the counterguerrilla efforts, Medici also had some exceptional assets to aid him in launching his administration. His predecessors had gained new technology and advice, mainly from the United States, and were as a result providing a far higher ratio of revenues to corporate and private incomes. Thus with a booming economy, Brazil stood on the threshold of opportunities for governmental investments in social and economic well being for the mass level of Brazilians to share. As the table in the appendix shows, several of the governmental initiatives undertaken in 1970 sounded as though real liberalism might be occurring. National and social integration and attempted rural improvements, together with land redistribution, held out hopes for the forgotten people of the land. Most of all, the illiterate population, which numbered almost half of all adult Brazilians, would be targeted for the MOBRAL (Mobilization for Brazilian Literacy) campaign. The Northeast was to come under renewed governmental investment toward overcoming its retarded development. States and local governments (*municipios*) were to begin receiving direct revenues from the federal government, replacing their own ineffective and inequitable tax levies and imposts. As the centerpiece of the program for national integration, the whole Amazonian region was to be opened up with new highways and riverine connectors. All of these plans, it should be noted, were expected to receive federal funding but also direct federal intervention.[20]

Since the Medici government acted under the optimum era of economic power and for a period almost equal to the length of the Castello Branco and Costa e Silva terms of the presidency combined, it would be fair to pause at this point to evaluate his regime's accomplishments. Leaving aside for the moment the guerrilla war that was waged and won in his term, his featured accomplishment was the dramatic TransAmazonica highway project, with the other programs taking lower billing and much less expenditure of funds. Although it had obvious appeals to pride, it appears to have had two primary motivations: keeping the Amazon basin from the potential control of foreign and domestic enemies of the government and serving to open up a huge colonization area with the intent of diverting migrant northeasterners away from Brazil's already urbanized Center-South areas and Brasilia. Although it did open up the area somewhat, the highway system has not drawn enough vehicular movement even to justify its maintenance, and it is thus appearing a decade later as a classic folly.[21] Other failures and mistaken or misdirected efforts contributed to the appearance of a regime that was either foolish or *entreguista* (disposed to deliver the country to outside purchasers for personal gain).[22] Not all of the Medici government's acts were judged faulty in execution; in some areas the criticism was that it was too aggressive and too consistently effective. An all-out campaign by the army in collaboration with state paramilitary forces succeeded, by the end of 1971, in eradicating all active *focos* while taking many guerrilla prisoners but also causing many more to "disappear."[23]

It seemed that Brazil in the 1970s conformed well to the adage, "success has many fathers, but failures remain orphans." When it became clear that the TransAmazon Highway inspired little commercial investment (except for the Carajas-Tucurui projects in central Para State, where rich mineral deposits and governmental assistance were irresistible, as described below), the maintenance, traffic, and ambitious colonization plans likewise suffered. But counterterrorism measures, hardly needed by 1972, tended to increase and inflict moral injuries on the government leadership. Giving the benefit of doubt, as Philippe Schmitter conceded in 1973, the acts of barbarism at the hands of the military and civil police may have taken place without the knowledge or means to prevent such abuses of the dissidents when they became political prisoners.[24] By failing to halt this state terrorism against its enemies, the probable result was to provoke greater numbers of dissidents to back the cause of the original Marxist guerrillas. Their suppressed evidence, in turn, provided justification to the military extremists of the hard-line to hold out against the growing opinion that authoritarian measures should be abandoned or at least ameliorated.[25] The real point is that the repressive measures did not end but, in fact, were expanded. Moreover, with an economic downturn beginning in 1974, with the state governments most affected initially, military police became the most visible part of the police force, as the state and local governments curtailed security expenses to meet budgetary limitations. The public response was thus to blame military authority for the repressive measures that only a minority faction believed were necessary. The most populous urban areas thereby increased the existing trend of antagonism toward continued military domination.

After winning with almost embarrassing majorities in the 1970 congressional elections, the serious setback suffered by the ARENA Party in the Center-South urban, industrial regions came as somewhat of a shock to the military leadership. Aside from the factors that have been suggested, these more politically sensitized areas more than likely also resented the imposition, with the old Congress's approval, of the fourth army general as next president, promising what seemed to be another five years of arbitrary and repressive rule.

Recession and Attempted Normalization under Geisel

Brazil was going through both an economic retrenchment and a transition of the two competing military factions when the military's selection of its new presidential team was being worked out in late 1973 to early 1974. The impact of the oil embargo was not significant, and the full effect on the economy of the quadrupled price of crude oil had not been fully felt. However, selection of General Ernesto Geisel—clearly identified with the Castello Branco moderate internationalists of the ESG line—had to be balanced with a certain number of trustworthy affiliates of the authoritarian bloc. The economy was also appearing overheated, and there were signs that the growth pattern of the past few years could not be sustained much longer. Promises of renewed liberalization emanating from the new leadership were therefore not to be dismissed as impossible, but the internal opposition within the military elite had available means to keep President Geisel in check, if it believed he was exceeding the agreed-upon limitations on his personal power by his declared *distensão* (decompression) program.

The 1974 elections of deputies and senators to the national Congress provided a rude awakening to the optimism of the new regime, which had anticipated no real challenge from the opposition MDB slate. When the vote was counted, the surprised ARENA Party and leadership groups found they now faced a more united, strong opposition of nearly half of the Chamber of Deputies and twenty new opposition senators (out of sixty-six total seats). With those numbers, the MDB group could limit but not overturn major policy initiatives of the president and his ARENA majority, particularly in the usual cases in which caucusing groups within a party (*sublegendas*) enjoyed freedom of choice.

In response to the disappointing congressional election results and consistent with his promised liberalization measures, Geisel let up on austerity measures such as a tight credit and money-supply doctrine, leading to an increase in inflation from 15 to 30 percent within his first year in office.[26] Expensively obtained capital goods and technology, imported from abroad for elaborate development plans made several years earlier, accounted for most of the mid–1970s inflationary spending, but the private consumptive sector also made its influence felt upon the sagging economy. The "decompression" program faced seemingly insurmountable difficulties of both political and economic origin. As Norman Gall expressed it:

Any real democratization, first of all, would mean such a large transfer of wealth to improve the consumption levels of the poor as to deprive the country of the capital needed for intensive economic development. Brazil is not unique in this, of course, as the conflict between the interests of consumption and capital-formation also pose one of the main challenges to the coherence and survival of advanced industrial democracies in future decades. This friction will become increasingly important, and will increasingly affect countries like Brazil, as huge sums will have to be saved and mobilized to finance the more complex technologies and organizations needed to maintain the flow of food and raw materials over greater distances to markets from soils and deposits that are less accessible or less productive naturally than those which have met the world's more modest needs in the past. . . . Countries like Brazil that originally were at the periphery of the world economy, consuming little while exporting wealth to the metropolitan centers, have become themselves centers of consumption, competing for resources with the older core areas.[27]

The point about turning to less accessible, more distant sources of raw materials brings up the huge capital investments in the Carajas mineral complex and the still-uncompleted Tucurui Dam, which is to furnish the cheap hydroelectric power needed to make the whole complex feasible. Located along or near the Tocantins River, the Carajas area has been estimated to contain high-grade iron ore in quantities equal to or even exceeding the total of previously known iron ores in the rest of the world, along with vast quantities of manganese and lesser amounts of tin, copper, gold, and diamonds that certainly merit immediate national investment.[28] Misfortune and perhaps also mismanagement have plagued the Carajas development project from the beginning of the 1970s, when Amazonian infrastructural investments were enthusiastically launched with the TransAmazon highway construction. Until 1984 very little mineral production was realized, principally due to two problems: divisions within the government over the issue of foreign investment and the retarding consequences of the existing state of underdevelopment in the whole area. Naturally, the first and the second problems were very much inter-related, since external investors were understandably slow to commit their money while the Carajas area lacked such things as serviceable roads and electric-power supplies. After the 1974 Organization of Petroleum Exporting Countries' (OPEC's) decisions, concerning the vast quantities of oil that Brazil imports, ended the Brazilian economic boom, fiscal constraints forced heavy borrowing and retrenchment on the government's planned investments toward both power-generating and road-building infrastructural programs.

Concerning the "misfortune" aspect, one could cite the economic consequences of the 1973 Middle East war—certainly in no way connected with Brazil's own policies or actions—that had come at the critical stage when major expenditures for development and importation of expensive technology were essential. Also, when newly elected President Geisel was promising decentralization and liberalization of his administration, the heightened consciousness of defensive nationalists worldwide, and very much present in Brazil, led them to turn to the previously undervalued and underprotected natural resources of their nation. Carajas soon became the focus of a nationalistic outcry against the government's leaders, whom they charged with both corruption and *entrequismo* (delivery of the national wealth to foreign interests for a share in the proceeds). Their anger was understandable; as further amplified below, the resources were being shared with an American consortium, U.S. Steel and Hanna Mining Company.[29] The sad aspect, however, was that Brazil could not hope to fund the Carajas project alone, and yet early receipt of its revenues was urgently needed to keep Brazil's fiscal resources solvent and its growing population fed. Equally sad, it would be too much to expect the nationalistic element to accept such an argument, and they did not.[30] The circumstances were tailor-made to serve the purposes of anti-regime agitators, many of whom soon bore the label of Marxists or Communists. Naturally, it was somewhat of a no-win situation for the government. The central region of the state of Para, especially around Arguinana and Maraba, has harbored an insurgent group variously described as Marxists and as members of a Catholic Christian *Comunidade* throughout much of the 1970s, managing to frustrate occasional military sweeps seeking to locate and destroy its organization.[31] Although the conflict in that region evidently began as a struggle on the part of *posseiros* (land squatters) of more than ten years' duration—therefore entitled to government protection of their holdings—to resist eviction and new developments, it soon grew to more than local civil war.

The mismanagement aspects chiefly concern the way that government officials planned and executed major hydroelectric projects such as the Tucurui Dam. This huge hydroelectric complex, when its power was available in 1985, became the world's fourth largest power station, capable of generating 8 million kilowatts, at an outlay of well over $5 billion. Because of the swirling political conflicts over Carajas and the already deteriorating TransAmazon Highway system, however, it, too, suffered from underinvestment and slow arrival of the massive supplies and construction equipment. In addition, it was soon discovered that the government would need to build a rail line of more than 500 miles from Maraba to São Luis in Maranhão State to supplement lighter cargoes sent via the Tocantins and Amazon rivers. Again, costs tended to get out of line, in view of uncertainties about repayment, due to the sparse population then in the area and foreign investors' reluctance to make firmer funding commitments. Compounding the problem, initial contractors failed to fulfill land-clearance projects in the half-million-acre area of Para backlands where the reservoir of the dam is soon to be filled.[32]

By 1977, when United States Steel quit the Carajas project, selling its interests back to Brazil for only $50 million dollars, some of the nationalists' arguments about the resource giveaways in the Amazon lost favor. Environmentalists and Amazonian anthropologists, however, raised further arguments against the government's actions. For example, the Tucurui Dam, to meet year-round-power-output requirements, handles 1,500 cubic meters of water per second in the dry season but must therefore withstand up to six times the load in the rainy season; if at such a time the dam were to break or even overflow, the entire city of Belem with a million inhabitants could easily become inundated.[33]

The administration's answer to these problems, and specifically to the inability to attract enough collaborative foreign investments, was to enlarge the project instead of abandoning or deferring it. Planning Minister Delfim Netto formulated what he called Grande Carajas, bringing in prospective lenders from Japan, Europe, and the World Bank (among others), to combine agricultural projects with an impressive array of steel, aluminum/alumina, copper, manganese, nickel, and gold-producing opportunities. It could well be the most extensive resource center in those commodities in the world: already Carajas with its estimated 18 billion tons of iron reserves of about 66 percent purity (world's largest) should in a few years be producing an estimated 35 million tons of ore per year. Not far away within Greater Carajas are what are considered the world's largest bauxite reserves, presently estimated at 4 billion tons, and in a similar time frame they should produce an estimated 1 million tons of pure aluminum, with additional fields that can be exploited if world demand justifies the investment. The area's copper reserves, averaging only 1 percent purity but mixed in with producible gold ores, have been estimated at 1 billion tons. Once production begins, the added gold production would raise Brazil to fourth rank in the world, amounting to at least 10 and perhaps 26 tons a year. Minor but significant reserves of manganese, tin, lead, nickel, and zinc also exist in the Carajas area.[34] Meanwhile, Brazil's petroleum production has risen to a point where (by conservation and alcohol-substitution measures as well) its crude oil imports have been cut in half.[35]

Clearly, the success or failure of major economic ventures on the scale of Grande Carajas, variously estimated to require somewhere between $30 billion and $60 billion, has far-reaching implications flowing from such ambitious development programs, affecting for good or for ill, the reputation of the ruling military regime. There is a high potential for serious mistakes and for senior officials to succumb to the temptations of financial corruption. Even greater potential exists for the general public to fail to appreciate the necessity for cooperation with foreign investors and to accept awkward compromises. At present, it seems premature to attempt any evaluation of the eventual success of the Carajas project. Some of the social consequences, however, have already appeared in the form of land-oriented protests coming in from all social classes, peasant to patron. To deal with them, the government created a new Ministry of Land Conflict, naming a general as first minister, who enjoyed the closest personal ties to the president. Significantly, the new minister was immediately placed on the ruling body for development, the Grande Carajas Council.[36]

President Geisel probably had the best possible preparation for the economic aspects of leadership, coming from the position as head of the giant state corporation Petrobras, which as a monopoly institution managed Brazil's petroleum resources: production, exploration, refining, research, technical services, and external procurement.[37] He enjoyed a well-established reputation for personal brilliance, liberal philosophy, and political skills that at least exceeded those of his mentor Marshal Castello Branco.[38] Even so, as president, Geisel could not rule effectively without the continued support of his predecessors' twin pillars: the armed forces senior command, which only occasionally presented a unified front, and the banking and industrial power bloc, which was centered in São Paulo State.

Events early in Geisel's administration nearly cost him all of his support and before the end of his term prompted an aborted coup plot. Those political problems, encapsulated in the next section, can be summed up by their relationship to the problems of succession, in the Brazilian context of negligible exposure to pressure groups outside the military hierarchy. It is possible to point with pride to the record of orderly presidential succession; it is not possible also to claim that the choices were by popular election.

CONFLICTS OVER LIBERALIZATION AND PRESIDENTIAL SUCCESSION

In times of crisis over policy issues, the two major factions, moderates and hard-liners, have found that neither could maintain stable ruling power without the support of the other. Ronald Schneider gave detailed accounts of the problems and the processes arrived at in the wake of the October 1965 elections that gave discredit to the regime and in the September-October crisis after President Costa e Silva's severe (later fatal) stroke, compounded by the terrorist kidnapping of U.S. Ambassador Elbrick.[39] The details are unknown about the midnight negotiations by Army (War) Minister Costa e Silva that had tamed the coup-minded hotheads of Rio's Villa Militar on October 5, except for the well-known results: to insure that Costa e Silva would become the next president by abolishing the existing political parties via the issuing of a second "institutional act." Interpolation of the more public and extensive consultations in the autumn of 1969, however, supports as a hypothesis the probability that an agreement was existing then, and probably had existed since 1965, calling for an alternation of the two factions in the presidency, to be rendered more secure by the placement of a senior member of the out-group in the "watchdog" post as army minister.[40] The evidence grows more convincing by the long delay, once General Medici had been agreed upon as the next president, undoubtedly caused by Medici's insistence upon having his own five-year mandate as president. It is also noteworthy that the pattern of alternation in the presidency and in the Army Ministry has been faithfully maintained.

Using this alternation hypothesis, some of the disturbing events and failures that occurred during President Geisel's administration are more easily placed in logical perspective. For example, it may explain Geisel's inaction, and occasional switches to hard-line thinking, on the occasion of two successive torture-murders of dissidents by the hands of military interrogators at the São Paulo headquarters of the Second Army. Thus an examination of the Herzog Affair, followed by the rapid sacking of the Second Army commander when the first was most embarrassingly followed by a second, similar death, can be used as a case study in what may be described as military pressure-group actions, as well as being an examination of political-crisis management.

A second case study considers the latitude of allowable risk taking by a president by considering a tentative plot against Geisel, preceded by his own machinations aimed at breaking the alternation by delivering the presidency to another moderate general. The casualties, not including probable loss of authority by the president, included Geisel's liberal Trade and Industry Minister Severo Gomes (who now sits among the opposition party as a senator) and Army Minister Frota.

The Herzog Affair and the São Paulo Hard-liners

Earlier, reference was made to the close liaison between military police units, long a *linha dura* center, and the SNI. The latter, created by President Castello Branco and first entrusted to General Golbery do Couto e Silva, reputedly the *eminence grise* behind the movement that ousted President Goulart, had grown so much as to be a threat to all other authority. Even President Medici, after successfully taming the guerrilla menace by 1972, had expressed alarm and attempted to rein in his former cohorts of SNI.

Despite efforts on the part of Geisel and Medici, a repressive campaign was continuing, especially in the São Paulo area, where the once-shadowy volunteer organization known as OBAN (Operation Bandeirantes) had now surfaced with official protection under the aegis of the army police investigative unit (CODI-DOI).[41] They had two major worries: fears stimulated by events in Portugal since its 1974 military revolution that a radical leftist influence would spread within its own ranks and the sudden outbreak of violence, arson, and sacking of governmental railroad facilities in the Greater Rio de Janeiro area. More enlightened consideration might have led to conclusions that Portuguese radicalism would not influence Brazilians unless there was already a climate of revolutionary discontent, just as the pillaging of the Rio Central Railways was of a mob-violence nature, brought on by intolerable overcrowding, hazards, and repetitive delays that had been costing the poverty-stricken commuters to Rio to lose whole days of wages. Surprisingly, President Geisel seemed to view the events in a manner no different from that of his São Paulo hard-liners.[42] As a result, purges, arrests, and charges extending upward to officers of colonel rank took place within the Brazilian armed forces.[43]

Another factor added to the incentives for more mindless waves of Communist hunting. Having suffered a setback in the 1974 elections, President Geisel was pressuring the ARENA Party to mount a comeback in the November 1975 municipal elections, logically believing the elections were his regime's strongest base. However, the political opposition took up the challenge. Using recently liberalized self-censorship rules by which the press tended to skirt the line while criticizing policies and the safer political personalities, the news media began waging a verbal war against the administration's mistakes, internationalist development policies, and austerity measures. Cities such as Rio de Janeiro and São Paulo became the battleground.

As news director for the São Paulo educational television station TV Cultura, Vladimir Herzog was among the corps of critical journalists. He had previously worked for the BBC in the same city and for two of the most critical print media, the weekly *Visão* and the major newspaper *O Estado de São Paulo*. In a massive sweep that totaled more than 200 dissidents, including 10 other journalists and a variety of lawyers, professors, union leaders, and MDB Party officials, Vladimir Herzog was issued a summons by the São Paulo staff of CODI-DOI. On the same day that he voluntarily appeared at the Second Army headquarters, his body was returned to his widow in an officially sealed casket. The required government investigative report considered only its autopsy and hearings, at which no other representation had been permitted, and the written confession his jailors claimed he had made, admitting that he belonged to the PCB (Communist Party of Brazil).[44] Supposedly, Herzog had hanged himself in his cell. The case was headlined and widely contested by opposition figures and the Catholic church, as well as the Jewish community of São Paulo. It soon became known that it was a false story after another journalist who had shared Herzog's cell appeared before cameras and press to give his version of how Herzog had been tortured, leading to his death at the hands of the brutal interrogators.[45]

It seems clear that President Geisel ought to have promptly purged the São Paulo army headquarters. However, the president's own mandate, by the alternation system, was insecure with Prota as minister. Evidently, what was decided instead, when the president summoned his second army commander, General Eduardo D'Avila, to a hastily convened conference in Brasilia, was that the regional army boss would conduct cleanup operations in São Paulo. D'Avila evidently did no such thing, until it was too late for him to act at all. A second torture-murder of an incarcerated dissident, metalworker Manoel Fiel Filho, in the same interrogation center only three months later led to the summary dismissal and retirement of General D'Avila.[46]

There was an interesting sidelight to the Herzog Affair, related with some authenticity (but uncorroborated) by the London newsletter *Latin America*. Evidently, with the fairly widespread knowledge of military dissidents and prominent civilians such as ex-Finance Minister Antonio Delfim Netto (comfortably exiled as ambassador to France), plans had been laid tentatively for December 1975 (following the local elections) for a *golpe* to remove Geisel from the presidency. The very center and presumably the acting leader of the coup attempt was to be General D'Avila of the São Paulo regional army. The conspirators had to be careful, because of Geisel's strong supporter, General Reinaldo de Mello, in command of the First Army in Rio de Janeiro. The two most salient issues that were troubling the hard-line nationalist faction, and thus uniting sufficient numbers potentially to unseat their president, were the *distensão* (decompression/liberalization) policy and the recently approved "risk contracts," which for the first time were to allow major foreign corporations to undertake oil exploration in Brazil. Apparently it was the sudden crisis stemming from the Herzog Affair that led to the postponement or shelving of Geisel's ouster.[47]

Meanwhile, Geisel decided he had to insist upon more direct and effective control over the military intelligence-police apparatus. Beginning in December, he set up a working group within the National Security Council, which was only technically under presidential control. The new controlling group included the president, the powerful head of the SNI, the civilian justice minister, the minister of the armed forces general staff (always a stronghold of moderates), and the general who headed the president's military staff (Casa Militar), which was his direct liaison to the military commands. By this move, he hoped to rein in the repression.[48]

By the Herzog Affair alone, President Geisel's regime suffered extensive damage both internally and abroad. It was all too clear that the official report on Herzog's death amounted to a whitewash. Such knowledge gnawed at the sensibilities of the MDB opposition and to many members of the ARENA Party as well. The incident also caused shame and consternation among moderate and uncommitted elements of the armed forces. Then, obeying a logic that was described as "responsible pragmatism," Brazil joined many other Latin American, oil-dependent nations in support of the Arab-African bloc's resolution in the United Nations General Assembly that labeled Zionism as racism. In doing so, Geisel, a Protestant, came in for even greater abuse from Catholic bishops and the Jewish community of Brazil for what they had perceived as official anti-Semitism.[49] After surviving those problems and unremitting hard-line pressure, Geisel sought to renew the promised *distensão* liberalization plans by taking what measures he could to procure an acceptable, liberal-minded successor in the presidency.

The Politics of Succession and the Prota Affair

It should be recalled that, in addition to the backing of the military high command, each president throughout the twenty-year military rule needed the firm support of an industrial pillar, of which São Paulo was the center. General D'Avila's dismissal was permitted only because he had lost the respect of his supporters in Brasilia, through acceptance of lavish gifts and honors offered him by Paulista leaders.[50] Even then, the military high command—evidently nervous about alienating their "second leg" in São Paulo—insisted upon publishing an effusive, congratulatory message to the general, coming from the army minister and backdated to the day of his cassation.[51] This was a small price also to guarantee support for the nominated replacement at São Paulo.

Presidents have an automatic right to name their ministers, who serve at the pleasure of the leader. Nevertheless, and perhaps especially because the presidents have been of the military also, it has been the army minister and the high command, which consists of the eleven top-ranked generals, who actually nominate senior officers for promotion and assignment. Furthermore, by the mid–1970s there appeared to be firm commitments within that group, as well as by their peers at the apex of the navy and the air force, ultimately to approve the major policies of the president and to control the processes of selection of the president's successor. Among those prerogatives, the agreement dating from

1965 called for alternation in the presidency of adherents to the moderate and hard-line persuasion. Based on those premises, which enabled each president to rely upon the grudging but externally unified support of the armed forces, Geisel's successor had to be a "hard-liner" general. Following past practice, and the wide-ranging discussions at the time General Medici was chosen as the emergency replacement of the hard-liner president in 1969 (Costa e Silva), the army with its dominant membership was to provide each of the successors, and the nominee should be a four-star general still on active duty. Exceptions to those rules were no doubt possible, but the tendency was to fear to propose any, to preserve "unity."

Despite Geisel's adroit moves to consolidate his position inside the military high command, which was also placed on the defensive by events of the past year, no clear means of control were available to the president while he had General Prota as his army minister. In looking over the list of hard-liner aspirants to become the next head of state in Brazil, Prota's was the most obvious name. However, the mandatory retirement age, either by attaining age sixty-two, or by completing twelve years in the general ranks, meant that Prota should be retired. This event, to which the president readily assented, still did not mean that Geisel was free also to dismiss Prota as one of his cabinet, even though that was a presidential prerogative. Doing so, with his known weakness to attack from the hard-line, would have meant that Geisel was unwilling to work cooperatively with the opposing army faction.

The other leg of the president's support, industrialists based mainly in São Paulo State, was being carefully cultivated by Geisel's minister of trade and industry, Severo Gomes, a Paulista with excellent to intimate personal relations with the majority of that community. With the Brazilian trade and economic growth declining, Minister Gomes played a very important role in attempting to satisfy his clientele's many requests for a more nationalistic policy concerning foreign businesses and investors. In this matter, Geisel and Gomes thought alike but were often unable to execute policies more pleasing to the Paulista front, due to a Congress and bureaucracy that had contrary leanings or commitments. There was another mutual interest between the trade and industry minister and the president, namely, to attempt to see through the envisioned process of liberalization that Geisel had promised at the time of his indirect election by Congress. In this undertaking, Gomes had the encouragement of only a minority of the São Paulo financial kings and few if any of the industrialists. Thus upon taking risky political soundings on behalf of the unorthodox presidential aspirations of a moderate general, Euler Bentes Monteiro, who had no chance at the presidency according to military elite's "insiders' rules" calling for a hard-liner president, Severo Gomes became vulnerable to losing his linchpin role in the cabinet.[52] Regretfully, on the insistence of the industrialists and a core of military leaders who found his speech making for the return to democracy intolerable, the president called for his resignation, even though he had personally encouraged the venturing of Bentes Monteiro as a controversial alternative to General Prota and the other "presidenciable" hard-liner on whom speculation was by then centering: General João Batista Figuereido, who headed the cabinet-level post of director of national intelligence in the powerful SNI.[53] The move tended to heighten tensions between the remaining two likely candidates and also to injure the president.

The one most significant thing President Geisel could do, in the existing circumstances, was to manage Congress so efficiently that the military elite's nominee would be insured of "election" by that formerly docile group when they voted in October 1978. Geisel made good on this requirement but not in the way a redemocratizing leader would be expected to act. Being unable to assure his military colleagues concerning the succession or of favorable results in congressional elections scheduled for November, he resorted to his one option: changing the rules of the electoral game. Lacking the needed two-thirds majority, as well as the finesse to swing the needed support his way, Geisel used emergency presidential powers in April 1977 to recess the Congress and issue a "package" of constitutional changes by decree. The changes expanded the Senate by one-third, with those new "bionic" senators chosen by state assemblies, where the existing proportions favored the ARENA Party. Of more immediate impact, he decreed indirect election of the state governors—eliminating even a prospect of publicly mandated rival power centers in key states—and added a quota of municipal councillors to the electoral college that would vote on the next president. Also included was the supposedly favorable change of altering the allocation of lower house (Chamber of Deputies) districts per state according to actual population, rather than by the number of eligible voters.[54] Although in the past that process had been the rule, and thereby the representation of the more rural, less literate regions had been kept artificially high, the administration may have been unaware of changing demographics. Instead of significantly increasing the pro-ARENA strength, which was greater in the North and Northeast regions, about equal strength was added to the representation coming from major urban centers, which had previously gained nothing from the large numbers of migrants, illiterate *favelado* inhabitants that had swelled the metropolitan centers since the 1960s.

With the April package unwillingly swallowed by the reassembled Congress, attention naturally turned to the question of the military elite's nominee for the presidency. Geisel wanted not to become a lame-duck president sooner than the law required, and the law prohibited open campaigning for the office before the middle of May 1978 (six months preceding the date of casting ballots). It appears that neither General Prota nor his apparent rival for the nomination, SNI Director General Figuereido, actually heeded the edict; of the two, however, Prota's political machinations were the most overt and apparently fruitful among the regional army commands. In the meantime, Geisel came to favor Figuereido, with whom he worked on an almost daily basis and who was in many ways a likely compromise. Figuereido enjoyed close relations with president Medici, but long before that he became the whiz-kid protégé of Geisel's political tactician, retired General Golbery. As various senior generals and prominent members of the Congress began making speeches extolling the admirable qualities of General Prota, Geisel and Figuereido naturally teamed in urgent but silent conspiracy to head off a gravitational shift within the army and the other services toward Prota's candidacy. In this way, inevitably, the establishment in Brasilia became engaged in a very intense, personalistic power struggle.[55]

The crisis came over the weekend preceding October 10, 1977, following key speeches on Prota's behalf by the ARENA Party leaders and retired General Jaime Portela, who had been President Costa e Silva's military staff chief. Quietly summoning Prota's replacement (well chosen by being himself of the same hard-line group), Geisel and Figuereido laid plans for Prota's dismissal for a mid-week holiday, when only a few generals and subordinate chiefs would be working in Brasilia. The drama was therefore brief, but it appears that Prota could have succeeded in reversing the tables and ousting Geisel, if his urgent directive summoning members of the army high command to Brasilia had not been an-ticipated and effectively interdicted.[56] Instead of gathering at the federal district's army headquarters (nicknamed ''Fort Apache'') to deliberate on Geisel's attempt to cast out Prota, presidential staff officers greeted the arriving generals and whisked them off to attend the ceremony installing General Fernando Belfort Bethlem, commander of the Third Army from Rio Grande de Sul, as the new army minister. If the military leadership thought it had been excluded from making the choice, it nevertheless accepted the outcome and pledged to support its president. One reason may well have been that Geisel portrayed himself as uncommitted as to the succession, citing a ''short list'' of his contemplated recommendations, from which the high command could presume it would still have some opportunity to deliberate upon the ultimate nominee. Although the list was probably unimportant, those opposed to the candidacy of Figuereido— then a three-star general and technically still below the zone for promotion— could note that his was the third name on that list.[57]

The strange business of the succession was essentially finished, in the face of growing interest from the press, when the president let it be known that he was sponsoring Figuereido as the nominee. One more tempest brewed briefly upon the abrupt resignation of General Hugo Abreu, chief of the president's military staff, who was angered at the way that his assurance to the high command that they would be further consulted, based upon prior agreements with the president, had proven untrue to his immense embarrassment. The tempest subsided, means were found to include Figuereido's name at the end of the four-star general list to be promoted in April 1978, and the ARENA Party's nomination and likely winner in the parliamentary (electoral college) balloting became fairly predict-able. For the first time, however, somewhat of a contest developed from the opposition MDP Party. After toying with the agreed-upon candidacy of Jose Magalhaes Pinto, popular Minas Gerais governor at that time and a former senator, they turned instead to the ''progressive'' military candidate that President Geisel had secretly favored: Euler Bentes Monteiro. With its enlarged electoral college numbers, however, the end result was the election of the ARENA candidate. Then, in the following month, elections to the new Congress went much as the elections of 1974, deprived as they were in both cases of the interest that always accompanies the election (directly) of governors of states and the national leadership.

THE FIGUEREIDO GOVERNMENT AND *ABERTURA*

Once the election of General Figuereido was insured, President Geisel seemingly pushed to recover the liberalizer reputation he had earlier sought but had not fulfilled. Although much of his plans was undoubtedly known by the new president-elect and perhaps shared in terms of how the plans were fashioned, the actions of Geisel as a five-month, lame-duck president must have won him few admirers and in retrospect could have been used to strengthen Figuereido's prestige if Geisel's plans had been shelved until mid-March 1979. However, Geisel acted in December to terminate most of the emergency powers of the presidency, most notably restoration of habeas corpus rights and cancellation of the draconian powers provided to the president by the odious Institutional Act #5. Discussions also began in earnest between Geisel, Figuereido, and Golbery, the presidential staff (*Casa Civil*) director, about how to manage future liberalizations with the meager majority of 5 percent in the lower chamber of the Congress.[58] It was appropriate for the decisions to be deferred until Figuereido had been inaugurated (along with the new Congress), but plans for a multi-party political system were by then appearing attractive.[59]

Bold Initiatives toward a Political Opening

In view of the divisiveness of the 1977–78 battles over the succession, one might have expected the Figuereido regime to display hesitancy and caution, figuratively feeling its way for awhile. In addition, the new president had to face several weeks of the most extensive and violence-prone industrial strikes in Brazil's recent history, only a month after his administration took office. With stern challenges to his authority coming from both right and left, it took determination and courage on the part of Figuereido just to press forward with his plans for the political opening (*abertura*). On the other hand, he might have lost too much credibility, as well as time, had he appeared uncertain at the outset. In retrospect, it appears that Figuereido enjoyed the best opportunity for wielding his powers in the direction of political liberalization at the very beginning because of the typical tendency for political followership to rally around a victor.

What was accomplished in the first nine months of the new government amazed even his critics at home and abroad. Using the ARENA bloc to maximum advantage to support radical reform measures, the new president obtained a general amnesty bill, applicable to all of Brazil's several thousand expelled and disenfranchised political convicts whose crimes did not include a felony. Within one or two months, by freeing "political prisoners" (i.e., those whose crimes were only as defined in the Law of National Security), he also had opened Brazil's airports to the return of thousands of political exiles. By the end of 1979, at his urging, Congress approved another bill cancelling the law that had set up the unpopular, two-party experiment in 1965. In other ways, such as the further minimizing of what was proscribed under the self-censorship process governing the news media, Brazilians were rapidly being treated to the refreshing atmosphere of freedoms that people in their teens and twenties had not previously experienced.

On the first anniversary of the six-year Figuereido government, the Congress faced the unusual task of reorganizing its leadership and that of several opposition parties also under the duly registered new political parties, which had realigned themselves through party conventions. As of March 1980 the result was to narrow the already thin lead of the governmental majority, now represented by the Democratic Socialist Party (PDS), to only 1 percent. In fact, the PDS would have lost its prior majority if it had not been able to split off one part of the major opposition party, the Democratic Movement of Brazil (PMDB), through the appointment of its leader Ibi Ackel as justice minister.

Should the multi-party system strategists in the president's staff have been able to anticipate this outcome? According to some observers' accounts, the key strategist had been General Golbery, and his concern was limited to only the one unquestioned outcome: that in allowing several political parties, the opposition could be kept so effectively divided that it would be unable effectively to block the government's proposals.[60] But Paulo Motta has pointed out that the former, many-partied system was the logical consequence of ongoing, unresolved differences of interests and ideologies between an urban, more liberal elite (of several party denominations) and an array of agrarian elite centers with their state governors as captains.[61] In view of the diversity of regional problems, the prevalence of what can be called traditionalism or personalism, and the pressures of military *tenentismo* both before and following the Vargas era, it was the judgment of Motta that Brazil is, but its nature, a multi-party state that by forcible limitation to two parties needed only an opportunity, as Jose Maria Bello had put (concerning another period) the matter, "to explode."[62]

The behavior of the liberalized, multi-party organization in Brazil seems to run in the opposite direction of that which theorists such as Maurice Duverger predicted, where the margins of control in a legislative body by a single, majority party or long-term coalition grow perilously thin. At such times, according to theory, there should be maximum discipline with the endangered party.[63] But Brazil's system is not parliamentary, and thus dissolution for new elections does not loom as a prospect to party defectors. Also, in the pre–1965 years there did not appear to be very much cohesion or stability within parties. But there were several other reasons as well by which to explain the number of the ARENA legislators who did not align with the pro-government (PDS) party. First, it seems clear that the pro-government bloc of the ARENA legislators bore a lengthy resentment of the way its support had been taken for granted during the past fifteen years. Thus once the law permitted official recognition of the de facto factions (known as *sublegendas*) in autonomous parties, and there were no longer the weapons under Institutional Act #5 available to the government leadership, the impulse to assert independence simply became too powerful to resist. Second, although there had on occasions been consultations with the pro-government legislators, most economic, foreign, and even domestic issues were undebated, and no compromises were allowed. Third, beginning in 1980, it was clear that Brazil was in a most precarious financial position, especially in regard to mounting indebtedness and the resultant growth-inhibiting repayment burden. But perhaps the most important factor leading to dwindling governmental support was the long-deferred, and now apparently unrealizable, expectation to have a more equitable share of the country's income among the middle and lowest sectors of the working population. Such a growing problem, now spreading into the middle class, seemed impossible to postpone any longer. Yet President Figuereido appeared unshakable in his backing of the economic strategy of his planning minister, Delfim Netto, whose role in the 1970s "Brazilian Miracle" still held him in favor.

Figuereido's government began putting together its winning strategy for the 1980 congressional elections soon after the formation of the six new parties.[64] With so little organizational time in prospect, the postponement of local elections slated for November 1980 (automatically extending the mandates of incumbents by two years and undoubtedly pleasing those local leaders) until the national elections of 1982 made good sense. Liberalization of wages was another priority move, combing, however, at an awkward time from the standpoint of adversely affecting the already rapidly rising rate of monetary deflation. By the 1980s the noted "crawling peg" of frequent, incremental adjustments to the cruzeiro-dollar exchange rate had been discreetly relabeled as the "trotting peg." Economic adversities continued to mount, as indebtedness for grandiose programs such as the Itaipu Dam (world's largest and undoubtedly costliest hydroelectic complex) and the previously mentioned Tucurui Dam ate up dollars without earning any revenue.

Aside from the usual party work in anticipation of the 1982 elections, the Congress that had for so many years been derided in the cartoon press for its passive and inactive role became the nerve center of a pro/anti-government scrimmage directly connected to the chances each foresaw of capturing a clear mandate. The prime object under contest was dubbed the "April Package," because of the time of its presentation as a group of constitutional changes. Having earlier anticipated the necessity of changing the 1967 Constitution under reduced majorities, the supporters of the new rule changes needed only a majority for the measures to become law. Even so, the furor did not die, nor did the rule changes become law until the end of the 1981 sessions just before Christmas. More adjustments soon appeared necessary and were again narrowly adopted in April 1982. This time, with gloom apparent, the government's plans included raising the minimum requirement for passage of constitutional revisions to a two-thirds majority; by that measure, the regime had expected to achieve its protagonist purposes and then to slam the door behind it, so that the loss of its thin majority in the wake of the 1982 elections could not jeopardize its recent gains by further changes. The two rules packages may be summed up as follows: combining in one election the choices of state governors, federal and state legislators, and municipal mayors and assemblies; requiring full slates of candidates for a party to have legal status in every district; prohibiting voters' past practices of ballot splitting between parties; and making the use of mass-media broadcast campaigning illegal before the start of formal campaigns as well as during the final four weeks.[65] The last time has been called the *Lei Falcao* (Falcao Law) after its originator in the mid–1970s, when it had been first applied with similar motivations.

President Figuereido suffered a serious heart attack requiring treatments and tests at a special hospital facility in Cleveland, Ohio, followed by complete rest, during the critical period of October and November 1981. The event is noteworthy in that, for the first time, the civilian vice-president Aureliano Chaves assumed the office of acting president. It was another sign to observers that the political opening was more real than prospective.

Despite the perceived unfairness of the election-rules changes, both political candidates and their many publics entered into the campaigns with enthusiasm and plenty of shrill debate. It appears, retrospectively, that the restriction that drew keenest disappointment among opposition parties was the extension of the Falcao Law limiting their means to wage a more public campaign. The fact that minor parties would have almost impossible odds, aside from obvious difficulties, in obtaining full slates of candidates in all state and municipal contests did not deter them from valiant efforts to comply. It seems that Brazilians are most apt to feel challenged, not frustrated or defeated, by majority-party tactics such as the PDS used to combat its opposition organizations. After all, Brazilians have always enjoyed the intensity of a variety of athletic contests.

When the votes were counted and made official, a full month following the election day, each side could claim victory for itself, and that in itself may not have been more than the PDS or the opposition had truly expected. With the combining of a moderate Peoples Party (PP) with the only other sizeable opposition party, the PMDB (Democratic Movement of Brazil Party, ex-MDB), what had been a fragmented opposition bloc now held 200 of the 479 seats in the lower chamber but prided itself more by having won nine state governorships. By the "packing" of the Senate—the indirectly chosen "bionic" third—there had been no prospect of taking effective control over the Senate. The PDS, on the other hand, had won twelve state governorships (and had another not subject to election), even though it trailed behind the vote of the other parties, combined, in terms of total popular vote. But the most critical outcome had to be the failure to capture a majority in the Chamber of Deputies, with its bloc of 234 PDS deputies needing another half-dozen just to attain a majority. In essence, the tokens of winning were small, for it would take much more than one act, such as an election, clearly to establish leadership.

In 1983, when the elected lower chamber gathered in Brasilia to reorganize its party and assembly leadership, a brief nuptial arrangement had been made with the Brazilian Labor party (PTB), which with thirteen deputies amounted to the second smallest party bloc. This was useful, though short-lived, since the (PTB) bloc president, Ivete Vargas (the niece of the party's founder in the 1940s, President Getulio Vargas), died. When Figuereido's planning and economic ministers attempted to sell the Congress on the necessity of complying with stringent austerity policies being dictated by the International Monetary Fund (IMF) specialists, the PTB bloc retreated from this weakened coalition rather than continue to face the mounting anger and defections of its mainly middle-class constituency.

Completing *Abertura:* The Agenda and the Obstacles

Transition to civilian leadership in the presidency has been attained but not in the expected manner, and for that reason alone, it does not appear prudent to assert that the process is secure, even for the six-year term of President Jose Sarney, which began in March 1985. Sarney was the awkward, compromise choice of the highly popular opposition presidential candidate, Governor Tancredo Neves of Minas Gerais. In the indirect (i.e., electoral college) elections held on January 15, the Neves-Sarney ticket soundly defeated the government's PDS candidate, Paulo Maluf, using the "Democratic Alliance" label that, for legalist purposes, combined the PMDB (itself a fracture-prone alliance) with dissidents from the PDS who reconstituted themselves as the "Liberal Front Party." However, after an exhausting, globe-spanning foray to thirteen countries in the two-month period before the scheduled inauguration, Tancredo Neves was hospitalized on the eve of his assuming the presidency. After a series of increasingly desperate surgeries, the septuagenarian president-elect left behind a mournful and distressed nation of Brazilians on April 21. Sarney, who assumed office in an uncelebrated manner on March 15, as acting president, became actual leader of the new administration with such intimations of likely failure and absence of legitimacy that he felt constrained to operate as the next president with a cabinet of ministers he had not chosen.

The military men Neves chose to head the services and armed forces general staff were committed to allowing *abertura* every chance at success without military intervention. Thus despite many unresolved issues of particular interest to the armed forces, there was by late 1986, no perceptible threat of military *golpe de estado* against Sarney. Is it valid, then, to adopt the term *redemocratization* for the existing status inside Brazil? The answer depends primarily upon one's definition of *democracy*. There does appear to be somewhat better representation of class interests and greater use of pluralistic practices than one found in Brazil before the 1950s. Military influences will without doubt be felt for a considerable future time, since their interests have been so thoroughly interwoven with those of other powerful political interest groups. Although history does not necessarily offer more than potential insights to future scenarios, there may be a useful parallel to the situation existing forty years ago when, under General Dutra's election to a five-year term, the army thought that it had put away forever the threats they saw in Getulio Vargas' populistic rule. As in the earlier case, one sees now some strong responses to the long negation of political liberties endured under his 1937–45 *Estado Novo* dictatorship.

With byway tests of relative strengths of the proliferating political parties on issues such as a major land-reform bill and direct elections by way of constitutional amendment, in addition to election of councils and mayors at the municipal level, Brazil's leadership has been afforded a gradualist approach toward fuller democratic norms. Although the outcome is never certain, the future agenda, which seems to have the president's support as well as that of his rivals in the Congress and state governorships, foresees authorization of a constituent-assembly role in March 1987 for the national Congress elected in November 1986. Although there was talk of calling for presidential direct elections in 1986 (greatly reducing Sarney's constitutional mandate, which runs to March 1991), the apparent compromise that has the strongest chance of occurring would see direct presidential elections as early as November 1988. This is what Tancredo Neves publicly advocated, while campaigning in the indirect elections in January 1985, but its fate lies in the hands of the constitution writers in the Congress.

Among the many obstacles facing any civilian administration in the near future, economic worries concerning Brazil's enormous debt burden and reviving the recession-plagued business climate must surely rank very high. The full impact of choosing to defy the lender community and the IMF is unclear, although the action does cut deeply into the already marginal lives of the majority. It remains a popular response–howerver imprudent it may be—that demogogic politicians can always turn to when they find no other campaign issue on which to build their appeals. Aside from this major problem, the five-year drought disaster afflicting the Northeast region and the unrelated ecologic threats that affect the wealthier, developed regions also demand more than Band-Aid approaches; they also tend to divide the political and social fabric within the country.

What about "militarism"? This, too, has to be a continuing concern to policy-makers, since the hard-line element is not without power in high places. Anti-corruption investigations and the possibility of trial of prominent past leaders could instigate an upsurge of fear and recriminations, but it does not seem apt to go unchecked, as was the case in the last incidents in 1982. Controversial figures, such as Governor Leonel Brizola of Rio de Janeiro, will continue to play a role in politics. Merely to insure his unimpeded assumption of governorship of the state required direct intervention by the president (Figuereido), including the sacking of several colonels and a general. That crisis involved an elaborate scheme to rig the computers used for the vote count and, failing there, a serious coup attempt.[66]

Another major obstacle to outmaneuver is the anti-democratic police/intelligence network that was built in the 1970s. Because of the convincing evidence of the deep involvement of some of the top officers in the Baumgarten affair, the power base of the SNI and its links to the state police and bureaucracy bases have been held on a short leash.[67] The presence of such a powerful and anti-democratic instrument at all levels will continue to inhibit the present and following administrations, unless and until some constitutional remedies have been instituted. The probable response in the interim will be to suppress the network by holding unused the threat of judicial actions against perpetrators of corruption, abuses of power, torturings, and outright murders. This stance may be acceptable simply because the practice appears to be followed in countries such as Argentina and Uruguay, where the events were more publicized and the anger more apparent among the populace.

CONCLUSIONS

Exact answers to theoretical questions posed earlier, and summarized below, are not yet available, due to insufficient historical perspective. The clearest conclusion this chapter has established is that, even in the narrowest of political regimes, an inevitable sharing of power becomes necessary to the maintenance of the regime's authority and external respect, through appearances of unity and leadership support. This is as true of military regimes, such as Brazil's over the past decades, as for its comparable predecessor, the *Estado Novo* regime of Getulio Vargas in the 1930s.

A second point concerns the discernible pattern of centralization and decentralization of authoritarian regimes, which can be traced through the narrative of events given in the appendix. Various of the military regimes came into power declaring an intention to popularize and liberalize their governments. But, as one sees, they all too soon responded to adversities and attacks by centralizing power once again. Thus the pattern under the Medici regime of contraction was to be followed in 1975 by decompression when the Geisel administration began. But it also centralized after 1976. The Figuereido regime declared itself for liberalization but found it necessary during critical stages in the 1983–84 period to retreat toward controls as its tenure grew shorter and electoral issues tended to weaken its powers further. This accordionlike expansion and contraction has its parallel in the degree of public approval the regime enjoys, as one can recognize from following Gallup and newsweekly popularity polls.

Brazil has once again shown its admirable trait of flexibility and respect for the rights of opposition parties or groups by the manner with which it handled the untimely death of the popular president-elect Tancredo Neves in April 1985. It speaks clearly for the political leaders' sense of legitimacy that the former PDS leader Jose Sarney, as vice-president-elect, was able to assume the office on the eve of Neves, scheduled inauguration (March 15) on a temporary basis and then to become president without notable objection, after Neves succumbed following repetitive, desperate surgery. Sarney had defected from the PDS to lead a sizeable splinter party calling itself the Liberal Front Party (PLF) into coalition with Neves' PMDB as the so-called Democratic Alliance. Although faced with suspicion and rivals eager to displace him as soon as possible, President Sarney has gained respect with his cautious but apparently popular attacks on inflation and recession and consolidated his power with the 1986 electoral showing of the PMDB. The new Congress will also act as a constituent assembly to redraft Brazil's Constitution.

FUTURE RESEARCH REQUIREMENTS

There is a lingering question about what factors have prompted the sharp centralization that took place during the Costa e Silva and Medici governments. We can infer that, like prior illegitimate regimes and others under attack, they responded in self-defense. But was there also a "military syndrome," whereby they failed to see typically Brazilian (sometimes barbarous) criticisms of their regimes, veiled in the Punchlike humor of news media such as Pasquim, as legitimate exercise of a free press? Although they undoubtedly thought they were clothed in the respectability of highly nationalistic campaigns to raise Brazil to its destined *grandeza*, their austere manner, to accompany the stringencies they imposed upon the majority of the working class by their policies, could not have made them popular figures.

Other questions have been raised. What combination of factors prompted Presidents Geisel and Figueiredo to pursue political liberalization at the risk of losing personal authority and the power to carry out their programs? Clearly, there were the most adverse economic conditions existing then and, when required, a broadened political base to give each the support necessary for meeting those crises. By 1983 the Argentinian turn toward democracy must have helped to influence President Figueiredo to continue, even though faced with growing opposition and economic adversities. It is likely that world opinion also had its effect, as the world turned its attention to such regimes' violations of human rights. The necessity of improving Brazil's image, as it found itself hemmed in by the necessity to negotiate rollover terms in the face of its indebtedness, also must have played a part in liberalization. Was the military elite endangered also by open division, leading to possible collapse if and when faced with internal violence or civil war? Even if implausible, this thought cannot have been remote from the minds of the military elite.

Other research questions also bear future investigation and become more valuable to students of Brazil who have profited from the investigations made in the 1970s by Peter McDonough and Kenneth Erickson. Which factor or factors most significantly affect the political community? Economic repression and injustice? Attacks upon human rights and self-dignity? Or is it a denial of the rights of political participation to no more than a narrow elite? After the past twenty years of Brazil's experience, opinions differ, and conclusions are still tentative. Given the evidence that the political system is once again normalized, these and other questions invite further investigation. The Brazilian polity may be the very best testing ground for answering such questions.

APPENDIX: MAJOR EVENTS IN BRAZIL'S LIBERALIZATION

June-November 1970	Programs of national and social integration, rural welfare, and land reform begun. Illiterates (ineligibles) not to be counted in apportionment of legislature.
March 1974	General Geisel inaugurated as fourth military president.
November 1974	Government suffers reversal in national elections, with twenty opposition senators and strong bloc in lower house.
February 1977	Succession battle begins, forcing resignation of liberal trade and industry minister Gomes, severing São Paulo support link, and weakening President Geisel.
April 1977	With the ARENA majority unable to pass an "electoral package" bill, Geisel uses emergency powers to dismiss Congress and decree laws restoring count of illiterates and indirect election of state governors.
October 1978	"Stacked" electoral college confirms election of the SNI director, General Figuereido, over an opposition nominee, General Euler Bentes Monteiro.
December 1978	President Geisel initiates liberalization, ending the emergency decree powers of president, restoring habeas corpus laws, and ending banishment of political exiles.
March 1979	Figuereido inaugurated and declares *abertura* (opening).
August-November 1979	Congress approves amnesty bill, passes law ending an artificial, unworkable two-party political system.
January 1980	Thousands of exiled politicians return and resume careers.
March 1980	Reorganized Congress leaves pro-government PDS with 51 percent majority in Chamber and 56 percent in Senate. Opposition begins as five separate parties.
October-November 1981	Figuereido replaced for fifty-three days by civilian vice-president due to heart attack. Electoral rules changes barely squeezed through Congress favoring the PDS.

April 1982	Further rules changes passed to help the PDS win elections.
August-November 1982	Election fever sweeps Brazil, despite restrictive laws. Heavy, orderly voting produces mixed view of results.
March-December 1983	Reorganized Chamber of Duties, briefly under the PDS control through co-opted miner PTB bloc, breaks up in conflict over austere wage/credit control bill being demanded by the IMF. Opposition accepts compromise bill, adding changes to revenue sharing and education laws.
January 1984	Recognizing narrowing odds on successfully controlling an open election, rebel PDS faction publishes manifesto committing a blocking third of the congressional assemblies to vote against a constitutional change to make the 1985 presidential elections direct. Massive campaign (*Diretas ja*) begins to pressure Congress.
February-April 1984	Crucial lower chamber vote, after intensive public campaign, fails by twenty-two votes to reach needed two-thirds majority. Symbolic impact unmeasurable, inasmuch as the measure could not hope to have won in the Senate.
July-August 1984	Large bloc of dissident PDS politicians opposed to the leading PDS candidate, Paulo Maluf, caucus and decide to form a new party, if their electoral college right to abandon the convention victor is successfully challenged. They are known as the "Liberal Front."
August-December 1984	Maluf defeats administration favorite, Interior Minister (ex-Colonel) Mario Andreazza at the PDS's convention, while the concurrent PMDB convention (now enlarged to welcome the new Liberal Front Party politicians) nominates Tancredo Neves, the moderate Minas Gerais governor. To weld the two groups together in what is called the "Democratic Alliance," former PDS leader Jose Sarney becomes Neves' running mate in the electoral college vote on January 15, 1985.
January 15, 1985	Tancredo Neves soundly defeats Maluf, 480 to 180.
March 14, 1985	One day before the scheduled inauguration, Tancredo Neves is hospitalized and operated on for severe, bleeding ulcers in the stomach. Jose Sarney becomes acting president in a scaled down ceremony before the dumb-struck Brazilian public realizes the severity of Neves' illness.

April 21, 1985   After a series of increasingly desperate surgical ef-
                                  forts, President-elect Neves succumbs, and Jose
                                  Sarney assumes the full powers of the presidency.

NOTES

1. Philippe C. Schmitter, "The 'Portugalization' of Brazil?" in Alfred Stepan, ed., *Authoritarian Brazil* (New Haven: Yale University Press, 1973), pp. 179–180.

2. Anthony J. Joes, *Fascism in the Contemporary World* (Boulder, Colo.: Westview Press, 1978), p. 188.

3. Thomas E. Skidmore, "Politics and Economic Policy Making in Authoritarian Brazil, 1937–71," in Alfred Stepan, ed. *Authoritarian Brazil* (New Haven: Yale University Press, 1973), pp. 3–46.

4. Guillermo O'Donnell, "Tensions in the Bureaucratic-Authoritarian State and the Question of Democracy," in David Collier, ed., *The New Authoritarianism in Latin America* (Princeton, N.J.: Princeton University Press), pp. 254–317.

5. *Latin America Regional Reports: Brazil* (London) RB 83–10 (November 25, 1983): 1–2. For a fuller, critical view of the role of the Law of National Security, see Jose Comblin, *A Ideologia da Segranca Nacional*, 3d ed. (Rio de Janeiro: Editora Civilizacão Brasileira, 1980).

6. Miguel Arraes, *Brazil: The People and the Power*, trans. Lancelot Sheppard (Middlesex, Engl.: Penguin Press, 1972), p. 75. For general but authoritative views on the Brazilian character, see Jose H. Rodrigues, *The Brazilians: Their Character and Aspirations* (Austin: University of Texas Press, 1968); Charles Wagley, *An Introduction to Brazil* (New York: Columbia University Press, 1963); Lloyd A. Free, *Some International Implications of the Political Psychology of Brazilians* (Princeton, N.J.: Institute for International Social Research, 1961); Hadley Cantril, *Patterns of Human Concerns*, pt. II, "Brazil" (New Brunswick, N.J.: Rutgers University Press, 1965); James Busey, "Brazil's Reputation for Political Stability," *Western Political Quarterly* 18, no. 4 (December 1965): 866–880.

7. Penny Lernoux, *Cry of the People* (New York: Penguin Books, 1982), pp. 313–332; Joaquim Quartim, *Dictatorship and Armed Struggle in Brazil* (New York: Monthly Review Press, 1971); "Pau de Arrara" (pseudonym), *La Violencia Militar en el Brasil* (Mexico City: Editora Siglo XXI, 1972). See also Peter Flynn, *Brazil: A Political Analysis* (Boulder, Colo.: Westview Press, 1978), pp. 520–522.

8. The principal concise source would be Alfred Stepan, ed., *Authoritarian Brazil* (New Haven: Yale University Press, 1973). Others include Ronald M. Schneider, *The Political System of Brazil* (New York: Columbia University Press, 1971); Flynn, *Brazil*; and the five essays in Richard Nyrop, ed., *Brazil: A Country Study* (Washington, D.C.: U.S. Government Printing Office, 1983).

9. The 1960 data were taken from *Latin American Statistical Abstract, 1975* (Los Angeles: University of California, Los Angeles, Press, 1976), Table 1403, p. 163. The 1976 index was calculated, based upon the data accumulated by Paulo Singer et al., reported in *Latin America Regional Reports: Brazil* (London) RB 80–04 (April 25, 1980): 6–7.

10. Information drawn from Donald Syvrud, *Foundations of Brazilian Economic Growth* (Stanford, Calif.: Hoover Institution Press, 1974), p. 51. His Table III–2 shows

a 91.9 percent rate of inflation but also points out that the rate was falling in the second half of the year. Concerning the argument about the late 1970's superinflation, the best support comes from reading Mario Henrique Simonsen's *Brasil 2002* (1974), since he was finance minister for Geisel and briefly planning minister for Figuereido.

11. James Rudolph, "Government and Politics," in Richard Nyrop, ed., *Brazil: A Country Study* (Washington, D.C.: U.S. Government Printing Office, 1983), pp. 233–288.

12. Schneider, *The Political System*, pp. 89–90.

13. Humberto A. Castello Branco, *Discursos, 1966* (Rio de Janeiro: Secretaria da Imprensa, 1967), p. 67.

14. Rene Dreifuss, *1964: A Conquista do Estado*, 3d ed. (Petropolis: Editora Vozes Ltda., 1981), pp. 90–92.

15. *Veja* (Rio de Janeiro), no. 68 (December 12, 1969): 31.

16. Ibid. Concerning presidential plans for June-July, see "Towards a New Democracy," *Latin America* (London) 3, no. 24 (June 20, 1969): 189–190; "Pessimism Returns," *Latin America* (London) 3, III no. 26 (July 4, 1969): 205.

17. "After the Kidnapping," *Latin America* (London) 3, no. 36 (September 12, 1969): 261–262. The MR–8 group took its name from the date of Che Guevara's death two years earlier.

18. "A Brazilian DeGaulle?" *Latin America* (London) 3, no. 41 (October 17, 1969): 303–304.

19. "Changing Horses," *Latin America* (London) 4, no. 12 (March 20, 1970): 94.

20. Syvrud, *Foundations of Brazilian Economic Growth*, pp. 260–273; Presidencia da Republica, *Metas e Bases Para A Acao do Governo* (Brasilia: Secretaria da Imprensa, 1970), pp. 31–34, 56, 108–110. This was the basic development plan of the Medici government.

21. Duarte Pereira, *Osny a Transamazonica: Pros e Contras*, 2d ed. (Rio de Janeiro: Editora Civilizacao Brasileira, 1971), pp. 404–410, passim.

22. The word is derived from *entregar*: to hand, pass, hand over.

23. Eugene K. Keefe, "National Security," in Richard Nyrop, ed., *Brazil: A Country Study* (Washington, D.C.: U.S. Government Printing Office, 1983), pp. 289–334; Schneider, *The Political System of Brazil*, p. 266.

24. Schmitter, "The 'Portugalization of Brazil?'" p. 181.

25. Peter McDonough, *Power and Ideology in Brazil* (Princeton, N.J.: Princeton University Press, 1981), pp. 232–233, 243.

26. Sylvia Hewlett, *The Cruel Dilemmas of Development* (New York: Basic Books, 1980), p. 53.

27. Norman Gall, "The Rise of Brazil," *Commentary* 26, no. 1 (January 1977): 45–55.

28. Pereira, *Osny TransAmazonica*, pp. 106–116.

29. Ibid., pp. 97–99, 275–276; Darrel R. Eglin, "The Economy," in Richard Nyrop, ed., *Brazil: A Country Study* (Washington, D.C.: U.S. Government Printing Office, 1983), pp. 186–232.

30. Pereira, *Osny Transamazonica*, pp. 93–101, 228, 276.

31. Lernoux, *Cry of the People*, pp. 267–277; "Fear of God," *Latin America* (London) 10, no. 50 (December 24, 1976): 394–396. The *foco* is also discussed in Donald Hodges, *Argentina, 1943–1976: The National Revolution and Resistance* (Albuquerque: University of New Mexico Press, 1976), p. 164.

32. "Serious Delays in Forest Clearing," *Latin America Regional Reports: Brazil* (London) RB 82–03 (March 12, 1982): 6.

33. "Tucurui: The Cost of Development," Latin American Regional Reports: Brazil (London) RB 82–03 (March 12, 1982): 5–6.

34. Compilations from *Latin America Regional Reports: Brazil* (London), RB 80–07 (August 8, 1980): 6–7; RB 82–08 (September 17, 1982): 4–5; *Latin America Weekly Reports* (London), WR 84–32 (August 17, 1984): 2; WR 84–39 (October 5, 1984): 12.

35. "Update: Petrobras Lists Achievements," *Latin America Regional Reports: Brazil* (London) RB 84–02 (February 10, 1984): 5, which notes approaching the target of producing half a million barrels a day, equal to half the domestic requirement.

36. "Carajas: Myth and Reality," *Latin America Regional Reports: Brazil* (London) RB 82–08 (September 17, 1982): 5–6. See also RB 84–02 (February 10, 1984): 4, which reports peasant uprisings at Petrolandia (40,000 population) on learning that many face displacement by 1986, when another dam will cover 340 square miles of land to supply Grande Carajas.

37. Hewlett, *The Cruel Dilemmas of Development*, pp. 110–116.

38. Schneider, *The Political System*, pp. 308; 371–372.

39. Ibid., pp. 169–170, 300–301.

40. Here is the pattern: Lyra Tavares (moderate) was army minister under President Costa e Silva. Continuity in the hard-line presidency was maintained by Medici, well-known as Costa e Silva's protege. Medici's army minister was Orlando Geisel, moderate elder brother of Ernesto. Ernesto Geisel's army minister was first Dale Coutinho, a hard-line member of whom little note has been taken. When Coutinho died, Geisel chose Frota as successor in the ministry (also hard-line). The pattern is less distinct concerning both President Figuereido (nevertheless cited as hard-line) and his army minister Walter Pires, whose career marked him among the field generals generally aligned with the hard-line. See Schneider, *The Political System*, app. B; Flynn, *Brazil*, pp. 475, 481. Another good source of insight would be Fernando Uricoechae, *The Patrimonial Foundations of the Brazilian Bureaucratic State* (Berkeley: University of California Press, 1980), esp. ch. 6, "The Gaucho Militiaman: "Lord of the Distances," which (p. 145) refers to political factionalism as a major contingency one has to deal with first for entry and then for promotions. The author also pointed out that officers of the commanding category—company, battalion, and so on—were always the important post for political purposes.

41. "News in Brief," *Latin America Regional Reports: Brazil* (London) 9, no. 13 (March 28, 1975): 104. Conversion and original sponsorship of the OBAN is also discussed in "Don't Let Them Die on the Table," ibid., 9, no. 5 (January 30, 1976): 36–37.

42. "Businessmen to the Rescue," *Latin America Regional Reports: Brazil* (London) 9, no. 29 (July 25, 1975): 229–230; "An End to Distensao," ibid., 9, no. 31 (August 8, 1975): 247; "Fool That I Was," ibid., 9, no. 32 (August 15, 1975): 250–252.

43. "Fool That I Was," *Latin America Regional Reports: Brazil* (London) 9, no. 32 (August 15, 1975): 252; "Nationalist Noises," ibid., 9, no. 35 (September 5, 1975): 276–277.

44. "Death of a Journalist," *Latin America Regional Reports: Brazil* (London) 9, no. 43 (October 31, 1975): 337–338.

45. "Troubled Times," *Latin America Regional Reports: Brazil* (London) 9, no. 44 (November 7, 1975): 346–348; Flynn, *Brazil*, pp. 496–498. The journalist Luis Costa was released two days after Herzog's death. His effect was more dramatic since he had

been rendered unable to walk from spinal injuries, had perforated eardrums, and missing teeth. His quick release suggests that panic reigned at the CODI-DOI at the time.

46. "Screwing Down the Lid," *Latin America Regional Reports: Brazil* (London) 9, no. 4 (January 23, 1976): 25–26.

47. "Gathering Clouds for a Rain," *Latin America Regional Reports: Brazil* (London) 9, no. 38 (September 26, 1975): 302; "Geisel Recovers," ibid., 9, no. 2 (January 9, 1976): 14–15. See also Flynn, *Brazil*, pp. 496–497.

48. "Geisel Recovers," *Latin America Regional Reports: Brazil* (London) 9, no. 2 (January 9, 1976): 15.

49. "A Jewish Problem," *Latin America Regional Reports: Brazil* (London) 9, no. 49 (December 12, 1975): 389–391. See also "Incipient Crisis," ibid., 9, no. 45 (November 14, 1975): 358–359; "Church Militant," ibid., 9 no. 50 (December 19, 1975): 394–396. Peter Flynn connected military authoritarianism with anti-Semitism effectively in his *Brazil*, pp. 71–74.

50. "Don't Let Them Die on the Table," *Latin America Regional Reports: Brazil* (London) 10, no. 5 (January 30, 1976): 36–37.

51. Ibid.

52. "Dropping the Gadfly," *Latin America Regional Reports: Brazil* (London) 11, no. 6 (February 11, 1977): 41–42; "Underdevelopment," ibid., 11, no. 7 (February 18, 1977): 49–50. See also Flynn, *Brazil*, pp. 497–507, passim.

53. Flynn, *Brazil*, pp. 497–507, passim.

54. "Do Not Pass Go," *Latin America Regional Reports: Brazil* (London) 11, no. 15 (April 22, 1977): 114–116. See also, "Hair on Their Chests," ibid., 11, no. 13 (April 1, 1977): 97–98.

55. *Latin America Political Report* (London) 11, no. 28 (July 22, 1977): 220–221. See also Flynn, *Brazil*, pp. 498–512, passim.

56. The principal source of this tale is "General Frota: The Loser in the Palace Coup," *Latin America Political Report* (London) 11, no. 41 (October 21, 1977): 323. See also "Frota Fired," ibid., 11, no. 40 (October 14, 1977): 313–314; "Pyrrhic Victor," ibid., 11, no. 41 (October 21, 1977): 324.

57. "Jumping the Gun," *Latin America Political Report* (London) 11, no. 28 (July 22, 1977): 221.

58. Flynn, *Brazil*, pp. 483–484.

59. Ibid., p. 486. See also, "Divide and Rule," *Latin America Political Report* (London) 12, no. 15 (April 21, 1978): 119.

60. "Divide and Rule," *Latin America Political Report* (London) 12, no. 15 (April 21, 1978): 119. See also Juan J. Linz, "The Future of an 'Authoritarian Situation,' " in Alfred Stepan, ed., *Authoritarian Brazil* (New Haven: Yale University Press, 1973), pp. 233–254; "Sentenca a Morte Ameaca ARENA e MDB," *Visao* (Sao Paulo), April 7, 1978, pp. 13–14; *Veja* (Rio de Janeiro), April 9, 1978, p. 17.

61. Paulo Roberto Motta, *Movimentos Partidarios no Brasil* (Rio de Janeiro: Fundaecao Getulio Vargas, 1971), pp. 73–82.

62. Ibid. Motta is citing Jose Maria Bello, *Historia da Republica (1889–1954)* (Sao Paulo: Companhia Editora Nacional, 1959), p. 170.

63. Maurice Duverger, *Political Parties* (London: Methuen, 1964), 11, esp. 330–337.

64. For a brief summary of the six parties initially formed, see Robert J. Branco, *The United States and Brazil* (Washington, D.C.: National Defense University Press, 1984), pp. 58–66.

65. Ibid. p. 54.

66. "Fraud Trails to Stop Opposition Victory," *Latin America Weekly Report* (London) WR 82–46 (November 26, 1982): 2; "Hard-liners Make a Last Attempt to Stop Brizola," ibid., WR 82–47 (December 3, 1982): 2–3; "Surprise Raid on Communists," ibid., WR 82–49 (December 17, 1982): 5–6.

67. The best account of the initially obtained facts behind the death of O Cruzeiro journalist-editor Alexandre Von Baumgarten was published by *Veja* in January 1983. See also *Latin America Regional Reports: Brazil* RB 83–02 (February 11, 1983); RB 83–10 (November 25, 1983): 2–3. Recent intimations of the administration's handling of the Baumgarten Affair are reported in *New York Times*, August 18, 1985.

7

Redemocratization in Uruguay

Ronald H. McDonald

Uruguay is undergoing significant changes in its political, governmental, and constitutional processes, changing from a military dictatorship to something else, which is still unclear. *Redemocratization*, a return to "democracy" as we commonly interpret the term, is perhaps a misleading and inappropriate description of the Uruguayan experience, since whatever happens, a genuine democracy, such as Uruguay enjoyed for more than half a century, is unlikely to reemerge.[1] The process being pursued is painful, uncertain, and contentious. But it is also inevitable, since the system that has governed Uruguay for the past decade cannot forever survive, perhaps the only premise on which all participants agree. Just what is to replace it and how long and whether it will last are the questions under debate.

For generations Uruguay, a small country without much military or economic significance beyond its own borders, drew pride from its functioning democratic institutions and heritage, a contrast with the authoritarian and unstable regimes that surrounded it. To recapture that pride is a national priority that perhaps only Uruguayans can understand, but it is a motive force in the country's politics.[2]

For generations Uruguayan politicians divided the dividends of national power among themselves and their supporters, and party politicians would like to return to the system that existed before the military regime. Military politicians have become habituated to having their own way for more than a decade, and they are indisposed, perhaps even frightened, to surrender that prerogative. New leaders, new viewpoints, new options, all are rejected by both sides, creating a political stalemate that could result in a compromise unattractive to all. The process of normalization has been slow and unstable. The debate on reestablishing civilian rule has involved the reinstatement of political parties and their leaders, a new or revised constitution, national elections, a free press, and the rules and processes to achieve these objectives.

The primary question to be resolved is the informal legal relationships that will emerge between civilian and military leaders—the willingness of the former to accept the anxieties and sensitivities of the latter and the willingness of the latter to accept the decisions and orders of the former. The only certainty in Uruguayan politics for the next few years is the uncertainty of change.

Uruguay is a country of political paradoxes. Historically one of the few South American countries with a strong heritage and record of democratic government, respect for individual and collective rights, freedom of expression and tolerance, it has nonetheless been ruled by one of the more repressive military regimes in the region for the past decade. Historically a stable country, Uruguay experienced a period of instability and violence in the 1960s unprecedented in the region. Once one of the more affluent and middle-class countries in the region, Uruguay has endured an extended period of economic decline since World War II, interrupted only briefly in the mid–1970s, at very high costs to the majority of the population, by the policies of the military regime. The Uruguayan military came to power without previous experience in politics or government, and this exercise has been traumatic for officers and elites of the organization. Unlike Chile, the rise of the military to power in Uruguay was gradual, with military influence and ultimately domination extending from one traditional civilian institution to another until total control was achieved. There have been strong political and organizational pressures in the military to return the country to civilian control, and this general objective has been a major preoccupation of the organization and its leaders for several years. An effort to achieve this end prompted military leaders to submit a new Constitution to the people of Uruguay in 1982 in a referendum through a carefully controlled process, with press censorship and limited debate. Chile's military government had previously done much the same and achieved a considerable majority in the vote. In Uruguay the referendum produced a defeat for the military government. An overwhelming majority of Uruguayans who went to the polls voted against the new constitutional proposal. In an extraordinary paradox, a military government's referendum, within a context of censorship and repression, was defeated by a popular vote by citizens who refused to give in to their military leaders. The examples of a military dictatorship being defeated in its objectives through a popular election and then having to confess this to its own people and the world are indeed few and far between.

There are few nations in Latin America that have sustained both a democratic and competitive political system over an extended period.[3] Just how Uruguay lost that tradition, the repression that followed in its wake, the stumbling efforts to reestablish it, and the political controversies and competition that surround it are the topics of this chapter. It has been a painful, anguishing experience for all involved and one whose ultimate outcome will not be known for a generation or more. Whatever the success or failure of formal legal processes, constitutions, elections, and changes in leadership, the ultimate balance between military and civilian influence will remain the central question and issue. Any resolution will require considerable time and effort. The results are by no means predictable.

The purpose here is to trace briefly the context and institutions of Uruguayan democracy; the unusual political, social, and economic factors contributing to its unique and gradual demise; the equally unusual political realities under its military dictatorship; and the gradual and awkward efforts to restore civilian and perhaps a somewhat democratic government to the country. The process of restoration has reached a critical stage, but it is likely that crises in the nation's politics will continue for a long time.

I

Uruguay's democratic tradition, which lasted just under three-quarters of a century, was preceded by a turbulent, anarchic period after independence and has been followed by a despotic military dictatorship that almost involuntarily came into being.[4] There are no direct analogies with the Uruguayan experience elsewhere in Latin America, but its democratic experiment and the causes of its current dilemmas do perhaps have relevance elsewhere in the region.

The gnawing reality in Uruguay's history has been its size, specifically its limited territory and its limited population. By any reasonable standard it probably should have become a province of one of its two large neighbors, Brazil or Argentina, with which it shares many similarities and traditions. Nationhood came to Uruguay more or less by accident. The concept of nation-state did not emerge as a result of the Spanish colonial experience but was determined subsequently as a result of civil wars and international interventions. The British were instrumental in promoting the Uruguayan independence, motivated by a desire to have a buffer state between Argentina and Brazil, two nations that the British regarded as potentially lucrative areas for investment. Being separated from Argentina by rivers, many Uruguayans saw independence as a desirable and viable option to incorporation in Argentina, particularly at a time when modern economic considerations were irrelevant.

Following independence the country was a traditional, agrarian society dominated by plantations and plantation owners, who pursued their personal economic interests. These pursuits often resulted in an internecine political conflict, with personal armies supported by landowners and their armies that ultimately produced a division between "liberals" and "conservatives," a familiar story in Latin American history. Sometimes these conflicts grew into civil wars, although rarely involving more than a few hundred, perhaps a few thousand, participants.

Lacking the modern equipment and uniforms of battle, these private armies and coalitions forged by like-minded landowners identified themselves by wearing colored ribbons in their hats (probably to avoid shooting at their own comrades). In Uruguay liberals wore red, conservatives white. It is from this distinction and confrontation that the basis for the contemporary Uruguay party system evolved: the "Colorados" (reds) and the "Blancos" (whites). Ultimately dearmed, the confrontation became the basis for a competitive, two-party system.

Throughout most of the nineteenth century the two parties and their armed militia engaged in regular battles, while national governmental offices alternated through an unstable process of coups and countercoups. The Colorados were the dominant force. The politics of the country remained tied to the land and those who owned it and to prominent families of which the most important was the Batlle family.

Like Argentines, and unlike most Latin Americans, Uruguayans were predominantly immigrants from Europe rather than a blend of Spanish and indigenous peoples. Before settlement there were few indigenous persons in the region. As a very arable land in the newly independent region, Uruguay attracted Europeans from Spain, Italy, Portugal, and Central Europe. Despite its civil wars, Uruguay was insulated from the major conflicts in Argentina and was considered a desirable location for many European refugees.

By the turn of the twentieth century, a remarkable political leader emerged from the Batlle family, Jose Batlle y Ordonez.[5] He had a vision for the country and the political skills to bring an end to the civil wars and establish a representative, democratic government that endured until the recent military regime. Batlle was a mixture of idealist and pragmatist, a newspaper publisher who founded the prestigious daily *El Dia*. Batlle sensed the importance of continuing European immigration and the opportunities for economic development being created by new technologies. He believed the future of his country lay in the cities and in industrialization, not in the rural areas. He wanted to end the control of the country by the traditional rural forces and bring an end to the continuing civil wars and violence they had created. He mistrusted strong leaders and wanted to contain their power, believing there was something endemic in Latin America that produced dictatorships and continuing instability. He also sensed that the future for a democratic polity in Uruguay lay in the capital city, Montevideo, and that whoever controlled Montevideo would control the country.

Battle's plan was simple. He arranged to divide political power over local regions (provinces) between the contending forces, the Colorados and the Blancos. At the same time, he began to build support among the rapidly increasing urban and immigrant classes, creating a visionary welfare and public works program, which anticipated those later implemented under the New Deal in the 1930s in the United States. His strategy of dividing power between the two parties and his advanced concept of social welfare and public services forged an unshakable coalition for the Colorado Party, which managed to win all national elections until the 1950s. Batlle died in 1930, but he remained an object of political controversy, debate, and respect for many years. His success generated electoral support and allegiance from other politicians in his party who tried to benefit from his reputation and success. His influence also drew opposition from the Blanco Party, as well as some Colorado politicians; others tried to absorb his legacy to their own benefit.[6]

Despite his political sagacity, Batlle's success and that of his party rested on one fundamental assumption, which was in fact the basis of Uruguayan democracy. That assumption was eventually to be challenged, discredited, and disproved. The assumption was that economic development and increasing standards of living for urban Uruguayans would continue indefinitely. It was an assumption that the combination of new technology and a strong traditional economy could guarantee a sustained process of modernization and industrialization. Unfortunately for Uruguayans, the assumption proved to be false. Their technology and access to technology did not keep pace with that of larger, more advanced countries, and their ability to industrialize was limited by the small size of their market. Their traditional economy, based on sheep, lamb, and wool, became unprofitable after World War II, as European nations found other sources for lamb and chose to replace it with beef and as synthetic fibers became a popular substitute for traditional ones, including wool. In small countries such as Uruguay, especially those at lower levels of modernization, exports are normally a critical factor in the welfare of their economies. Uruguay's exports declined and with them its economy, its standard of living, and eventually its political life.[7]

Newspapers in Uruguay, perhaps because of the small size of the country, have traditionally been national ones, available throughout the country and read by a large percentage of the population. Batlle's influence in national politics came in part from his newspaper, and journalists historically have been a critical factor in Uruguayan politics. Many who succeed as journalists ultimately pursue political careers. Most who succeed in politics ultimately become involved in journalism. Newspapers, and more recently broadcast media, are influential, political, and inseparable from the Uruguayan concept of politics and government. This reality, characteristic also of other democratic societies, must be kept in mind as one traces the fall of Uruguayan democracy and evaluates the importance of the resulting censorship of the press and repression of journalists.

By the end of World War II, Uruguay had achieved a remarkable society that was democratic, stable, and by Latin American standards prosperous and middle-class, with government programs that could be considered visionary by either European or North American standards. The first serious study of Uruguayan politics, published in the 1950s, described the country as the "Switzerland of Latin America."[8] The process of economic decay, however, had already set in by then. It was a gradual process which for many years did not disturb most persons' lives. But its results were cumulative and eventually set the stage for major disruptions in the country's political life. Military coups are a common experience in Latin America, and the restoration of democracy is not unknown. But both processes in Uruguay have been unique by virtue of their gradualness.

Chile lost its traditional democratic government with extraordinary force and speed. Argentina, with the election of President Alfonsin, restored a democratic regime with rapidity. The dissolution of Uruguayan democratic politics occurred slowly and methodically, and its reestablishment seems to be proceeding in the same manner.

II

The fall of Uruguayan democracy approximates the decade of the 1960s.[9] To understand it one must appreciate the unusual relationship in the country between economics, demographics, and politics. There was also a complex change in the professional elite of the military, motivated from their viewpoint by patriotic and nationalistic concerns but conditioned by personal opportunism and a broad mistrust of civilian politicians.[10]

What might be termed the political decay of Uruguayan democracy was distinctive. There was no catalysmic strike by the military against a civilian regime. The military absorbed power slowly, over several years. It is almost impossible to identify with clarity exactly when Uruguay changed from a civilian to a military regime. Economic conditions, the general pattern of decline and stagnation, also occurred gradually; there was no precipitous decline in life-styles, unmistakable as the general pattern was. Having committed itself to a visionary program of public education, Uruguay continued through the period to produce an exceptionally large number of highly educated youths, education extending for many through the university level. As was common elsewhere in Latin America, in Uruguay the National University had an alluvium of Marxist traditions that provided simple, persuasive explanations for the troubles of the country and its economy. The sluggish and deteriorating economy could not generate employment opportunities at a pace fast enough to absorb youths relative to their levels of education. Revolutions and anti-establishment political activity are primarily the domain of the young, who, depending on one's point of view, through their altruism, idealism, or their naive adolescent innocence are most likely to engage in rebellious activity. Slowly, Uruguay's youth, at least a substantial portion of them, became radicalized; it was from them that the revolutionary Tupamaro movement emerged. The Tupamaros were perhaps the most sophisticated, urban terrorist movement to be seen in Latin America.[11] Ultimately, they succeeded in destroying what Batlle had sought to construct—an urban basis for Uruguayan democracy. The Tupamaro movement was not entirely a youth movement, but its origin and leadership were.

Like all confrontations in Uruguay, that between the Tupamaros and the government authorities, including the military, was protracted, extending over more than a decade. The objectives, ideology, and strategies of the Tupamaros were complex but effective. Their ultimate purpose was to provoke the Uruguayan military to intervene militarily and destroy what the Tupamaros could not, the Uruguayan democratic system. Their rhetoric was largely Marxist, but they were essentially a nationalistic movement. The inability of civil authorities to deal with the Tupamaros, accompanied by a growing level of confusion and conflict, created increasing concern within military elites about internal security and, ultimately, a proclamation that the situation was one of internal war. The challenge by the Tupamaros helped resocialize the country's military elite and increase their political awareness. The inability of civilian politicians to deal with the Tupamaros also increased the military elite's political concern.

During the 1960s there emerged a strong mistrust by military leaders for party politicians. Batlle's solution to the nineteenth-century political instability, dividing power among the contestants, ultimately produced a political system based on clientele politics. Although the Colorado Party won most elections, the electoral laws and procedures guaranteed individual leaders a share of the national power and patronage, and each had an organization and relationships not dissimilar to those found in political organizations in the United States a century ago. These interests were strong and made it difficult for politicians to make unpopular decisions, which the military thought should be made to confront the challenges of the Tupamaros and the economic decline.[12]

There was also an institutional change in Uruguay's government during the 1960s, which proved to be unfortunate. Batlle, out of his fear of strong presidents becoming dictators, had urged the elimination of the presidency and the substitution of a collegial executive modeled after the system he had observed in Switzerland. Such a system was ultimately implemented in Uruguay by a constitutional referendum in 1953, weakening administrative leadership at the time economic conditions were beginning to deteriorate. The collegial executive consisted of nine members, six from the majority party and three from the minority party, again a system of power sharing. The collegial executive system was ultimately removed in a 1968 referendum, returning the country to a presidential system within a context of virtual political paralysis.[13]

Economic realities continued to worsen during the 1960s. Demand and income from traditional exports continued to decline, without adjustments in the agricultural sector to exports that were in demand. Industrialization, based on import substitution, required high tariffs, quotas, government subsidies, and, in a few cases, nationalization of industries that otherwise could not have survived. Batlle's programs had created high expectations and high government expenditures for education, social security, health, transportation, and culture. The government increasingly faced the reality that revenues could not pay for expenditures, and it responded by deficit financing. This in turn increased inflation and interest rates, slowing economic development and eroding the standards of living of many Uruguayans.[14] Economic decline also decreased the number of jobs available for those entering the work force, increasing unemployment and a condition in which large numbers of educated youths, especially those who had acquired a university level of education, could not be absorbed into the economic system. Having assumed that economic opportunity and security would always persist in Uruguay, the new reality created disenchantment, alienation, and eventually a hostility by many youths toward their society, a cohort mentality that created generational divisions as well between youthful political activists and the older generations. The economic decline also reinforced the military's opinion that civilian politicians had become unable to manage the country, and a new system had to be found.

The actual sequence of events leading to military domination, like most trends in Uruguay, was gradual. At first the military pressured the civilian government to take strong actions, which it ultimately did by declaring a state of siege, technically termed the *medidas prontas de seguridad*, or the "temporary security measures." This declaration, entirely legal in the formal sense, allowed the government to suspend many individual liberties, to limit the freedom of the press, and to take stronger measures to counteract the Tupamaro movement. One by one the military began to press hard on the traditional political and governmental institutions of the country—the legislature, the national parties, the press, the National University, and, ultimately, the presidency. In the late 1960s the military assumed responsibility for counteracting the Tupamaros after the police had failed to do so. At the insistence of the military, a National Security Council (COSENA) was established in February 1973 to "advise" the president on security problems. The COSENA was an instrument of the military commanders. Later that year the president, on the advice of the COSENA, dissolved the national congress and ruled by decree, in effect staging a coup against his own constitutionally elected regime. The president, Juan Maria Bordaberry, tried to consolidate his power further, which angered many military leaders. Finally in July 1976 the military forced Bordaberry to resign and imposed its own choice for president on the country.

Exactly when the military took power depends on one's interpretation. The dissolution of the congress, the suspension of party activities, and the control over the press were completed by 1973. By 1976 the military officers were making decisions as the government. The process of replacing a civilian, democratic regime with a military one in Uruguay had taken almost a decade.

III

Life under the military in Uruguay was a grim shadow of the previous democratic heritage. The highest priority of the military rulers was to exterminate the Tupamaros, which they did effectively, ruthlessly, and promptly. Large numbers of Uruguayans were arrested, tortured, and imprisoned without the benefit of legal procedures or even the most fundamental concern for human rights. Anyone suspected of having connections with or sympathy for the Tupamaros was detained and interrogated. Some traditional party leaders went into exile, others were arrested or detained, and a few were ultimately killed. Newspapers and the broadcast media were further censored, a blow to institutions that had played a central role in the nation's democratic processes. The National University was taken over by the military, faculty and administrators were fired, and classes were suspended. Individuals were subjected to periodic searches, roadblocks were set up for inspections, and opposition to the government was met with maximum force from the military authorities.

At first no single dictator emerged. Some officers had more influence, authority, and power than others, but the process of governing was essentially collegial, controlled by the internal bureaucratic politics of the military institutions. Some civilians were recruited to high government positions to lend an element of credibility to the government. Almost from the beginning of the dictatorship, military leaders announced their intention to return the government ultimately to civilians, but the questions of when, how, and under what conditions went unanswered. The military inherited an economy that was in shambles and confronted it with a new set of economic policies that were a major departure from traditional ones.

The military's economic policies can be described as monetarist, aimed at reducing inflation and controlling the expansion of the money supply, less government subsidy to national industries and state-controlled industries, less protection from imports, a de facto reduction in state-supported programs, and at least the objective of a free exchange rate for the Uruguayan peso.[15] The architect for these programs was Alejandro Vegh Villegas, and the programs were comparable to what was being pursued in the 1970s in other South American countries, notably Chile, Argentina, and Brazil. Vegh was subsequently replaced by Valentin Arismendi and later by Lusiardo Aznarez; Vegh was brought back to the position of minister of economy in December 1983.

By the mid–1970s the government did achieve a free convertibility of the peso to the dollar and a "free" exchange, which was, nonetheless, ultimately controlled by the Central Bank, which subsidized the peso through a process of mini-devaluations, again a policy similar to that being pursued by the Chilean military. The monetary policy was supplemented by a series of laws that facilitated the growth of an "off-shore banking industry," the movement of funds into and out of the country without taxation or penalties. This in turn stimulated foreign deposits, especially from Argentina, for which Montevideo was becoming a relatively safe haven for savings. Argentina also became by the mid–1970s a major source for capital investment in Uruguay, particularly in real estate and construction, and, along with Brazil, a continuing source of income from tourism.

Notwithstanding its serious dependence on imported energy and the escalated costs of that in the 1970s, Uruguay's economy gradually recovered, and aggregate economic growth was impressive for several years. This, however, did not translate into rising living standards for the majority of Uruguayans; indeed, the opposite occurred. Unemployment increased; those dependent on welfare, social security, and education found themselves less well off; and what evidence there is suggests that income distribution in the country became less equal. Structural disequalibriums in the export economy persisted—what the country produced was not in demand internationally, and compromises in the prices of Uruguayan exports had to be made.

The military regime was especially harsh on the nation's press after 1973. Some newspapers and magazines were closed, others were forced to suspend publication temporarily, broadcast stations were sanctioned, and censorship was either imposed by the government or self-imposed by those media that continued to function. Given the close relationship between the media and politics in Uruguay, this was a particularly serious control and an offensive one to most Uruguayans. Reporters were harassed—some arrested—and advertisers were intimidated by the bureaucracy with which they necessarily had to do business.[16]

Traditional party leaders fared no better. Most found themselves under arrest, in exile, their political and personal rights suspended. One of them was Jorge Batlle Ibanez, a prominent Colorado politician, whose father—also a prominent Colorado politician—was a nephew of José Batlle y Ordónez. Another was Wilson Ferreira Aldunate, a leading politician of the Blanco Party. Both men had been senators and presidential candidates. Batlle remained in Uruguay, at times under arrest, and was prevented from engaging in political activity. Ferreira went into exile in 1973 and has become a leading critic from abroad of the military regime, and, under a free electoral system, the most likely to be elected president of the republic. There were many other political leaders who suffered at the hands of the military, but it is interesting to note that those of the Blanco Party, historically considered the more conservative of the two, have been among the most vociferous opponents of the regime.

After coming to power and being unaccustomed to exercising power, the military in Uruguay split into factions, ranging from hard-liners to reformers. The military institution was unequipped to deal with such divisions as well as the opposition from civilian politicians. As a result it created the Armed Forces Commission on Political Matters (COMPASPO), comprised of officers whose task it was to design new institutions and processes for the country, as well as to promote unity within the divisions of the military. The assumption of power created considerable tension within military elites, and dozens of officers were eventually removed, mostly forced into early retirement. Divisions emerged on ideological and generational lines. The size of the military was increased as were expenditures for it. The regular military almost doubled to approximately 24,000 men and was supplemented by another 20,000 police, which constituted a paramilitary force. Estimates of government expenditures for the military suggest as much as 40 percent of the national budget by the mid–1970s.[17] The military ultimately came under the control of General Gregorio Alvarez, who finally was named president of the republic.

The rise of military influence in Uruguay was accompanied by a decline in presidential leadership. This decline was caused in part by historical misfortune and in part by the incompetence, ambition, and inexperience of those who occupied the office. To understand how the Uruguayan military came to dominate the presidency as an institution, it is important at this point to review briefly the sequence of events that contributed to its decline. It extended over a considerable period, from approximately 1967 to 1976.

In 1967, following a constitutional referendum, the weak nine-person council of state was replaced by a presidency. The winning candidate was a Colorado politician, retired General Oscar Daniel Gestido. Coming to power at a critical time in Uruguayan history, Gestido seemed to have considerable qualifications for the position. As a former general, he was acceptable to the military. As a Colorado, he was identified with the majority political force in the country. As a conservative he seemed qualified to lead the country through the worsening economic crisis. Unfortunately for Uruguay, he died at age sixty-six from a heart attack, only 280 days after taking office.

Gestido was succeeded by his vice-president, José Pacheco Areco, a young (age forty-seven) Colorado politician. Relatively insignificant and unknown, Pacheco was nonetheless a professional politician, and many thought he was a good balance for the presidential ticket headed by Gestido, a somewhat enigmatic and politically untested person. Pacheco had the misfortune to preside over the country during a time of serious economic decline and political revolution. His methods were harsh, arbitrary, and unimaginative. Under his presidency the military had a state of siege imposed and began challenging the country's traditional political institutions. Neither a popular nor charismatic politician, Pacheco cooperated with the military in an effort to strengthen his own personal power.

Pacheco was succeeded in the election in 1972 by Juan Maria Bordaberry, a Colorado politician with close ties to wealthy, rural Uruguayans. Bordaberry actually received fewer votes than his principal opponent, Blanco leader Wilson Ferreira Aldunate, but because of the unusual Uruguayan electoral system, Bordaberry won. Political parties were permitted multiple presidential candidates. The candidate who received the largest vote from the party with the overall largest vote was the one elected, even though a candidate from another party might as an individual have received more votes. Bordaberry's position was weakened by virtue of the fact that he had not received a plurality of the vote.

Bordaberry also had to run against a new opposition movement, the *Frente Amplio*, or Broad Front. This movement was a coalition of minor groups— including Christian Democrats, Socialists, Communists, and some dissident factions of the two traditional parties—and indirectly had support from leaders of the Tupamaros. In some ways the front resembled *Unidad Popular*, or Popular Unity, which had been the coalition in Chile that had made possible the election of Salvador Allende a short time before. The front won 31 percent of the vote from Montevideo and about 18 percent nationally. Its success further weakened Bordaberry's political position and created considerable alarm among military leaders.

Bordaberry liquidated the final remnants of Uruguayan democracy. Under pressure from the COSENA, he dissolved the national congress and replaced it with the Consejo de la Nacion, or National Council, which was controlled by the military. His arbitrary and incompetent rule, combined with his ambition to extend his tenure in office, finally angered the military leaders to the point that they forced him to resign in July 1976.

In a legalistic gesture, the military selected the head of the National Council to occupy the presidency, seventy-nine-year-old Albert Demicheli. Within two months, he in turn was replaced by an aging conservative lawyer, Aparicio Mendez, also named by the National Council. Mendez was given a term in office of five years, but he was little more than a puppet for the military officers. By the time of his selection, the presidency had become impotent and totally under military control.

General Alvarez, during the five years of the Mendez presidency, came to dominate if not totally control the nation's politics, and he was named to succeed Mendez beginning in September 1981 as president. Ten years before he had been named chief of the armed forces joint staff and subsequently secretary of the COSENA. In 1978 he had been promoted to rank of lieutenant general and selected to be commander in chief of the army; he retired in 1979. Although officially retired when he was made president, his selection was the final step in the military conquest of the institution.

As the military came more into direct control of the government its campaign against civilians increased. In an effort to control traditional politicians, it issued the infamous ''Decree number 3,'' which prohibited most persons who had been elected to the congress in 1971 from holding public office for fifteen years. In 1978 it proclaimed the ''Law of a State of Emergency,'' which decreed that Uruguayans could be imprisoned for holding anti-government ideas even if those ideas were not formally written or published or resulted in any direct actions by the individuals. Arrests continued, an estimated 50,000 to 60,000 thousand Uruguayans were detained for political reasons during the 1970s, the highest per capita level in the world. Detention often meant persecution, torture, and sometimes death. There was no single cause or person responsible for the rise of military politics in Uruguay, but the ultimate change was dramatic. The task of redemocratizing the country would prove to be difficult and tedious.

IV

Speculation about redemocratization began almost as soon as the military was firmly entrenched in the government. Even the most authoritarian military officers realized that in a country with such strong democratic traditions, some plan to normalize the nation's politics had to be devised, and for political reasons the hope for that had to be extended to the Uruguayan people. But the military was also determined not to allow the country to return to what it considered the political and economic chaos that had existed previously and to insure that it was committed to a continuing role and participation in any subsequent government.

The strategy questions for managing redemocratization were assigned to COM-PASPO, and they generated considerable controversy among the military officers and ultimately divisions within their organizations. The basic division was one of how long the military should stay in power, but there were also questions of what kind of institutional framework would be acceptable and what policies the regime should pursue in the meantime.[18] Being inexperienced in ruling, some officers sought an example in the Peruvian military regime and advocated major, structural reforms in the society; others looked toward the Brazilian military regime and advocated a gradual restoration of civilian rule. Still others, including President Alvarez, tried to conceive a political solution that would be consistent with the country's own distinctive traditions. One of the unifying themes in the process was the general assumption that traditional Uruguayan parties and leaders were responsible for their having to assume power and that a return to the old politics in Uruguay was unacceptable.

For the civilian politicians the objective was to return to the old politics, essentially a politics based on clientele relationships in which politicians serviced their constituents in return for their political loyalty, a service that reached substantial levels given the extent of the government bureaucracy and the range of public programs. For Colorados patronage meant control over the social programs such as education, welfare, and social security, and for the Blancos it meant control over programs that affected or regulated the traditional sectors of the economy.[19]

Politicians in both parties, rather than giving in to military demands, decided to play politics with the military leaders. Being oppressed, or even in exile, became in a strange way a political asset for Uruguayan politicians, for it established their political credentials as opponents to the military leaders. The one assumption that both military and civilian leaders accepted was that somehow Uruguay would ultimately have to be returned to civilian rule and that one group could not achieve that without the cooperation of the other. This provided a basis for political bargaining, and it has proved to be an extended and contentious process. So far the civilians have proved to be better politicians than the military.

Before becoming president, General Alvarez was instrumental in having the military submit to the Uruguayan electorate a new Constitution to be voted upon in a referendum scheduled for 1980. The draft was made public to the voters only a few weeks before the referendum, and although censorship of the press was eased, there was little opportunity for public debate. The text reduced the role of traditional parties and politicians, outlawed extremist parties, sustained the role of the COSENA in matters of national security, and in effect provided the military a virtual veto over government policy. Although there was little opportunity for public debate, most Uruguayans apparently knew fairly well what to expect in the document. The referendum was held on November 30, 1980, with about 80 percent of those eligible voting. In what can only be described as one of the most extraordinary events in recent Latin American history, the proposed Constitution was defeated. Approximately 880,000 voters voted against it, 642,000 for it. Normally, under military governments in Latin America referendums are approved, since elections can be controlled. The defeat was humiliating for the Uruguayan officers.

The traditional parties, leaders, and the press had generally opposed the referendum, and for them its defeat was a victory. It strengthened the resolve of civilian leaders to hold out for as much as they could get from the military in the process of restoration, and it increased the stakes in the negotiations between military and civilian leaders. The experience also seems to have increased the resolve of many military leaders that they needed to get out of power as soon and as easily as possible, retaining what they could of their political influence. The military subsequently initiated discussions with civilian political leaders about plans to restore civilian rule and elections. The discussions were difficult since neither side was experienced in negotiating with the other, and many key civilian leaders were prevented from participating by virtue of the fact that they were either in exile or had their political rights suspended by the regime.

The position of President Alvarez was further complicated by deteriorating economic conditions. The worldwide recession had an enormous impact on the Uruguayan economy, and conditions were worsening. It had become increasingly apparent to many Uruguayans, including his officer peers, that President Alvarez had ambitions to run for the presidency himself in the anticipated elections, and his political motives became suspect.

The regime announced a new process for restoring democratic government in Uruguay that would consist of three principal steps. First, elections would be held in 1982 to reconstitute the political parties, at least the three the regime found acceptable: the Colorados, the Blancos, and the Civic Union Party, a small, conservative Catholic group. These elections were designed to select representatives, about 500 of them, for the internal organization of the parties. They were the first such elections ever held to determine internal party leadership and the first elections held nationally since 1973. The assumed objective of the military was to dilute the control of traditional politicians over the parties. The results were less than the military expected. The strongest opponents of the regime in the Blanco Party, supporters of Wilson Ferreira Aldunate, won an overwhelming victory in that party's elections. Opposition sectors in the Colorado Party also won a commanding victory, with most support going to Julio Sanguinetti and Enrique Tarigo. Former President Pacheco, who had basically supported the military regime, received only 25 percent of the vote in the election for Colorado delegates. About 11 percent of the ballots cast were blank, a protest vote to the process.

The second step in restoring democratic government involved the approval of a new Constitution, or revisions of the 1967 Constitution. It was assumed that the party elections of 1982 would produce delegates to participate in this process. These negotiations proved to be very difficult and were complicated by the breakout of popular protests in the country against the government for the first time since the military had assumed power. On September 25, 1983, a protest demonstration in Montevideo of workers and students drew an estimated 80,000 persons. In November 1983 outlawed labor organizations mounted another protest, which was met by force from government troops, resulting in several deaths and many injuries. In December 1983 the two traditional parties held national conventions, resulting in the nominations of Wilson Ferreira Aldunate as the

Blanco candidate, although he was still in exile, and Julio Sanguinetti as the Colorado candidate for the presidency. For its part, the military still insisted that the COSENA be made a part of a new institutional framework and that extremist parties not be permitted to participate in the electoral process.

The third step that the regime envisioned was the holding of national elections in November 1984. One of President Alvarez' close associates announced the possibility of forming a fourth party with the objective of promoting his candidacy. At this time cracks began to appear within the military high command. Other officers let it be known that if President Alvarez intended to run for the presidency he would have to first resign his presidency. By mid–1984 doubts circulated about whether the November 1984 elections would be held and, if they were, under what conditions and whether Alvarez would try to control the outcome of the elections. It is ironic that the process of trying to restore democracy in Uruguay has been as protracted and contentious as was the process of destroying it.

V

Although military leaders have tried to move Uruguay toward a process of redemocratization, political realities in the country have remained the same. Civilians—both political leaders and the general population—have resisted efforts by the military to impose their terms and conditions on the process. The military by some means may eventually relinquish power to civilians, perhaps even to traditional party leaders, but they are unlikely to be depoliticized in the process. They can reassert power and control the country whenever they wish, depending only on their ability to form internal coalitions within their organizations. Political stalemate, economic crises, increasing political protests and violence could galvanize such a coalition. Continuing economic stagnation and a decline in personal income could threaten the viability of any civilian regime, just as it has for the military regime. The possibility for a venting of popular hostility, a radicalization of Uruguayan politics in the absence of military repression, is great.

Being a small country situated between two relatively large ones, Uruguayans are sensitive to the political trends in each. For many years Uruguayans prided themselves on their ability to sustain a democratic society while their neighbors were unable to achieve one. The gradual process of redemocratization in Brazil and the rapid one in Argentina have stimulated Uruguayans to try to restore what was once the major object of national pride, their democratic tradition. In characteristically Uruguayan ways, the processes of political and economic decay were slow, tentative, and uncertain. It is unlikely that Uruguayan politics can or will return to what existed before the military regime. The military may relinquish power to civilians and competitive elections may again be held, but the experience of the past two decades cannot be erased. The political tensions between the judgments of military leaders and the judgments of civilian leaders will continue, but in all likelihood so, too, will the deeply rooted democratic tradition engrained in the majority of Uruguayans, a tradition that possibly will limit and control the options of both groups.

NOTES

1. An earlier analysis of many of the themes raised in this chapter can be found in Howard Handelman, "Uruguay," in Howard Handelman and Thomas G. Sanders, eds., *Military Government and the Movement toward Democracy in South America* (Bloomington: Indiana University Press, 1981), pp. 215–286.

2. This point is developed in one of the first and most comprehensive studies of Uruguayan politics, Russell H. Fitzgibbon, *Uruguay: Portrait of a Democracy* (New Brunswick, N.J.: Rutgers University Press, 1954).

3. The context of recent Uruguayan politics is well analyzed by Marvin Alinsky, *Uruguay: A Contemporary Survey* (New York: Praeger, 1969).

4. A balanced, if somewhat optimistic, interpretation of the Uruguayan tradition can be found in G. Pendle, *Uruguay: South America's First Welfare State* (London: Royal Institute of International Affairs, Oxford University Press, 1954).

5. The character of Jose Batlle y Ordonez is well described in Milton I. Vanger, *José Batlle y Ordónez of Uruguay: The Creator of His Times, 1902–1907* (Cambridge: Harvard University Press, 1963).

6. Perhaps the best study of Batlle's political system is contained in Philip B. Taylor, *Government and Politics in Uruguay* (New Orleans: Tulane University, 1960).

7. Russell H. Brannon, *The Agricultural Development of Uruguay* (New York: Praeger, 1968), pp. 1–23.

8. Fitzgibbon, *Uruguay*.

9. I have discussed this elsewhere, in Ronald H. McDonald, "The Rise of Military Politics in Uruguay," *Inter-American Economic Affairs* 28 (Spring 1975): 25–43.

10. A useful, if somewhat unfocused, study of the Uruguayan armed forces is Gabriel Ramirez, *Las Fuerzas Armadas Uruguayas en la Crisis Continental* (Montevideo: Tierre Nueva, 1971), esp. pp. 1–210.

11. There are many studies of the Tupamaros. The best in English is that of Arturo C. Porzecanski, *Uruguay's Tupamaros: The Urban Guerrilla* (New York: Praeger, 1973). The sophistication of the Tupamaros is challenged by Abraham Guillen in his provocative book *Philosophy of the Urban Guerrilla* (New York: William Morrow, 1973). Guillen dealt extensively with the Tupamaros, and although he generally supports their objectives, he is critical of their strategies and tactics.

12. The best analysis of interest politics in Uruguay is Phillip B. Taylor, "Interests and Institutional Dysfunction in Uruguay," *American Political Science Review* 58, no. 1 (March 1963): 62–74.

13. A further analysis of this is in Martin Weinstein, *Uruguay: The Politics of Failure* (Westport, Conn: Greenwood Press, 1975).

14. The context of these problems is discussed, if in a somewhat biased way, by Jose L. Buzzetti, *Historia Exonomica y Financiera del Uruguay* (Montevideo: n.p., 1969), pp. 54–75.

15. Further background on Uruguayan economic history is in M.H.J. Finch, *Historia Economica del Uruguay Contemporaneo* (Montevideo: Ediciones de la Banda Oriental,

1980), or in English by the same author, *A Political Economy of Uruguay Since 1870* (New York: St. Martin's Press, 1982).

16. Many of the same problems are discussed by Edy Kaufman, *Uruguay in Transition* (New Brunswick, N.J.: Transaction Books, 1978).

17. Data regarding the size of the military are at best estimates, as are data regarding expenditures. The latter is partially disguised in budget information released by the government. In 1965 Uruguay ranked only 91st of 121 countries in the world in percentage of GNP spent on the military; see McDonald, "The Rise of Military Politics."

18. This is extensively discussed by Handelman, "Uruguay," pp. 274–276.

19. This style of politics is well analyzed in Nestor Campiglia, *Los Grupos de Presion y el Proceso Politico* (Montevideo: Arca, 1969). See also William Berenson, *Group Politics in Uruguay: The Development, Political Activity, and Effectivenes of Uruguayan Trade Associations"* (Ph.D. diss., Vanderbilt University, 1975).

8

Military Regimes, Democracy, and Political Transition in the Southern Cone: The Chilean Case

Manuel Antonio Garreton, M.

In this chapter I describe, in a schematic presentation, the various meanings of *democracy* in the countries of the Southern Cone that lived through military regimes and the conditions, after the failure of these regimes, under which the transition to political democracy was begun. In the second part of this chapter I apply these ideas to the problem of transition in a contemporary Chilean situation, starting with an analysis of the political situation between 1983 and 1985.[1]

DEMOCRACY AND POLITICAL TRANSITION IN THE MILITARY REGIMES OF THE SOUTHERN CONE[2]

It is now commonly recognized that democracy plays the same preponderant role in the intellectual political realm of the eighties as the questions of development and revolution or socialism played in the fifties and sixties. It is also necessary to recognize that the theme's omnipresence is accompanied today, as it was in the past, by a certain ambivalence or ambiguity. This stems from the various meanings attributed to the term both by its different national contexts and by the various sociopolitical actors involved in a single national context.

In the Southern Cone countries the question of political democracy has arisen in recent years as a consequence of the failure of the military regimes inaugurated in Brazil in 1964 and later imposed in Argentina, Chile, and Uruguay or as a response to the kind of domination that these regimes established.[3] In contrast to other authoritarian or military regimes, or to traditional dictatorships in Latin America, these regimes, in some way, presented themselves as attempting a capitalist or bourgeois revolution. Their rationale was to end populist society and to reconstruct domestic capitalism, reorganizing society from the top down and reinserting this domestic capitalism into the international system.[4] The Armed Forces came to constitute the principal actor, endowed with the repressive power necessary to implement the project. The various capitalist factions and the technocratic and intellectual groups of the dominant bloc were associated with the Armed Forces and had control over the project's "substance."

From this project of capitalist reconstruction and reinsertion emerges a first idea, a path toward the question of democracy. On the horizon lay the hegemonic aspiration to replace the "compromise state" (*Estado de compromiso*) and to achieve the anti-populist utopia: eradicating politics or returning to its nineteenth-century grandeur and exclusivity. The military regime emerged as a historic condition necessary for carrying out social transformations but not as the culmination of these transformations. At stake was a new type of political regime that, in order to be entrenched in the political culture and to claim historical legitimacy, had to retain the name of "democracy." What it meant was a "new democracy," where alternatives for changing the system and the sectors that represented them would be excluded. A restricted political arena would be formed despite recognition of popular sovereignty expressed in the polls vote, and there would be a safety valve: the military veto. This new democracy required bringing about the maturation of the social transformations introduced by the authoritarian capitalism of the military regime. The initial Brazilian "opening" (abertura), the plebiscites in Chile and Uruguay of 1980, and the numerous aborted institutional proposals in Argentina were illustrations of this political project. This concept of democracy seemed to combine well the concepts of "national security," the image of a society projected from the "free market" and from the mechanisms necessary for "governability."[5]

The military regimes, however, were unable to implement the hegemonic dream of the capitalist classes, who believed they were losing everything in the populist societies or in the revolutionary tide and looked to these authoritarian regimes as their last hope.[6] Perhaps it was the difficulty of building, within the dominant bloc, as internally hegemonic nucleus that would insure state control over the social transformations; or the narrowness, incompetence, or dogmatism of the project of transformation; or the limitations of the corporate pressures or expectations within the dominant bloc; or the civil society's resistance to the substance of military domination; or the inadequacy of the military protagonist; or the external limitations on the project of capitalist reconstruction and reinsertion; perhaps it was a combination of all of these factors. What is certain is that the political project of transition to a new democracy, which confirmed the hegemony of the capitalist classes within the new social ordering, remained without a real foundation. Authoritarian capitalism was unable to insure the viability of the political model. In the midst of the foreign debt, local unemployment, world recession, destruction of the productive structure, incapacity of state action, wars in some cases, and the resurgence of the civil society, the transition to a new democracy became a call for crisis management and the proposal of a solution that would keep the house of domination afloat. For the dominant sectors democracy became a lesser evil that had to be accepted before it was too late. Even in the case of Brazil, in which redemocratization seemed to parallel relative success in the process of capitalist transformation and its sociopolitical consequences, it ceased to be an exception with the advent of the economic crisis.

The concept of new democracy thus gave way to two other ideas of democracy. A second concept or meaning of democracy is that which arose most concretely in opposition to the pattern of military domination. Here, democracy is the combination of legal and political institutions that belong to the liberal representative system, in which all types of individual liberties are sanctioned along with basic human rights, political competition and pluralism, electoral formulas, the division of powers, and so on. The central question is the establishment of the rule of law and the principle of popular will, both of which are expressed in an institutional framework that sets the rules of the game. For those countries that had experienced democracy previously, it means a recuperation or a restoration of democratic frameworks within which competition for alternate projects was to take place. Recognition of the precariousness of a formula that does not insure a content different from the domination embodied by the military regime results in the linking of this concept of democracy to the idea of social pacts or agreements. In them, limitations to social change are sanctioned, and the popular sectors find themselves in a position of subordination.[7]

This democratic proposal usually comes from groups near the center of the political spectrum, from international pressures, or from institutions that hold a broad base of legitimacy in society. It is necessary to recognize that during times when the military regime faces crises or when repression worsens, this proposal tends to acquire intensity and hegemony, becoming capable of unifying the spirit of the society's numerous sectorial demands and of its factional struggles. But its weakness lies in the fact that once the moment of crisis is gone, it loses credibility because it does not take into account the diversity of interpretations contained in the struggle or resistance to military regimes and thus remains relatively abstract. Neither would there seem to be a resolution of the problems that prompt the crisis of democracy and the introduction of military rule. This proposal presents a response to the form of domination but not to its content, thereby risking a precarious solution that, while responding to the interest of a politically diverse class, can lose legitimacy when social conflicts break the initial consensus. In these countries a proposal for democracy that is not tied to a social-transformation project, and thus to a sociopolitical bloc capable of expressing it, becomes elusive and can cause democracy to be short lived.

The inadequacies contained in the previous concept of political democracy lie at the source of a third meaning of democracy, which is found in countries with authoritarian capitalism and military rule. This third concept is linked to the ideological evolution of the left. Starting with a critique of the formality of bourgeois or liberal democracy, and confronting it with the concept of a real or substantive democracy, even when the foreseeable end of liberal democracy was implied, the left or leftist sectors have been reassessing political democracy. The critique of real socialisms, the self-criticism of the Latin American revolutionary experiences of the sixties and seventies, the international Marxist debate, and, most importantly, the experience of military dictatorship that led the left to speak the language of human rights and individual liberties have guided the reassessment of the substantive meaning of political democracy. This implies a profound adjustment in a theoretical tradition that used to see political democracy only as a higher form of bourgeois domination and as a trap or barrier to popular victories and for changing the system of domination. The political-historical memory of the left leads to political democracy as the most suitable ground to establish popular classes as a political actor. This concept of democracy is as yet defensive and not a foundation for democracy that can be widely generalized. Even so, it moves from the area of available means to the area of goals and values to be weighed in the balance. This does not imply abandoning the struggle to transform society. On the contrary, it implies a recognition that in Latin America the feasibility of political democracy is tied to a dual foundation: on the one hand, it is based not on a tradition of individualism but on the idea of forming a collective actor; on the other hand, political democracy involves the fight for equality in all areas of social life. The idea of democracy also implies a model of development and social change that responds to popularly expressed demands. Political democracy and social transformation emerge as inseparable concepts. The form of domination expressed by military regimes is challenged not only by political rule but also by an alternative content to the domination that the regimes embody. The relationship of democracy and socialism is thus reestablished: socialism emerges as a requirement for feasible and stable political democracy but also must be seen as a tendency whose triumph depends on political and democratic support of the majority. There is clearly a dual risk present in this proposal: first, the principle of social transformation may be abandoned under the pretext that democracy is in danger, and second, there exists a temptation to renounce the democratic principle when the possibilities for transformation reach a quagmire and revolutionary opportunities emerge. Both risks correspond, in turn, to the various tendencies that make up the left.

The concept of a transition to democracy has various meanings, then, in accordance with the three preceding ideas developed under military regimes. For the dominant sectors, transition implies a maximum goal of the institutionalization of exclusive authoritarian rule and in times of crisis of a faltering of military rule, a minimum goal of defending gains in capitalist development. In its more classical conception, transition implies the ending of military rule and consolidation of the legal and political institutions of representative democracy. The concept of transition to democracy held by the left sets the same requirements as those of the classical conception, but it includes the need for an active participation of popular demand to implement social transformation.

The failure of the Southern Cone military regimes' project establishes certain stipulations for a transitional process and for the future feasibility of political democracy. In truth, such a failure does not mean that there has been no transformation in society.[8] The characteristics of the transformation that has occurred constitute the inevitable inheritance that will mark any future transition or democratic project.

It is possible to identify two extreme cases. In one case the transformations went the route of an incomplete and perverse modernization, with enormous structural inequalities and marginalizations but also the generation of new classes, class factions, or social actors. Brazil would seem to be the case of a military regime that produced a relatively high degree of industrialization, state expansion, and the emergence of new social forces, but at the same time, segmentation of the social masses and social inequality were heightened. This process of transition, then, presents the challenge of insuring a political channel for the newly created forces, and social conflict is characterized by the confrontation surrounding the costs or results of the transformations.

The other extreme is exemplified by situations such as the Chilean case in which the capitalist project carried out by the military regime meant stagnation or reversion of industrialization, a lessening of the state's role in the development and redistribution of national resources, a decrease in the existent bases of the previously dynamic social forces, and their decline and impoverishment without the formation of new dynamic centers.[9] Here, the crisis of military rule coincides with a crisis of national identity. The conflict is posed not in terms of the redistribution of the products of transformation but rather as one of national reconstruction. Here, a transition to political democracy contains an invisible component, that is, the constitution of political actors, which redefines the classical problem of transition between two political regimes.[10] In short, in these cases the military regime meant a return to square one and lost years in which no accumulation was possible, and then it required the reestablishment of a regime for a clean new start.

Transitional processes that are generally determined by the failure of the historical project of the military regimes and by crises in military rule present precarious conditions for such processes and for an eventual democratic future. First, two sociopolitical forces exist that did not adhere to a democratic project but rather accepted it as a lesser evil: the capitalist class and the Armed Forces. They do not seem to have lost their predominant position. Regarding the former, there does not seem to have emerged a solid political right (a party) committed to democratic values. In the case of the Armed Forces, their eventual withdrawal from political power through negotiated or imposed conditions, which allows them to maintain their institutional integrity, their physical resources, and their external contacts, leaves them in a situation of disproportionate power with respect to the rest of society, with the possible exception of the Argentinian case. The existence of the right and of Armed Forces subjected to democratic rules only by the demands of the present juncture is an inheritance of a type of transition that constitutes a threat of reversion.

Second, in crisis of military rule, there are still at least two unresolved problems concerning the opposition forces that would constitute the supporting foundation for democracy. The first refers to the need to supersede creatively the typical partisan models that have marked the relations between politics and social movements: the "populist matrix" and the "vanguard party." Both belong to the type of society that authoritarian capitalism tried to bury. In spite of efforts in the right direction, and partially due to the phenomenon of repression, the attempts of renovation and of the formation of a new matrix for political and partisan action seem to be still only half way along.[11] Momentum from the grassroots was not able to resolve the problem of political representation at a global level. The formation of a new type of party, in any case ideal, is a pending task that will have to be confronted simultaneously with the challenges of the transition to and with the establishment of democracy. The second problem refers to a consensus within the opposition forces beyond agreements on democratic rules and one that deals with long-term projects of social transformation. Clarity still does not seem to exist on an alternative model for development; that is, foundations have not been created for a sociopolitical bloc that would insure that dimension of transformation without which political democracy will always be precarious.

Third, and relating to the above, the material bases for political democracy are extraordinarily fragile.[12] It has already been said that the economic struggle between the different social sectors in countries of dependent capitalism tends to be a zero-sum game. If the constrictions on a new process of industrialization or the lack of space for it are going to reinforce this zero-sum game, the democratic game will have a very weak base and a permanent tendency toward instability. The question again arises of the compatibility between dependent capitalism and political democracy and of the affinity of the first with authoritarianism. This does not mean a return to determinisms but rather a recognition that such a condition reinforces the importance of a collective democratic political will and of democracy as a hegemonic idea in order to compensate for the weakness of the economic foundations.

The existence of Armed Forces not overthrown militarily by insurrectional movements and of ample and diversified middle classes, among other factors, gives the transition to democracy in the Southern Cone a radically different character from that of the Central American political processes. In the latter, the fall of a dictatorship tends to co-exist in a single process with an initial revolutionary moment for the construction of a new society. In the Southern Cone, the termination of military regimes tends to disassociate from the process of constructing a new society, or if one wishes, the possibility of a new society is played out within the framework of political democracy once this is obtained. If this is true, the socialist alternative can be defined here as a dual movement: the struggle to terminate military rule and to establish a political democracy and the constitution of a political force capable of proposing a socialist project and of converting it into a hegemonic and majority proposal. I will attempt to illustrate these ideas in the current Chilean situation.

CRISIS AND POLITICAL TRANSITION IN THE CHILEAN CASE[13]

It is common to affirm that Chile is living through the worst crisis in its history. From a political perspective this crisis can be defined on two levels: as a crisis of military rule and as a general national crisis. The first refers to the regime's lack of a social project aside from its pure survival once the economic model implanted in 1975 collapsed. The second, in turn, can also be politically defined on two levels. On the one hand, there is a legitimacy crisis inasmuch as there exists no legitimacy of any project, of any authority, or of any mechanisms for conflict resolution in the various social spheres. On the other hand, it is a representation crisis as far as the social transformations that have occurred make the representation of society by traditional political actors difficult and as far as there does not exist an arena where this representation could be exercised. As indicated above, this crisis can be summarized in the problems of the reconstructing national unity and of the possibilities of historical feasibility.

The perception of a national and global crisis can impede the best analyses of solving formulas to the extent that from each of these formulas there is the demand of resolving all of the problems of society. Methodologically, it is useful to distinguish clearly the problems and dilemmas related to the ending of military regimes and the establishment of an alternative democratic regime, that is, the process of transition, from the problems and dilemmas that refer to a process of consolidation and democratic stabilization and that include the more profound structural transformations of society. This distinction is founded on the above-mentioned hypothesis that for the Southern Cone dictatorships, including Chile, there is no single moment when the end of a political regime coincides with the building of a new society or when the establishment of political democracy coincides with a process of general democratization. In other words, we are not confronting a revolutionary situation characterized by the total collapse of a regime, the establishment of a provisional government, and the construction from there of a new social order. We are, instead, facing the question of a transition between two political regimes that leaves pending the problem of the global transformation of society.[14]

In this chapter I analyze the Chilean political situation until 1985 from this transitional perspective, referring first to the military regime itself, later to the problems of the opposition, and then to possible changes of scenario, finally, I schematically suggest some problems of an eventual democratic consolidation.

On several occasions we have attempted a periodization of the Chilean military regime with the purpose of placing the immediate junctures within the wider perspective of its dual character: response against the preceding society and an attempt, today a complete failure, to generate a new social order.[15] We have thus shown that the period 1973–76/77 was characterized by the almost exclusive predominance of the repressive and destructive aspect of a regime that lacked a definition of a clear project of social and political reorganization, apart from the economic model. This period was also characterized by the destruction or freezing of social organizations and by the personalization of military political power.[16] The period from 1976–77 to the beginning 1981, while keeping the repressive dimension intact, was characterized by the importance conferred on the aspects of societal transformation through the conversion to a new type of capitalism that is dependent on the world capitalist system and by an authoritarian political model sanctioned by the 1980 Constitution.[17] Since mid–1981 the progressive collapse of the economic model has caused the military regime to enter a phase of recurring crises, not necessarily implying, however, a terminal phase. The phase is characterized by the fragmentation of supporting sectors, the decomposition of the state's nucleus of leadership, the incoherence of government policies, the isolation of Pinochet, and the growth and organic consolidation of the opposition.[18] In synthesis, this is a phase in which the central question for the regime is that of its survival at any cost.

In 1983, after the massive discontent was made public through the national protests, which from the start mobilized vast middle-class and popular sectors, the regime initiated a period known as "opening" (*abertura*), which ended in November 1984. This was not to mean, however, an opening oriented toward change in the regime or toward a transition; rather, its two objectives—rebuilding the block of civil support and channeling or encapsuling the opposition—aimed at insuring the basic goal of the regime's survival according to the timetable and means of the 1980 Constitution.[19] This basic calculation for survival or self-maintenance, the principle parameter for all actions undertaken by the regime, is the same one that predominated in November 1984 when the state of siege was declared. The lifting of the state of siege in June 1985 expressed a response to external pressures and does not necessarily indicate the beginning of a new opening but only a slight and almost exclusively formal easing of the repressive authoritarian rule.

From the perspective of the military regime, one can thus predict for the future a scenario that combines openings, closings, liberalizations, and hardenings, attempts within the context of fulfilling the political project established in the 1980 Constitution, that is, the shifting from a *military regime* in the strict sense of the term to an authoritarian regime beginning in 1989.[20] All of this would be accompanied by a worsening of intense repression.

We are in the presence, then, of something not rightly called a "transition" but rather a continuity, a consolidation, and an authoritarian transformation. For this, the regime has three principle elements in its favor. First, there is the strong will of Pinochet to stay in power and the cohesion of the Armed Forces around him to the extent that he unifies in his person the political and the hierarchical-military leadership.[21]

Second, the 1980 Constitution wields legitimacy among the Armed Forces and groups of civil support as a mechanism for conflict resolution and as a consensual continuity project where all other internal consensus has been lost. This makes the transition problem in the Chilean case extremely difficult in that, if a military collapse is improbable, this transition ought to move through a decision compelled by society such that the Armed Forces relinquish power. Now in our case, this would imply changing a decision already made in the 1980 Constitution that would establish the reconstruction of an internal military consensus. That is never a simple process in this type of Armed Forces.

Third, despite a progressive erosion in the civil support bloc, until 1985 there had not been a consolidation of a true opposition from the democratic right that could unify an effective demand for liberalization and democratization for the corporate vindications of the capitalist sectors. One the one hand, what could be called the "capitalist" or "business-entrepreneur" class is still confined in a corporate and traumatic consciousness with respect to a democratic past, limiting itself to partial criticisms of the economic policy of the military regime and never questioning its validity as such. Here, the Chilean capitalist class confirms its enormous political or hegemonic weakness and its inability to establish projects that are more than merely adaptive or defensive of its positions. On the other hand, with respect to the political right, only a few isolated sectors have formed themselves as groups in clear opposition to the dictatorship. On the whole there has been a configuration of a phenomenon that could have great importance in the future. This consists of the increasingly consolidated presence of two rights. One of them defines itself in terms of basic loyalty to the military regime and perceives itself in terms to be the latter's heir; herein are found the nationalist and the sectors tied to the "Chicago model" of economics and social organization (Union Democratica Independiente) despite deep discrepancies and antagonisms found within these two groups. The other, while not questioning the legitimacy of the regime or its constitutional framework, keeps its distance and proposes steps and mechanisms that approach a restricted type of political democracy. This grouping includes sectors of the old National Party (Partido Nacional) and, partially, other groups of this party assembled in the National Union (Union Nacional). If one adds to these last two sectors the groups on the right already incorporated into one of the opposition blocs, the Democratic Alliance (Alianza Democratica), one can consider that here exists the foundation for a future democratic right, which is indispensable in the process of consolidation. But the formation of such a right is necessarily slow, even uncertain, and a large question mark remains concerning the union between political and socioeconomic right.

From the perspective of the opposition, there are also factors that have contributed to blocking a transition. First, there is a two-dimensional problem in the political opposition. The first dimension refers to the fact that from the moment in which the political opposition appeared in the public arena after the first national protests, it paid the price of the current climate of certainty surrounding the imminence of the regime's fall. Thus the opposition perceived a maximum goal (the overthrowing of Pinochet and the end of military rule), bu this very imminence caused the opposition to skip the necessary stage of formulating a strategy and a proposal for change in order to avoid an institutional vacuum. In the absence of a strategy and a concrete proposal, and without abandoning its maximum goal, the opposition became absorbed in organic proposals that accentuated the problems of partisan identity and exclusions (Democratic Alliance [Alianza Democratica], Popular Democratic Movement [Movimiento Popular Democratico], and the Socialist Bloc [Bloque Socialista]) initially and later attempts at overcoming these blocs in the Democratic Intransigence (Intransigencia Democratica) and the Civic Front (Frente Civico), the latter failing up to mid–1985.[22] This was accompanied by an unrestrained confidence that the social mobilization, seen as a continuous extension of the movement of Protests, would by itself be able to destabilize the regime and bring it to a collapse or cause a separation between Pinochet and the Armed Forces, which in turn would bring the latter into negotiating a solution with the civilians. Neither the drafting of a truly political strategy, such as the one attempted by the Democratic Alliance, nor one of an insurrectional nature as insinuated by the Communist Party was able to transform itself into a coherent and viable strategy.[23] The result is that the mobilization tends to erode away and to be reduced to a militant base, allowing the government to take advantage of the situation politically in terms of condemning "disorder and insecurity."

The second dimension of the political opposition's problems is related to its internal relations. One must not fall for the myth that a united opposition in itself is enough to terminate military rule. Historical experience shows this hypothesis to be false. On the other hand, in Chile, at the moment when a minimal public space was created, moreover an informal one, the opposition did not fill it in a multi-party manner assembling all of the groups but rather through blocs that were accompanied by a very heavy ideological weight. Accepting as fact these two elements (that oppositional unity is not a condition *sine qua non* of the termination of military rule and that ideological weightiness makes the opposition's organic unity enormously difficult, capable of transforming it into an impossible goal), there are still two levels at which a certain consensus within the opposition is necessary to advance a process of transition. On one level, there is the need for the elaboration of a consensual formula that goes beyond the declaration that "Pinochet leave." It must allow a resolution of the legitimacy crisis in which a minority supports the regime and the Constitution and a majority wishes for their termination and substitution by a democratic system. In the foreseeable transitional scenario, there will be an unavoidable process of negotiation surrounding a formula to substitute the timetable and mechanisms imposed by the 1980 Constitution so as to recognize military sensitivity. But it is evident that we are facing a government that has absolutely no desire to negotiate or to change the timetable or mechanisms that it had imposed. A negotiation must be forced. This cannot be accomplished without strong social pressure and mobilization that is organized for this specific end and endowed with not only the required magnitude but also with flexibility of form and rhythm so as not to repeat the cycle of protests that terminated in the stage of siege at the end of 1984. This is the second level at which an opposition consensus must be established: a consensus surrounding the necessary tasks to organize mobilizations to support the proposal of transition (like the mobilization in Brazil that proclaimed "direct elections").

Until 1985 one factor that made this type of opposition consensus difficult was the differences regarding what the potentialities of the Chilean political situation were. Some saw at most a transition toward a democratic regime, and others perceived an insurrectional and revolutionary dynamics. The other factor was that the weight of doctrine and the political and organizational interest involved led the Christian Democracy (CD), or Democracia Cristiana, accompanied in this by rightist sectors, to reject any formal agreement of transition with the Communist Party (CP), or Partido Comunista, using as a pretext the more insurrectional position of the latter. (One must remember that long before the CP had changed direction from its more traditional line toward new forms of struggle, the CD had maintained a position of reluctance to any agreement with the CP.) Finally, this reinforces a defensive tendency in the CP that leads it to reaffirm more radicalized lines, trying to surpass and at the same time to take over the social mobilization.

A second big problem for the opposition, beyond its political expression as such, is the disintegration of the traditional relationship between political party structures and social organizations and movements.[24] After the first national protests, a growing distance tended to become evident between the political and the social world, between a principle of instrumental and institutional action, although precarious and therefore distant, and a much more expressive-symbolic and radicalized principle distrustful of institutions and compromises. Both elements, in turn, separated themselves from atomized, anomic, and frightened masses. There are several factors that contribute to the explanation of this disarticulation of the matrix of sociopolitical action. On the one hand, structural transformations led toward the reduction of spaces for the formation of social movements, increasing the volume of the unemployed or independent. On the other hand, institutional changes hindered social organization and reinforced the atomization. To this must be added the systematic repression exercised against organizations, leaders, and the social base. Finally, one must consider as a contributing factor the enormous difficulty of the political leadership in adapting to the new circumstances and their maintenance of styles and proposals that do not always take into account these considerations or the demands of the new generations within the popular sectors. This distance became even sharper in the popular urban youth world, whose radicalization, a product of the subjugation suffered during these years, was translated into a certain involution of a rebellious and communitarian type whose projection in the truly political arena was diffi-cult.[25] All of the above impedes and further obscures the concerted political action of a sociopolitical opposition that is unable to transform the majoritarian social discontent into an effective and equivalent political force.

In synthesis, from the narrow perspective of a change of political regime—of a transition from a dictatorship to a political democracy—the Chilean situation until 1985 seemed clearly blocked.[26] There appeared to be three factors or agents needed to unleash a transitional process and whose combination would determine various possible scenarios. Since all three seemed to be blocked until 1985, if one projected the situation without variants, the regime would continue until 1989 and only in that year would the opportunity arise for some change or point of inflection, and this is still uncertain.

The first factor is the military regime itself. A transition could be unleashed either through a crisis of breakdown of the dictatorship or by deliberate intent, Brazilian style. In both cases we face a transition from the top down.'' But I have already said that in the Chilean case there exists no transition from the top down. However, there does exist a project to maintain the dictatorship and to convert it into an exclusive authoritarian regime starting in 1989, a project crystalized in the Constitution imposed in 1980.

The second factor that could unleash a transitional process is the sociopolitical opposition. A transition from below was blocked, in my judgment, by the lack of insurrectional or revolutionary feasibility and the absence of consensual strat-egies for a political formula to change the regime.

The third factor capable of unleashing a transition process is an external element situated above both regime and opposition. There could be an institution to mediate between the two (the king in Spain), or a political arena such as a plebiscite (Uruguay), or elections that resolve the conflict in some way (Brazil), or an event such as death (Spain) or war (Argentina, Greece, and so on) that leads to the collapse of the regime or to one of the just-mentioned formulas. In Chile the conditions for an event such as the last few mentioned did not exist; neither did a mediating institution appear. There did not exist a political space where the majority could express itself against the regime and inflict political defeat.

But this picture cannot be evaluated in static terms. Each one of the elements that make it up tends to vary, altering the total situation and making a change in political scenario possible. In this sense three fundamental events of 1985 could have important consequences for an eventual change of scenario.

First, the magnitude of repression (one must remember the assassinations and throat cutting of Communist leaders among other tragic crimes perpetrated by the repressive apparatus of the regime) reached such extremes as to imply the complete visibility of the state's responsibility, the internal struggle between its components, a greater distance between judicial power and the regime, and the scandal between a few of its members leading to their distancing from the regime. The depth and irreversibility of these events is yet to be seen, but it is a fact that all of this had a direct expression in the political processes to which I refer below.

Second, at the level of the middle class and certain popular sectors, there developed a type of mobilization that partially overcame the purely agitational aspect of the protests and that was tied to a dimension of social and political organization of the corporative demands. Examples of this are a few worker strikes and the electoral mobilization in student and professional organizations, with a clear defeat of the pro-regime forces. Even if these forms of mobilization do not become generalized within other sectors of the populations, they complement the models of the pro-regime forces and tend to destabilize this type of dictatorship.

Third, on a truly political level, the measure initiated by Cardenal Fresno that culminated in the signing of the National Agreement for a Transition to Full Democracy (Acuerdo Nacional para una transicion a la plena democracia) is, perhaps, the most significant political event of 1985 in terms of the possibility of a change in the described scenario and in spite of the limitations to which I referred.[27] On the one hand, and although this and other aspects could be reversed, the church assumes the role of a mediating institution, which has been lacking in the Chilean situation, a role that goes beyond its already crucial role of denunciation and the defense of human rights. On the other hand, civilian political sectors that had identified with the regime, upon adhering to the agreement, now constitute a semiopposition, maintaining ambiguity with respect to the timetable of the 1980 Constitution but ceasing to be an active part of the regime. This relative split, along with its highly positive significance for a transition, has two limitations: the loss of influence within the regime and the "bunkerization" of the regime, as well as the limited influence of this classical political right in the economic sectors of the capitalist class, which is preoccupied solely with its corporate problems and is always ready to be co-opted by the economic policies of the dictatorship that it supports after all. Finally, although it began gradually to lose its profile, the agreement sanctioned for the first time on the part of the opposition an institutional proposal like the plebiscite, which is an indispensable element in this type of transition.

It is appropriate to point out, despite the extremely positive elements already mentioned, two big limitations to the National Agreement. One of them refers to the initial exclusion of the Communist Party and important socialist sectors. This reproduced the fragmentation of the opposition forces, reinforced the more polarizing tendencies in the Communist left, and abandoned part of the socialist left to isolation without possibilities for development. The other limitation refers to the somewhat imprecise content regarding "consensus" for transition, around which to allow negotiation to occur, and insufficiency regarding the "consensus of consolidation" to the extent that neither a project nor a coalition appears in outline for the combination of democratic stability with the dimension of social transformation.

None of these limitations invalidates the importance of this first partial agreement (partial in content and in its extension along the spectrum) by sectors that want a democratic regime for Chile. Moreover, the National Agreement places the primary theme of 1985 on the carpet: the permanence or the termination of the dictatorship. It is because of this that the government responded to the church, to the National Agreement, and to international pressure in the only manner suitable to its sole objective of staying in power: it reaffirmed what is stated in the Constitution and denied and refused any type of negotiation that would open the doors to a process that would accelerate its termination.

For the future, then, the regime's perspective is to maintain the closure and repression, to attempt to buy or co-opt potentially destabilizing discontent sectors via economic solutions, to insure internal cohesion of the army around Pinochet, and to postpone any institutional negotiation or modification until a moment of extreme weakness. Meanwhile, time passes and the proximity of 1989 plays in the regime's favor. The credibility of its survival allows a continued ambiguity of American politics and the risk of some form of recuperation of the political right, preserving the conformity of the capitalist class. What all of this would mean is the generation of the conditions to "reelect" Pinochet in 1989, in accordance with the terms of the 1980 Constitution.[28]

Because of this, time is short for an opposition that wishes to set into motion a political transition. The absence of change in the near future would imply entering into the dynamic of the events leading to 1989.

Between 1983 and 1985 the fundamental theme of the opposition was social mobilization. This was normally understood by its agitative aspects and did not achieve a connection with a coherent strategy other than that of expressing discontent and rejecting the regime. It lacked, as I have said, a formula or proposal of transition or change that would unify and channel it. In 1985 the presence of the church in the directly political scene, the experience of the state of siege, and the signing of the National Agreement favored placing the subject of negotiation in the forefront, without its being supported by a precise transitional proposal. It lacked clarity on what to negotiate, inasmuch as the agreement is a general framework of principles and not an instrument of interlocution or negotiation. Those themes also became completely disconnected from the social mobilization. In other words, neither mobilization nor negotiation, which there never was, inserted itself into a political strategy, and both elements created an artificial ideological debate, unaware of the absolute indispensability of both dimensions.

There seem to be three major tasks facing the opposition in the immediate future if a transitional process is to take place. One would have to add to this the reinforcement of the active mediational role on the part of the church.

The first task is to propose a consensual and unifying formula for change that incorporates all sectors, leaving aside questions of ideology. The formula must be based on the collective historical memory of the Chilean people as the only way to give meaning and goals to the sociopolitical mobilization. The theme of an honest plebescite or elections fulfills this requirement.

The second task is to abandon exclusions or, if one wishes to use positive terminology, to include the Communist Party and the socialist sectors of the Democratic Popular Movement (DPM) in a formula like this one and in the operations that will carry it out. Without this inclusion, the tendencies toward polarization and massive frustrated radicalization will make a changed scenario ever more difficult. There is no possible development of the more democratic tendencies within youth and popular sectors without such inclusions.

The third task has to do with the opposition's responsibility to propose unifying goals of partial or sectorial democratization that, while not terminating the regime, give meaning to the daily mobilization and once more tie the political leadership to society. The intermediary goals of democratization, on the other hand, hold unexpected dynamic effects for the maximum goal of ending military rule.

Perhaps the delay and difficulty of democratic transition in Chile is due to the simultaneous presence of several problems: those belonging to an authoritarian regime, those lying in the transition itself, and those that deal with the democratic consolidation toward the future. All of the political actors move in these three dimensions. The contemporaneous presence of all of them greatly impedes clarity with respect to goals and strategies referring strictly to the end of the regime. The regime, for its part, has a single goal: survival. This gives it an enormous advantage over the opposition. It would seem that the social leadership and the intellectual political opposition class ought to make an effort not to leave out any of these three dimensions, but they have to have the clarity to deal with them separately and not to confuse the strategies for each of them.

If the future of a democracy certainly depends partially on the manner in which it is established, that is, on the characteristics of the transition process, however, it is possible to make a relative abstraction of them when the scenario is uncertain and to indicate what would be the conditions of a stable Chilean democracy in the future, whatever the transitional scenario might be.[29]

Taking into account the factors that made this political democracy possible in the past and those that provoked its crisis, as well as those changes that occurred during the military regime's operation, we could list schematically those lessons that facilitate the consideration of a long-term and stable democratic regime in Chile.

The first seems to be the reformulation of a model for development in which the state reassumes a leadership role and where a material base is created for a progressive process of "substantive" democratization.

The second is a renewed articulation of the relationship between state and civil society that, although it cannot be entirely different from that in operation until 1973, will have to emphasize the greater autonomy of social organization with respect to the political leadership and the transfer of power and effective participation at grassroots and mid-levels.

The third, on a strictly political level, is that the inclusiveness of the system, whereby all of the sociopolitical sectors continue playing by democratic rules, must exist. This inclusiveness supposes the organic constitution of a democratic right, the reorganization of the socialist left, and the presence of the Marxist-Leninist left. Any exclusion will just weaken the political system and hinder the Armed Forces' strict subordination to political power. In the heart of this democratic spectrum must be resolved the problem of constituting a majority capable of reestablishing, with proportions and content appropriate to the new situation, the founding agreement between middle class and popular sectors, between the center and the left, that made political democracy and the dynamic of social change possible in Chile and whose rupture contributed to unleashing the crisis in democratic rule.

NOTES

1. The final version of this work was completed while I was a Fellow of the Kellogg Institute of the University of Notre Dame and at the Center for Iberian and Latin American Studies at the University of California, San Diego. The editors and I are grateful to Kathy McKnight for her translation of the original Spanish version of this chapter.

2. In this part I have used material from other works, especially from *Democracia, transicion Politica y alternative socialista en el Cono Sur* (Madrid: Leviatan, 12, 1983).

3. For a discussion of the theme of democracy in Latin America in recent years, see, among others, DESCO, *America Latina 80: denicracia y movimiento popular* (Lima, 1981); *Revista Critica y Utopia*, #1 a 4 (Buenos Aires); *Revista Pensamiento Iberoamericano* 1 y 2 (Madrid).

4. For a characterization of these regimes, see D. Collier, ed., *The New Authoritarianism in Latin America* (Princeton, N.J.: Princeton University Press, 1979; the second part of Manuel Antonio Garreton *El Proceso Politico Chileno* (Santiago: FLACSO, 1983, chapter 1 in idem 5 *Dictaduras y democratizacion* (Santiago: FLACSO, 1984).

5. A vision of this style appears in Brian Crozier, Samuel P. Huntington and Watanuke, *The Crisis of Democracy* (New York: New York University Press, 1975).

6. A recent evaluation of this authoritarianism is in A. Portes and A. Kincaid, "The Crisis of Authoritarianism: State and Civil Society in Argentina, Chile and Uruguay" *Research in Political Sociology*, vol. 1 (1985); and in chapter 1 in Garreton, *Dictaduras y democratizacion*.

7. Two counterposed visions on the theme of acts are in A. Foxley, *Para una democracia estable* (Santiago: CIEPLAN, 1985); and G. O'Donnell, *Pactos politicos y pactos economico-sociales. Por que si y por que si y por que no* (Foro Cono Sur, Rio de Janeiro: ILDES, 1985, mimeo).

8. An evaluation of these transformations is in C. Filgueira, *Acerca de las condiciones sociales de la democracia en el Cono Sur* (Rio de Janeiro: 1985).

9. See J. Martinez and E. Tironi, *Las clases sociales en Chile. Cambio Y estratificacion, 1970–1980* (Santiago: Sur, 1985).

10. See Garreton *El Proceso Politico Chileno*; idem, "The Political Evolution of the Chilean Military Regime and Problems in the Transition to Democracy," vol. 2 in *Transitions from Authoritarian Rule*, Guillermo O'Donnell and Philip Schmitter eds. (Baltimore: Johns Hopkins University Press, 1987).

11. About the concept of a matrix of political action, see Garreton *El Proceso Politico*.

12. See F. Fajnzylber, *Reflexion sobre limites y potencialidades economicas de la democratizacion* (Foro Cono Sur, Rio de Janeiro: ILDES, 1985).

13. In this part I have used material from *La problematica de la transicion a la democracia en Chile. 1985. Una sintesis* (Santiago: Documento FLACSO, 1985); and from *Transicion a la democracia en Chile: avances, obstaculos y dilemas en 1985.* (Revista Mensaje, Santiago: January-February 1960).

14. A general view of this type of transition in Guillermo O'Donnell and Philip Schmitter, *Political Life after Authoritarian Rule: Tentative Conclusions about Uncertain Transitions* vol. 4, of Guillermo O'Donnell and Philip Schmitter eds. *Transitions from Authoritarian Rule* (Baltimore: John Hopkins University Press, 1986).

15. A detailed analysis is in Garreton, *El Proceso Politico*; and idem, *The Political Evolution.*

16. On the evolution of repression, among others, see Organization of American States, *Report on the Situation of the Human Rights in Chile* (OAS, SERL/V/II. 66. Doc 17. 9/17/1985).

17. Above all, for this period, see Samuel Valenzuela and Arturo Valenzuela, eds., *Military Rule in Chile: Dictatorship and Opposition* (Baltimore: Johns Hopkins University Press, 1985); P. Vergara, *Auge y caida el neo-liberalismo en Chile* (Santiago: FLACSO, 1985).

18. Vergara, *Auge y caida.* See also Garrenton, *El Proceso Politico*; G. Bajoit, *Les Mouvements sociaux et politiques au Chile, 1980–85* (Santiago: 1985, mimeo).

19. About the processes that led to the institutionalization of 1980, see Manuel Antonio Garreton, *Political Process in an Authoritarian Regime: The Dynamics of Institutionalization and Opposition in Chile, 1973–1980,''* in Samuel Valenzuela and Arturo Valenzuela, eds., *Military Rule in Chile: Dictatorship and Opposition* (Baltimore: Johns Hopkins University Press, 1985). On the opening, see C. Huneeus, *La politica de la apertura y sus implicancias para la inauguracion de la democracia en Chile* (Revista de Ciencia Politica, Santiago: 1985), 2:1.

20. The Constitution establishes the maintenance of the present scheme of power until 1989, when Pinochet can be reelected for another eight years through a plebescite. Starting in 1989 some mechanism of restricted representation will be established, and the Armed Forces will have a power of veto. See an analysis in G. Arriagada, "La Constitucion conduce a la democracia?" *Revista Hoy* #358, Santiago:1984.

21. On the Armed Forces under the military regime, see A. Varas, *Militarization and the International Arms Race in Latin America* (Boulder, Colo.: Westview Press, 1985), ch. 8.

22. The Democratic Alliance (Alianza Democratica) includes a small sector of the right, the Christian Democracy (Democracia Christiana), the Radical Party (Partido Radical), the Social Democracy Party (Social Democracia), and one of the Socialist parties. The Democratic Popular Movement (DPM), Movimiento Democratico Popular, includes the Communist Party (Partido Comunista) as a principal force, the other Socialist Party, the MIR, and other groups. The Democratic Intransigence (Intransigencia Democratica) tries to group national and partisan personalities of those independent conglomerates mentioned, without the Christian Democracy having adhered to them. The Civic Front (Frente Civico) was an unsuccessful initiative of the Socialist Party that is in the Democratic Alliance. The Socialist Bloc (Bloque Socialista) tried to unify some socialist sectors that are in the alliance with newer parties such as those of MAPU and the Christian

Left (Izquierda Christiana). Recently, some socialist sectors in the PDM are also at-tempting a fusion.

23. In 1980 the Communist Party made a certain change of direction from its traditional line, accepting the route of insurrection as one of the possible roads. Since then the armed action of the Frente Manuel Rodriguez has developed. It has the sympathy of the CP, although the CP does not reduce its strategy to this form of action. In fact, there would seem to be a permanent internal confrontation between the traditional sectors of the CP, more prone to the political route, and radicalized sectors of the youth that opt for more insurrectional forms of struggle.

24. On this relationship, Garreton, *El Proceso Politico*.

25. See E. Valenzuela, *La rebelion de los jovenes* (Sur, Santiago: 1984).

26. See M. A. Garreton, "Chile: la transicion bloqueada" *Revista Mensaje*, (January-February, 1985).

27. The agreement was published by, among others, Las Ultimas Noticias, August 27, 1985. All of the parties of the Democratic Alliance endorsed it; the National Party and the National Union (both on the right); the Christian Left, the MAPU, and later a vast number of personalities and social organizations endorsed it.

28. On the ambiguity of the American policy, see the discussion in *Prospects for a Democratic Transition in Chile* (Hearing before the Subcommittee on Western Hemisphere Affairs of Foreign Affairs, House of Representatives, 95 Cong. 1st sess. July 16, 1985); P. Bell, "Democracy and Double Standards: The New View from Chile" *World Policy Journal* 2, no. 22 (Fall 1985). See also Manuel Antonio Garreton, "Transicion a la democracia en Chile e influencia externa. Dilemas y perspectivas," a Working Paper (Notre Dame, Indiana: The Helen Kellogg Institute, University of Notre Dame, 1985).

29. This topic has been further developed in "Chile: In Search of Lost Democracy" in J. Harlyn and S. Morley, eds., *Latin American Political Economy: Financial Crisis and Political Change* (Boulder, Colo.: Westview Press, forthcoming).

9

Military Breakdown and Redemocratization in Argentina

David Pion-Berlin

Dankwart A. Rustow wrote that democracy was unlikely to develop unless preceded by a "prolonged and inconclusive political struggle" in which the "protagonists represent well entrenched forces" (like social classes), the conflict is polarized, and the issues hold "profound meaning for all concerned."[1] He reasoned that if people were not engaged in fundamental conflict, they would have no reason to invest in democracy's complex rules of conflict resolution.

If Rustow's words hold any meaning, Argentina should be a perfect candidate for redemocratization. Few countries in the region, or the world for that matter, have been so plagued by persistent, uncontrolled, and unresolved confrontations between social classes, political groupings, and government and the opposition during a period of authoritarian rule broken intermittently by fragile and short-lived civilian regimes. From 1948 to 1977 Argentina ranked (among 125 countries) 22 in political riots, 19 in protest demonstrations, 7 in politically motivated strikes, and 4 in assassinations and imposition of governmental sanctions.[2] There is a deep yearning in Argentina these days for problem solving through negotiation and compromise to overcome the turbulence of the past.

However, desire is a pre-condition and not a guarantee that democratic procedure will be followed. Rustow said that adversaries must commit themselves to the new rules but that this is cultivated through practice and the successful settlement of certain disputes. If democratic values are learned, Argentina is off to a good start. The nation's electoral and judicial processes have been dusted off after lack of use and put to the test. The completion of presidential and congressional elections with full political party participation, the termination of the Beagle Channel dispute through a plebiscite, and the bringing to justice in civilian courts of former military officials guilty of widespread human rights abuses during the "dirty war" are all positive signs.

While the benefits of democratic rule are becoming apparent, so are the costs of authoritarian rule. There is reason to believe that those social classes that most aggressively played the military card in the past may have second thoughts the next time around. These classes swallowed a bitter political and economic pill during the most recent phase of bureaucratic-authoritarian rule (1976–83) that has called into question the assumption that such regimes have the best interests of the propertied sectors in mind. In the final portion of this chapter, I examine the military regime's policy performance and responsiveness and its impact on attitudes toward authoritarian governance.

The prelude to democratic transition was the breakdown of the military regime of 1976–83, which is the first subject of this chapter. Although there is voluminous literature on the causes of military coups, very little has been written on the causes of military withdrawal from power.[3] The decline of the armed forces is an important object of inquiry, since it may itself have a bearing on social support for democracy.

The armed forces were not pressured to leave by a militant opposition. In fact, the first five years of their reign was marked by an absence of protest from the working class. Unions were intervened and strikes were scattered and quickly repressed; the Peronist Party was barred from political activity and could not mount a successful underground resistance. This contrasts sharply with the Argentine government of General Juan Ongania (1966–70), whose downfall was precipitated by violent clashes between the military and students and workers from the city of Cordoba in 1969. The entrepreneurial classes, which had pinned their hopes on the Ongania regime, could point the finger at the lower classes but could not do the same during the "Proceso," when a relatively autonomous regime revealed to the public its own inadequacies. The Argentine image of authoritarian leadership, which is strong, businesslike, and able to "get the job done," may have been tarnished somewhat after 1980 as a disunited, insecure, and indecisive military could not steer clear of political and economic calamities. This bodes well for redemocratization.

Why did the regime break down? Most certainly, the military's defeat at the hands of the British in the Malvinas War made the return to civilian rule all but certain. After having dashed the hopes of Argentines for a swift reconquest of these South Atlantic islands, it was not surprising that the navy and air force refused to take part in the post-war government. This left the army hopelessly isolated and prepared to cede control to a more confident civilian opposition. However, although the Malvinas War hastened the military's downfall, it was not in our view the cause. The decline was not as precipitous as Argentina's surrender to the British would suggest. Rather, it began two years before the war and was an unintended result of a pattern of self-defeating behavior on the part of the armed forces. The regime displayed remarkable unity during the first four years of rule, only to come unraveled thereafter. The loss of faith in programmatic objectives (primarily economic) and the emergence of personal and ideological cleavages within the ranks contributed significantly to the regime's demise.

Morris Janowitz, in his study of the military establishment, explained how the armed forces must have a mission in the absence of warfare if they are to govern successfully. Clarification of and commitment to a set of goals will in turn promote greater social cohesion within the ranks.[4] But when objectives are lost or confused, factions emerge or resurface. Such divisions will not only limit its governing capacity but threaten the military as an institution, as officers pursue personal or ideological ends while ignoring corporate responsibilities.[5] Under these circumstances, it takes an unusually deft military leader to manage internal dissent sufficiently to permit policy enactment.

Such was not the case in Argentina under the leadership of General Roberto Viola in 1981. Torn by conflict and self-doubt, the armed forces were left without complete control over the state apparatus. This inadvertently created a power vacuum that the opposition finally filled. There were five stages to this process, discussed in the following pages.

STAGE 1: THE VIDELA GOVERNMENT AND ITS "LIBERAL" MISSION

The military junta of General Jorge Videla, which overthrew the government of Isabel Perón on March 23, 1976, had a mission that differed from its predecessors in a few fundamental respects. First, the coup was strongly reactive. A guerilla movement (led by the Peronist-affiliated Montoneros) had surfaced in the early 1970's and, for the first time in Argentine history, seriously challenged the military's traditional monopoly over the means of coercion. The military was single minded in its determination to eliminate the guerilla threat. But this presented it with a dilemma: How would it justify prolonged rule, should the war against the "subversives" end quickly and successfully?

The military presented the more goal-oriented aspect of its plan in the Act of National Reorganization proclaimed on March 24, 1976. Known as the "Proceso," the act set out a series of clearly defined political, social, and economic objectives and strategies to be pursued by the regime. By committing itself to a phased restoration of "proper moral values," national security, economic efficiency, and "authentic representative democracy," the military assigned itself tasks that demanded an extended rule.[6]

Within the Proceso, the economic program was quickly elevated to a position of pre-eminence. The newly designated minister of economics, José A. Martínez de Hoz, announced strict austerity measures in April 1976, which launched the government on an unprecedented free-market (or, as is commonly referred to in the Latin American setting, liberal) crusade to eliminate inflation and unshackle the economy from the fetters of state control. The Economics Ministry became a super ministry within the cabinet. Seldom were its directives challenged by the junta, nor could other departments successfully take issue with economic decrees that affected their own bureaucratic interests.[7] Some would argue that next to General Jorge Videla, Martínez de Hoz was the most powerful individual in the regime, by virtue of his expertise and the centrality of economics in the junta's overall plan. The preoccupation with economic variables at the expense of political ones would become the characteristic trademark of the government.

What led the military to choose the free-market approach? This was a peculiar and indeed remarkable decision, given its historical penchant for state intervention and subsidies. Beginning in the 1940s the armed forces acquired business concerns with the founding of the Dirección General de Fabricaciones Militares— the Argentine equivalent to the military industrial complex. Since these industries drew heavy subsidies from the state, the military had vested interests in rejecting economic models that proposed across-the-board cuts in fiscal spending.

First, the junta wanted a strategy that would depart from the previous Peronist program, whose wage-price-control policy it associated with hyperinflation, economic stagnation, and social unrest. The liberals' philosophical rejection of controls seemed to be the perfect choice. More significantly, the military's endorsement of the plan resulted from considerable lobbying efforts by the economics minister. Initially, Martínez de Hoz spent nearly one-third of his time traveling from barrack to barrack, explaining to military men the rationale and objectives behind his stabilization project.[8] Even officials who were never particularly fond of the minister or of his views admitted they were impressed with his style, logic, and command of the facts.[9] This led many of them to approve of the liberal plan, despite their misgivings. Martínez de Hoz was aided in his efforts by the fact that the armed forces had no strong ideological pre-dispositions and were consequently less biased and more open to new arguments.

In pursuing its principal object of reducing inflation, the free-market plan went through three phases.[10] The first tried to control excess demand through wage restraints. The decline in workers' incomes (wages fell 56 percent in real terms in the first two years) did reduce consumption, but this effect on inflation was offset by the freeing of prices and the devaluation of the peso. In June 1977 the government turned to a restrictive monetary policy: interest rates, normally controlled by the Central Bank, were set free; private banks could charge borrowers and reward depositors with whatever rates the market could bear. The intent was to curtail the flow of credit to the private domestic sector while building up the nation's savings capacity. Here again, results were unimpressive, as export surpluses and swelling peso accounts contributed to the growth of the money supply.

To rescue his anti-inflationary operation, Martínez de Hoz decided in December 1978 to trail the rate of devaluation of the peso behind the domestic rate of inflation (the plan was called the *"tablita"*). With an overvalued currency, the minister hoped to attract cheap imports and, in theory, induce a convergence between domestic and international prices. The plan yielded no results the first year (1979) and mildly positive results the second (1980) but still left Argentina with enormously high rates of inflation. Furthermore, the exchange-rate program had ruinous effects for domestic firms, (industrial production fell 19 percent in real terms from 1979 to 1981), which were driven out of business through the price advantages afforded to foreign corporations. The agricultural export sector faired only slightly better, as export prices became less attractive abroad; while wages began to rise in response to the exchange rate, real income of the workers remained below levels found at the beginning of the decade.[11]

Virtually every socioeconomic sector of Argentine society—from laborers and small shop owners to large industrialists and agriculturalists—opposed the economic policies. Yet the military remained remarkably unaffected by complaints from such powerful pressure groups. Rather than gauging its performance by the setbacks suffered by industrial and agricultural sectors, the junta concentrated on a set of macroeconomic variables. On the insistent advice of their economics minister, it noted positive trends in the rate of inflation (which had declined by 52.1 percent from 1979 to 1980), international reserves (they increased sixfold from 1976 to 1980), deposits in official and private banks (which grew seventy-five fold from 1976 to 1980), and state participation in the economy (which declined from 1975 to 1977 and then increased moderately from 1978 to 1980).[12] Comments made by military officers in January and February 1980 reflected some impatience with the stubbornly high rates of inflation but general approval of the minister's performance.[13]

The military's acceptance of overwhelmingly unpopular economic remedies attested not only to their commitment to the monetarist program but to the effectiveness of a political strategy that insulated state leaders from societal demands. By coercively demobilizing popular classes and denying the dominant classes their traditional "entrance ways" into state policy-making circles (i.e., by limiting personal contacts with military elites), Videla created a pressure-free environment that allowed the government to function as if special interests did not matter. Consequently, the regime displayed a high degree of unity in the face of an angry public. Ironically, the regime's isolation from society contributed to its stability during the first four years.

STAGE TWO: A LOSS OF FAITH

The turning point for the regime occurred just days after the fourth anniversary of the coup, with the collapse of several of Argentina's most important banks. In the last week of March the Banco Intercambio Regional (BIR) went under; several days later three more of the nation's largest financial institutions—Banco de los Andes, Banco Oddone, and Banco Internacional—followed suit. Together, these four banks held deposits that equaled 8 percent of the financial resources of the country.[14] All of them had grown impressively owing to the policy of freed interest rates. For instance, the BIR alone had acquired 350,000 savers with 1.67 billion pesos in deposits, or 3.5 percent of the country's total. By April the government had liquified its assets and had intervened in the three other financial institutions.

Many industries that were indebted to these banks could not meet repayment obligations, owing to the June 1977 freeing of interest rates and the overvalued exchange rate, which allowed foreign competitors easily to outbid local industry for market shares. The collapse of industry left banks with so many bad debts that they could no longer do business. Their failure touched off a financial panic, as depositors withdrew funds and demanded foreign exchange. Despite the Central Bank's best efforts, it could not stop the flight of capital that ensued—the first since the military had taken over.

The economics minister tried to localize the problem, claiming it was one of irresponsible management and lending policies on the part of these few firms and not symptomatic of the financial sector as a whole. But the minister's confidence was not shared by all within the armed forces. For the first time, there appeared subtle yet visible discrepancies in regime behavior and perceptions. The commander-in-chief of the navy, General Armando Lambruschini, noted on April 24 that "no society can tolerate sectors which exceed in a clear manner, the great limits of reason and justice." In reference to recent practices he called speculation "the greatest enemy of economic freedom in the realm of production."[15] Whereas Martínez de Hoz had insisted on a narrow definition of the crisis, Lambruschini painted a foreboding picture of the entire financial sector. Then the general took the unprecedented step of disclosing to the press that the navy's "misgivings" about the financial situation were brought to the attention of the junta. The decision by a member of the junta to publicize internal displeasure over the economic policy, particularly in light of the navy's historical penchant for liberal-orthodox programs of the kind Martínez de Hoz had advocated, was significant.

Several times during late April and May, Martínez de Hoz and his entire ministerial cabinet were called before high-ranking officials from all branches of the armed forces. The minister insisted that these meetings with the military had been planned months in advance and were therefore normal.[16] But the intensity at this time of high-level contacts and intentional public disclosures suggested that the military was not only deeply troubled by the events of April but convinced that its own policies were linked to the current crisis. In a reference to the economics minister, the commander-in-chief of the air force, Brigadier General Omar Rubens Graffigna, said, "We (the junta) do not remain indifferent to those responsible for the regime's problems."[17]

This did not indicate a readiness to abandon ship. General Leopoldo Galtieri reaffirmed the armed forces support, noting that no one (inside the armed forces) wanted to change the economic philosophy to satisfy the left or the right. By omission, Galtieri's remarks underscored the nature of the disagreement at the time; it was not over objectives but rather over strategies. Although not revealed then, it later became apparent that the financial crisis had touched off the first major confrontation within the ministry of economics—again over strategy. Alejandro Estrada, the secretary of commerce, argued along pure liberal lines, saying that financial difficulties could be avoided in the future by freely floating the currency on the world market and removing all guarantees on deposits. The minister disagreed and persisted with the *tablita*. But the secretary made clear that the loss of faith signaled by the flight of capital was not limited to investors but had crept into the economics ministry and into the ranks of the military as well.[18] Owing to the measures of success they had set out for themselves, the flight of capital should have worried the armed forces. They had been advised to ignore balance-of-trade deficits, since the massive influx of capital from abroad would more than compensate for a loss of export earnings, but the surge in demand for dollars jeopardized the country's reserve position. The problem was compounded by the large percentage of funds in short-term (thirty-ninety day) deposits. Any change in market conditions could result in a sudden and dramatic outflow of funds. It seems likely that by the summer of 1980 the armed forces were reevaluating their commitment to the program in light of the indicators.

STAGE THREE: POLITICAL SUCCESSION

The financial crisis complicated efforts in July and August of 1980 to find a successor to General Jorge Videla, whose term in office was to end in March 1981. The military and Videla in particular were committed to an orderly transfer of presidential power. Should they succeed, it would set a precedent, since every previous succession had been the result of a palace coup. In the midst of governmental change, Videla wanted to preserve a sense of institutional coherence and unity. He also wanted to insure that changes in personnel would not lead to alterations in the principal tenets of the Proceso. But given the unprecedented failure of Argentina's top banks and loss of reserves, would new leadership feel compelled to make economic policy changes?

Videla faced a dilemma. Although personally committed to the liberal economic program, he knew full well by August 1980 that other members of the armed forces were less than enthusiastic about the prospects of economic continuity. Videla's option was to extend his term, in deference to his economics minister. Martínez de Hoz sensed that his program would be scrapped under a new administration and urged Videla to stay in power another two years to give him enough time to produce results. Videla declined, cognizant of the fact that to evade procedure would have been unprofessional and would have fostered greater dissension in the ranks.[19] Thus the corporate interests of the military were placed above the desires of the Economics Ministry to complete the liberal mission.

On October 3 it was announced that the junta had chosen General Roberto Viola to succeed Videla. The decision was not surprising. Viola had been a classmate of Videla in the 1950s and served loyally under him as commander-in-chief of the army from 1978 to 1979. He was considered the moderate choice, the one likely to symbolize best the institutional continuity of the military. Yet Viola's selection was hardly automatic. The delay by a week in the announcement of a successor revealed the apparent squabble that lay under the surface: the navy had voted against Viola, while the army and air force had approved. The vote suggested the degree to which internal cleavages now fell along economic lines: the navy had become the champions of neo-classical economics and was clearly advocating Martínez de Hoz's position here. What were their objections to Viola?

Although Viola unquestionably supported the basic tenets of the national reorganization scheme of the armed forces, he differed tactically and stylistically with his predecessor. He believed that policy could not be made in a vacuum; it would have to be fashioned in light of the politically possible. That could only be surmised in consultation with important socioeconomic sectors (such as organized labor). This would conceivably upset the liberal economic strategy, which thrived on an insular style of policy-making. Viola was more the politician in contrast with Videla, who preferred to administrate rather than negotiate. Viola favored pragmatic compromise; Videla was the dogmatist.

These stylistic differences could not and did not determine overall policy outcomes in an institutionalized process. But within the parameters set by the regime, changes in executive tactics could be important. Martínez de Hoz realized this in the fall of 1981 and lobbied the junta and Viola to preserve the economic course he had originally set.

But the liberal's power base during the lame-duck presidency of Videla had narrowed, and Martínez de Hoz found it exceedingly difficult to convince the generals to stay the course. In one final effort to salvage the pieces of his plan, he called meetings with Videla and Viola in December and again in January to press for continuation. Viola refused to commit himself to the *tablita* and General Videla did nothing to convince him otherwise. To the contrary, a month later, on February 2, Martínez de Hoz was placed in the embarrassing position of having to go before the Argentine public to announce a 10 percent devaluation of the peso. The success of the economic plan hinged on the maintenance of a monthly devaluation rate below the level of inflation. The latest measure would exceed this limit and jeopardize the plan. In one stroke, the minister had undercut his anti-inflationary strategy, but he had done so at the urging of both General Viola and General Videla. Martínez de Hoz had no choice but personally to go before the Argentine public to announce the devaluation: Viola refused to allow his newly designated economics minister, Lorenzo Sigaut, to do so and thereby inherit all of the burdens of the previous plan. But in sharing the responsibility with the Videla government, Viola placed the onus on the regime itself.

In sum, the military preserved institutional integrity through its scheduled transfer of power. But in the process, it abandoned its zealous commitment to the liberal plan. By discarding a key component of the plan, it left itself with a motivational void. What would provide the incentive for continued rule?

STAGE FOUR: THE VIOLA GOVERNMENT AND REGIME DISUNITY

On March 29, 1981, General Roberto Viola assumed the presidency, but his government lasted less than nine months. By December 11 it had been ousted in a coup led by the army's commander-in-chief, General Leopoldo Galtieri. The rebellion against the president revealed the depth of disagreement and confrontation within the regime that had culminated in the coup of December. The military had led itself down a treacherous path of divisiveness, beginning with public discrepancies and followed by internal factioning and rebellion.

Viola sketched out his political formula in a series of speeches beginning with his inaugural address on March 28.[20] His plan of national integration envisioned the gradual normalization of intermediary organizations (i.e., unions and political parties), restoring some of the rights lost during the previous five years. Viola's proposal called for dialogue between the government and opposition to forge a national consensus on political transition. He left his long-term plans purposefully vague. But his promises to reinstate political party rights pointed the way toward conventions, selection of candidates, and elections—in short, a strategy of re-democratization.

In a speech in May 1981 General Leopoldo Galtieri outlined a different agenda for the future. While not renouncing Viola's political opening, or *abertura*, Galtieri cautioned against electoral interpretations, saying, "las urnas estan bien guardadas" (the ballot boxes are well guarded), and he emphasized that there would be no rapid phaseout of the Proceso.[21]

Apparently, Galtieri never consulted with Viola before making his discrepant remarks, nor did he feel any obligation to do so. This contrasts sharply with the Videla government, where the president enjoyed unswerving loyalty from his commanders-in-chief (first Viola and then Galtieri) and could avoid public disclosures that would raise embarrassing questions about regime solidarity.

Public discrepancies of June turned into confrontations in September. President Viola broached the subject of presidential succession in 1984. He said the next chief executive could not be chosen without political party participation or survive without broad-based popular support.[22] These remarks were taken as a hint that elections were on the agenda. The military quickly countered however, categorically ruling out elections for president in 1984, saying that the junta would designate a successor.

Within a week of his earlier remarks, Viola recoiled completely from the subject of an electoral timetable, arguing that the armed forces would "not offer fertile ground for those trying to hurry the work of democratic reorganization."[23] The president drew himself closer to the junta but in doing so simply reinforced the image of a weak leader and provided increased ammunition for his political foes. By this time, Viola's latitude as chief executive had narrowed considerably. His reported incessant consultations with the junta about practically all matters of state raised questions about the regime's own decision-making roles. Were the presidency and the government itself losing their authority?[24] Were Galtieri and his supporters gaining ground?

The internal disputes that plagued the military regime during the second half of 1981 opened up opportunities for the political opposition. In the first organized expression of solidarity among the major political parties since the coup, a coalition was formed in July called the Multipartidaria (Multiparty).[25] The Multiparty called for a prompt initiation of a phased plan for redemocratization and a nationalist-expansionist-oriented economic platform, which included tariff protection for industry, lower interest rates, liberalized credit, and substantial real wage increases.[26]

The government's response to the proclamation was cautious. Viola did not want to denounce the group, since some of its demands were his own. But at the same time he could not commit himself to the coalition's timetable without jeopardizing his already tenuous position with Galtieri's hard-liners, who were opposed to speeding up the transition.

Despite having set the stage for renewed political activity in 1981, Viola could not capitalize on it. One option would have been for him to generate a popular base of support as a counterweight to his right-wing opposition from within. He could then hold up the specter of a civilian offensive against the military should Galtieri and his allies threaten a coup. Instead, he found himself distanced from the political parties. With newfound confidence, the Multiparty said it would now pursue its objectives with or without government support.

At the same time, the birth of the Multiparty isolated the president even further from officers who perceived the political coalition as a direct threat. The challenge of the Multiparty was that it seized the initiative, thus underscoring the fact that the military had granted it the political space to do so. The opposition clarified the options for the regime: either commit itself to a phased withdrawal or become more resistant. Unquestionably, the military had the capacity to crush the parties, as it had done before. But those favoring a return to repressive rule were restrained by Viola's retention of executive power. Through the presidential office and the ministry of the interior (now run by Horacio Liendo, a loyal supporter of Viola and strong advocate of negotiation with labor), Viola controlled a large part of the coercive apparatus of the state. To clamp down on the political parties and the labor movement could mean usurping his authority. At the time (August and September 1981) Galtieri's forces probably lacked sufficient backing to do so. In the interim, the military seemed incapable of projecting power: it could neither make effective use of repression nor legitimize itself through linkage with populist sectors. Hence the basis of regime stability was in doubt. Because such a situation was untenable, stronger efforts were made in October and November by Galtieri loyalists to alter the balance of power within the regime. These efforts culminated on December 11 when General Galtieri removed General Viola from office and assumed the presidency.

The ouster did nothing to reunify the armed forces. Instead, it laid bare the bitter internal power struggle that had been waged for months prior. There seemed to be an amalgamation of right-wing nationalists and economic liberals behind Galtieri. Generals Christino Nicolaides of the Third Army Corps and Juan Trimarco of the Second Army Corps as well as the secretary-general of the army, Alfredo Oscar St. Jean, comprised an important part of Galtieri's support group. On the other side was a coalition of politically moderate and economically nationalist officers, such as General Jose Villareal of the Fifth Army Corps and General Horacio Liendo, the interior minister. Alliances crossed over service lines, with Almirante Jorge Anaya, newly appointed commander-in-chief of the navy, an apparent Galtieri loyalist, and coup instigator from early on.

Galtieri's motives were ideological (he favored a return to neo-classical models with a strong repressive state) and personal. By removing Viola, he could become president and have the option of retaining his position as commander-in-chief (which he did), thereby centralizing power. All the while, Galtieri's strategy was to lay the problems of the Proceso on Viola's doorstep. By personalizing the difficulties the regime was facing, Galtieri could assume power and "clear the name" of the armed forces—as well as his own. Instead, his machinations inadvertently precipitated a decline in regime performance. His personal drive for power widened divisions within the military, which Videla had deftly controlled. Neither Galtieri nor the armed forces could disassociate themselves from Viola's legacy; it was their own.

Perhaps Galtieri understood this. In his inaugural address, he presented a demoralized and insecure military to the Argentine public. He said this was "an hour of uncertainty," adding that "the time for words and promises had been used up."[27] The junta did not expect Argentine citizens to stand united behind them, so the government would have to earn the nation's confidence, he said. The press reflected the general sentiment in and out of government. One newspaper said that "for the first time the unity of the actors in the 'Proceso' appears fractured."[28]

I have argued that the descent of the military regime during this year could best be attributed to successive failures to manage governmental conflicts and to redefine and coalesce around the objectives of the Proceso. This is not to suggest that the political or economic goals embodied in the Proceso were either beneficial to Argentina or worthy in their own right. Indeed, given the tremendous loss of life at the hands of state security forces and the dramatic decline of Argentine industry resulting from the application of the liberal model, many serious objections could be raised about the political economy of the regime.[29] However, the source of immediate tension for the regime did not lay in the unpopularity of its programs (which was great) but the declining chances that its actors could remain unified in whatever goals and strategies they had set for themselves. Without a consensus and a sense of mission, the military could easily lose sight of its objectives and fail to justify continued intervention in the political process. In the final stage of military rule, President Galtieri tried to reestablish a sense of purpose for the armed forces.

STAGE FIVE: THE GALTIERI GOVERNMENT GOES TO WAR

Galtieri began his term as head of a military government now weakened by a year of factional conflict. However, his initial political and economic strategies did nothing to heal the wounds or bolster the confidence of the armed forces. First, his political ploys confused fellow officers. His apparent object was to chart a middle course between continued dictatorial rule on the one hand and a rapid transition to electoral politics on the other hand. Resurrecting ideas that had been used in the past by the military, Galtieri called for the creation of a unitary movement for political change. This would "represent, in organic fashion, an independent current of national opinion which until now has remained diffuse."[30] The president would build a military-civilian coalition that would gradually accumulate sufficient support to return Galtieri to office as an elected official in 1984. Clearly, Galtieri would have to reduce the competitive advantage of the multi-party opposition or risk an embarrassing electoral defeat as occurred in 1973 at the hands of the Peronists.[31] With that in mind, he began to popularize his government with the appointment of civilian governors and state administrators in January. He then met secretly with key Peronist leaders (unaware to the rest of the military) in an apparent effort to strike a deal. In exchange for labor support, he would relax union restrictions, invite some Peronists into his government, and remain as president through 1984 while delaying elections indefinitely.

Yet Galtieri would not abandon competitive politics altogether. His announcement upon the sixth anniversary of the coup that a political party law would be passed by mid-year that would restore the party system and commence a serious dialogue about redemocratization left democratic forces cautiously optimistic. But Galtieri's maneuvers left the commanding officers confused. The exposure of the meetings with Peronists angered the military. The two-track political plan left the impression that the government was erasing with the left what it had written with the right. If its aim was to arrange a military-civilian power-sharing formula, why restore political party rights? What was the overall objective of the junta: to maintain power, share it, or relinquish it? These were questions posed by division and brigade army generals in a meeting with Galtieri the first week of March. They demanded that they be kept informed about all of the president's activities and insisted that a cohesive strategy soon be devised. But even more serious were their objections to the continuation of the present economic policies.

Galtieri had chosen Roberto Alemann to be his minister of economics. Alemann was an even more devout exponent of pure economic liberalism than Martínez de Hoz. The minister's initial measures included a complete freeze on all public-sector wages (affecting some 1.6 million workers) and a plan to turn portions of the military industrial complex over to the private sector—all in an effort to trim the budget deficit from 8 percent in 1981 to 2 percent for 1982.[32]

The plan placed an onerous burden on the working class, provided no relief for indebted industry, and was sure to antagonize military industrialists. But Alemann received strong support from Galtieri.

The minister of the interior, General St. Jean, candidly expressed the sentiment of many other officers when he said there was a "contradiction between the political orientation designed to procure democracy and a rigid economic policy that must necessarily be harsh."[33] How could Galtieri prepare the way for his own electoral victory with an economic program that was clearly unpopular? At the same meeting of early March, a document was drawn up and endorsed by a large number of high-ranking officers. It referred to the "failure" of the Proceso's economic plan, which had "gravely" affected the credibility of the armed forces, and emphasized that no further positive results were likely should Roberto Alemann continue with his orthodox model for economic recovery.[34]

Galtieri's mishandling of the Peronist meetings, his poorly devised two-track political plan, and his ill-fated defense of the economics minister weakened his own authority and widened the fissures within the military establishment. It was imperative that Galtieri shore up his own position and that of the regime itself. It was in this context that he chose the military option.

In embarking on an invasion of the Malvinas on April 2, 1982, the military had finally implemented a plan that had been first seriously considered in December 1981, directly after the Galtieri coup. Under strong prodding from navy commander Admiral Jorge I. Anaya (who backed the new government on condition that they break the deadlock over the Malvinas) the junta decided on January 6 to go ahead with an invasion.

The military made two miscalculations. The first was to assume that the British would not respond with a full show of force. The armed forces were so confident in their prediction that they sent into battle eighteen- and nineteen-year-old conscripts with only two weeks' training and no experience in the cold South Atlantic climate. General Menendez, who directed the operation, had never commanded any fighting units and had very little knowledge of the terrain. According to the Calvi Report issued after the war, the soldiers were told by their superiors that the operation would be for symbolic purposes, since no enemy response was anticipated.[35] Since the military was not anticipating a major armed confrontation, it would appear that in their eyes the Malvinas operation carried minimal risks. But the British sinking of the ship Belgrano and their subsequent land invasion thoroughly exposed Galtieri's errors of judgment and sent the generals scurrying to find an honorable way out of the conflict.

During those first few weeks, the Malvinas operation (referred to by the military as Operation Rosario) had its desired effect: the military, having floundered for months without a purpose, suddenly had one and rallied to Galtieri's side. Had the military found a way to rescue the Proceso? It would appear not. The generals quickly wrote the Malvinas operation into the Proceso's script, claiming that it had always been the logical sequel to the defeat of the guerillas and the subsequent normalization of the political and economic spheres. The military hoped to convey the impression that the operation was not a response to failed domestic policies but, on the contrary, an important chapter in the military's larger mission to restore national security and sovereignty.

It was clear that regardless of the war's outcome, the regime's plans were in trouble. As early as April the military spoke about removing Alemann as economics minister, which was a clear admission of defeat for laissez-faire economics. But more seriously, there was no indication that the war effort had expanded Galtieri's political appeal. The president's second miscalculation was to have thought that his "movement of national opinion" would win a greater public following once the battle for the Malvinas was underway.

The estimated 250,000 people that crowded in front of the presidential palace on April 6 to back the Malvinas operation also shouted their disapproval of the regime itself. In fact, organized labor and the multi-party coalition made it clear to the president that at war's end they would press for a swift restoration of their social and political freedoms. Consequently, the war had not altered the agenda of the opposition nor drawn it into Galtieri's "movement." Whether Operation Rosario ended in victory or defeat, the masses had no intention of abdicating to the junta. A victory in the war would have bought some time for the regime; the defeat simply hastened a degenerative process already underway. The postwar government led by General Reynaldo Bignone could do nothing more than schedule elections according to the timetable proposed by the multi-party coalition. When Raul Alfonsin assumed the presidency in December 1983, military rule in Argentina officially came to a close.

The Argentine military invited its own defeat. Far from being overcome by a formidable opposition, the armed forces through their own blunders and inadequacies opened up a political space that their adversaries gladly filled. The regime did not consciously hand power over to the civilians; the withdrawal was largely unpremeditated. Rather than performing as a rational and unitary actor, the military regime fell into disarray.

This is not to suggest that the military lacked a broad opposition and therefore ruled legitimately. To the contrary, it very quickly lost its popular mandate of March 1976 by carrying out a "dirty war" against the guerillas, which left thousands of innocent victims in its wake. It then became imperative to extend its repressive apparatus to society at large. Despite having been perched atop a precariously narrow base of support (limited mainly to the financial capitalists) the regime held its balance with relative ease for the first four years—but only through the effective use of coercion.

It is conceivable that in the absence of viable protest, the force of inertia would propel the regime's policies forward indefinitely. However, Guillermo O'Donnell pointed out that should performance be ruled unsatisfactory—within the biased set of indicators chosen by the regime itself—this can weaken the confidence of the ruling coalition and promote internal divisions.[36] With the military badly divided, it will be unable, in A. Stepan's words, to "dominate the entire state apparatus, much less agree on an inclusionary or exclusionary design to impose on society."[37] To bring the full weight of the state's repressive apparatus to bear upon a political opposition, the regime must be unified and resolute in carrying out its objectives. The task of organizing a complex security force is made difficult when lines of authority break down as they do in an organization riddled with dissent.

In the Argentine case, it is clear that after the bank failures and capital flight in 1980, and the subsequent transfer of power from Videla to Viola, consensus regarding the critical ideas and strategies of governance had disappeared. Factions that previously had laid dormant now emerged. Political hard-liners and economic liberals teamed up against political moderates and economic nationalists. The clash between these subgroups diverted the military's attention long enough to allow democratic forces to regroup. Under these circumstances, military subgroups will often cultivate support from influential social actors to improve their own internal bargaining positions. However, in the Argentine case, the regime's imperviousness and autonomy from social groups worked to its disadvantage once the will to repress had evaporated. Viola could not solidify his position with the Multiparty, since it was distrustful of a figure who himself had been a sponsor of the "dirty war." Galtieri's natural alliances were limited by the exclusionary nature of the monetarist practices of Martínez de Hoz (leaving only the financial sector in support). Hence the political game was played out internally, with Galtieri grabbing enough of the uncommitted officers ultimately to prevail.

But Galtieri's views were no longer "hegemonic" within the regime: gone were the themes of internal warfare and spirited free enterprise that had unified the military under Videla. Still badly divided, the regime could not agree on a strategy of either renewed repression or political liberalization. The failure to achieve consensus among elites is damaging to a regime such as this one, which cannot win popular legitimacy or even anchor itself with a social class. Faced with a more formidable opposition, Galtieri sought a new unifying theme and thought he had found it with the invasion of the Malvinas. But by war's end, it was evident that the armed forces had neither regained the confidence of the public nor healed their own wounds and thus returned to the barracks in defeat.

It is difficult under any circumstances to speculate on the chances for a lengthy and stable period of democracy. More so in the case of Argentina where democracy has been a short interlude between periods of military rule. One noted scholar of Argentina said that "nothing is more foreign to Argentina than anti-militarism."[38] The statement was intended to convey the idea that social groups themselves have been eager to elicit the support of the armed forces, and the armed forces have complied. Since the fall of Perón in 1955, each civilian president has seen his full term abruptly cut short by military intervention; succeeding military governments survived longer than the ones before; and each succeeding democratic government remained in power for a shorter duration. If these simple trends are of any significance, the future is not bright for the Alfonsín government.

However, there are reasons to believe that this time the democratic phase may
be more durable. There are two approaches to the problem. One is to comment
on the positive aspects of redemocratization since 1983 that have fostered greater
loyalty for democratic procedure. The other is to examine the drawbacks of
authoritarian rule, which may give pause to social classes and political forces
and even the military itself when contemplating another coup.

There are lessons to be learned from the most recent experience of bureaucratic
authoritarian rule in Argentina. The first has to do with comparative expectations
and economic performance. The dominant capitalist classes had hoped that the
bureaucratic authoritarian regime of 1976–83 would repeat the fine economic
record achieved by its predecessor between 1966 and 1970 and with politically
more stable conditions. Under the direction of Economics Minister Krieger Vasena, the government of General Juan Carlos Ongania impressively achieved
4.0 percent real growth and kept inflation at a moderate 28.0 percent, while
pursuing one of only three successful stabilization programs in South America
during the 1950s and 1960s.[39] The program reaped benefits for the propertied
sectors, as their share of national income increased from 54.6% in 1967 to 57.9%
in 1970. More specifically, the large transnational and national conglomerates,
whose magnates are thought to be the principal agents behind the formation of
the bureaucratic-authoritarian state, experienced a large increase in profits (in
part due to declining real wages in 1967 and 1968) and sales compared with the
pre–1966 period. According to O'Donnell, this period constituted the "reconstruction of the economic dominance of the grand bourgeoisie."[40] Unfortunately,
the Ongania government had not prepared itself for the sudden worker-student
uprisings in Cordoba in 1969 and could never complete its economic project,
having been overwhelmed by these political events. The bourgeoisie was confident that the Videla government would be different. Representing a similar
ruling coalition of classes, it was confronted at the outset by a formidable guerilla
movement and a mobilized working class. The higher level of "threat" would
invite the necessary amount of force to secure a stable economic environment.
Indeed, during the first year and a half there was reason for the propertied sectors
to be optimistic, since inflation rates declined from 347.5 to 160.4 percent, the
economy grew by 6.4 percent in 1977, and the share of national income going
to the working class plummeted from 45.7 percent in 1975 to 31.2 percent in
1976.[41] By 1979, however, wage earners had recouped some of their losses as
corporate profits declined.

More important than these relative shifts were the absolute losses. The average
rate of industrial growth at factor costs was -2.8 and gross fixed investment
figured at -0.5% for the period. After disaggregating the industrial sector by
size of firms, it is clear that even some corporate giants did not fare well after
1978. Of the top five private firms of 1977, four experienced a decline in sales
revenue in real terms after 1978, and only one held its position in rank.[42] The
post–1977 recession left a trail of failed companies in its wake. The regime
insisted this was proof that resources were being reallocated toward more pro-

Table 9.1
Economic Performance in Comparative Perspective: Two Argentine Regimes[a]

	Democratic	Bureaucratic-Author
	(1973-75)	1976-82)
Real GDP growth[b]	3.0	-.1
Inflation rates	139.6	178.0
Investment	4.4	-.5
Industrial growth	2.4	-2.8
Agricultural growth	3.5	2.0

[a] all figures are in percentages
[b] figures represent the average annual growth rate for period

Sources: GDP data for 1973–1982 data from Fundacion de Investigaciones para el Dessarrollo (FIDE) *Coyuntura y Desarrollo: Anexo Estadístico XIV* (Buenos Aires, April 1983), p. 16. Inflation data for 1973–75 are from the World Bank; for 1976–82, from Victor E. Tokman, "Global Monetarism and Destruction of Industry," *CEPAL Review* 23 (August 1984): 116. Investment represents gross fixed investment, and data are from Fundacion de Investigaciones para el Desarrollo, *Coyuntura y Desarrollo*, p. 16; industrial performance, from idem, *Coyuntura y Desarrollo*, p. 18; agricultural performance data, from idem, *Coyuntura y Desarrollo*, p. 18.

ductive sectors. However, one study reveals that of every ninety-nine workers who lost their jobs in the industry, fifty-two went over to low-productivity occupations or swelled the ranks of the unemployed.[43] These facts could not have but disillusioned the most ardent supporters of military rule who had claimed authoritarian leadership would always place the highest premium on rational and efficient growth.

Not only did this regime fail to measure up to the first bureaucratic-authoritarian regime, but it could not even compare favorably with the previous period of civilian rule. Table 9.1 indicates that in every respect the performance of the economy under military rule was considerably worse than that found under the shaky Peronist civilian government of 1973–76, whose thorough mismanagement of the economy beginning in mid–1974 led to its own demise. Consequently, a comparative view of this latest period would call into question the utility of this brand of authoritarian rule.

Certainly not all economic outcomes, successful or unsuccessful, could be attributed to policy itself. Governmental manipulation of interest rates, bank credit, exchange rates, and tariffs can condition but ultimately not control the direction of an ostensibly free-market economy. Nonetheless, victims of economic misfortune are quick to blame the authorities whether or not they are responsible, and they did so in the Argentine case. On the fifth anniversary of the coup, the Sociedad Rural Argentina, representing the largest cattle ranchers and wheat growers in the nation (including the family of Martínez de Hoz) cited (among other measures) the exchange-rate policy of December 1978 as a "great error," which had contributed directly to declining export sales and higher internal costs. It said that "urgent" corrective measures must be taken to forestall further economic decline.[44]

A leading association of giant national and transnational conglomerates in Argentina is called the Consejo Empresario Argentino (CEA). The CEA was formed in 1967 (with the endorsement of then Economics Minister Krieger Vasena) to serve as a channel of communication between government and the business community. The CEA's enthusiastic approval of Krieger Vasena's economic program from 1966 to 1969 was ample proof that the grand bourgeoisie was pleased with state policies then. Twelve years later this same organization on the third anniversary of the 1976 coup issued a position paper that took the government to task for failing to "apply the principles outlined in March of 1976 in a permanent and coherent form" and specifically criticized the ministers' policies on public spending, inflation, salaries, and exchange rates.[45] This was a significant document because it provided evidence that the Proceso had failed to satisfy even the upper stratum of the bourgeoisie.

The striking aspect of all of this was its unpredictable character. Given the posited linkages between the bureaucratic-authoritarian state and its governing agents on the one hand and these classes on the other hand, one would have predicted a different set of outcomes. José Martínez de Hoz was himself formerly a member of the SRA and president of the CEA. Having been born into a powerful and distinguished landed family and as past chairman of the board of Acindar Corporation (the nation's largest private steel company), it was presumed that with his appointment the interests of the dominant classes would be well protected. Yet they were not.

The problem is more serious than simply a failure to perform. If that were all, the private sector might very well conclude that with the right economic plan, a new authoritarian coalition could govern satisfactorily. The issue, however, is also one of policy responsiveness. The dominant classes in Argentina and elsewhere in Latin America had thrown their weight behind military coups before, in hopes of establishing a strong regime that could withstand the assaults of the popular classes. The bureaucratic-authoritarian regime would, they hoped, allow a coherent set of economic policies aimed at facilitating the accumulation of capital to emerge uninterrupted and unobstructed by popular protest and yet be sensitive to the bourgeoisie's own needs. The state would disarm social and political groups that challenged the state's dominant economic project while remaining open to unofficial flows of influence from the privileged classes. It was thought that the state "moved in time with the upper fractions of the bourgeoisie," so that the regime's autonomy was consequently limited and its policy preferences fully sensitive to the demands of the propertied elite.[46]

The Ongania government of 1966–70 seemed to fit the description fairly well; the same could not be said for the Videla government of 1976–81. Despite repeated efforts by representatives of the pampa bourgeoisie and medium and large industrial establishments, the regime remained intractable; neither interest rate nor exchange rate nor tariff policies were appreciably altered to satisfy the concerns of these powerful economic sectors. The government was unresponsive not only to the data, which suggested a continued decline for industry and a downturn for agriculture after 1978, but to the specific complaints lodged by representatives of these sectors. The Unión Industrial Argentina pleaded with the government to enforce anti-dumping legislation to protect local business against unfair competitive practices of foreign corporations. Although such measures were finally approved, they came much too late for Argentine industry. The Confederación Rurales Argentina explained to the economics minister the fact that interest rates (which were 98 percent in nominal terms and 26 percent in real terms in 1980) were making it prohibitive for farmers to finance the purchase of new equipment to raise yields. Many had already gone into serious debt; others were selling out, as the cost of inputs rose faster than the domestic price of their commodities. The minister refused to provide credit on more lenient terms and responded with a ghastly logic: if there were those who were selling out, others must be buying. The high cost of borrowing will challenge the new owners to avoid the inefficiencies of the past, raise levels of productivity, and contribute to the economy's growth.

The military became impervious to societal pressures through exclusionary tactics. Policy-making was undertaken in a well-insulated environment. This in turn enabled the regime to gauge its performance with a set of indicators that had significance not for societal groups but for state officials. Monetary contraction, increased savings, and reserves were valued over investment, consumption, and income redistribution. While the commanding officers and their economic technocrats congratulated themselves on the basis of highly selective evidence, labor and entrepreneurial sectors were made to bear the costs in income, purchasing power, and profit losses.

Martínez de Hoz had promised the private sector early on that his administration would not sway from its original plan. Initially the bourgeoisie was all smiles, but ironically, it was precisely that commitment to stay the course that later revealed to them the inherent dangers of authoritarian rule. It is a lot easier for powerful social classes to set the armed forces loose against weak civilian leaders than it is to rein them in. Authoritarian rule shows its darker side when its economic policies fail to achieve prosperity and when its policy-makers shield themselves from private-sector influence. These classes may now believe that their interests cannot be left unguarded at the doorstep of the military and will prefer a more open system susceptible to influence. If so, this can only strengthen the hand of democracy.

It is too early to tell just how deep the capitalists' sense of betrayal toward the previous regime runs. But a poll taken in August 1985 indicates that upper-class support for military intervention has already eroded. When asked to rank twelve social organizations or institutions according to reputation, the public placed the military at the bottom of the list. When disaggregated by income groups for the first time, it was found that the upper class had a more negative assessment of the armed forces than the middle-income sectors.[47] Furthermore, parties of the right, which have traditionally represented these same classes, have called for subordination of the military to civilians, democratic socialization of military officials, and reduced conscription.[48] These facts could augur in a trend away from the political culture of militarism so prevalent in Argentina.

The regime's autonomy may have contributed to its stability during the first four years. But ironically, it may undermine future efforts to restore authoritarian rule. Free from popular protest from below and defiant of significant fractions of the upper class, the military brought into sharper focus its own performance and in the process laid bare its own inadequacies. The claim made by monetarist technocrats in 1976 that previous stabilization efforts under authoritarian rule had never been given a fair chance to succeed could not be used again to justify another coup. The "proper political climate" *had* been achieved; the military simply could not take advantage of it, and its self-inflicted wounds should strengthen the forces of anti-militarism and democracy in the foreseeable future.

NOTES

1. Dankwart A. Rustow, "Transitions to Democracy: Toward a Dynamic Model," *Comparative Politics* 2 (April 1970): 337–363.

2. Charles L. Taylor and David Jodice, *World Handbook of Political and Social Indicators*, 3d ed., vol. 2, *Political Protest and Government Change* (New Haven: Yale University Press, 1983).

3. The writings on military coups are too numerous to mention. A noteworthy example is found in Abraham F. Lowenthal, ed., *Armies and Politics in Latin America* (New York: Holmes and Meier, 1976). On military withdrawal from power, see Christopher Clapham and George Philip, *The Political Dilemmas of Military Regimes* (London: Croom Helm, 1985). See also Guillermo O'Donnell, *1966–1973: El Estado Burocratico Autoritario: Triunfos, Derrotas y Crisis* (Buenos Aires: Editorial de Belgrano, 1982).

4. Morris Janowitz, *Sociology and the Military Establishment* (Beverly Hills, Calif.: Sage Publications, 1974).

5. The costs of factionalism are discussed by O'Donnell. He explained how the Argentine coup of 1966 was made possible once the armed forces had resolved their differences. See Guillermo O'Donnell, *Modernization and Bureaucratic-Authoritarianism: Studies in South American Politics* (Berkeley, Calif.: Institute of International Studies, 1979). Another author demonstrated how the post-coup military of Peru held together only because of General Juan Velasco's careful management of dissent from within. See J. Garcia, "Military Factions and Military Intervention in Latin America," in S. W. Simon, ed., *The Military and Security in the Third World: Domestic and International Impacts* (Boulder, Colo.: Westview Press, 1978).

6. Revista de Educación del Ejército, "El Proceso de Reorganización Nacional como Respuesta Institucional de las Fuerzas Armadas," *Revista de Educación de Ejército* 31 (1979): 55–93.

7. In an interview, General Horacio Liendo, ex-minister of labor under President Videla, described his frustration in not making headway in labor negotiations because of the recalcitrance of the economics minister who had sufficient backing in the government to block any wage adjustments.

8. Interview with José A. Martínez de Hoz, July 1984, Buenos Aires.

9. Interview with an army general, former junta member, and president of Argentina, July 1984, Buenos Aires.

10. José A. Martínez de Hoz, *Bases para una Argentina Moderna* (Buenos Aires: Companía Impresora Argentina, 1981).

11. Industrial growth data are from Fundación de Investigaciones para el Desarrollo, *Coyuntura y Desarrollo: Anexa Estadística XIV* (Buenos Aires, April 1983), p. 9. Workers' income data are from Republica Argentina, Ministerio de Economía, *Instituto Nacional de Estadística y Censos: Indice de Precios al Consumidor y Salarios Industriales* 109 (January 1982): 1531.

12. Fundación de Investigaciones para el Desarrollo, *Coyuntura y Desarrollo; El Mercado*, August 24, 1978, p. 97; August 30, 1979, p. 159; August 27, 1981, p. 18.

13. Estimates of the military's views were made by reading press reports from January to March 1980 in *La Nacion, La Prensa*, and *El Economista*.

14. *Latin America Weekly Report*, April 4, 1980, p. 6; May 2, 1980, p. 1.

15. *La Nacion Weekly*, April 28, 1980, p. 5.

16. Interview with José A. Martínez de Hoz, 1984, Buenos Aires.

17. *El Economista*, September 18, 1981, pp. 1, 4, 5.

18. Interview with Alejandro M. Estrada, July 1984, Buenos Aires.

19. Interview with J. A. Martínez de Hoz, July 1984, Buenos Aires.

20. *La Nacion*, March 29, 1981, p. 22.

21. General Galtieri also said, "In the last fifty years other military procesos, faced with the proliferation of criticism, took the wrong path and thought elections were the solution to the political problem. The history of those successive failures, the after effects of which we are still suffering, leaves us with the hard but wise lesson that we must not make the same mistake." *Latin America Weekly Report*, July 3, 1981, p. 10.

22. *El Economista*, September 18, 1981, pp. 1, 4, 5.

23. *La Nacion Weekly*, October 2, 1981, p. 5.

24. In a tone suggestive of an ultimatum, the junta demanded on October 1, 1981, that Viola present them a detailed plan for economic recovery by October 12.

25. The parties involved were the Radicals, Justicialists (Peronists), Christian Democrats, Intransigent Party, and Movement of Integration and Development.

26. Multipartidaria, *La Propuesta de la Multipartidaria* (Buenos Aires: El Cid Editor, 1982).

27. *La Nacion Weekly*, December 28, 1981, p. 1

28. *El Economista*, December 11, 1981, p. 1.

29. Amnesty International estimates that more than 15,000 people were arrested and unaccounted for by the junta. Most of them have been discovered or presumed to be dead.

30. *Latin America Weekly Report*, February 26, 1982, p. 6.

31. General Alejandro Lanusse paved the way for elections in 1973. However, the military's candidate, Brigadier Ezequiel Martinez, received 2.9 percent of the vote compared with the Peronists's 49.5 percent. Galtieri described Lanusse's strategy as a "leap into the void."

32. *Buenos Aires Herald*, January 3, 1982, p. 1; *Latin America Weekly Report*, January 29, 1982, p. 12.

33. *Noticias Argentinas*, April 1, 1982, p. 1.

34. *La Nacion Weekly*, March 8, 1982, p. 5.

35. A. Gavshon and D. Rice, *The Sinking of the Belgrano* (London: Secker and Warburg, 1984); G. Makin, "Argentina Approaches to the Falklands/Malvinas: Was the Resort to Violence Foreseeable?" *International Affairs* 59 (Summer 1983): 391–403.

36. O'Donnell, *Modernization and Bureaucratic-Authoritarianism*.

37. Alfred Stepan, *The State and Society: Peru in Comparative Perspective* (Princeton, N.J.: Princeton University Press, 1978), p. 85.

38. Alain Rouquié, *Poder Militar y Sociedad Politica en la Argentina, II: 1943–1973* (Buenos Aires: Emecé Editores, 1982).

39. A comparative analysis of this program is found in Thomas E. Skidmore, "The Politics of Economic Stabilization in Postwar Latin America," in James M. Malloy, *Authoritarianism and Corporatism in Latin America* (Pittsburgh: University of Pittsburgh Press, 1977), pp. 149–190.

40. O'Donnell, *1966–1973: El Estado Burocratico Autoritario*, p. 215.

41. Fundación de Investigaciones para el Desarrollo, *Coyuntura y Desarrollo* 60 (August 1983): 35.

42. *El Mercado*, August 24, 1978, p. 98; August 30, 1979, p. 160.

43. Victor E. Tokman, "Global Monetarism and Destruction of Industry," *CEPAL Review* 23 (August 1984): 113.

44. Sociedad Rural Argentina, *Boletín de la Sociedad Rural Argentina* 469 (April 15, 1981): 2, 3.

45. Consejo Empresario Argentino, "A Tres Años del 24 de Marzo de 1976," Memorandum, March 24, 1979, esp. p. 17.

46. Guillermo O'Donnell, "State and Alliances in Argentina, 1956–1976," *Journal of Development Studies* 15, (October 1978): 25.

47. *Latin America Weekly Report*, August 16, 1985, p. 10.

48. Walter Little, "Civil-Military Relations in Contemporary Argentina," *Government and Opposition* 19 (Spring 1984): 207–224.

10

U.S. Foreign Assistance Policy and the Redemocratization of Latin America

David Carleton and Michael Stohl

Analysts of recent U.S.-Latin American relations are frequently trapped by the myths propagated by the personnel and supporters of our two most recent presidents. These myths represent a picture of the world that each administration would prefer us to believe. These mythmakers paint the policies of their own administration in the best possible light and the policies of the other as ineffective and dangerous. If accepted, these mythologies order our perception of events and can lead to serious oversimplification and misunderstanding. As in most myths, within each we can find a kernel of truth. But largely in the interest of U.S. domestic political concerns, these kernels have been magnified and distorted. Thus to understand accurately the U.S. role in redemocratization, we must break through the constraints imposed by these political and ideological myths.

The myths offered by President Carter and his supporters include:

Myth 1: President Carter made an ''absolute commitment'' to human rights and democracy in Latin America and, to that end, pursued and punished gross violators of human rights by denying them U.S. foreign assistance. In this way, he pressured authoritarian regimes to embark upon a democratic path.

Myth 2: The Reagan administration purposefully abandoned the Carter human rights policy and ended the use of foreign assistance as an instrument for punishing dictators. Instead, Reagan chose to embrace Latin American dictators who joined him in the more pressing fight against global communism.

On the other hand, President Reagan and his supporters hold that:

Myth 3: The Carter policy served only to reduce U.S. ties to authoritarian regimes and thus merely reduced U.S. leverage over them. It therefore did little to promote liberalization.

Myth 4: President Reagan is deeply committed to human rights and democracy and promotes them with established U.S. influence by means of "quiet" or "traditional" diplomacy. This policy has made a significant contribution to the present wave of democratization in Latin America.

These myths have dominated and structured public discourse on U.S.-Latin American relations in recent years. In this chapter we attempt to avoid the pitfalls of these myths. First, we briefly discuss the enduring themes of U.S.-Latin American relations, which allows us to place the Carter and Reagan policies in historical context. Second, we take a hard look at U.S. opportunities and potentials for contributing to positive regime change in Latin America.

PRELUDE: U.S.-LATIN AMERICAN RELATIONS SINCE INDEPENDENCE

> The United States seems destined by Providence to plague Latin America with misery in the name of Liberty.
>
> —Simon Bolivar, 1828[1]

> I tell you now that the success of the democratic enterprise in this hemisphere is not a matter of indifference to the United States. Democracy is at once the foundation and objective of our cooperation.
>
> —Secretary of State George Shultz, 1984[2]

The United States has been involved intimately in Latin American affairs since the Latin nations fought for and won their independence from Spain early in the previous century. In the nineteenth century, following the demise of Iberic power, Britain quickly assumed the dominant role in Latin America. Nevertheless, given its proximity, the United States had a natural interest in the region. Although aimed at European expansion in North America, the declaration of the Monroe Doctrine (however weak the U.S. ability to enforce it) began the process of building U.S. hegemony in the entire hemisphere. For the most part, however, early U.S. activities in Latin America consisted of pursuing economic inroads. Substantial and sustained U.S. involvement did not begin until after the Civil War. The Spanish-American War in 1898 opened this century as U.S.-Latin American relations moved first through the period of the Big Stick and Dollar Diplomacy and then through the more pleasing sounding periods of the Good Neighbor Policy, the Alliance for Progress, the Mature Partnership, the New Dialogue, and now the Caribbean Basin Initiative.[3] Whereas the former policies made little pretense of real concern for democracy (although the theme may always be found in presidential addresses), the latter policies have brought with them a great deal of rhetoric about democracy and development. With hindsight, however, it would not be too great an exaggeration to suggest that the conception of democracy employed (when, indeed, one was considered at all) had far more to do with capitalism and private enterprise than with any notion of democracy in a political sense. It certainly had little to do with the expansive liberal interpretation of democracy represented by the American or French revolutionary traditions (life, liberty, and the pursuit of happiness or liberty, equality and fraternity). Here, we summarize and discuss the interaction and contradiction of these policies and the promotion of human rights and democracy in Latin America from 1898 to the mid–1970s.

The first decades of this century were characterized by the frequent use of the U.S. Marines, the favored instrument of the Big Stick. This was particularly true in Central America and the Caribbean, where U.S. influence was greatest. In addition to the U.S. intervention in Mexico during that country's revolution, the United States intervened militarily on fifteen occasions between 1898 and 1934.[4] In all, 1903, 1904, and 1911 were the only years during this thirty-six-year period in which the United States was not occupying all or part of at least one Central American or Caribbean country. Beyond occasional rhetoric, this heavy-handed behavior had little to do with the pursuit of democracy. What discussion or consideration there was of democracy, furthermore, was paternalistic. It was assumed (or, actually, declared) that U.S. political and economic involvement in the Latin American nations "naturally" had a "civilizing," liberalizing, and democratizing effect. But if this occurred, it certainly was a side effect of U.S. intervention rather than its primary purpose. To the contrary, intervention was almost always intended to secure narrowly defined U.S. political and economic interests in the region.

In contrast to later years, the reasons for intervention were discussed unapologetically and, hence, openly. The United States most frequently intervened to insure payment of loans made by U.S. banks and to insure the maintenance of a favorable business climate, although there were instances in which intervention was clearly meant to secure political interests. The reasons for U.S. intervention were discussed by Smedley D. Butler, a general in the marines and commander of several U.S. expeditionary forces, who wrote about this experiences upon his retirement. His striking candor warrants quoting him at length.

I spent thirty-three years and four months in active service as a member of our country's most agile military force—the Marine Corps. I served in all commissioned ranks from a second lieutenant to major-general. And during that period I spent most of that time being a high-class muscle man for Big Business, for Wall Street and for the bankers. In short, I was a racketeer for capitalism . . . Thus, I helped make Mexico and especially Tampico safe for American oil in 1914. I helped make Haiti and Cuba a decent place for the National City Bank to collect revenues in? . . . I helped purify Nicaragua for the international banking house of Brown Brothers in 1909–1912. I brought light to the Dominican Republic for American sugar interests in 1916. I helped make Honduras "right" for American fruit companies in 1903.[5]

In short, during the first several decades of this century U.S. policies did little to promote democracy. Rather, U.S. policies in this period were guided by economic and political interests.[6] In several instances they were propelled by racism.[7] All of this was justified by the explicit or implicit notion of manifest destiny.[8]

With the 1930s and the adoption of Roosevelt's Good Neighbor Policy, U.S.-Latin American relations took a new course. The marines were returned to their barracks—in the United States. Both the political will of the Roosevelt administration and the contraction of economic ties as a result of the Depression led to somewhat more benign relations between the United States and the Latin nations. In effect, the Good Neighbor Policy can be viewed as the consummation of Taft's Dollar Diplomacy. The latter was designed to supplant U.S. military power with economic might. Taft thought that as U.S. economic involvement in Latin America increased, a commonality of interests would develop and there would be less need for the marines to impose the U.S. will. However, the United States continued to find it necessary, despite Taft's plans, to intervene militarily on a frequent basis throughout the 1920s. The Good Neighbor Policy brought Taft's plans to fruition in the 1930s and 1940s.

By the 1930s the United States was in a much better position vis-à-vis British economic power in Latin America. By this time the United States was the clearly dominant economic power in Central America and the Caribbean and was increasingly influential in South America. Moreover, the United States was interested in devising some means to insure its interests without repeated military intervention, a policy that met with increasing opposition at home and that was proving increasingly ineffective (culminating, particularly, in the debacle in Nicaragua in the late twenties). In this context, the Good Neighbor Policy largely consisted of a tradeoff. The United States foreswore direct military intervention in pledges made at the 1933 Montevideo Conference and the 1936 Pan-American Conference in Buenos Aires, and in return the Latin American nations agreed to economic rules and behavior that were conducive to U.S. economic interests.[9]

Although it is unclear whether it was a conscious policy, the United States simultaneously developed additional security for its interests in the form of indigenous dictatorships. Although direct U.S. military intervention declined during this period, the United States took an active role in establishing or maintaining several dictators; they included Ubico in Guatemala, Hernández in El Salvador, Trujillo in the Dominican Republic, Andino in Honduras, Batista in Cuba, and Somoza in Nicaragua. This was particularly true once World War II began. During the war the United States was far more concerned (naturally) with securing its geopolitical needs than with promoting liberty in Latin America. It was interested in stemming German inroads in Latin America and in maintaining pro-American regimes. These dictatorships were an economical way (in both human and financial terms) to insure U.S. interests, and therefore democratic forces were aided.[10] Thus U.S. policies vis-à-vis democratization during this period were, at best, ambiguous. Although U.S. policy continued to do little to actively promote democracy, there was nevertheless a decline in direct military involvement.

The growing economic power of the United States, which had allowed Roosevelt to substitute economic for military domination in the hemisphere, reached hitherto unimagined heights following World War II. United States political and economic power was unparalleled. As a consequence of this global hegemony, the United States assumed new international roles. In effect, the United States became the defender of both private enterprise (or international trade and investment) and the free world (or the non-Soviet world). These inter-related roles had two sides to them. On the one hand, they clearly served the economic and political interests of the United States. The defense of international private enterprise mainly benefited U.S.-based multi-national corporations, and the defense of the free world guaranteed U.S. political hegemony in the world. On the other hand, U.S. policy-makers clearly believed that these roles also had a positive, moral side. There was a sincere even if, as it developed, misguided belief that the promotion of private enterprise was the only way to promote democracy and, in turn, that defense against communism was a necessary precursor for private accumulation. Thus in the years immediately following the war, the United States assumed a more dominant and active role in the world and believed (at least in the abstract) that there was a commonality between the pursuit of U.S. interests and the pursuit of democracy and liberty in Latin America. Moreover, largely due to the U.S. role in the fight against Nazism, policy-makers in the immediate post-war era thought that they had a certain mission to promote freedom and democracy.[11]

The possible contradictions of these U.S. goals—the simultaneous promotion of its own economic and political interests and the promotion of democracy worldwide—was not immediately apparent. U.S. policy-makers have often had to deal with the realization that what was best for international accumulation and their political interests actually undermined democracy in particular countries. This contradiction and policy-makers' attempts to deny/or accommodate the conflict have been the principal cause for the confusion and inconsistency of U.S. rhetoric and policy toward Latin America in the post-war era.

The principal watershed in the United States' management of this contradiction was the Cuban Revolution. The Castro revolution and its aftermath have effectively skewed U.S. Latin American policy. While allowing for periodic and personal differences among administrations, the enduring thrust of the past two decades of U.S. policy in this hemisphere was best summarized by President Kennedy. Upon contemplating the future of the Dominican Republic following the overthrow of Rafael Trujillo, he is reported to have made the following argument. ''There are three possibilities in descending order of preference: a decent democratic regime, a continuation of the Trujillo regime or a Castro regime. We ought to aim at the first, but we really can't renounce the second until we are sure that we can avoid the third.[12]

From the Cuban Revolution onward, U.S. policy, whether guided by Dem ocrats or Republicans, has had at its bottom line the prevention of "another Cuba" in the Western Hemisphere. This political interest, with all of its associated economic interests, has been foremost in U.S. policy. This interest has repeatedly clashed (at least in the minds of policy-makers) with the promotion of democracy. The openness and tolerance of democratic systems have been seen as offering opportunities for the left. The diverse individuals and groups subsumed within the left are purportedly able to subvert and manipulate democratic rules to their advantage. In this way, democratic systems can be used to impose Cuban-styled regimes. There are thus inherent dangers in democracy. These weaknesses of Latin American democracy increase the probability of another Cuba in ways that authoritarian regimes do not. In the absence of a safe democratic alternative, the United States has repeatedly lent its support to more trustworthy dictators. In has, in other words, repeatedly opted for the security of Kennedy's second option.[13] As Brazilian Otto Maria Carpeare has written, the security of the marines "was exchanged after 1945 for the Big Stick of the Latin American generals."[14]

That U.S. policy-makers have repeatedly chosen the security of dictatorships over the uncertainties of democracy is evidenced in many ways. It is seen most clearly in the events that followed the Cuban Revolution, but the same attitudes were foreshadowed by U.S. policy toward Guatemala in the early 1950s.

The regime of Jacobo Arbenz came to power in perhaps the fairest election in Guatemalan history.[15] It was the second election following the revolution against Ubico, and power was transferred smoothly from Arevelo to Arbenz. The political conflict that developed between Arbenz and the United States, and the U.S. response, has been well documented elsewhere.[16] In short, the United States saw its geopolitical interests at stake and took a variety of active steps to overthrow the democratic government. In its place, the United States acquiesced in the establishment and maintenance of one, if not the most, abusive regime in the hemisphere.[17] The point is that even in the early 1950s the benefits of supporting democratic regimes were not as important as the risk of a geopolitical setback.[18] The United States thus consciously overthrew a democratic regime.

The contradiction among U.S. interests simply became clearer after the Cuban Revolution. The contradiction was manifested in a variety of ways during the 1960s and 1970s. In virtually every instance, U.S. policy-makers chose political and economic interests over their concern for democracy. When push came to shove, in other words, the ideals of U.S. foreign policy were subordinated to perceived security goals. President Kennedy's 1961 formula held firm. This conflict outcome was demonstrated in a number of specific cases.

The Kennedy administration began with a call to idealism.[19] This applied to foreign as well as domestic policy. The United States, especially in Latin America, would work to attain the American ideals of liberty and democracy. But these ideals were quickly subordinated to Cold War imperatives. As implied by the quote above, the clearest sign of this took place in regard to the Dominican

Republic. When the military moved against Juan Bosch in 1963, Kennedy declined to lend active U.S. support to the constitutionalist forces.[20] This predilection of the Kennedy administration had already been foreshadowed, however, in its earlier response to military coups in both Argentina and Peru. When the Argentine military moved against President Frondizi and the Peruvian military prevented the victorious Aprista candidate Haya de la Torre from assuming power, both in 1962, the administration made little fuss. It very quickly recognized both military regimes.

Thus although there was little effective action in the direction of democracy on the part of the Kennedy administration, there was at least the pretense of idealism and a great deal of rhetorical support for democracy. After his assassination, and the escalation of conflict in Southeast Asia, however, the promotion of regional democracy (even rhetorically) was not actively pursued by the administration of Lyndon Johnson.

Johnson almost immediately recognized the military governments of Honduras and the Dominican Republic, a decision Kennedy had refused.[21] More important, however, was the Johnson administration's involvement in the 1964 Brazilian coup and the 1965 Dominican crisis. If possible, Johnson, even more than Kennedy, was obsessed with Cuba. Eric Goldman quoted him as having said that "any man who permitted a second Communist state to spring up in this hemisphere would be impeached and ought to be."[22] Having begun with this premise, Johnson's behavior is not surprising. At the very least, the Johnson administration welcomed the Brazilian coup with open arms and likely was an active conspirator in the coup.[23] By 1964 the United States had made its displeasure with the elected government of Joao Goulart well known. The military regime, which replaced Goulart, was immediately recognized, and U.S. foreign assistance to Brazil was greatly increased. The increased aid and welcome reception were likely seen as a signal by other Latin militaries.

The Dominican intervention represents yet another example of U.S. fears of "another Cuba" leading it to oppose democratic forces. In the spring of 1965 military officers staged a coup in an effort to reinstate elected President Juan Bosch (overthrown in a 1963 military coup). The fighting itself was confined to Santo Domingo. The Johnson administration unilaterally intervened with approximately 25,000 marines after having convinced itself, with little evidence or apparent difficulty, that the revolt was Communist inspired and directed. After the Bosch supporters were contained, the United States sponsored elections in which former Trujillo lieutenant Joaquin Balaquer became president. There is still controversy over the character of those elections.[24] In the end, however, Kennedy's second option was the result. The conservative oligarchy retained power, a situation that did not change until at least the middle of the Carter administration.[25]

The most aggrieving case in which U.S. support for democracy was subordinated to geopolitical interests, however, took place during the Nixon administration. We refer to the case of Chile from 1970 to 1973. Again, this case has been thoroughly documented elsewhere and does not require reiteration here.[26] The U.S. position in regard to Chilean democracy was best captured by Henry Kissinger's statement concerning the possible election of Marxist Salvador Allende: "I don't see why we need to stand by and watch a country go Communist due to the irresponsibility of its own people."[27] In short, the Nixon administration had very little regard for the democratic system in Chile. To secure U.S. interests, it actively sought first to subvert the system and then to overthrow it. The results of the administrations' "success" are now well known. Many thousands of Chilian citizens continue to suffer under the brutal rule of Pinochet's police state.

Beyond these specific cases, or crisis situations, the contradiction of U.S. goals has been more generally evidenced in the nature and content of U.S. assistance to Latin America. More precisely, it is evidenced in the changing content of U.S. foreign assistance. With great fanfare and a promise of development and democracy, the Kennedy administration launched the Alliance for Progress in 1961. In the spirit of pan-Americanism, the United States would provide long-term capital to promote domestic industrialization, and, in turn, the Latin American nations would enact the needed social and political reforms defined as necessary to insure societal progress. It was an effort to attack the basic causes of Cuban-style revolutions and the social and economic inequalities so prevalent throughout Latin America. On the surface, the Alliance for Progress had a good deal of merit.

In practice, however, the alliance suffered for a number of reasons. First, the United States never committed the quantity of resources necessary to effect the changes sought. Second, the resources it did commit were not directed toward the most democratic nations in the region. The two highest aid recipients from 1961 to 1966 were Panama and the Dominican Republic, and Mexico and Uruguay were two of the lowest.[28] Third, the plan was politically unrealistic. It called for the ruling Latin American oligarcies to effect the very reforms that would dramatically reduce their own power. Moreover, alliance funds went directly to these ruling groups, and thus the program worked to strengthen the very groups that were preventing progress. Not surprisingly, most regimes enacted at most only cosmetic reforms. More surprisingly, the United States did not object. The reform aspects of the Alliance for Progress were quickly dropped. The content of U.S. assistance was increasingly made up of various kinds of military aid. A program that began with the idea of attacking the root causes of political instability increasingly focused instead on containing the manifestations of dissent. The United States increasingly turned to the Latin American military institutions to guarantee its strategic interests. In this environment, the first years of the alliance saw many democratic regimes fall victim to military coups.

Although the changing nature of U.S. assistance was by no means the sole determinant, it certainly contributed to the wave of authoritarianism that swept Latin America from the mid–1960s to the mid–1970s. The United States provided a great deal of the material, training, and strategy that the new Latin dictators relied upon. The full complement of material that the United States has supplied that has been employed consistently for the purpose of repression has been documented by, among others, Michael Klare and Cynthia Arnson.[29] The United States has also disseminated counterinsurgency or internal-security strategy through its military courses at the School for the Americas (known elsewhere as the School for Juntas or, simply, the Coup School) and has apparently provided varying levels of more specific advice on the nefarious topic of torture.[30] It has done the same thing regarding the use of counterterror or death squads.[31] At the very least, the United States must share some responsibility for the consistent behavior evidenced among the military personnel it trained and equipped. Thus U.S. assistance increasingly has worked to strengthen authoritarian forces in an effort to secure U.S. geopolitical interests. It has done little to effect changes conducive to democracy.

The pattern of U.S. Latin American policy from the end of World War II to the mid–1970s is thus fairly clear. The United States has repeatedly been faced with the contradiction between its idealistic goal, the promotion of democracy, and its perceived strategic, political and economic interests. When a choice has had to be made between these goals, the United States has consistently chosen its more material interests. It has thus done very little to promote democratic development in that region and in fact has contributed, in the interest of security, to its subversion. It is not necessarily the case that there has been a lack of desire for democracy, but there certainly has been an unwillingness to accept potential costs in its pursuit. That is, if security were guaranteed, there would be little doubt that U.S. policy-makers of both parties would choose to promote democracy over authoritarianism. But security is never guaranteed. U.S. policy-makers have therefore been unwilling, in almost every instance, to risk the loss of any material interests to promote democracy.

This is the context within which we must examine the Latin American policies of the Carter and Reagan administrations and their role in the present wave of regional redemocratization. To do so, we first discuss the domestic opportunities for democratic development and the role that the United States can potentially play in that development.

DOMESTIC OPPORTUNITIES AND CONSTRAINTS

This discussion of the opportunities and constraints for democratic development in Latin America is guided by a particular concept of democracy. The nature of democracy has been the source of considerable debate in recent years. Criticisms of ethnocentric standards imposed on other societies are familiar. With particular regard to Latin America, Howard Wiarda has urged "modesty, circumspection and sensitivity" in the application of the concept of democracy.[32] He has cogently argued that the Latin culture offers its own tradition and interpretation of democracy and that we should strive to evaluate these societies on their own terms. Although we are sensitive to these concerns, we also worry about the problem of cultural relativism and the possibility of broadening the concept of democracy as much that it loses much of its meaning. To be useful empirically a concept must have fairly clear lines of demarcation. Unfortunately, concerns over empirical clarity and cultural sensitivity may at times contradict one another. Although we recognize the potential for criticism, we have chosen to conceptualize democracy in a fairly traditional Anglo-American fashion.[33]

We would argue that a regime must meet certain minimum standards of behavior to be correctly labeled democratic. Beyond these thresholds, political systems may vary considerably and remain democratic, but the thresholds must be met. We conceptualize three general thresholds: (1) the objective application of laws and regulations; (2) the public accountability of governing elites; and (3) the respect of individual human rights. Laws must be applied without prejudice or preference for particular individuals, groups, or classes. There must be, in other words, equality before the law. Governing officials must be accountable to the public. This standard obviously requires that the system be inclusionary. Thus, for instance, the generally exclusionary system in Colombia would be a borderline case, despite its regular elections. Clearly, however, the requirement for accountability is most usually fulfilled by way of regularized elections, although alternative means are theoretically possible. Finally, to be labeled democratic a regime must insure its citizens' basic human rights. Democratic systems must insure a variety of political and civil rights, as well as the rights of the person. These are primarily negative rights; they are freedoms *from* government actions. Governments must not violate the sanctity of the human body or prohibit the flow of information and the expression of ideas or prohibit social interaction, organization, and participation. Importantly, these negative rights are not resource dependent; all governments, from the richest to the poorest, have the ability to insure these rights.

We turn to the potential for the development of such political systems in Latin America. One is immediately struck with the difficulty of such development. The constraints on democracy are considerable. The constraint discussed most frequently is the colonial heritage of Latin America and its associated culture. The colonial structure imposed by Spain and Portugal was strictly hierarchical and laid great emphasis on obedience to authority. The culture that developed with and around these structures is characterized by its corporatist and elitist beliefs and thus often contradicts the basic tenets of democracy.[34] Related to these factors is the Latin cultural history of personalism. This serves to foster an "us versus them" political atmosphere in which the notion of a loyal opposition, essential to democracy, is almost impossible.[35]

The colonial experience set in motion another major impediment to democratic development, namely, the highly unequal social structure and, related to this, land-tenure system. The land-tenure system in Latin America has traditionally been marked by large landholdings in a few hands. This has produced a social structure in which the vast majority of the population is economically and socially marginalized. As in other regions, these marginalized sectors have been largely excluded from the political process. As long as the social structure remains highly skewed, with most of the population precariously close to the margin of survival, political participation is likely to be opposed from above and difficult (if not dangerous) from below.

A third constraint on democratic development is the changing nature and strength of the military institutions in Latin America. Frequently, the military is the strongest political institution in society and consequently wields a great deal of influence. The strictly hierarchical structure of the military provides a poor model upon which to build democracy. More troubling, however, is the changing nature of the Latin American military. The military has increasingly oriented itself toward internal rather than external security and, commensurate with this, has developed its own ideology of national security.[36] This ideology has been characterized as "anti-politics."[37] Specifically, it calls for the depoliticalization of society. Such attitudes regarding political participation are not conducive to democracy.

Finally, the relatively low level of economic development in Latin America also makes democratic development more difficult. For many years it was believed that economic development in itself was the key determinant of democracy.[38] It increasingly has been questioned. The pressures created in the development process may well undermine democracy.[39] Notwithstanding the transition process to a developed economy, which Samuel Huntington and others have correctly identified as a difficult period for democracy, it is generally true that higher levels of development make democracy easier. This is true in that as resource scarcities have been overcome, conflicts over resource allocation have been reduced, although the transition periods often have been stormy, and both longitudinal and cross-sectional analyses of the relationship between economic development and conflict have produced an inverted, U-shaped relationship.[40] In an environment of plenty, in short, consensual politics is simply much easier. In the environment of resource scarcity found in all of the Latin American countries, politics is likely to be more conflictual and, hence, democracy more difficult.

Although the constraints on democracy that we have discussed are formidable, we may identify at least a few opportunities for democracy. First, despite all of the above constraints, there are specific cases in which democracy has worked well. Costa Rica offers the most obvious case, although the imperfect cases of Colombia, Mexico, and Venezuela also offer hope. Moreover, many countries, even if presently non-democratic, have experienced significant periods in which democracy worked well. Pre–1973 Chile and Uruguay offer the best examples of this. Finally, the successful transition processes from dictatorship to democracy in Spain and Portugal provide some reason to believe that they can be replicated in Latin America as well.

Second, there can be little question that there is a strong desire for democratic processes throughout Latin America. The response to the present wave of redemocratization in most cases has been overwhelming. Furthermore, in those dictatorial countries that remain, significant numbers have been risking their lives working for the development of democracy. The desire and commitment to democracy remains one of the most important determinants of successful transition.

Finally, the Latin culture places a great deal of emphasis on the individual. The individual is accepted as inherently unique.[41] When this attitude is channeled to respect for the rights of individuals, it is conducive to the growth of democracy.

We must conclude that the prospects for democracy are complex and uncertain. There is a variety of domestic factors that work both for and against democratic development. On the surface, it would appear that the constraints are more compelling than the opportunities and that democracy is thus a very difficult proposition. Clearly, however, whether or not democracy develops depends upon the interaction among these factors and with both international influences and historical circumstances. Moreover, we would argue that the prospects for democratic development depend at least in part upon the form of the authoritarian regime in power. Not all dictatorships are the same. We may differentiate between personalistic dictatorships and institutionalized or bureaucratic-authoritarian regimes. In short, the existence of the latter makes democratic development all the more difficult.

Personalistic dictatorships have been the historical norm in Latin America. One individual, usually an active or retired member of the military, rules by virtue of personal loyalties to him and by his skill and ability in playing competing interests off against one another. Such dictatorships, which generally sit above an oligarchy and are dependent upon their support for survival, are relatively easy to depose. Once the individual is delegitimized in the eyes of key elites, it is almost impossible for him to stay in power. Such personalistic dictatorships usually leave the scene quickly and quietly. Their demise is rarely associated with a violent coup or a bloodbath. Even Getulio Vargas, perhaps the consummate personalist dictator, stepped down from the Brazilian presidency quietly when he lost the key support of the military. Similarly, once Somoza and Batista had lost the support of key business and middle-class leaders, their regimes quickly disintegrated. Although personalistic dictatorships may be quickly overthrown, there is no guarantee that they will be replaced by democratic regimes. But a key step in instituting democracy, the weakening of the authoritarian order, is easier when facing a personalistic rather than an institutionalized dictatorship.

Since the 1960s we have witnessed the formation of what has been variously called institutionalized, bureaucratic-authoritarian, or national security dictatorships. In such regimes, authority does not rest entirely in one individual or simply on the will of the traditional oligarchy but rather in the military institution as a whole.[42] This form of military dictatorship, begun in Brazil in 1964 and followed in Peru, Chile, Uruguay, and Argentina, has a greater sense of structure, and hence the feel of permanence. These regimes have come to power with a far more extensive agenda than previous military regimes. In the past, the military has assumed control to restore order and stability. This done, it has returned power (with a watchful eye) to civilians, either democratic or dictatorial. But these new regimes come to power with their national security ideology, referred to above, so that they are interested not only in restoring order but also in the reshaping of the entire political and economic system and the long-term economic development of the society. These new goals require the military to retain power for the foreseeable future, and they thus institutionalize their rule rather than vest it in a single individual. Such a dictatorship is much more difficult to dislodge. If a legitimacy crisis is encountered, the president may be removed and replaced, while the dictatorship remains intact. Far more dramatic change is usually necessary to weaken and overthrow such a regime. Thus we would expect that different types of pressures would be necessary to manifest democratization in these different types of dictatorships.

THE U.S. ROLE

> There *are* new democratic trends in Latin America. With great care, empathy, prudence, and a sustained, coherent policy, these might be encouraged and developed. With sensitive foreign policy officials, the judicious use of assistance funds, and a sense of restraint and modesty as to what the United States can accomplish, there are things the United States can and should do to aid Latin American democracy. Some of these can be accomplished unilaterally, some multilaterally; there are a variety of levers and techniques available.
>
> —Howard Wiarda[43]

This review of the domestic constraints upon and opportunities for democratic development in Latin America leads us to examine the potential role that the United States can play in fostering regime change and to examine how much and what type of influence the United States can bring to bear.

Liberal analysts have for some years correctly questioned the notion of "exporting revolution." They have argued that revolutions are fundamentally homegrown phenomena. External actors can aid revolutionary change but not cause it. Lacking the proper domestic circumstances, no amount of external assistance or intervention will cause a revolution. In considering the prospects for "exporting democracy" and the role that the United States can play, we argue that the opportunities are roughly the same as for exporting revolution. The United States can aid democratic development, but it cannot in and of itself cause or create democracy (that is, short of a complete U.S. invasion and occupation of a country). Lacking the proper domestic circumstances, neither the United States nor any other external actor can create democracy. Given proper domestic opportunities and circumstances, however, we believe that the United States can aid the process. At the very least, as we shall discuss, the United States can decline to take actions that are detrimental to the process.

In discussing the potential U.S. role, it is important to distinguish between what can be done in the short and long term. U.S. influence is greatest in effecting the long-term prospects for democracy. Unfortunately, the greatest emphasis is almost always placed on what the United States does in the short term. Although U.S. influence can be crucial to the outcome of a short-term crisis situation, the United States' options are constrained by the realities of the immediate situation. If a regime is confronted with a significant insurgent challenge, the United States can be instrumental in determining which side emerges victorious, but if neither is democratic, there is little the United States can do to foster a democratic outcome. In the long term, however, the United States can take actions that promote the development of a democratic option. Thus we believe it is important to separate out the potential influence of the United States in the short and long term and to judge U.S. policies accordingly.

We must also distinguish between positive and negative actions on the part of the United States. The former refers to those steps the United States can take to promote democracy and democratic forces. The latter refers to those steps the United States can take to oppose or weaken new or existing dictators. Each type of action brightens the prospects for democratic development but in different ways.

For the most part, the policy instruments available for positive and negative actions are the same. They are simply manipulated in opposite directions. For instance, foreign aid is one possible policy instrument. If it is increased to a new democratic regime, it is a positive action, and conversely, if it is reduced to a dictatorial regime, it is a negative action. Again, however, each in its own way can aid democratic development.

The United States has at its disposal a variety of policy instruments. Not the least of them is rhetoric. Given its global dominance, the United States can have an impact by merely ''talking up'' or ''talking down'' particular regimes. The latter is rarely done, in the name of diplomacy, but except for an occasional bruise to U.S. diplomatic relations with particular dictators, it can be a relatively painless way to support democracy.

Second, the United States can manipulate the distribution of its foreign assistance. This is the area that has received the greatest attention to date from both Congress and the general public. The United States can rapidly increase or decrease both economic and military bilateral aid, and similarly, it also can actively support or oppose multi-lateral aid to particular regimes. This approach has been criticized on the grounds that reducing or cutting off aid simply eliminates U.S. influence.[44] This ignores the fact, however, that once the stick of aid termination is employed, the United States can then rest its influence on the carrot of aid resumption.

Third, the United States can use its political clout in various international organizations and forums to support and oppose regimes. This is likely to have less impact than bilateral actions, but used in conjunction with other available policy instruments, it may be effective. It is also likely to be relatively painless.

Finally, the United States may manipulate several economic instruments to support democracy or oppose dictatorship. These steps, by present diplomatic standards, will be considered drastic. Objectively, however, they appear reasonable steps to take if one seriously intends to weaken authoritarian regimes. The United States can rescind or refuse to grant most-favored-nation-status to dictatorial regimes. It can also reduce or eliminate official support for U.S. multinational operations in these countries, through the use of agencies such as the Export-Import Bank. Finally, when appropriate, the United States can cut import quotas for goods from these countries. At present, the United States does in fact manipulate each of these economic instruments but only in pursuit of its geopolitical interests; for example, each of these instruments has been employed against Communist countries. They are available for use in the promotion of democracy as well. None of these short-term instruments are likely, in and of themselves, to lead to the collapse of a dictatorial regime or the emergence of a democratic regime. They would contribute to and aid these processes.

Domestic factors are so important in the short term that it is extremely difficult to effect domestic change from the outside. It is difficult to work against particular regimes and produce an almost immediate result. The potential influence of the United States is therefore greater in the long term, even if the results are less clear. Given the nature of the long-term instruments available, it is difficult to associate particular regime changes with particular policies, but that does not mean that the policies are not influential. Thus we believe that the United States has a much greater role to play in promoting general democratization in the long term than with changing particular regimes in the short term.

In addressing the instruments available for influencing long-term change, we again begin with rhetoric. Positive U.S. rhetoric is a particularly potent instrument for effecting long-term change. It can dramatically alter the international environment or atmosphere. A strong and active U.S. rhetorical commitment to the concepts of democracy, liberty, and human rights can set the tone for debate, both in and outside of specific countries. This was evidenced by the response to President Kennedy's strong rhetorical support for democracy. He received a very welcome reception on his trips to Colombia and Venezuela in 1961 and to Mexico in the following year. These trips stood in marked contrast to the disastrous trip that then Vice President Nixon took through Latin America in 1958. The point is that moral persuasion and the pressure of publicity can greatly assist change (a point that Amnesty International demonstrates every day). If the United States makes a strong and enduring rhetorical commitment to democracy in Latin America, it can have a significant positive impact. The impact will be all the greater if U.S. actions are consistent with its rhetoric.

These actions largely rely on the manipulation of the instruments already discussed. The United States can manipulate foreign assistance, political support in international forums, and economic instruments. The difference in their use to promote long-term change is that instead of being applied for or against particular regimes, they can be used systematically against dictatorships in general. If the United States would systematize its response to dictatorships in this fashion, it could avoid paternalistic charges of superpower interference in the internal affairs of specific governments. Such a policy would also likely be effective. For example, if the United States would establish a systematic policy of dramatically reducing or eliminating military aid in cases in which the military overthrows a democratic regime, it could very well have a significant impact on the frequency of such coups.

Beyond the manipulation of these instruments, the United States can also aid processes that begin to break down the domestic constraints on democracy that we discussed above. These, obviously, must be long-term goals. Most importantly, the United States can support changes that will improve the existing social structure. The most significant of them is the support—with both funding and technical advice—of meaningful land reform. Finally, the United States can also work to minimize the role of the military in Latin American societies by reducing the flow of repressive equipment and by restructuring training programs to emphasize an apolitical military role and an external orientation.[45]

In sum, there is a wide variety of policy instruments that are available to the United States to support democratic development in Latin America. We have tried to emphasize that these potential U.S. actions are likely to effect change only at the margin. The principal impetus for democratic development must come from within each of the Latin American nations. The United States has the potential, however, to aid this process. Finally, and this is a point to which we return below, most of these policies involve costs vis-à-vis U.S. political and economic interests. The United States must reestablish priorities and risk aspects of its political and military dominance, as well as economic advantages, in order to promote regional democracy.

THE CARTER AND REAGAN POLICIES

It is time to return to the myths of U.S.-Latin American relations that we reviewed at the start of this chapter. We are trying to sort out what role the United States has played in the recent redemocratization in Latin America. The Carter and Reagan administrations, at least on the surface, took very different approaches toward the regional respect for human rights and democratization. At the lowest level, the competing myths can be seen as an effort by each administration to claim credit for the present redemocratization. The Reagan administration pointed out that most (though not all) of the democratic regime changes have taken place "on their watch." They then leave us to draw the logical conclusion that they are somehow responsible for many of these changes. Carter proponents argue instead that Reagan has actively embraced the region's dictators and that he is merely reaping the democratization benefits of the seeds that the Carter administration sowed. There are also other possibilities; it may be that both, or neither, administration has played a significant role in these changes.

Now that we have reviewed the history of U.S.-Latin American relations and addressed the potential role that the United States could play in promoting democracy, we are in a better position to break through these myths and construct an accurate picture of the role played by each administration. Beginning with an understanding that both administrations were constrained by the same historical context and faced the same difficulties of democratic development, one is likely to dismiss the implicit premise of each administrations' argument that the United States can virtually create or destroy democracies at will. If so, a very different picture of recent U.S.-Latin American relations is likely to emerge.

We argued above that both U.S. rhetoric and actions could have an important impact upon democratic development; thus we first compare the rhetoric of the two administrations and then examine their actions. In each case, we try to assess both the short- and long-term impact of each administrations' policies.

U.S. Rhetoric

The Carter administration was marked by strong and consistent rhetorical support for the concept of human rights. Carter affirmed his support for human rights in his inaugural address, when he proclaimed that his was an "absolute" commitment. Both he and his leading foreign policy advisors repeatedly asserted the importance of human rights in U.S. foreign policy.[46] Although he was clearly capitalizing upon the political backlash against the amoral character of the Nixon-Kissinger-Ford foreign policy, there can be little doubt that Carter was sincere in his support for human rights. Thus, in short, the Carter tenure of U.S. foreign policy was characterized by the use of strong official rhetoric in support of human rights.[47]

Several members of the Reagan administration have attempted to separate the concepts of human rights and democracy. In an effort to differentiate the two administrations, they have argued that the two are somehow unique, and that whereas Carter supported human rights, Reagan has—in contrast—supported democracy. But as we discussed above, a respect for human rights is a defining characteristic of democracy. The two are inseparable. Clearly, whatever support Carter lent to human rights must be seen as support for democracy as well.

Carter argued that U.S. foreign policy needed to be morally consistent in that it could not justifiably criticize the abuses committed by U.S. adversaries while ignoring abuses by U.S. allies. Beginning with this premise, he tended to make rhetorical pleas for human rights generally, rather than simply referring to specific countries. Although debate continues over Carter's actions vis-à-vis particular regimes (as we discuss below), his administrations' rhetoric, particularly in the first two years, was frequently cast at the general level. Rhetoric was used relatively infrequently to effect short-term changes in specific cases. Rather, the rhetorical efforts of the Carter administration were general and aimed at effecting long-term changes by creating an international environment supportive of human rights progress and democracy.

The perceptible result of the Carter rhetoric, not surprisingly given the emphasis of the rhetoric, appears to have had very few short-term effects. Few of the most repressive regimes at the time even moderated their behavior, and none relinquished power. Furthermore, the long-term effects of the rhetoric have been minimized by the fact that the Reagan administration dropped most of the Carter rhetoric. The Carter rhetoric thus appears more as a four-year anomaly than as a consistent U.S. policy.[48] Nevertheless, the rhetoric did produce several successes. Indications are that it did at least in part create a new environment, focus debate, and raise the hopes of oppressed peoples. Many Latin American victims of human rights abuses, most notably Jacobo Timerman, have given Carter credit for these achievements.[49] Carter's success was further evidenced by his trip to Latin America in 1984. He received a tremendous welcome in each country he visited. Leonel Brizola, governor of Rio de Janeiro, stated that "millions of Brazilians are delighted that Jimmy Carter should come here so that they can publicly express their gratitude for everything he did."[50] There can be little doubt that Carter's strong rhetoric *helped* produce hope and change in Latin America.

President Reagan ran a campaign in 1980 that was highly critical of the Carter human rights policy. He argued that the policy was immoral, ineffective, and detrimental to U.S. security interests. Ignoring the actual policy, Reagan argued that Carter's approach was immoral because it established a double standard that focused U.S. complaints on U.S. allies, while the more abusive Soviets and their client states were ignored. Furthermore, it was ineffective because it served only to reduce U.S. influence in the offending countries and was dangerous because it undermined the stability of strategic U.S. allies.[51] There could be little doubt, therefore, as the Reagan administration assumed office that there was going to be a change in U.S. policy.

At the start of the Reagan administration there was little or no rhetoric concerning either human rights or democracy. Secretary of State Haig proclaimed in his first news conference that U.S. interest in terrorism would replace the previous interest in human rights.[52] Throughout Haig's tenure in office, the administration's rhetoric was almost solely concerned with combatting international terrorism and anti-communism (issues the administration saw as linked).[53] Over time, however, the promotion of democracy clearly replaced the administration's original emphasis on terrorism. The virtues and promotion of democracy have been the major focus of several Reagan speeches, and the administration has proposed the creation of a U.S. institute to encourage democratic development. It is important to point out, however, that even after the administration introduced a concern for democracy into its rhetoric, there was little doubt that such concerns remained less important than the Reagan rhetorical confrontation with international communism and Soviet influence.

Reagan's rhetorical support for democracy has also been undermined or at least muddied at times by the seemingly contradictory statements by administration officials. Early in the administration there was Vice President Bush's now infamous toast to Philippine dictator Ferdinand Marcos: "We love your adherence to democratic principles—and to the democratic process."[54] During this trip to Brazil in 1981, Reagan stated that under his tenure U.S.-Brazilian relations were returned to normal after the "strain" of Carter's emphasis on human rights.[55] Then in 1982 President Reagan made matters more difficult (if not downright embarrassing) when he argued that the Guatemalan regime, arguably the most ruthless and aggrievous regime in the hemisphere, was getting "a bad deal" in terms of criticism for human rights abuses.[56] Also in 1982, while in Argentina, U.S. Ambassador Kirkpatrick publicly praised the status of Argentine labor unions under the junta.[57] That status consisted of being terrorized into submission. More recently, Under-Secretary of State for Latin American Affairs Langhorn Motley, upon returning from a visit to Chile and General Pinochet, stated: "My impression is this destiny of Chile, in Chilean hands, is in good hands."[58] Such statements must unfortunately raise questions about the sincerity of the administration's rhetorical support for democracy.

Reagan's sincerity is further tarnished by the apparent double standard in his administration's human rights reports. A comparison of the reports on El Salvador and Nicaragua is illustrative. Abuses in the former are presented as "allegations" and "charges," and emphasis is given to government denials, while in Nicaragua abuses are presented as facts and government denials are dismissed. Furthermore, although the reports given proper weight and respect to the findings of the Nicaraguan Permanent Commission on Human Rights, they go to some length to trivialize the findings of Tutela Legal, the human rights commission of the Catholic Archdiocese of San Salvador.[59] There can be little doubt that these transgressions are due to Reagan's primary concern with anti-communism, since in the administration's view, there is a threat of communism in each of the countries involved in the above statements. Nevertheless, such rhetorical inconsistencies do not aid the process of promoting democracy and, in fact, create serious credibility problems for the administration.

The Reagan administration would assert that its rhetoric, in the short term, has had some positive effect on both El Salvador and Guatemala. El Salvador has held several elections and has seen at least a moderation of repression. Guatemala has not gone nearly as far but has at least planned for elections to be held in 1985. Even these very limited successes are hampered, however, by the administration's narrow definition of *democracy*. The administration has consistently stressed that elections equal democracy and has downplayed or ignored guarantees of human rights, which are equally necessary elements of democracy. Without the objective application of laws and a respect for basic human rights, elections do not equal democracy. Thus the elections in El Salvador and those planned in Guatemala are, at best, very limited successes and are as notable for their public relations efforts as for their commitment to the democratic process.

The long-term effect of the Reagan administration's rhetoric, it appears, will also be limited. The promotion of democracy is just not seen as the central thrust of the administration's Latin American policy. It was only added to the rhetorical package several years into the administration, and it is still clearly of secondary importance to anti-communism. In this environment the credibility and, hence, the impact of the administration's rhetorical efforts are severely hampered.

Overall, in comparing the rhetoric of the two administrations, we must conclude
that successes have been moderate. This is particularly true as regards short-term
changes or improvements in specific countries. It could be argued that the Carter
administration enjoyed its greatest success in the long run. By virtue of its consistent
and strong rhetorical support for human rights, it had a significant impact upon the
international environment and raised the hopes of Latin American masses. By contrast, the credibility of the Reagan administration's rhetorical support for democracy
has suffered because of its inconsistencies, and it is thus difficult to establish a plau-
sible causal path for administration success.

U.S. Behavior

As our discussion of potential U.S. actions indicated, there is a wide variety
of actions open to the United States to promote democracy. However, the United
States has never used the full complement of available actions to promote Latin
American democracy consistently. U.S. actions tend to be concentrated in one
or two areas. U.S. actions since the mid–1970s, in large part due to their visibility
and flexibility and the fact that they have received a good deal of attention from
Congress in recent years, have involved the distribution of its foreign assistance.
Thus although we discuss the other areas of potential U.S. action, most of our
discussion in this chapter focuses on U.S. military and economic assistance.

It is also worth noting at the outset that U.S. actions have been directed almost
entirely toward short-term effects. The United States has never implemented a
systematic response to dictatorships. At the start of the Carter administration it
appeared as if such a policy was possible, but as Carter realized that the promotion
of human rights might be costly in other areas, he quickly shifted to a case-by-
case approach to human rights promotion.[60] Such an approach necessarily involves focusing on short-term problems in specific countries, rather than a general
and systematic stance against authoritarianism. Thus our discussion of the impacts of the actions we review below are by default limited to short-term effects.

It is not at all surprising that the economic instruments we discussed—the
denial of most-favored-nation status, the refusal to insure or subsidize U.S.
exports, and the reduction of import quotas—have been virtually ignored. They
are not widely seen as diplomatically acceptable, and thus they are rarely even
considered in the debate. Congress did act, however, to deny U.S. government
subsidies for U.S. exports to Chile. This action was supported and upheld by
the Carter administration. In contrast, Reagan made an effort early in his administration to have this restriction lifted.[61]

The pattern is much the same as regards the use of U.S. political influence
to promote democracy. The contrast is between a few widely spaced actions by
the Carter administration and a complete lack of action by the Reagan administration. In his first year in office, Carter pressed the cause of human rights in
the Organization of American States. Largely due to administration efforts, the
Seventh General Assembly was devoted almost entirely to the issue of human

rights, and a strongly worded resolution was passed that rightly dismissed the
notion that anti-regime violence justified human rights abuses. Although this
effort was a success, it was both the beginning and the end of Carter's use of
U.S. political influence in international organizations.[62] However, Carter did
score another success by way of U.S. political influence. When the military
intervened and stopped the counting of ballots during the 1978 national election
in the Dominican Republic, Carter intervened personally. After he expressed the
United States' grave concern over the matter, the military withdrew and allowed
the election to proceed unimpeded.[63] Unfortunately, to date there are no similar
instances in which the Reagan administration has used U.S. political influence
to promote democracy in the region. Instead, in one of its few relevant actions
in an international organization, the Reagan administration voted in February
1981 against having the United Nations' Human Rights Commission give special
attention to the situation in Chile.

The Reagan administration established its image early on with a number of
actions designed to distance itself from the Carter White House. Within the first
four and a half months of the administration, Reagan warmly welcomed to the
White House President Viola of Argentina, the chairman of the Brazilian Joint
Chiefs of staff, and the commander of the Chilean Air Force. He also sent
Vernon Walters to Guatemala to visit Lucas García, the most brutal of Guate-
mala's recent string of ruthless dictators, and sent a U.S. military delegation to
Argentina with the expressed purpose of improving relations with the junta.[64]
In the words of Abraham Lowenthal, this "rush to embrace authoritarian regimes
cost Washington credibility with opposition groups and democratic forces in
Latin America."[65] These actions simply did not aid the process of democrati-
zation.

Concerning the use of foreign assistance to promote change, it is important
to recall that Congress has codified a good deal of legislation tying foreign
assistance to human rights practices. Beyond a variety of country-specific legislation, Congress has passed legislation that forbids the distribution of both
economic and military aid to regimes that are "gross violators of human rights."
It has also directed the executive branch to vote against loans to "gross violators"
in the international development banks.[66]

Through a combination of actions taken by Congress, actions taken by Carter,
and unilateral decisions taken by aid recipients, U.S. military assistance was cut
off to eight countries during the Carter administration:[67] Argentina, Bolivia, El
Salvador, Guatemala, Haiti, Nicaragua, Paraguay, and Uruguay. Although this
seems like a very significant development, and Carter has been severely criticized
for it by conservatives, it was not as drastic a change as it appeared on the
surface.[68] Many of these countries were receiving only low levels of military
aid, and half of these nations voluntarily cut themselves off from aid. Carter

reinstated aid to El Salvador before leaving office, economic aid continued to flow to most of these countries, military spare parts continued to be delivered, and so, too, did military equipment and aid already "in the pipeline."[69]

Although the changes in aid distribution made during the Carter administration were thus minimal, they were nevertheless severely criticized by President Reagan. As a result, Reagan has tried to reinstate aid to several of these regimes, particularly Chile and Guatemala but with only minimal success. Reagan certified that the Pinochet regime had made significant human rights progress and asked for a renewal of military aid to the regime in March 1982. Congress, however, refused this request. Given the administration's greater interest in Central America, Reagan has made a more concerted effort to renew U.S. military aid to Guatemala. The administration has frequently floated the idea, and in January 1983 it lifted the U.S. arms embargo against Guatemala and authorized the sale of $6.3 million worth of military spare parts. It then budgeted $10.25 million worth of military aid for Guatemala for fiscal year 1984, but this was subsequently barred by Congress.[70] Although the Reagan administration has thus been only partially successful, it has shown a clear disposition to reinstate U.S. aid to two of the severe violators of human rights who were cut off during the Carter years.

The situation has been much the same in the area of multi-lateral assistance, although in this area the Reagan administration has been more successful. In the 1977 International Financial Institutions Act, Congress directed the United States not to vote for International Development Bank (IDB) loans to gross violators of human rights. In line with this legislation, the Carter administration consistently abstained or voted against loans to Argentina, Chile, Guatemala, Paraguay, and Uruguay. In the first eight months of his administration, Reagan reversed the Carter policy and ordered U.S. delegates to the IDBs to again vote in favor of "economically feasible" loans to Argentina, Chile, Paraguay, and Uruguay. He then reversed the policy toward Guatemala in October 1982.[71] Thus the United States now supports multi-lateral aid to all of those Latin American countries denied that support during the Carter administration, whether or not their human rights situation has improved.

Beyond this fragmentary evidence, it is also possible to conduct a more systematic analysis of U.S. foreign aid distribution during the two administrations. We have done so elsewhere and have shown that, as a package, there was surprisingly little difference between the administrations.[72] An empirical analysis of these issues is severely hampered by the political biases and methodological inadequacies of existing measures of human rights and democracy.[73] To overcome many of these problems, we employed four somewhat overlapping measures. If the four would yield similar results we would be confident that the particular inadequacies of each measure were not significantly skewing the results. Two ordinal scales were created, one from the information in the annual reports of Amnesty International and the other from the reports of the U.S. State Department.[74] The other two measures used are the political and civil rights scales published annually by the Freedom House organization. The two ordinal

Table 10.1
**Spearman's Rank-Order Correlations Between U.S. Per Capita Military and
Economic Assistance, and Four Measures of Human Rights/Democratic
Development**

	Military Aid Per Capita		Economic Aid Per Capita	
	Carter Admin.	Reagan Admin.	Carter Admin.	Reagan Admin.
Amnesty Int. Scale	-.33	.09	-.13	.04
State Dept. Scale	-.05	-.09	-.05	-.07
Political Rights Scale	-.07	-.01	.10	.06
Civil Rights Scale	-.17	-.07	.12	.10

* : Significant at the .05 level or better

scales focus narrowly on human rights violations, whereas the other two measures are more general attempts to measure democratization. We acquired data for 1977 to 1983 on twenty-three Latin American countries.[75] We have computed the Spearman's rank-order correlations between these indicies and U.S. per capita military and economic assistance. The information is aggregated by administration, and the results are presented in Table 10.1.[76]

These results are fully consistent with our earlier study (which included countries from other regions as well). In short, there is very little difference between the two administrations. None of the correlations are statistically significant, and they are not meaningfully large. It is interesting to note that military aid is more likely than economic aid to be negatively correlated with higher levels of human rights abuse. At least at the margin, the two administrations appear to have given less military aid to the most abusive regimes in the region (although, again, these negative correlations are not significant). What explains this lack of difference? First, as we tried to make clear above, the Carter administration in reality did far less than is generally perceived or expected. Second, despite its wishes, as outlined immediately above, the Reagan administration has generally been unable to persuade Congress to reinstate bilateral military aid to those regimes previously cut off. Moreover, even in those cases in which Congress has gone along, the administration has been able to procure only low levels of assistance. Thus the unwillingness of the Congress to go along with the Reagan priorities may be skewing the results. If the administration had been able to do as it wished, the results might be different. In effect, Congress may have forced Reagan to do "as well" as the Carter administration in directing U.S. foreign assistance away from Latin Americas' most abusive regimes.

In sum, the two administrations present, at best, a mixed bag. Of the two, the Carter administration took more actions in direct support of human rights and democracy. Carter was instrumental in saving (indeed, improving) democracy in the Dominican Republic. He took steps to end U.S. subsidies for exports to Chile, denied support to abusive regimes in the IDBs, and reduced military aid to several regimes. In contrast, the Reagan administration has taken few if any positive steps. Instead, it has all too frequently chosen to receive warmly and on occasion even praise some of the regions worst dictators, renewed the subsidy of exports to Chile, renewed U.S. support in the IDBs, and tried repeatedly to restore U.S. military aid to those regimes denied aid by the Carter administration. The Reagan administration has done very little actively to support democratic development. Carter achieved one major success (in the Dominican Republic) and took several other positive even if relatively minor steps. The most significant negative aspect of the actions taken by the Carter administration is that they did not measure up to the administration's rhetoric. The actions reviewed above do not appear to be a true reflection of an "absolute" commitment to human rights and democracy.

CONCLUSION

We have sought to establish the role that U.S. foreign policy has played in the recent redemocratization in Latin America. Members of both the Carter and Reagan administrations have argued that the policies they pursued have aided the process. They have, in effect, claimed a good deal of credit for redemocratization. At the same time, each has argued that the policies of the other administration have hindered the process or at the least have not aided it. We must clearly reject these latter politically motivated claims. The positive regime changes have not been confined to the years of one or the other of the two administrations. Democracy was reinstituted in both Ecuador and Peru during the Carter administration, and significant steps were taken toward democracy in Bolivia, Brazil, and Panama as well. The remainder of the new democratic regimes have formally been initiated during the Reagan administration (although the administration cannot arguably take any credit for several of these cases, most notably that of Argentina). Thus, clearly, neither administration can claim sole credit for regional redemocratization. However, this still does not answer the question of whether either administration played a sizeable role in these regime changes.

We have examined the nature and impact of both the rhetoric and actions of the Carter and Reagan administrations. Based on this examination, we must conclude that the Carter administration played a more positive role in redemo-cratization than did the Reagan administration. The actions taken by the two administrations in support of democracy were minimal, but Carter clearly did a good deal more than Reagan. Carter's actions, however, were not as positive as his administration's rhetoric. If his behavior and rhetoric had been more consistent, Carter would have taken considerably more far-reaching and system-atic actions. Nevertheless, he did take several positive steps and achieved a number of successes that Reagan has not matched and, indeed, in a number of instances tried to reverse. More important in the long run than these records of behavior, however, is the rhetoric employed by the two administrations. Carter employed strong and consistent rhetoric in support of human rights. His rhetorical consistency and obvious sincerity strengthened credibility and, hence, the impact of the rhetoric. Carter's rhetoric successfully reshaped the international envi-ronment and focused international attention on the issue of human rights. Reagan has lent rhetorical support to democracy, occasionally with great force, but his credibility and sincerity have been undermined by inconsistencies and the per-ception that the promotion of democracy was an afterthought to the anti-com-munism of his foreign policy. Thus in his use of rhetoric as well as his actions, Reagan has played a less significant role than did President Carter.

It is important to emphasize a caveat to the above conclusion. As we have tried to stress throughout this chapter, even the more active Carter administration affected the redemocratization process only at the margin. There are few cases in which the United States was instrumental in a country's transition to democ-racy. Neither administration can rightly claim substantial credit for the region's regime changes. What we can say on the basis of this examination is that the Carter administration was inclined to aid the process and did so marginally but that the Reagan administration has declined to do even as much. There can be little question that the principal impetus for redemocratization has come from within Latin America. This impetus appears to have derived in large part from the economic difficulties encountered by the region's military dictators. Most of these regimes assumed power with the expressed justification that they could run the economy rationally and well. As economic problems have worsened or proven intractable, the regimes have lost a good deal of their own internal confidence and cohesiveness and have lost a good deal of the legitimacy with which they began, particularly among the middle classes.[77] These regimes lost further justification for their existence as the military absorbed the very corruption for which it criticized its predecessors and as regional insurgency and terrorism declined. Finally, no small amount of credit must go to the changing nature of the Catholic church in much of Latin America. Whereas the church had tradi-tionally supported oligarcic forces and authoritarianism, in many countries the church has now assumed a prominent role in the movement for human rights and democracy. This development has mobilized many formerly disaffected people and greatly increased the pressures for change.[78] The point, simply, is that neither the Carter nor the Reagan administration was instrumental in creating

or nurturing any of these democratic forces. But of the two, the Carter administration went considerably farther than the Reagan administration in aiding these
forces and nurturing the hope of eventual success.

Although we have concluded that U.S. foreign policy has done relatively little
to help bring Latin America's new democracies into being, it remains to be seen
whether the United States will help nurture and strengthen these regimes. There
is particular concern that the harsh remedies for the debt crisis, imposed by the
International Monetary Fund (IMF) and supported by the United States, will
create too great a burden for the fledgling democracies.[79] The sacrifices demanded
by rigid stabilization policies could lead to an early demise for many of these
new regimes. Furthermore, it remains to be seen whether the United States will
provide these regimes with financial assistance, a reduction in import restrictions
to promote their exports, and easier terms for debt renegotiation. Thus far the
signs are not encouraging that the United States will choose to help provide the
economic assistance to support democracy in this manner.

It is important, as we noted at the outset, to place recent U.S. policy toward
Latin America in historical perspective. In our review of U.S.-Latin American
relations we saw that the United States has consistently chosen to pursue its own
political and economic interests first and then, when it did not conflict with those
interests, to pursue democratic development. The problem has been that there
are few instances in which actions to promote democracy have not put some
U.S. interest at risk. Thus while U.S. policy-makers have sincerely believed in
the benefits of democracy, they have been unwilling to assume any of the costs.
The United States, in the abstract, has wanted to pursue both goals of democratization and "national security." A narrow conception of the latter has, however, always received higher priority, and hence we find the consistent pattern
that the United States has done little or nothing actively to support democratic
development in Latin America. The United States has not tapped its full range
of potentially useful policy instruments, and when it has employed some of this
potential, it has tended to do so inconsistently.

The Carter and Reagan policies can be seen as consistent with this history.
This is particularly true of the Reagan administration, which has shown a clear
preference for *anti*-communism rather than *pro*-democracy as the basis of policy.
This preference places it squarely in the mainstream of twentieth-century U.S.
Latin American policy. The Carter policy, on the other hand, represents at least
a minor anomaly. It is clear that Carter deviated somewhat from this history.
However, when one considers his policies toward the Third World as a whole,
rather than just looking at Latin America, his policies look more traditional. It
is increasingly recognized that he, too, accepted a broad notion of the U.S.
national interest and that when this interest clashed with his views on human
rights, he, too, chose to subordinate the latter.[80] In cases in which he perceived
a clear U.S. interest at stake—for example, South Korea, the Philippines, In-
donesia, Pakistan, Iran, Zaire, and El Salvador in 1980—he did not push his
human rights policies. Thus what differentiated Carter from his predecessors and

his immediate follower in the presidency was his perception of Latin America. Unlike the others, Carter did not believe that the United States had vital national interests in danger anywhere in Latin America.[81] He could thus afford to pursue human rights and democracy in Latin America. The point is that the Carter policy did not represent a new set of priorities vis-à-vis democracy and U.S. political and economic interests, but rather, it represented only a new evaluation of the threats to national security in Latin America at that moment. As such, it was only a small break with the history of U.S.-Latin American relations.

What must be clear by this time is the simple fact that if the United States wants to promote democracy in Latin America, it must be willing to risk occasional damage to either of its political and economic interests. Thus far, U.S. presidents have not exhibited such a willingness. As long as these priorities remain unchanged, the United States is likely to remain peripheral to the forces of democratization in the region. This has been the pattern throughout the last century. The United States has not stood at the center of the fight for Latin American democracy. The policies of the Carter administration represented a slight deviation from this pattern and in so doing had a marginal but clearly positive impact on the present wave of democratization. The policies of the Reagan administration have since returned the United States to its historical pattern. Thus although it is a mixed and complex issue, it is generally true that the present redemocratization is occurring despite U.S. policies rather than because of them.

NOTES

1. As quoted in Andre Gundar Frank, *Dependent Accumulation and Development* (New York: Monthly Review Press, 1979), p. 82.

2. Secretary of State George Schultz, "Democratic Solidarity in the Americas," *Current Policy* #550. U.S. Department of State, February 8, 1984, p. 2.

3. See Abraham Lowenthal, "Ronald Reagan and Latin America: Coping with Hegemony in Decline," in K. Oye, R. J. Lieber, and D. Rothchild, eds., *Eagle Defiant: U.S. Foreign Policy in the 1980s* (Boston: Little, Brown, 1983), pp. 311–336.

4. They were: Cuba, 1898–1902; Honduras, 1905; Cuba, 1906–9; Panama, 1908; Honduras, 1910; Panama, 1912; Cuba, 1912; Honduras, 1912; Nicaragua, 1912–25; Haiti, 1914–34; Dominican Republic, 1916–24; Cuba, 1917–23; Panama, 1918; and Honduras, 1919. See Jenny Pearce, *Under the Eagle* (Boston: South End Press, 1982).

5. Quoted in Pearce, *Under the Eagle*, p. 20.

6. This is demonstrated by the following quotes, the first by U.S. Senator Albert Beveridge in 1898 and the second by Under-Secretary of State Robert Olds in 1927. As quoted in Ibid., p. 9:

[American factories] are making more than the American people can use. . . . Fate has written our policy . . . The trade of the world can and must be ours. And we shall get it, as our Mother England has told us how . . . We will cover the ocean with our merchant marine. We will build a navy to the measure of our greatness. Great colonies, governing themselves, flying our flag, and trading with us, will grow about our ports of trade. Our institutions will follow . . . And American law,

American order, American civilization and the American flag will plant themselves on shores hitherto bloody and benighted by those agents of God henceforth made beautiful and bright.

Our ministers accredited to the five little republics, stretching from the Mexican border to Panama . . . have been advisors whose advise has been accepted virtually as law in the capitals where they respectively reside . . . We do control the destinies of Central America and we do so for the simple reason that the national security absolutely dictates such a course . . . Until now Central America has always understood that governments which we recognize and support stay in power, while those we do not recognize and support fail.

7. This is aptly demonstrated by the following vision expressed by President William Taft in 1912, as quoted in *Ibid.*, pg. 17: "The day is not far distant when three Stars and Stripes at three equidistant points will mark our territory: one at the North Pole, another at the Panama Canal, and the third at the South Pole. The whole hemisphere will be ours in fact as, by virtue of our superiority of race, it already is ours morally."

8. Which can be seen clearly from the following excerpt from an 1898 editorial in the *New York Times* as quoted in *Ibid*, p. 10: "There can be no question of the wisdom of taking and holding Puerto Rico without any reference to a policy of expansion. We need it as a station in the great American archipelago misnamed the West Indies and Providence has decreed that it shall be ours as a recompense for smitting the last withering clutch of Spain from the domain Columbus brought to light and the fairest part of which has long been our heritage."

9. See Dick Steward, *Money, Marines, and Mission: Recent U.S.-Latin American Policy* (Lanham, Mass.: Union Press of America, 1980).

10. The U.S. attitude was demonstrated by FDR's response when questioned about U.S. support for Rafael Trujillo: "I know he is an S.O.B., but at least he is our S.O.B." See ibid., p. 35.

11. One might argue that the trickle-down economic theory lay at the heart of political development theories as well. See Seymour Martin Lipset, *Political Man* (New York: Anchor Books, 1960), on the relationship between democracy and development.

12. Arthur Schlesinger, *A Thousand Days* (New York: Houghton Mifflin, 1965).

13. Karl Meyer, "The Lesser Evil Doctrine," *The New Leader* 46 #21 (Oct 14, 1963), p. 14.

14. Quoted in Steward, *Money, Marines, and Mission*, p. 104.

15. Even this election was tainted, however, when Arbenz's chief opponent, Colonel Javier Arana, was assassinated. There were reports at the time that he had been assassinated on orders from Arbenz himself.

16. See, most recently, Richard Immerman, *The CIA In Guatemala* (Austin: University of Texas Press, 1982); Stephen Schlesinger and Stephan Kinser, *Bitter Fruit: The Untold Story of the American Coup in Guatemala* (New York: Doubleday, 1983); G. Bowen, "U.S. Approaches to Guatemalan State Terrorism, 1978–1985," in Michael Stohl and George Lopez, eds., *Terrible Beyond Endurance?: The Foreign Policy of State Terrorism* (Westport, Conn.: Greenwood Press, forthcoming).

17. Jeffery Paige has offered the term *homicidocracy* to capture its true character. For a detailed discussion of the nature of the Guatemalan regime, see Amnesty International, *Guatemala: A Government Program of Political Murder* (London, 1981).

18. It should be stressed that most analysts now dismiss the notion that Arbenz was a Communist or a Communist dupe and that there really was a risk to U.S. geopolitical interests. Nevertheless, the important point is that U.S. policy-makers believed that this was the case at the time.

19. This call to idealism should not be confused, however, with a policy that was anything but counter-revolutionary. See R. Walton, *Cold War and Counter Revolution: The Foreign Policy of John Kennedy* (Harmondsworth, Eng.: Penguin, 1972).

20. Kennedy's ambassador, John Bartlow Martin, thought Bosch was weak. Martin was to play a significant role in the 1965 intervention. See John Bartlow Martin, *Overtaken by Events: The Dominican Crisis from the Fall of Trujillo to the Civil War* (New York: Doubleday, 1966).

21. See Richard Barnet, *Intervention and Revolution: The United States in the Third World* (New York: World Publishing Co., 1968); J. Slater, *Intervention and Negotiation: The Unitd States and the Dominican Revolution* (New York: Harper and Row, 1970); and Abraham Lowenthal, *The Dominican Intervention* (Cambridge: Harvard University Press, 1972).

22. Eric Goldman, *The Tragedy of Lyndon Johnson* (New York: Knopf, 1969).

23. See ibid.

24. See Slater, *Intervention*; Lowenthal, *The Dominican Intervention*; E. Herman and F. Brodhead, *Demonstration Elections* (Boston: South End Press, 1984).

25. This is a point to which we will return. See also Slater, *Intervention*; Lowenthal, *The Dominican Intervention*.

26. For a review of the case, see James Petras and Morris Morley, *The United States and Chile: Imperialism and the Overthrow of Allende* (New York: Monthly Review Press, 1975); Armando Uribe, *The Black Book of American Intervention in Chile* (New York: Beacon Press, 1975).

27. Seymour Hersh, "Censored Matter in Book about CIA Said to Have Related Chile Activities," *New York Times*, September 11, 1974.

28. William Furlong, "Democratic Political Development and the Alliance for Progress," in H. Wiarda, ed., *The Continuing Struggle for Democracy in Latin America* (Boulder, Colo.: Westview Press, 1980), pp. 167–184.

29. Michael Klare and Cynthia Arnson, *Supplying Repression: U.S. Support for Authoritarian Regimen Abroad* (Washington, D.C.: Institute for Policy Studies, 1981).

30. See A. J. Langguth, *Hidden Terrors: The Truth about U.S. Police Operations in Latin America* (New York: Pantheon Books, 1978); J. Ellman, "School for Democrats and Dictators," *The Guardian Weekly*, May 29, 1983, p. 14.

31. See the frank discussion by U.S. Colonel John Webber, quoted in Pearce, *Under the Eagle*.

32. Howard Wiarda, "Democracy and Human Rights in Latin America," *Orbis* 22, no. 1 (1978): 137–160.

33. We recognize the validity of the argument that one must have a "full belly" before being able to exercise many of the derivative political rights in this formulation of democracy. We also recognize that because of economic concentrations some citizens are more equal than others, and hence we recognize the utility of thinking in terms of economic democracy. But for our particular purpose, this narrow conception of democracy is more useful.

34. See Howard Wiarda, "Corporatism and Development in the Iberic-Latin World: Persistent Strains and New Variations," in F. Pike and T. Stritch, eds., *The New Corporatism* (Notre Dame, Ind.: University of Notre Dame, 1974); pp. 3–33; John Sloan, "State Repression and Enforcement Terrorism in Latin America," in M. Stohl and G. Lopez, eds., *The State as Terrorist* (Westport, Conn.: Greenwood Press, 1984), pp. 83–98.

35. See Furlong, "Democratic Political Development," p. 170. However, as the experience of Spain and Portugal have shown during the past decade, this culture can be altered.

36. See Alfred Stepan, "The New Professionalism of Internal Warfare and Military Role Expansion," in Alfred Stepan, ed., *Authoritarian Brazil* (New Haven: Yale University Press, 1973), pp. 47–68; Edward Herman, *The Real Terror Network* (Boston: South End Press, 1982); George A. Lopez, "National Security Ideology As An Impetus to State Terror" in Michael Stohl and George A. Lopez, eds., *Governmental Violence and Repression: An Agenda for Research* (Westport, Conn.: Greenwood Press, 1986), pp. 73–95.

37. Brian Loveman and Thomas Davies, eds., *The Politics of Anti-Politics* (Lincoln: University of Nebraska Press, 1978).

38. See Lipset, *Political Man*.

39. Samuel Huntington, *Political Order in Changing Societies* (New Haven: Yale University Press, 1968).

40. See Bruce Russett, "Inequality and Instability," *World Politics* 16, no. 3 (1964): 422–44.

41. See Furlong, "Democratic Political Development" p. 174.

42. See Alfred Stepan, *The State and Society: Peru in Comparative Perspective* (Princeton, N.J.: Princeton University Press, 1978); Guillermo O'Donnell, *Modernization and Bureaucratic-Authoritarianism* (Berkeley, Calif.: Institute of International Studies, 1973).

43. Howard Wiarda, "Can Democracy be Exported? The Quest for Democracy in United States-Latin American Relations" (Unpublished working paper for The Wilson Center, Washington, D.C., 1984), p. 18.

44. See Jeane Kirkpatrick, "Dictatorships and Double Standards," *Commentary* 68, no. 4 (1979): 34–45.

45. See John Samuel Fitch, "Human Rights and the U.S. Military Training Program: Alternatives for Latin America," *Human Rights Quarterly* 3, no. 4 (1981): 65–80.

46. See Sandy Vogelsgang, *American Dream, Global Nightmare* (New York: Norton, 1980).

47. See David Carleton and Michael Stohl, "The Foreign Policy of Human Rights: Rhetoric and Reality from Jimmy Carter to Ronald Reagan," *Human Rights Quarterly* 7, no. 2 (1985): 205–229.

48. Even Carter was not wholly consistent. As the administration progressed, Carter put less emphasis on human rights. The last two years of the administration saw far fewer references to human rights than did the first two years.

49. "Rights Victim Is a Potent Presence as Senators Assess Reagan Choice," *New York Times*, May 20, 1981.

50. See Alan Riding, "A Latin Spring: Democracy in Flower," *New York Times*, November 27, 1984.

51. For the most comprehensive review of these criticisms, see Kirkpatrick, "Dictatorships and Double Standards."

52. "Comments," *New Yorker*, February 1981, pp. 31–32.

53. Haig in particular was apparently opposed to an administration emphasis on human rights. It was reported in 1982 that Haig considered human rights to be "sissy stuff, fancy pants stuff." See Bernard Weintraub, "Reagan's Human Rights Chief, No Liberal Mole," *New York Times*, October 19, 1982.

54. Raul Mangilapus, "Buttery Toast in Manila," *New York Times*, July 10, 1981.

55. Steven R. Weisman, "Reagan, in Brazil, Warns on Trade," *New York Times*, December 3, 1982.

56. "Guatemalan Vows to Aid Democracy," *New York Times*, December 6, 1982.

57. Bernard Nossiter, "New Political Category," *New York Times*, February 13, 1983.

58. See Lydia Chavez, "Has the U.S. Softened Its Line on Pinochet?" *New York Times*, February 24, 1985; "Four More Years in Chile," *New York Times*, February 25, 1985.

59. For a discussion of political bias in the human rights reports, see Americas Watch, Helsinki Watch, and the Lawyers Committee for International Human Rights, *Critique: Review of the Department of State's Country Reports on Human Rights Practices for 1983* (New York: Americas Watch, 1984); idem, *The Reagan Administration's Human Rights Record in 1984* (New York: Americas Watch, 1985).

60. See Lars Schoultz, "U.S. Diplomacy and Human Rights in Latin America," in J. Martz and L. Schoultz, eds., *Latin America, The United States, and the InterAmerican System* (Boulder, Colo.: Westview Press, 1980), pp. 173–205.

61. Juan De Onis, "U.S. Lifts Carter's Ban on Trade Assistance for Chile," *New York Times*, February 21, 1981.

62. See Schoultz, "U.S. Diplomacy."

63. See Michael Kryzanek, "The 1978 Election in the Dominican Republic: Opposition Politics, Intervention, and the Carter Administration," *Caribbean Studies* 19 (April-June 1979); 51–73.

64. Edward Schumacher, "U.S. Military Wooing Argentina, but Rights Issue Could Intervene," *New York Times*, April 8, 1981.

65. Lowenthal, "Ronald Reagan and Latin America," p. 329.

66. The intent of congressional initiatives in the 1970s vis-à-vis foreign assistance was meant to address gross human rights abuses and, by implication, was intended to aid democratic development. However, Congress left a large loophole for executive interpretation of U.S. geopolitical interests, and the executive branch has made great use of this loophole. For discussions of this as well as reviews of the human rights legislative package and its development, see Lars Schoultz, "Politics, Economics, and U.S. Participation in Multilateral Development Banks," *International Organization* 36, no. 3 (1982): 537–574; David Carleton and Michael Stohl, "The Foreign Policy of Human Rights: Rhetoric and Reality from Jimmy Carter to Ronald Reagan," 7, no. 2 (1985): 205–229.

67. For a discussion, see Carleton and Stohl, "The Foreign Policy of Human Rights."

68. See especially Jeane Kirkpatrick, "Dictatorships and Double Standards"; idem, "Establishing a Viable Human Rights Policy," *World Affairs* 143, no. 4 (1981): 323–334.

69. Further, Argentina, Brazil, Uruguay, and originally both El Salvador and Guatemala chose to withdraw their requests for aid because they viewed the State Department's human rights reports as a violation of their national sovereignty. On this, see John Salzberg, "The Carter Administration—an Appraisal: A Congressional Perspective," in V. Nanda, J. Scarritt, and G. Shepherd, eds., *Global Human Rights: Public Policies, Comparative Measures, and NGO Strategies* (Boulder, Colo.: Westview Press, 1982), pp. 11–22. Financial aid and equipment "in the pipeline" was denied to Chile, but this was in response to Chile's lack of cooperation in the Letelier case rather than its domestic human rights behavior. For a discussion of this, see Roberta Cohen, "Human Rights

Diplomacy: The Carter Administration and the Southern Cone," *Human Rights Quarterly* 4, no. 2 (1982): 212–242.

70. "Congress Bars U.S. Aid for the Guatemalans," *New York Times*, November 18, 1983.

71. Raymond Bonner, "U.S. Now Backing Guatemalan Loans," *New York Times*, October 10, 1982.

72. Carleton and Stohl, "The Foreign Policy of Human Rights."

73. See John McCamant, "A Critique of Present Measures of 'Human Rights Development' and an Alternative," in V. Nanda, J. Scarritt, and G. Shepherd, eds., *Global Human Rights: Public Policies, Comparative Measures, and NGO Strategies* (Boulder, Colo.: Westview Press, 1981), pp. 123–146; Christopher Mitchell et al., "State Terrorism: Issues of Concept and Measurement," in M. Stohl and G. Lopez, eds., *Government Violence and Repression: Agenda for Research* (Westport, Conn.: Greenwood Press, 1986).

74. For a detailed discussion of how these scales were constructed, see Michael Stohl, David Carleton, and Steven Johnson, "Human Rights and U.S. Foreign Assistance from Nixon to Carter," *Journal of Peace Research* 21, no. 3 (1984): 215–226; Carleton and Stohl, "The Foreign Policy of Human Rights"; Mitchell et al., "State Terrorism."

75. The countries included are: Argentina, Bolivia, Brazil, Chile, Colombia, Costa Rica, the Dominican Republic, Ecuador, El Salvador, Guatemala, Guyana, Haiti, Honduras, Jamaica, Mexico, Nicaragua, Panama, Paraguay, Peru, Surinam, Trinidad, Tobago, Uruguay, and Venezuela.

76. Thus the per capita aid figures were summed for 1977–80 for the Carter administration and for 1981–83 for the Reagan administration. These figures were then correlated with the human rights-democracy scales for the last available year of each administration (1980 and 1983). This was done for the sole purpose of simplifying the presentation. The year-by-year correlations were computed and were not significantly different from those generated with the aggregated data. Our conclusions are thus unaffected by the use of the aggregated rather than the year-by-year data.

77. See Edward Epstein, "Legitimacy, Institutionalization, and Opposition in Exclusionary Bureaucratic-Authoritarian Regimes," *Comparative Politics* 17, no. 1, (1985): 37–54.

78. See Penny Lernoux, *Cry of the People* (New York: Doubleday, 1980); Scott Mainwaring and Eduardo Viola, "New Social Movements, Political Culture and Democracy: Brazil and Argentina in the 1980's," *Telos*, no. 61 (Fall 1984.)

79. See Riordan Roett, "Democracy and Debt in South America: A Continent's Dilemma," *Foreign Affairs* 62, no. 2 (1983): 695–720.

80. See Stephen Cohen, "Conditioning U.S. Security Assistance on Human Rights Practices," *American Journal of International Law* 76, no. 2, (1982): 246–279; Stohl, Carleton, and Johnson, "Human Rights"; Carleton and Stohl, "The Foreign Policy of Human Rights."

81. Stephen Cohen, "Conditioning U.S. Security Assistance."

Bibliographic Essay
George A. Lopez and Michael Stohl

Scholars of comparative politics have produced a plethora of literature on the questions of democracy, its breakdown, sustenance, and restoration through the established journals of the field, such as *Comparative Politics*, *Comparative Political Studies*, *Journal of Inter-American Studies and World Affairs*, and *World Politics*. In fact, the volumes mentioned in this essay notwithstanding, it is difficult to conceive of thoroughly researching the topic of redemocratization without assessing these important journals. So, too, the topic has been an important theme of scholarly conferences and research presentations held under the auspices of the Woodrow Wilson International Center for Scholars, Smithsonian Institution, Washington, D.C. 20560, and the Helen Kellogg Institute for International Studies at the University of Notre Dame, South Bend, Indiana 46556. But a good deal of theoretical work and case study analysis does exist in book form, and it is on these works that this bibliographic essay focuses.

Most modern analysts of the democratization and liberalization processes depicted in this volume would draw their theoretical vantage point from the literature of democratic theory best exemplified in the approaches of Robert A. Dahl and Arend Lijphart. The former has produced three critical books: *After the Revolution* (New Haven: Yale University Press, 1970); *Polyarchy* (New Haven: Yale University Press, 1971); and *The Dilemmas of Pluralistic Democracy* (New Haven: Yale University Press, 1982). In Lijphart's *Democracy in Plural Societies* (New Haven: Yale University Press, 1977) more recent scholars have found, among other formulations, the theoretical contours of the consocial concept of democracy. The classic study of the collapse of democratic systems remains the impressive multi-volume compilation of Juan Linz and Alfred Stepan, eds.,

The Breakdown of Democratic Regimes (Baltimore: Johns Hopkins University Press, 1978). The contributors provide both frameworks for understanding the deterioration processes in political orders and case studies from Europe and Latin America as to how such developments actually unfolded.

The work of Linz and Stepan paralleled the examination of the rise of counter-democratic tendencies in the form of corporatism and authoritarianism. This theme as a "new" governmental form, especially in Iberian and Latin societies, was studied in detail and in the best traditions of comparative scholarship by a number of researchers. The major intellectual parameters were set by Guillermo O'Donnell in *Modernization and Bureaucratic-Authoritarianism* (Berkeley: University of California Press, 1973). Extensions of O'Donnel's work and country-focused examinations of corporatist regimes appears with the work of Alfred Stepan, ed., *Authoritarian Brazil* (New Haven: Yale University Press, 1973); *James M. Malloy, ed., Authoritarianism and Corporatism in Latin America* (Pittsburgh: University of Pittsburgh Press, 1977); Howard J. Wiarda, *Corporatism and Development* (Amherst, Mass.: University of Massachusetts Press, 1977); Philippe C. Schmitter and Gerhard Lehmbruch, eds., *Trends in Corporatist Intermediation* (Beverly Hills, Calif.: Sage Publications, 1979); and David Collier, ed., *The New Authoritarianism in Latin America* (Princeton, N.J.: Princeton University Press, 1979).

As the liberalization of regimes began and as the possibilities of democratic openings emerged, the literature in the field closely scrutinized these developments in light of the authoritarian tendencies that preceded them. The work of Constantine C. Menges, *Spain: The Struggle for Democracy Today* (Beverly Hills, Calif.: Sage Publications, 1980); Howard J. Wiarda, ed., *The Continuing Struggle for Democracy in Latin America* (Boulder, Colo.: Westview Press, 1980); Howard Handleman and Thomas J. Sanders, eds., *Military Government and Movement Toward Democracy in Latin America* (Bloomington: Indiana University Press, 1981); Jorge Braga de Macedo and Simon Sarfaty, eds., *Portugal Since the Revolution* (Boulder, Colo.: Westview Press, 1981); Jose Maravall, *The Transition to Democracy in Spain* (New York: St. Martin's Press, 1982); John Herz, ed., *From Dictatorship to Democracy* (Westport, Conn.: Greenwood Press, 1982); Thomas Draper, *Democracy and Dictatorship in Latin America* (New York: H. W. Wilson, 1981); and Fred Eidlin, ed., *Constitutional Democracy* (Boulder, Colo.: Westview Press, 1983), are most noteable in this regard. The most recent studies that draw from what appears to be the experience of substantial liberalization and continued redemocratization include Wayne A. Selcher, ed., *Political Liberalization in Brazil* (Boulder, Colo.: Westview Press, 1985); and two volumes: Julian Santamaria, *Transitions to Democracy in Southern Europe and in Latin America* forthcoming (Guillermo O'Donnell, and Philippe Schmitter, eds., *Transitions from Authoritarian Rule*) (Johns Hopkins University Press, 1986).

Index

About the
Editors and Contributors

WILFRED A. BACCHUS is Assistant Professor of Political Science at the University of Connecticut, Stamford, and a member of the Center for Latin American and Caribbean Studies of the University of Connecticut. His publications on Brazil have appeared for the Foreign Policy Research Institute and in *The Journal of Political and Military Sociology*, and *Armed Forces and Society*. His recent research, concentrating on the Brazilian military elite, will be published by Greenwood Press in *Mission in Mufti: Brazil's Military Regimes, 1964–1985*.

GORDON L. BOWEN is Associate Professor of Political Science at Mary Baldwin College in Straunton, Virginia. His many publications about Central America and U.S. foreign policy have appeared in *Latin American Perspectives, Commonweal, Armed Forces and Society* and in a number of recent edited collections, including *Revolution and Counterrevolution in Central America, Terrible Beyond Endurance?* and *Human Rights and Third World Development* (both Greenwood).

DAVID CARLETON received his Ph.D. from Purdue University in 1986. His research interests include problems of political economy, human rights, and state violence, especially in Latin America. His publications have appeared in *Human Rights Quarterly*, *Journal of Peace Research* and in a number of edited collections.

MANUEL ANTONIO GARRETON, M. is Professor of Sociology of la Facultad Latinoamericana de Ciencias Sociales (FLACSO) in Santiago, Chile. Until 1973 he was the Director of Social Sciences at the Catholic University of Chile. He has been a Visiting Fellow at the Woodrow Wilson Center (Washington, D.C.), at Oxford, and at the Kellogg Institute of Notre Dame. In addition, he has been a Visiting Professor in Mexico, Peru, and at the Universities of Chicago and California, San Diego. He has published in four different languages and his books include *El proceso político chileno*, (with Thomas Moulian) *La unidad popular y el conflicto politico en Chile*, and *Dictaduras y Democratizacion*.

SANDRA WOY-HAZELTON received her Ph.D. from the University of Virginia and currently serves as Deputy Director for Academic Affairs, Institute of Environmental Science and Adjunct Assistant Professor of Political Science at Miami University, Oxford, Ohio. Her field research in Peru focused on popular participation and political parties, and her publications include chapters in *Citizen and State Participation in Latin America* (Booth and Seligson, eds.) and in *Revolutionary Peru: The Politics of Transition* (S. Gorman, ed.) and chapters on Peru in *The Yearbook on International Communist Affairs*.

WILLIAM A. HAZELTON received his Ph.D. from the University of Virginia and is currently Associate Professor of Political Science and Director of the International Studies Program at the University of Miami, Oxford, Ohio. His research has focused on the role of Latin American states in the international system and his publications include chapters in *The Dynamics of Latin American Foreign Policies: Challenges for the 1980s* (J. Lincoln and E. Ferris, eds.) and in *Latin American Foreign Policies: Global and Regional Dimensions* (E. Ferris and J. Lincoln, eds.).

GEORGE A. LOPEZ is Associate Professor of Government and International Studies and a Faculty Fellow at the Institute for International Peace Studies at the University of Notre Dame. His research work on terrorism and human rights has appeared in *Terrorism: An International Journal*, *Human Rights Quarterly*, *Chitty's Law Journal*, and in a number of co-edited works (with Michael Stohl), including *The State as Terrorist* (1984) and *Government Violence and Repression: An Agenda for Research* (1986), both from Greenwood Press.

RONALD H. MCDONALD is Professor of Political Science at the Maxwell School, Syracuse University. He has traveled extensively in Latin America and written on Latin American politics. He is author of *Party Systems and Elections in Latin America* and research articles in *Journal of Politics*, *American Journal of Political Science*, *Inter-American Economic Affairs*, *Western Political Quarterly*, and *Current History*. He has also contributed numerous chapters to edited volumes on Latin American politics. In 1980 he was a Fulbright Lecturer at the University of the Republic, Montevideo, Uruguay. Presently he is completing a new book, *Parties, Elections and Public Opinion in Latin America*, which will be published in 1987.

LAURA NUZZI O'SHAUGHNESSY is Associate Professor of Government at St. Lawrence University, Canton, New York. Her research has centered on the political processes of revolutionary regimes and post-reconstruction policies. She has done field research in Mexico and Central America from 1974 to the present. She is co-author (with Michael Dodson) of "Religion and Politics" in *Nicaragua: The First Five Years*, and co-author (with Luis Serra) of *The Church and Revolution in Nicaragua*.

DAVID PION-BERLIN is Assistant Professor of Political Science at the Ohio State University. His thesis, *Ideas as Predictors: A Comparative Study of Coercion in Peru and Argentina*, won the 1985 Western Political Science Association Award for the Best Dissertation in Comparative Politics. He has published on problems of repression, political economy, and military breakdown in a number of edited books and in *The Journal of Inter-American Studies and World Affairs*, *PS*, and *Comparative Political Studies*.

RICHARD STAHLER-SHOLK is a Ph.D. candidate from the University of California, Berkeley, who has conducted extensive field work in Nicaragua. His research interests include problems of democratic transition and political change, particularly in Central America. He has been a rapporteur for the Wilson Center and for the group that wrote *Comparative Aspects of the Transition from Authoritarian Rule* (1981).

MICHAEL STOHL is Professor of Political Science at Purdue University. He has been a Fellow at the Richardson Peace Institute and a Fulbright Fellow to New Zealand. He has published widely on problems of insurgent and state terrorism, including articles in *Journal of Peace Research*, *Human Rights Quarterly*, and *Chitty's Law Journal*. In addition, he has edited *The Politics of Terrorism* and co-edited four other books.